THE ESSENTIAL
ALLOTMENT GUIDE

My thanks to Stephen Liddle
for his illustrations

THE ESSENTIAL ALLOTMENT GUIDE

John Harrison

A HOW TO BOOK

ROBINSON

ROBINSON

First published in Great Britain by Robinson in 2009

Copyright © John Harrison, 2009

9 10 8

All rights reserved.
No part of this publication may be reproduced, stored in a retrieval system, or
transmitted, in any form, or by any means, without the prior permission in writing
of the publisher, nor be otherwise circulated in any form of binding or cover other
than that in which it is published and without a similar condition including this
condition being imposed on the subsequent purchaser.

A CIP catalogue record for this book
is available from the British Library.

ISBN: 978-0-7160-2212-1 (paperback)
ISBN: 978-0-7160-2243-5 (ebook)

Printed and bound in Great Britain by Clays Ltd., St Ives plc

Robinson
is an imprint of
Constable & Robinson Ltd
100 Victoria Embankment
London EC4Y 0DY

An Hachette UK Company
www.hachette.co.uk

www.littlebrown.co.uk

How To Books are published by Constable & Robinson, a part of Little, Brown Book
Group. We welcome proposals from authors who have first-hand experience of their
subjects. Please set out the aims of your book, its target market and its suggested
contents in an email to Nikki.Read@howtobooks.co.uk

CONTENTS

Fig. 1. A typical allotment.

1

WHY GET AN ALLOTMENT?

'Why get an allotment?' may seem a strange question to ask in a book about allotments; after all, you must at least be thinking of getting one to be reading this. Yet all the rewards that allotments can offer may not be apparent at first.

I've been growing fruit and vegetables for 30 years now and on an allotment for the last six. What took me by surprise was the difference between allotment growing and just growing at home in the back garden.

The general view of allotments is that they are just a patch of land where people grow vegetables and that's about it, but that is a very narrow and somewhat outdated view.

Since the Second World War, land and property prices have increased hugely in real terms, despite the odd blip. Builders have crammed more and more houses into less and less land so that the modern house has a garden that is hardly bigger than a patio. And don't forget the increase in flats and maisonettes with no garden at all. For those people, the allotment provides their only real opportunity to grow anything outside of a pot.

Even if you're fortunate enough to have a reasonable sized garden, the demands on it to be a children's play area or a decorative addition to the house rarely leave room to grow any serious quantities of vegetables and fruit. So the allotment steps in and provides that room.

If you do have a large garden, there are other benefits of an allotment that are not to be ignored. Because your plot will be on a site with other people interested in growing their own, you have a source of advice on hand. Books are helpful, but the opinion of an experienced grower on the same site can often get you to the solution faster.

Allotments provide green spaces in the city and that's a precious resource in itself. It is quite amazing how you can feel miles away from the pressure of city traffic and being overlooked by simply walking onto the oasis the allotment site is. Many a fine summer evening I've just sat and watched the sun sink behind the boundary trees, feeling as if I'm a million miles away from any cares. That to me is priceless.

Allotments help the ecology by providing some green space in the concrete jungle, increasing bio-diversity. I've seen frogs and toads, newts and lizards, and even the most beautiful grass snake basking in the leafmould.

There is formal evidence that allotments are good for your mental health as well as your physical health. Obviously caring for your plot gets you out into the fresh air and provides exercise. Clearing and digging is just as good for you as running on a treadmill in a gym. It is productive and much more fun, as well as costing an awful lot less.

We live isolated lives nowadays. People move for a job to different areas of the country and hardly have time to speak to their immediate neighbour, let alone become part of a community. The allotment provides that vital contact and inter-action we so need for our mental well being. Talking with workmates, where we are always on our guard in case the boss finds out what we really think, is not the same.

Often we don't meet many people outside of our small group of family and friends but allotment holders are a diverse bunch. On our small site you can find a retired consultant surgeon chatting with a builder's labourer, and a bank manager being advised on growing by a car mechanic. You couldn't find a more different group of people but they all share a love of their plot.

This opportunity to see how others live and to develop a real community is often ignored but it is important both to the individual and to repairing our fractured society.

One great development on allotments nowadays that would not have been much seen 30 years ago is the number of women and children enjoying the allotment. The image of the typical allotment holder is no longer a retired man in a flat cap, but on many sites it is more likely to be a young woman. The allotment community has developed so much recently that some of the children I know pester their parents to come down to the plot to meet their pals.

You may wonder why people bother 'growing their own'; after all, vegetables aren't too expensive and you can buy anything you want at any time of year in your local supermarket. However, those fruits and vegetables in the supermarket, strawberries at Christmas and tomatoes in January, have often been shipped around the world at huge cost in 'food miles'. It's obviously far better for the environment to eat locally produced food when you can and you don't get more local than an allotment.

Despite having vegetables available out of the home season, the supermarkets offer quite a narrow range. For example, you may find three or four types of potato but I have the choice of 400 types I can grow. When we plan a meal, we don't just have potatoes with it; we may have Valor or Arran Pilot or Anya. We don't have tomatoes; we have Green Zebra or Ailsa Craig or Sungold.

The taste of home grown is incomparable. If you have not tasted a pea picked, podded and eaten in one motion on the plot you are in for a wonderful surprise.

Allotments do cost money. As well as renting your plot, you have the cost of seeds, fertilizers and so forth but you will still save money. Exactly how much will depend on your circumstances and how much you would have spent on fruit and vegetables. My best estimate is that in 2009 a family of four would save about £1,500 a year, assuming they prefer their food without pesticide residues and eat organically.

Of course, that calculation does not include your labour but at least you're not spending the equivalent of one year's allotment rent on one month's gym membership.

On the subject of organic growing, to me the mystery is how commercial organic growers manage to supply the market at the price they do. Modern farming has concentrated on reducing labour costs with increased mechanization and it is certainly far cheaper just to spray a crop of cabbages rather than pick off caterpillars by hand. I would not qualify as an organic grower, as I do believe there are times where the use of weedkillers and chemical fertilizers makes sense. However, organic growing on an allotment scale is far easier than on a farming scale due to the diversity of crops in an area. Industrial scale farming does encourage pests to develop to biblical proportions.

You may not be 100 per cent organic but you can grow in the certain knowledge that your vegetables are free of invisible, tasteless but poisonous pesticide residues by simply not using any.

2

A BRIEF HISTORY
OF ALLOTMENTS

Although this book is aimed at helping you to grow produce on an allotment, you might be interested in a little of the history of the allotment which can be said to go back over a thousand years to when the Saxons would clear a field from woodland which would be held in common. Following the Norman Conquest, land ownership became more concentrated in the hands of the manorial lords, monasteries and church. The Reformation in the 1540s confiscated much of the church lands but they were transferred via the crown to the lords.

In the late 1500s under Elizabeth I common lands used by the poor for growing food and keeping animals began to be enclosed, dispossessing them. In compensation, allotments of land were attached to tenant cottages. This is the first mention of allotments, although not quite as we know them today.

By the 1790s the population of Britain had grown, the industrial revolution was changing society and the people were moving from agricultural jobs in a rural economy to the towns with their 'Dark Satanic Mills'. Unfortunately, this made the poor purely dependant on buying food and without the benefits of a social security system. The poor could literally starve for lack of money to buy food or the land on which to grow their own food.

By the nineteenth century the pace of change had increased and the General Enclosure Acts of 1836 and 1840 made it possible for landowners to enclose land without reference to Parliament as long as a majority of them (in value and number) agreed to do so.

The General Enclosure Act of 1845 and later amendments attempted to provide better protection for the interests of small proprietors and the public. This was enacted in no small part due to fear of civil unrest and revolt, and provided for land to be set aside for allotment use.

The act required that the commissioners should make provision for the landless poor in the form of 'field gardens' limited to a quarter of an acre. This was really the beginning of the allotments we have today in Britain.

However, the act actually failed to provide much land for the use of the poor. Of the 615,000 acres enclosed only around 2,200 acres finally became allotments.

By the second half of the nineteenth century, the urban allotment development began to emerge, as evidenced by the 'guinea gardens' brought into use on the outskirts of Birmingham. These, however, gradually disappeared as the outward spread of the city led to them being closed and the land used for building purposes.

The Allotments and Cottage Gardens Compensation for Crops Act 1887 obliged local authorities to provide allotments if there was a demand for them. The local authorities resisted complying with the act, and revision was required to strengthen it. An echo of the situation today!

The Smallholding and Allotment Act 1907 imposed responsibilities on parish, urban district and borough councils to provide allotments, and further legislation in 1908 consolidated previous acts and resolved various anomalies.

To the Victorians, allotments were a productive use of time, keeping the poor away from the evils of the demon drink and providing wholesome food for a workforce housed in tenements and high density terraced housing without gardens to speak of. How much of this was charity and how much self-interest is hard to judge, a well fed workforce being more productive.

The Great War of 1914–18 found Britain suffering food shortages as a result of German blockades and for those left behind growing their own food became a priority, which in turn increased the need and demand for allotments.

One source of land suitable for allotments but not large enough for general agricultural use was the land owned by railway companies. These parcels of land were often allotted to the railway workers and this is the reason that you will often see allotments by railway lines to this day.

Following the Great War and the end of the food shortages, there was a decrease in demand for allotments and this, combined with increased need for building land for housing, reduced the number of allotments over the next 20 years.

The Second World War arrived and once again Britain was blockaded and food shortages became the norm. The pressure was far greater than in the First World War due to the U boat campaigns in the Atlantic; and what shipping did get through was better employed bringing war material than foods that could be produced at home.

Such was the demand that even public parks were pressed into use for food production. The famous 'Dig for Victory' campaign exhorted and educated the public to produce their own food and save vital shipping space.

This was the peak for allotments and by the end of the war Britain had an estimated 1.4 million plots under cultivation. The contribution of the allotments and 'Dig for Victory' campaign should not be underestimated. Agricultural production is generally more efficient in terms of labour but not in terms of land usage. Those allotments and home growers were estimated to be producing 1.3 million tonnes of food annually.

Immediately after the Second World War the demand for allotments began to fall. Public parks became leisure gardens once more and, of course, there was huge pressure on housing stocks so suitable land was at a premium. This is despite the fact that rationing of some foods continued right through to 1954.

The result of demands for more and more building land saw the re-establishment of the Allotments Advisory Body which in 1949 recommended a scale of provision of 4 acres per 1,000 head of population. This, in turn, led to the passing of the Allotment Act of 1950.

Even so, there was a sharp decline in allotment provision to around 500,000 by the beginning of the 1970s. The decline continued during the 1970s but at a much slower rate. During the 1970s there was a huge upsurge in interest in self-sufficiency and home food production epitomized by the television series *The Good Life* which ran from 1975 to 1978.

By the 1980s the mood of the country had changed. The 'good life' was now to be found in the City, and the rate of decline again increased, encouraged by the continuing rise in land and housing costs, which created an incentive to hard-pressed local authorities to sell allotment land for high prices to housing developers.

By 1996, according to a House of Commons report, there were around 297,000 plots available and, although definite figures do not appear available, since then the rate of decline appears to have decreased whilst at the same time there has again been an upsurge of interest in growing food crops.

Concerns about the genetic modification of foodstuffs, chemical pollution and contamination of our food, and the desire for the ultimate in freshness have seen empty plots filled and waiting lists appear for sites that previously had high vacancy rates.

It is possible that this increase in demand, combined with a willingness to demand provision of allotments as allowed for under statute, will see numbers rise from present levels.

3

HOW TO FIND AND CHOOSE
AN ALLOTMENT

We were lucky when we moved house; the first thing I noticed was an allotment site a hundred yards away around the corner. It's surprising how well hidden many allotment sites are though, so you might have to do a little detective work to find one.

Your first port of call should be your local council. They will manage allotments in their area and will know of privately run allotments outside of their control.

Sometimes the council receptionist may be unsure who handles allotments. If you try Parks, Recreation, or Leisure Services you should find someone who knows. Another good source of information is your local library.

Once you have tracked down the local sites, it's well worth visiting first to check out the facilities on offer, such as an on-site shop, parking, toilets and running water. Have a chat with any plotholders you meet to discover what it's really like there. Unfortunately, some sites suffer from vandalism and it's worth finding out what the risk is like in advance. The other big benefit of chatting to a few plotholders is that you will learn which plots grow well. Some plots always seem to get flooded, others are really fertile. Useful information!

If there is a waiting list, as there is with many allotment

sites, have a chat with the site manager or representative. If he or she knows that you are keen and will make something of your plot, it's surprising how quickly a site can come vacant. Sadly many people take on a plot only to find it is more work than they expected and leave an overgrown mess behind them when they give up. It does no harm to let the site manager know that you appreciate what is involved.

Allotments are, by and large, fairly traditional places. Telling the site manager you want to make friends with your weeds or you intend to plant by the phase of the moon may not help your cause.

You might consider seeing if there is someone on the site who is struggling, perhaps getting older and finding it hard to keep things in order. Offer to share and help. You benefit from advice and the older plotholder from younger muscles. Do be diplomatic: it's better to ask them to help you by teaching than imply that they are not as fit as they once were.

Official waiting lists may well contain a number of people ahead of you who have already found a plot or were not serious and have lost interest. If the site manager is on your side, then you'll often find one comes free faster than expected.

Not all sites in an area may be full. If your nearest site has a waiting list, ask about others in the area. There may well be a reason that a site has vacancies, perhaps vandalism has been a problem. Nevertheless, if you get onto a site, then you can start improving things. I've seen near derelict sites turned around in a year by new blood, willing to put in a bit more and do something for the community rather than just moan and give up.

Local horticultural societies are a good source of information. Try the library and check the local papers for information about when they meet. Often allotment holders will be members and you'll get to know that a plot is about to come free or someone is finding it hard going and would like to share.

If there are no allotments available in your area and the waiting list is such that you need to put your name down at birth to stand a chance, then all is not lost. In response to a petition the Government recently stated:

'The provision of allotments is the responsibility of local authorities. Under existing legislation (the Smallholdings and Allotments Act 1908) there is a duty on local authorities (except for inner London boroughs) to provide allotments where they perceive a demand for them in their area. If an allotment authority is of the opinion that there is a demand for allotments in its area, it is required, under Section 23 of the Small Holdings and Allotments Act 1908, to provide a suffi-cient number of allotments and to let them to persons residing in its area who want them.

'Written representations may be made to the local authority on the need for allotments by any 6 resident registered electors or persons liable to pay council tax, and the local authority must take those representations into account (section 23(2) of the Small Holdings and Allotments Act 1908). The Council must assess whether there is a demand for allotments in their area. If the Council then decides that there is a demand for them, they have a statutory duty to provide a sufficient number of plots. In terms of the duty to provide under section 23 of the Small Holdings and Allotments Act 1908 there is no time limit for provision once it has been established that there is a demand.

'Furthermore, statutory allotments are protected via Section 8 of the Allotments Act 1925 which requires that local author-ities seek the Secretary of State's consent for disposal or appropriation to another use. Consent cannot be given unless the Secretary of State is satisfied that certain criteria are met. Clarified criteria were issued to local authorities in February 2002.'

The phrase 'there is no time limit for provision' is very telling. What this means in practice is that even if your local authority admits there is a demand, they can take their own time, perhaps many years, in providing allotments.

You can get your council to make allotments more of a priority if you're willing to get a bit political. You can get the address of your local councillors, often off the web, and write to each one about the problem. Even if you send them all the same letter, make sure it's personally addressed and legible. Mailmerge is a wonderful tool!

Get the local press involved – nothing moves politicians more than the press. If the politicians think they can get votes out of something, then they'll help if they can. Make sure you have your arguments worked out before meeting the press. If you can get a photo of a group of would-be allotment holders outside the gates of a site – headline 'Locked Out' – I guarantee the council will take notice.

Councils have a duty to prioritize their spending and setting up an allotment site isn't cheap. Democracy is about getting your view heard and making the allotment a priority. Ask questions such as, 'How many people use the leisure centre and how much did it cost to set up and how much to run?' Then you can put the argument that allotments offer their voters better value.

It may take a while, but you will win if you keep pushing and then the real work and pleasure of growing your own begins.

If you find a site with vacancies and you are lucky enough to have a choice of plot, then be aware that the site manager may well want to allocate you the tough one. It's quite simple from his point of view: if you stay the course and work hard, his problem plot has been improved; and if you don't stay the course, then maybe you will have half cleared it.

Having said that, don't worry too much about a weedy plot. Fertile soil grows weeds well and they're easily cleared. If you can, avoid plots next to a boundary, especially one with over-hanging trees that will shade your crops from the top and steal water and nutrients below.

If you take a spade with you when you pick your plot, you can always dig down a spit (the depth of a spade) or two and see how deeply cultivated the plot is. The subsoil is usually a lighter colour than the topsoil or you could hit a clay layer. The deeper your topsoil, the better your crops will grow. You may as well benefit from the hard work that has gone before you if you have the chance.

4

HOW MUCH TIME DOES AN ALLOTMENT TAKE?

A lot of people underestimate the amount of time an allotment is likely to take them to cultivate. Obviously it will vary with the season and there will be times when inclement weather keeps you off the plot. Even if you are willing to dig with an umbrella in one hand and spade in the other, you can't actually dig over well when the soil is wet and claggy.

That aside, 'How long do you spend on the plot?' is a question I'm often asked but the answer isn't quite so easy as it may seem at first. For a start, there is the time you just spend with fellow plotholders putting the world to rights. Some days you can spend a good hour or two just chatting and get nothing done that you planned. Nothing wrong with that; it's a hobby not a job.

To try and give some guidance though, I'll assume you have a 10 rod plot; that's 300 square yards or 252 square metres for those who accept decimal currency.

In the dark winter months of December, January and February you don't need to spend a lot of time on the plot. Apart from possibly catching up on digging that should have already been done, harvesting a few leeks and Brussels sprouts and perhaps spreading some compost and manure, there's nothing much to do unless it's really mild and the weeds are growing. If you pop down for half a day twice a month that will be sufficient.

March and April are when things start to take off for the season. You'll be sowing and planting, hoeing the weeds down and so forth. In these months the equivalent of three or four days is probably needed. It depends to some extent how you handle it. In the Government's excellent advice for the 'Dig for Victory' campaign it stated, 'But once weather and soil are right, we should take time by the forelock and get on with the job – not leaving everything to the week-end, if we can help it, but seizing any opportunity of an evening – when it's fine – to put in a little time on essential work on the plot. Little and often will help us along far better than crowding a lot into the week-end that may turn out wet.' This advice is just as true today. There's always something to do on an allotment and if you get a couple of hours in of an evening, then your plans will not be in ruins if the weekend turns out to be awful.

May, June and July will find you running to stay still. The weeds are growing, so a lot of time is taken just keeping on top of them. Sowing, planting and cultivation are at their peak and yet just an hour or two a day would be sufficient. That is every day, of course, and it's bound to pour with rain on one or two days. If you plan on one full day each weekend and a few evenings, you will be OK.

August is a little quieter, but if we're lucky you'll be spending time watering as the sun blazes down. The problem with August is that the holiday fortnight often comes when just missing a day's watering in the greenhouse could kill the crop. The answer is to come to an arrangement with another plotholder and look after each other's plots when away.

September is a little busier. Things are coming to the end and the harvest is in full swing. Add to that any catching up if you took a break and you're probably going to need a good day and a half each week.

October and November bring the season to a close with

clearing, tidying and digging over. Say three or four days each month.

If you total this very rough estimate up, you'll see it comes to about 44 days a year, less than a day each and every week albeit concentrated into the growing season. Don't forget your chatting time and some time just to stand still and admire your plot, watch a robin clearing the bugs from where you've just dug and to see the sun set.

5

PESTS AND PROBLEMS

Slugs and Snails

Of all the creatures on the planet, slugs and snails are hated the most. I once asked another plotholder what he thought their purpose in the greater scheme of things was and the answer was, 'To test us!'

A row of seedlings comes up and the next day they've vanished – it's the slugs. That lettuce you came to the plot to pick for tea is reduced to a stump – it's the slugs – and you cut open that cabbage to find there's a couple more slugs staring back at you.

I don't want to dishearten you, but you never get rid of the slugs. What you can do is effectively control them and reduce the damage to a minimum. Incidentally, when we have a crop with a bit of damage, I always point out that if it's not good enough for the bugs to eat, it's not good enough for us.

Nematodes

The best control is to use nematodes, sold under the trade name of Nemaslug. This uses the nematode *Phasmarhabditis hermaphrodita*, which was discovered by scientists at the government research institute in Bristol. You get a powder, a bit like yeast, which you mix according to the instructions and water onto the plot. This puts 300,000 microscopic allies to work for you in every square metre.

You won't see much evidence of the nematodes' work. Most of the slugs will have died underground or under rocks where they've been waiting for dusk before coming out to eat your crops. Any that do die on the surface may well get eaten by birds or hedgehogs, but don't worry, the nematodes only kill slugs and neither the wildlife nor you will come to any harm.

Potatoes are very susceptible to slug attack later in the season than most other plants. So you can delay applying nematodes until 6–7 weeks before harvest, when the tubers are most likely to be eaten by slugs. Nematodes are far more effective than pellets because they kill the slugs underground where the vast majority spend their days.

Unfortunately, this method is not very effective on heavy clay soils for some reason and, it must be said, it's not a cheap control method. Neither is it effective for the whole season. After six weeks or so the nematode population falls back to natural levels and slugs re-colonize the plot so you may need to re-apply them.

Pellets

The second best control method is the slug pellet. These come in two types: the metaldehyde and the ferramol. Metaldehyde pellets have come in for a bad press as there has been speculation that the pellets could harm our bird and hedgehog allies if they eat a poisoned slug.

In fact there is little hard evidence to back this but I found the ferramol pellets (sold under the trade name of Growing Success) to be more effective, especially in showery weather. The good news is that the ferramol pellets are safe for wildlife and pets, although it must be said that the conventional pellets contain a repellent and are unlikely to be eaten by pets anyway.

Ferramol pellets are more expensive than conventional ones but if used correctly will only cost you about an extra pound or two for the whole season. Many people use slug pellets incorrectly and wastefully, throwing them on by the bucket full. They think the more pellets they use, the fewer slugs there will be, but actually you are better to broadcast the pellets thinly and after a few days or a week re-apply. I've been told that over-applying them is actually less effective anyway as a surplus of the attractants in the pellets means the slugs get confused and ignore them so there's no benefit. As with all these things, read the instructions carefully.

Encourage your allies to help you. Hedgehogs eat slugs so, if you have one on your site, be grateful. Many birds will eat them and, if you keep chickens, they will happily eat them as a nutritious treat. Toads and frogs go for them as well. If you have the room and are allowed, a small pond on the site will encourage these allies to live on the site and work for you. On raised beds, make a little ramp in and out of the bed and small black beetles will be able to get in and out. They eat slugs too.

Traps and Hunting

Slug traps will catch them, but they don't seem to make much of a dent in the numbers even though the trap may fill. All you need is a jar half buried on its side at an angle so the top is level with the ground and put some beer in it. The slugs crawl in for a drink and drown. Happily one presumes. Emptying the traps is pretty distasteful though.

Just leaving a plank or even a black plastic bag on the surface will attract slugs. Turn them over to expose the slugs and then deal with them as you will.

Barrier Methods

You can try to stop the slugs from reaching seedlings and young plants by creating a barrier. Horticultural grit, crushed eggshells or anything else that has sharp edges may work for you. Didn't for me, but you might be lucky.

Another method I've seen is to surround young plants with a copper ring. I've also seen copper wire (electrical wire with the insulation stripped off) stapled around raised beds and you can also buy copper tape. Very expensive if effective. In fact, I would suggest barrier methods as a whole are best left for potted plants on a patio than an allotment.

Birds

Birds are a great ally, eating a multitude of bugs and slugs but they're also a pest. I've watched pigeons sitting on electric cables over our site and I swear they're deciding whose brassicas to devastate next.

I've seen people hanging CDs on strings and ribbon strips of plastic to flutter and scare them away. I've also seen birds perch on those CDs and happily sit on a scarecrow's head as well! The only real answer is to net vulnerable plants. However, don't just drape nets over crops, as the birds peck through the gaps whilst sitting on the net. Ensure some space between net and crop.

Another happy trick of the pigeon family is to pull sprouting onion sets and garlic out of the ground and scatter them around. I think they pull them up, don't like the taste and cast them aside in disgust before trying the next one in the row. Horticultural fleece will keep them off until the crop is established and safe.

Cats, Rats and Mice

Cats can be a problem. Well, to be accurate, their toilet habits can be a problem. The neighbourhood cats will absorb any vacant space into their territory and then they leave a message for the other cats via their droppings that your plot belongs to them.

Drive off the cat who has toileted in your plot and in short order another will take his place. There's not a lot you can do. Throwing rocks at him is not only a serious criminal offence but you could be devastating the little old lady across from the site whose only companion is Tiddles.

Leaving some transparent 2-litre fizzy drink bottles around full of water often works for some reason. Possibly the cat is scared by the distorted reflection. Cats also detest the smell of citrus fruit, so scattering orange or lemon peel around can force them off. On the plus side, the cats will keep the rats and mice down.

Rats and to some extent mice present a health risk. They continually urinate as they move around and their urine carries Weil's disease, particularly in water. They can do some damage to crops as well. Trapping or poisoning is the only answer to serious infestations. Rats, especially, are attracted by poultry feed being left around so, if you are keeping poultry on your plot, do not overfeed, leaving grain in the pen. Store feed in metal bins if possible, since rats will easily gnaw through a plastic container if they have a reason.

Compost can be a problem as well, especially if you bring kitchen waste from home. Never put cooked foods, meat or bones in your compost heap.

Mice have a reputation for eating peas just after planting. The traditional remedies are soaking the peas in paraffin or putting prickly leaves like holly or gorse into the planting trench.

Rabbits

Rabbits are bad news on an allotment site. Not only do they like to eat what we grow but they also like to burrow, with our tilled ground making a good starting point for that. The best defence is to fence them out and this is best tackled on a site-wide basis. The fence needs to have a mesh size of 1 inch (2.5cm) or smaller and to be 3 feet (90cm) high with about 6 inches (15cm) buried at about a 45 degrees angle into the ground outward of the site.

If you can't fence them from the whole site, then you need just to fence your plot. Although shooting rabbits is allowed, you must know what you are doing and the legal implications, which are a bit beyond the scope of this book. If you shoot one, his pals will take his place so you'll need to fence anyway.

Vandals and Thieves

It's a sad fact that many allotment sites suffer from vandalism and theft. Sometimes it's just a minor annoyance like the theft of my pumpkins and squash near to Halloween but at other times it's much more serious like the smashing of all the glass in the greenhouses, breaking into sheds to steal and even the burning down of sheds.

This problem seems to be almost the norm in many urban areas and leads to some plotholders simply giving up. Just as you will feel violated if your house is burgled, vandalism of or theft from your plot has a severe emotional impact. It's almost worse in a way as at least you can see a reason for the burglar – he wants to take your property to make money.

The vast majority of vandalism and theft is undertaken by children, often as young as ten if not younger. They do it out of boredom, for the lack of anything better to do.

Theft is not generally very profitable on an allotment site. Let's face it, the value of stolen tomatoes or pumpkins is next to nothing. Tools like spades, which cost a packet new, are very cheap second hand. Even rotavators have a pretty bad weight to value ratio.

How to Reduce Theft and Vandalism

A few ideas that you may find helpful:

Increased Occupancy

Increased occupancy on a site will result in more people being around and thereby deterring the culprits from coming. Since most of the problems will occur at night, when plotholders are unlikely to be around, increased occupancy is only going to deter, but it will assist.

Security Fencing

Security measures such as fencing will help keep out the troublemakers. If they can't get in, they cannot cause trouble. Even if they do get in, their escape route is made more difficult, which will add to the deterrent effect. You can also get non-setting paint which is going to deter when they have to explain why their new trainers and clothes are ruined.

Security Lights

If mains power is available on a site, infrared-activated security lights will deter night time raiders, who don't want attention drawn to them. Care should be taken that the lights do not cause a nuisance to people in the locality. They will often be activated by a passing cat so alerting the neighbourhood at 4 am to the presence of a tomcat is not going to make for good relations.

Security Cameras

Security cameras can offer a solution. Nowadays these are available in low-light models and infrared with radio links to a computer that only records if movement is detected. Prominent signs warning of their presence would provide a deterrent effect. They do, to be truly effective, require somebody on the other end to call the police if necessary.

Hedges

A lower cost and ecologically more beneficial method is to plant a hedge by the boundary. Plants such as Hawthorn and Pyracantha have nasty thorns that will make getting in well nigh impossible.

Unfortunately, these take up space. Vegetables do not tend to do well under the rain shadow of a hedge and hedges obviously take years to grow to such a stage as to be effective. Once grown they will also require trimming to keep them in bounds. However, gardeners are used to doing things today for which the benefits will not be apparent for a number of years.

On the plus side, they increase bio-diversity and provide food for birds, shelter for pest-predators, etc.

I've seen young tearaways break open a security fence but

I've never seen anyone get through a thick, thorny hedge. To surround a whole site with hawthorn isn't as expensive as you might imagine; the planting labour is where the cost really can mount. Perhaps a 'Site Sunday' where everyone does a few feet of the boundary is the answer.

Social Inclusion
Since most of the trouble is likely to come from local children, possibly the best answer to reducing vandalism is to include children and the site's neighbours.

If the local community is aware of an allotment site, considers it of value and has some sense of ownership, then they are more likely to dissuade children from undertaking acts of vandalism against the allotment and to report unusual happenings on the site.

If the children themselves appreciate the allotment site and know the plotholders, then they are less likely to want to cause trouble. Better still, if they actually have a plot themselves they will discourage their compatriots from causing trouble.

Events such as open days and offering tours to the local community help in these aims. Donations of surplus produce or other services to a neighbourhood will assist as well.

In other words, making friends with the local scallywags can pay back as they become your best security guards.

One final word on security. I've heard of people lying in wait for vandals and inspecting their sites by torchlight. You are putting yourself at risk both physically and legally. Discuss the problem with your local police. They have the skills and training to handle these problems and will advise you as to how you can help them and yourself.

Your local councillors and officials also have an interest in reducing petty crime, so it's often well worth discussing with them what can be done. Whatever happens, don't let them win.

6

HEALTH AND SAFETY

At the risk of sounding like Granny warning of dangers whatever you do, I think it is worth considering a few points when you are on your allotment.

Tetanus or Lockjaw

This very serious infection kills one in three people who contract it. It is caused by a bacterium that lives in the soil, especially manured soil. The bacteria enter the body through a cut or open wound and a few days or weeks later the illness hits. You may not even be aware of the cut – bacteria are very small!

A tetanus jab will prevent it but not cure it. You can usually get the jab from your doctor – and it is not a painful one any more. If you are unsure about your vaccination record and immunity, ask your GP.

Exercise

Allotments and gardening provide you with a lot of physical exercise. This is good for you but don't overdo it. Especially on cold days, warm up a little first before starting to dig over your plot. Break up large jobs into small manageable sections and take a break between them. When lifting, use your legs, not your back. I twisted my back humping leaves into a leafmould bin some four years ago and it still gripes at times. Smaller loads don't really take that much longer.

Telephone

If you own a mobile phone, it's probably a good idea to have it with you on the plot. Imagine the scenario – you are the only person on the site, something happens to immobilize you and you could be there all day waiting for help.

Tool Using

Proper tools make jobs a lot easier and safer. Old spades and forks have handles sized for smaller people than we are today. A longer handle will not only make the job easier but helps prevent back strain. Get the right sized tool for you.

Rotavators and Other Power Tools

A large rotavator can be a bit of a strain to control and take a while to get used to. Just like when you learnt to drive a car, you need to develop the correct reflexes. Those tines that happily break up the soil will do the same to your feet if you are not careful, so sensible footwear please. Power strimmers, shredders, etc, all have their dangers as well. Read the manuals and follow the instructions carefully.

Often it is a good idea to wear ear-defenders or earplugs with noisy engines going nearby and safety goggles will protect your eyes from flying debris from a strimmer.

I know it is pretty obvious, but don't try to clear a blocked shredder with the power on. If they can shred a branch, they will make easy work of your fingers.

Clothing

Having seen people happily trying to use a fork in sandals, it needs to be said. Sensible shoes and especially 'toetectors' can save you from a forked foot or worse. Shorts are great in summer, until you kneel in a red ants nest (happened to me!) and ants in your pants are no fun at all!

Pesticides and Other Chemicals

Just follow the instructions with great care. And if you take children to the plot, keep the chemicals where the kids can't get them. Young children have magical abilities to open child-proof caps, unlike adults!

7

CHILDREN ON THE PLOT

Unlike the strictly male province allotments used to be, now many plots are taken by mothers, who will bring their children down with them to the allotment. This is great, even I have been known to smile at the sound of children happily playing, but please be aware that an allotment site is not a playground.

There are dangers around; greenhouses are perhaps the biggest one. Children running around playing hide and seek have been know to run into them. Horticultural glass is thin, so breaks easily. However, it can cut just as badly as ordinary glass. Often people have ponds on plots but even more potentially dangerous are water barrels. Leaning into a barrel to investigate a bug floating can end up with your little one head down in deep water.

Also, you don't want your children to be a nuisance. When they're in a group and egging each other on, things can quickly get out of hand. Do teach them that Mr Smith's strawberries are his and scrumping is not allowed.

Another point you must consider is their vaccination status. They must be covered for tetanus, but, then again, they should be covered for this anyway as grazed is the natural state of children's knees.

Now I'm certainly not saying don't bring the children, but just be aware that your safe haven may not be so safe for them. Keeping them occupied and an eye on them is the key.

If they're coming to the plot, make it fun for them. Don't expect them to try and dig your heavy clay with a spade designed for filling buckets with sand on the beach! Proper small tools are available, which will make their efforts productive.

Find things they actually enjoy doing and can make into a game. Pick off the caterpillar or squash the slug are particularly loved by kids and very useful too.

If they enjoy digging, find a place where it is useful to you or at least does no harm. A small patch of their own will encourage them to grow but stick with the fast developing crops like radish at first.

Another good one for children is the sunflower. They're quick to grow and impressive. We had a largest sunflower competition for the children on our site, which proved popular.

Involving children in your crop growing will nurture an interest for life and often their participation in the growing process means they are more likely to taste and enjoy the flavours of fresh vegetables and fruit.

Sometimes unusual vegetables can be helpful in this. My nephew loved the 'purple space cauliflower' I grew. Well, actually, it was a variety called purple graffiti but he didn't need to know that. The exceptionally sweet tomato, Sungold, was treated like a sweet and so the habit of trying and eating vegetables was developed.

Allotments offer great opportunities for education as well. Ask questions such as (sorry to those who use imperial measurements!), 'How many onions will go into a 3 metre row if they are spaced at 10cm apart?'

Or, 'We have an area of 5 metres each side. How many sweetcorn can be planted in there at a spacing of 50cm each way?' Tip: they can draw a plan. Talking of which, that brings up the concept of scale drawings.

However, it's not all mathematics. Handicrafts come into allotment growing as well. Make a scarecrow or a string of

CDs to scare the birds. This is before we even touch on the ecology and biology. I'm a great believer that we under-estimate the power of children to learn if they are interested, often well beyond what you might expect. I once had a lovely lecture on how insects develop immunity to pesticides through natural selection from a ten-year-old.

There will come a point when the kids discover other things, like loud music, and allotments are no longer cool. Don't worry. One day they'll come back to it and remember fondly the lessons learned.

8

PLANNING THE PLOT

'If a man fails to plan; he plans to fail'

A new plot is a great opportunity. You can adapt it to meet
your needs, rather than working within the constraints of
somebody else's plan. Don't try to micro-plan it, though. You
will find that things change with time so let's work with broad
brush strokes and create a general framework which you can
work within and alter later to suit your changing needs.

The first thing is to decide where to put your permanent
fixtures, sheds and greenhouses. Obviously a greenhouse
needs somewhere light but a shed could be best sited in a
shady spot, leaving the sunnier places for growing crops. If
you have piped water available, then site the greenhouse near
to the tap if you can. You'll be watering in the greenhouse
even when it's pouring with rain.

If your site doesn't have water available, then don't forget
to allow some space for water butts. Even if you do have
mains water, it's not a bad idea. Guttering is quite easy to fit
to a shed and many greenhouses incorporate guttering as part
of their design.

An internal water butt in the greenhouse is a good idea as well.
It's really bad for your greenhouse plants to get watered with
freezing cold water. Having a butt in there will ensure your water
is at the same temperature as the interior of the house. It also has
a small benefit in that it acts as a heat store, absorbing heat in the

warmth of the day that is released in the cold of the night.

Do check the site rules. On many sites the places where you can put 'buildings' are laid down in them. Sometimes the rules are strictly enforced and at other times not, so it's wise to run over your plans with your site manager before starting any major works, despite what others may have done on the site in the past.

You'll find you need a working area to store things such as piping (for cloches) and canes, scrap wood and sheets of glass. If you can, plan it so that the worst places for growing get used for fixtures, freeing more valuable growing space.

Your compost heaps can also go in a shady spot but, if all things are equal, then put your heaps in the middle of the plot. You'll be taking material to and from the heaps all the time and this way you minimize the distance you have to trundle your barrow. It's always a good idea to save yourself work if you can. That gives you a bit more time just to sit and enjoy your plot. On that note, don't forget to have a space where you can sit down and have a break. Some plots on our site even boast barbecue spots. I've seen allotments with small grass lawns, complete with slide and Wendy house to keep the youngsters amused while Mum and Dad get on with cultivating.

The next item to consider is the permanent plantings. A comfrey patch is not going to be moved and neither is an asparagus bed so this is the time to decide where they're going. Incidentally, comfrey does quite well even in shady, wet parts of the plot. If you have some space for a butt by the comfrey patch, it will save you carting the cut leaves to the butt when making your own liquid feed.

The other permanent area is the fruit beds. Fruit bushes and cane fruit are bird magnets so keeping them all together makes sense as you can construct a fruit cage to protect them.

This may all seem a little daunting at first glance so here's how I do it. First draw a plan of your plot. Measurements don't have to be to the inch but it's helpful to have them to the foot. Mark on it any existing fixtures, trees around the edges giving shade, etc, pathways, water taps and anything else relevant. Don't forget to mark where north is so you can align things like raised beds properly.

Draw this up neatly, to scale if you can, back at home. On another sheet of paper, make a list of what is to go on the plot like the compost bins, comfrey patch and so forth.

Then you can sketch them in on the plan. Most often you will find you actually need three allotments to get everything in you want! That's when you go back to the drawing board, as they say. Perhaps a dozen blackcurrant bushes are more than you really need.

Once you've a plan that seems workable, go back to the plot and try to imagine how it will work in practice. Often things just fall into place but it is easier to have something to work to.

The space that's left after all these permanent beds and fixtures is where you will grow your vegetables. Don't forget them! Now is the time to think about raised beds and whether they're for you.

Raised Beds

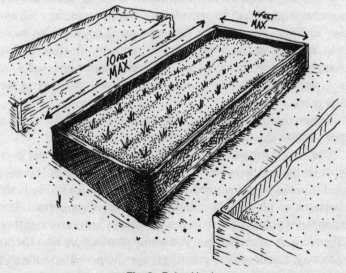

Fig. 2. Raised beds.

There was a time when every gardening programme on the television seemed to be about decking and pergolas. Now it's about raised bed growing, and everyone taking on a plot seems to think they have to start by putting in raised beds.

In some circumstances raised beds make a lot of sense. If you have a terrible heavy clay soil that is going to take years to improve and to be productive, raised beds are a fast way to get growing great crops. If you have a waterlogged area and plants are drowning, then a raised bed can be the answer, especially if drainage is difficult to put in. However, your raised bed will need watering more often if we have a decent summer.

There is a psychological benefit to raised beds. They impose order and make the plot feel more manageable although they don't really make them more manageable. When you come to weed after a holiday you can weed a bed at a time and feel you have won, at least in part at the end of the day. On the other hand, I can hoe half the plot in the time it takes to hand weed two raised beds.

For some crops raised beds make a lot of sense but for potatoes, squash and sweetcorn they don't provide any advantage and may actually be a disadvantage. They can also make crop rotation difficult and they're not very flexible if you change things as the years go on. Finally, raised beds are a lot of work and a bit of an expense to construct properly in the first place.

Before discussing how to construct a raised bed, let's take a look at the theory of them and their benefits.

The important point to a raised bed is that you do not ever walk on the soil and compact it. This gives you a deep, friable, well-drained soil allowing the roots to go down. Raised beds are supposed to be planted at higher densities than normal. For example, if your crop is spaced at 6 inches (15cm) in rows a foot (30cm) apart, in a raised bed you would plant at 6 inches (15cm) each way. The density of planting is also supposed to shade and suppress weeds, but I've not noticed it working that way.

Because you have paths between and around the beds which are not productive, to gain extra from raised beds you really need to double the crop yield. I've yet to see that achieved in practice but they are great for carrots, parsnips and root crops which love the depth of topsoil you provide.

In the winter you should not need to dig over a raised bed because the soil hasn't been tramped down. Having said that, my experience is that they do benefit from forking over or tilling with a Mantis to keep the soil condition.

The optimum bed size has a length of 10 feet (3 metres) and a width of 4 feet (1.2 metres). If the bed is any longer, the temptation is to step on it to get over to the other side, unless you're very self disciplined. The width is ideal as you can easily reach to the centre of the bed from the side. If possible, run the beds north to south so sunlight evenly hits both sides. It's not critical but it is best practice.

Between beds you need a path with a minimum width of 18 inches (45cm) or you won't be able to kneel in them when weeding or planting; and to the sides the paths should be at least 2 feet (60cm) wide so you can get a wheelbarrow up and down. If you have five or more raised beds, then make some of the long paths 2 feet (60cm) wide so you can get a barrow from one side to the other easily. Do note those are minimum widths for the paths. Increase by 6 inches (15cm) if you have room.

You're not limited to a rectangular shape. If you feel creative and want some squares or even triangles, then feel free. Just keep in mind that you don't want them so wide that you cannot easily get to the centre.

Having decided where your raised beds are to go, first scrounge your wood! If you can find old scaffold planks, these are ideal. They may look a little rough but they will last for years, especially given three good coats of preservative like Cuprinol.

Builders' reclamation yards are a good source of second-hand boards at a low price. Do not use wood that is too thin, like floorboards, because it will rot and be too flimsy to hold the pressure the soil will exert upon it.

Mark out on the plot where the bed is to go and then double dig the bed (see page 86). Make sure the soil is broken up well at the base and any perennial weeds are got out. In the corners, use something like a fence post cut to the height of the boards plus an inch or two below and nail the boards to them. Check the bed is square and level (as for a greenhouse base) and then fix some posts – 2" x 1"/5cm x 2.5cm is ideal – to the outside. It's a good idea to attach one in the centre of the run to help withstand the pressure of the soil which will try to bend the boards out.

Now you can fill the bed with compost or a manure/soil mix, etc, then leave for a week to settle before planting. For the paths around the bed, lay some weed suppressant matting and cover with wood chippings if you get them on your site.

One of the charming things about allotments is the innovative use of other people's rubbish. I've seen raised beds edged with old wine bottles (placed neck-end down), old telegraph poles, broken down decking and reclaimed floorboards doubled up to provide strength. Be creative, re-use and recycle.

Crop Rotation

We've now covered all the hard landscaping of the plot but there is one thing left to think about in your planning: your crop rotation.

If you grow the same vegetable in the same place for year after year what will happen is that the nutrients in the soil will become unbalanced as some plants use more of one nutrient than another. The pests and diseases will begin to concentrate and after a few years your crop yield will collapse. Often you will come across growers who have an onion bed or runner bean trench that they use year on year. Eventually things catch up and they'll see problems develop; not all old boys' methods work.

The most important rule of crop rotation is to avoid growing the same thing in the same place for two years running. Obviously this does not include your permanent crops like asparagus.

The longer the period between a crop returning to the same position the better but for an allotment a simple three year rotation will be adequate.

	Year 1	Year 2	Year 3
Plot 1	Potatoes	Brassicas	Everything Else
Plot 2	Brassicas	Everything Else	Potatoes
Plot 3	Everything Else	Potatoes	Brassicas

In the winter before Year 1 add manure to Plot 1 for the potatoes, which also prefer their soil somewhat acid. Also add lime to Plot 2 for the brassicas which like their soil neutral. In Year 2 manure Plot 3 and lime Plot 1. Just carry on through the plots as the years go by.

This basic system works up to a point but, of course, your crops are unlikely to fit in quite so precisely.

A four- or even five-year rotation is more effective at preventing a build-up of problems. You can adapt on the above principle quite easily. For example, legumes will do well in the same pH as the brassicas so you could arrange it:

- Potatoes followed by green manure and lime in the winter
- Legumes (the bean family) followed by manure (brassicas like manure as well)
- Brassicas
- All the rest

Perhaps you grow a lot of onions. If so, then you could tuck them in between brassicas and all the rest. It does take a few years to develop a rotation plan that works for you and even then you adapt it as your growing patterns change.

Don't worry too much about rotation. I've had people, who have obviously been very concerned about getting it right, send me the most intricate plans. Just provide what each crop needs and avoid repeat planting and you will be fine.

9

CLEARING THE PLOT

You've got your allotment and looked at the site, admiring those tidy plots by the gate as you come in, when the site manager shows you to your plot. It's that one in the back corner. No, those aren't crops – they're weeds! Six foot high weeds and probably a tribe of pigmies living in there as well.

The chances are that the previous tenant decided to give up the plot after harvesting his summer crops, or he may have moved house and neglected to inform the authorities formally so the plot has stood vacant for six months until the rent became due. So where do you start?

This is the time to hold your nerve; do not panic. Take a good look at what you have on the plot. What weeds are growing? Nettles, docks, buttercups and daisy all indicate that your soil is acidic. Docks love damp conditions. Horsetail or mare's tail (*Equisetum arvense*) also likes acidic soil.

You will now have an idea of what your soil is like. Weeds are actually a good indication of soil fertility. Lush tall weeds indicate good fertility, so the more weeds on your plot, the better the soil. That's positive thinking.

Do wear some stout shoes or boots for your inspection, there can be all sorts hidden in the undergrowth. Old bits of wood with nails sticking up, broken glass and sharp edged tin cans are sadly pretty common.

If the plot is really overgrown with tall weeds and brambles, it's worth hiring a brushwood cutter or strimmer for a day. Take along some loppers as well to deal with thick stalks and cut the lot down to about 6 inches (15cm) high.

Pile the waste up and at the end of the day the plot will look a hundred times better. Get all the rubbish in a pile as well. If allowed on your site, you can burn that rotten wood, reserving any decent pieces you find. You'll find a use for them eventually.

What happens to the rubbish depends on your site. Some have a skip, others don't and you'll have to take a trip to the local tip.

One word of warning: watch out for hazardous waste. Often asbestos sheets were used for roofing sheds and makeshift fences. Chemicals long since banned may have been left in bottles on the plot, or even old cans of used oil, which was used as a preservative on fences and sheds.

If you find this sort of waste, seek advice from your council on how to handle it. Often the council will send out men in moonsuits to pick it up (especially for asbestos), or tell you where you can take it.

Having brought the weeds down so you can see the plot and cleared the rubbish, you now have to decide what you want to do. Most of us nowadays prefer to be organic but that is going to involve a lot more work and time than the chemical route.

The easy way is to spray the whole plot, except for any permanent crops like rhubarb or asparagus, with a weedkiller. The best for this job will be glyphosate, which is often sold under the trade name of Roundup™ . The beauty of this is that the chemical is taken down into the roots through the leaves and kills the perennial weeds but de-activates when it touches the ground. It's safe to plant in the next day but you need to leave the weeds for a couple of weeks to give it time to work its way into the roots.

Once the weeds have died off, you can dig over or rotavate your plot. A word of warning: never rotavate a weedy plot, unless they are dead weeds. Perennial weeds will grow back from a fragment of chopped up root. I've seen a chap rotavate a plot with quite a few dock leaves on it. It looked fine for a couple of weeks after which he had a plot full of docks. Not what you want, at all.

Even if you're going down the organic route, you might like to consider using a spray just to clear the plot and then go organic. It will save your back!

To clear the plot organically, first decide how much time and energy you have. I certainly could not clear a plot in one go or even in one week. To hold back growth until you have time to get to a section of the plot, cover that section with thick plastic, old carpets or tarpaulins (if you have them). Most of the weeds will die if you leave an area covered for a year or so. However, I do not want areas out of production for that long so I just use covering as a holding method to stop growth until I can get around to clearing it. Many allotment sites do not allow the use of old carpets nowadays as too many plotholders have moved away leaving them behind, so check first. Old carpets are also no longer organically approved for use, despite being fine a few years ago, but I must admit to preferring to recycle an old carpet than using hydrocarbon produced plastic.

Deal with one small section of the plot at a time. I can manage an area about 6 feet (1.8 metres) long by 15 feet (4.5 metres) wide in one go but younger and fitter people will be able to do more.

With a spade, start to remove the surface grasses and short-rooted weeds. Stack the resulting 'turfs' upside-down so that they eventually form a loam. You will need to dig out any deeper rooted perennials (like docks). These are the devil to deal with when established.

Initially I just added the perennial weeds to a cool compost heap but found that they happily grew back from the roots. You can try chopping them (to weaken them) and add them to a hot compost heap but other methods are drowning in a barrel of water for three weeks or tying up in a plastic bin bag for a few months. This definitely kills them.

Having completed clearing, then dig over with a fork to break up the soil and extract any weed roots. Be on the look out for bindweed as this spreads from a small bit of root.

The trickiest weed to clear is horsetail (or mare's tail). It will grow back from a small amount of root and the roots are thin, hard to see brown coloured and they break easily. Just to add to the fun, they go all the way down to Hades – well 6 feet anyway. Pull out what you can and be prepared to keep hoeing them off for a few years to come.

As you clear a patch, consult your overall plan and prepare the ground accordingly. If it's getting late in the season, then consider a green manure. Not only does it hold nutrients in the soil, it crowds out the weeds. As you get towards the end of your plot you will probably find weeds sprouting behind you. They never stop! Most of these will be annual weeds whose seeds have been germinated by your clearance exposing them. Don't worry – you can just hoe them off.

If it is early enough in the season, do plant up as you progress. This way you get to see some rewards for all your hard work.

You will often hear of people growing potatoes to clear the ground. The fact is that the preparation of the soil to grow potatoes is what clears the ground. Sorry, whether you are an organic or chemical grower, the initial clearing of an overgrown plot is hard work, but it is incredibly rewarding when you get to the end and look back at the result.

10

CONSTRUCTIONS ON THE PLOT

On a journey through France we happened on an allotment site. The plots were well laid out and each one shared an identical semi-detached brick-built shed with his neighbour. Comparing that with our allotment sites, looking more like a shanty town with sheds of all shapes and sizes, green-houses constructed from this and that and water butts made from food product storage barrels, I knew which I preferred. One of the charms of our allotments is the individuality of the plots, the use of recycled materials in innovative ways.

Now before you commence building a scale model of the Taj Mahal on your plot from old packing cases, do check the rules. Most sites are free and easy but some stipulate what you are allowed to build and where. It's quite usual for there to be a rule against permanent concrete footings being laid. After all, you may move on, taking your shed but leaving a concrete base for the next tenant to try to remove.

Paths
On our site, there is a formal pathway between each two plots, allowing access. Other sites may differ, as they say. Sometimes these are just slabs laid down and sometimes just

grass, which always needs cutting but does provide some clippings for the compost heap.

If you are putting down a semi-permanent path, laying weed matting underneath will make life easier in the long run. Often sites have wood chippings delivered. What's a problem to dispose of to the tree surgeon is a useful material for the allotment holder. I love wood chippings for temporary paths as well. The material rots down and, when I no longer need the path, it can just be dug in.

If you don't want to use weed matting under a path, then six or so layers of newspaper will suppress any weeds.

Sheds

A shed on a plot is immensely useful – somewhere to keep your tools dry and make a cup of tea when the sky darkens. It's amazing how many secondhand sheds are advertised in local papers but often, if you just let people know that you are looking for a shed, one will be offered in short order. Sometimes DIY stores will get rid of ex-display models for a pittance at the end of the season. It does no harm to ask.

Although you may not be able to lay concrete, concrete slabs will provide perfectly acceptable foundations for sheds and are easily removed by the next tenant. It's a good idea to place the shed on bricks so air can circulate under the shed. A shed manufacturer told me that placing them directly on the ground or a concrete base without ventilation so that they rotted was what kept him in business.

There are things you can do to make your shed more secure – good padlocks and so forth – but any shed, like any house, can be broken into. I've even heard of secure sheds being set fire to by frustrated thieves. If you're on a site suffering from thieves and vandals, then don't keep anything of too much value in there. Chaining up tools, padlocked again, may help as will putting your postcode on in fluorescent paint as a deterrent, but any security system can be circumvented if they're determined.

There is an argument that less damage is done by thieves if you leave the door unlocked on the basis honest people wouldn't enter anyway.

Allotment Fridge

Fig. 3. Plant pot fridge.

On a positive note, I mentioned having a cup of tea in your shed. A bit of camping equipment and you're on your way. The trickiest thing is actually keeping the milk cool in hot weather. However, there is an easy and cheap way to have a fridge in your shed. It's ideal for keeping cans of drink cool as well and it doesn't use any energy.

Take a tray or large pot saucer and put about an inch (2.5cm) of water in it. Put your bottles or tins in there and cover with a clay pot, soaked in water.

The water will evaporate from the pot and it will suck up more water from the saucer below to evaporate. The evaporation causes the temperature to drop and, hey presto, you've got a green fridge for your plot.

We used something similar many years ago when we had milk delivered. The milkman came after we'd left for work and in the summer the milk would turn if just left outside. This method kept it relatively cool until we came home in the evening.

Coldframes

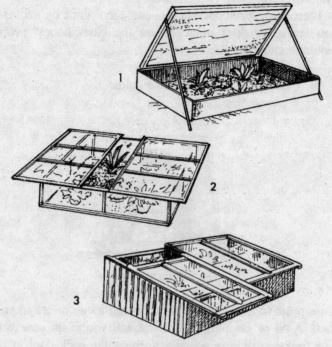

Fig. 4. Coldframes.
(1) Wooden box frame with polythene lid.
(2) Purpose-made aluminium and glass coldframe.
(3) Home-made frame.

Coldframes are immensely useful for any grower. They enable you to bring things on early, keep things late and harden off (the process of acclimatizing plants to outdoors that have been started in a greenhouse).

They really are quite easy to build using scrap wood from pallets and a couple of opening window lights. Just keep an eye out for a replacement window company ripping out old windows and ask if you can have them. They'll be glad to have less in the skip.

Ideally the side edges of the coldframe should slope about

30 degrees to maximize the amount of sunlight getting in, but even level frames are better than no frames.

With solid sided coldframes, seedlings can be drawn to the light, which causes them to become spindly or leggy. Lifting the seed tray onto a brick or a couple of upturned pots, thereby bringing it nearer the glass, will help.

Another idea I have used is to line the coldframe with polystyrene. A 'lot of electrical stores have polystyrene packaging from display models and you can often find sheets that have been on top of a washing machine or such like. You can also buy, very cheaply, a roll of polystyrene wallpaper to line your frame.

There are three benefits to a lined frame:

1. The white interior reflects more light onto the plants
2. The lining stops cold drafts from any gaps in the frame
3. Polystyrene is an insulator so it holds warmth better

Horticultural Fleece and Netting

I'm a great lover of horticultural fleece. It's cheap to buy and lasts a few years if looked after whilst it keeps plants safe from frosts and pests. For many crops, like potatoes, it's fine just laid across the top but the wind can easily carry it away. You can peg it down, but those pegs damage the fleece and it can rip free in a strong wind. I tried holding the fleece down with bricks but the sharp corners of the bricks tend to cause rips as well. Eventually I hit upon the answer: old 4-pint plastic milk containers filled with water.

The smooth plastic with rounded edges means that they won't damage the fleece and the water makes them as heavy as a brick. They only last a year, but that's no problem. Recycle them and save some more empties.

With some plants, like carrots, laying the fleece on the foliage squashes it down and can damage it. So we break up old bamboo canes into about 2 foot (60cm) lengths and push these into the soil, pop one of those empty milk containers on the top of the cane and lay the fleece over. Once again, the smooth plastic does no damage and they keep the fleece about a foot above the soil, which allows the foliage to grow whilst keeping the carrot fly at bay.

With larger crops still, you can make a miniature poly-tunnel with fleece, using alkathene water pipe. This is the pipe that they use for running mains water to houses and is thicker than a hosepipe but flexible enough to make into a hoop. You can buy it in rolls from most builders' or plumbers' merchants.

You can cut it to length with a sharp knife. You need to allow enough length to have a bit of a straight side. As a rough guide, for a bed 4 feet (1.2 metres) wide, you need it about 8 feet (2.4 metres) long. That's worth remembering when you're buying fleece as well; it comes in different widths and you want it down to the soil surface at the sides.

Once again your old bamboo canes come into use. Break them into lengths and insert half into the pipe and half into the ground. Tie some bamboo canes lengthways between the hoops and then drape your fleece over.

The supports for fleece also work well for netting but do remember that birds can sit on netting and eat your crops through the spaces. So support netting at least 6 inches (15cm) off the crop.

Bamboo Canes – Safety Tip

Often you may use short canes to mark out where a row is and so on. That's fine until you absent-mindedly bend over and poke yourself in the eye. If you just put something over the top of the cane, then it will be easier to see and it will also cushion the cane if you do forget. I have seen it done with old yogurt pots but the best thing I've seen for these were the tubes that those tablets for sterilizing false teeth come in. You can always claim you were given them!

Greenhouses

Fig. 5. Greenhouse.

Like sheds, there tend to be lots of greenhouses available secondhand and, in the best traditions of allotmenteering, we don't want to buy a new one. Often people just give them away. You may need to replace some glass and you will need to buy a few components but you can end up with a rather good greenhouse for about a fifth of the cost of a new one.

You want to site your greenhouse on level ground in a sunny spot and as far away from public roads as you can. Boys do enjoy throwing stones and the sound of breaking glass.

If you're planning where to put your greenhouse in winter, consider what things will be like in the spring. A tree to the south when in leaf will be shading your house until the sun gets above it; this can make a huge difference in how warm your greenhouse will be.

Avoid building at the base of a slope as these are often frost pockets where cold air collects in a layer. This will cause your greenhouse to be colder, defeating the object. Ensure the land is well drained because this will enable you to cultivate the border soil at any time of year without it being too sticky.

Always choose the largest greenhouse you can find; you can never have too much of a good thing. I guarantee that you will wish it were larger in the middle of the growing season. A 10 x 8 foot (3 x 2.5 metres) one is a good size, but I have seen two smaller houses joined together to make one large one. It doesn't matter what it looks like, as long as it does the job.

Now some tips from the heart on buying and moving a secondhand greenhouse. You may see adverts saying that the house has already been taken down and dismantled, but one of those shouldn't be your first choice. If you take the old house down, then you will know how it goes up and you will be sure you have all the parts.

When you go to collect and disassemble the house, this is what to take with you:

- A notebook and pen
- A felt tip marker pen
- Some WD40 easing oil
- A metal hacksaw and spare blade
- A digital camera
- Some small bags
- Some good quality gloves
- A pair of pliers
- A spanner or two of a size suitable for the bolts
- Possibly a step stool or similar

The camera isn't strictly necessary but it is so useful to have a few photos to refer to when you come to put it back up. The marker pen means you can label struts, and the notebook is so you can record what the labels are: FTL for Front Top Left strut, etc. Beware, parts may look exactly the same at first glance but have small differences. Mark them up.

Start by removing the glass. This is where the pliers come in useful for removing glazing clips that may have been there for years. Usually the glass will be standard 2 foot (60cm) square or 18 inches by 2 foot (45cm x 60cm). Mark any unusual shapes or sizes and note where they come from for later.

Usually greenhouses are glazed with horticultural glass, which is only 3mm thick and quite fragile. Also, glass becomes brittle with age and the chances of breakage are fairly high. This is where the gloves come in. Please, I can't say this enough, please be careful. Wear those gloves.

The step stool, on a firm base please, can be useful when you start working on the top of the roof. Take out the side panes first, then the roof. That way, if you do slip, you are less likely to break that precious glass.

The glazing clips go into the bag of bits and the glass may as well go straight into the car or van. It shouldn't take more than an hour to deglaze a greenhouse with two of you on the job.

Now you can start to take it apart. It will depend on your vehicle how much you take apart. If you have a large van or if the greenhouse is within walking distance of your plot, you could even get away with moving it in one piece. Two people can easily carry an aluminium frame greenhouse.

Otherwise it is a matter of taking it apart. Often nuts and bolts will be oxidized and stuck; that's where the WD40 easing oil comes in or the hacksaw as a last resort for really stuck bolts.

Start from the top and work your way down. When you have, say, ten glazing bars the same, wrap them together with some parcel tape. Trust me, go slowly on this part of the job and the erection at the other end will go quickly.

It's been my experience that you are bound to need some more greenhouse nuts and bolts and some glazing clips. Old bolts have been sawn, some will have stripped threads and often glazing clips are bent out of usable shape when they're removed. They're cheap enough and available easily from most DIY stores and garden centres. It is best to buy a load before you start re-building.

Once you have the new greenhouse on the site, you need a base for the house. Since most sites don't allow permanent concrete bases I'd suggest using 3 inch (8cm) square fencing posts laid on the ground. They are available treated quite cheaply, although they will benefit from a few extra good coats of a preservative like Cuprinol since they will be in contact with the ground.

If your plot is a bit wet, dig a little trench under where the sides will go and put some gravel in. This will stop water standing under the posts.

Now, it is critical that the base is square and level. A spirit level will enable you to check that things are level but square is not so easy. Measure the diagonals; they should be equal when the base is square. If you want to make sure that an angle is a right angle (90 degrees) use the 3:4:5 rule. Measure three feet on one edge, four on the other and the distance between those points should be five feet when things are square. Yes, it is Pythagoras' theorem from school!

I have two greenhouses on my plot. One has a border all round the edge with slabs up the middle as a hard path and the other just has a border on one side and the rest is slabs. Lay these before you start building and you have something firm to stand on.

With a bit of luck and helped by your notes, you will get the frame up fairly quickly. Especially with a larger greenhouse, it's a two-person job.

Having got the frame up, the next job is to glaze the greenhouse. Start from the top because you can manoeuvre better without the glass in the frame below you. This is where you discover you are really short of glazing clips and many of those you have are twisted and unusable. You did buy some extras, I hope? My 10 x 8 greenhouse uses 200 glazing clips. Incidentally, I found the W clips by far the easiest and best.

Once again, **take great care handling glass**. Glass weakens with age and hairline cracks can cause a pane to break when you least expect it. Work slowly and safely; do wear those gloves.

Once you have your greenhouse up, there are a few fittings you might like to buy. First, and in my opinion a must for an allotment house, is an automatic vent window opener. These are not expensive, take moments to fit and can save your crop from being cooked on a hot day when you are not there.

A louvre window for lower down is a useful addition to ensure a good airflow in hot weather. You can also get automatic openers for these.

If you have young children on the plot with you, then do keep in mind the dangers a glasshouse can present. You may want to replace the glazing below roof level with safety glass or even polycarbonate. Expensive, it's true, but safety is important.

Greenhouse Bench

Fig. 6. Greenhouse bench.

In my small greenhouse, I have a bench, which is great for starting things off and growing in pots. Having looked at the prices, I decided to build my own. This only took a few hours and cost me a tenth of buying one.

I used pressure treated timber throughout, so it won't rot. For the legs I used two 8 foot (2.4 metre) fence posts cut in half, with 2" x 1" (5cm x 2.5cm) bearers lengthways and 1" x ½" (2.5cm x 1cm) slats across with a gap between to make the shelf surfaces. To keep it stable a couple of struts made from 2" x 1" (5cm x 2.5cm) wood run at 45 degrees on the back.

Compost Bins

Fig. 7. Compost bins made from pallets.

No allotment is complete without a compost bin. Of course you can get plastic bins, often subsidized from the council, or from the shops, but the traditional allotment compost bin is made from old pallets and scrap wood.

For a starter, you need seven pallets and some posts. Position the pallets into an 'M' shape and then drive the posts into the ground inside the pallets or on the outside if they won't go inbetween the laths. To hold the corners together and stable, use some wire to tie them together – old wire coat hangers are fine, just twist them tight with pliers.

Usually a pallet has more laths on one side than the other, so put the side with more onto the inside. To keep the heat in, stuff the space between the sides of the pallets with cardboard and you have a perfectly functional pair of compost bins in an hour.

The two spare pallets form the fronts. These are wedged up with posts at an angle to hold them in place.

Preserving Wood and Especially Posts

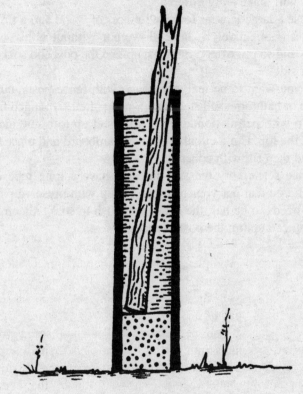

Fig. 8. Post soaker.

When buying new wood, fence posts, etc, you can specify pressure treated. This means that a preservative has been forced into the wood. It will last longer than untreated wood, but where it is in contact with the ground for years it is well worth treating it further.

You can buy Cuprinol or similar but don't go for cheap (or

expensive!) fence paint. Your wood is in contact with the soil and fence paints will not do the job.

Cuprinol recommend three good coats applied with a brush but it's better to soak it. Rot tends to start at the cut edge endgrain of wood, so just soaking the ends and painting the body will make a big difference.

I use a large jam-jar for small pieces of wood and a flower bucket – effectively a large flowerpot without holes – for posts and so on. After 5 minutes, up-end the post and soak the other side.

If you want to be really thorough with fence posts, take a piece of bathroom soil stack down-pipe, often scrounged from a skip with permission, and fill with soil up to a few inches from the top. Cut a circular piece of cardboard and place that in and then fill with concrete.

Once set, empty the soil and you have a long tube into which you can put your post and fill up with preservative. It only needs to be half the depth you wish to soak, remember, as you can upturn the post to soak the rest.

11

LIVESTOCK

Keeping some livestock on the allotment is a very natural step from growing your own crops. I've seen everything from bees to horses kept on allotments but generally the most popular thing is to keep some hens.

But before we go ahead and convert the plot into an urban farm, there are a few points to consider.

Does your site actually allow you to keep animals? Sometimes this will be banned under the rules, in which case you need to try to get the rules changed. This can be an uphill task, but you do have an ally in the Government who recommend (in the Fifth Report of the House of Commons Committee for Environment, Transport and Regional Affairs in June 1998) allowing the keeping of livestock. Quote that and you are halfway there!

Usually the objections that are raised against keeping livestock on the allotment are also things you should consider carefully.

Will your animals be safe?

Unfortunately, allotments are not immune from thieves and vandals. The worst I have heard of is a shed full of hens being set on fire. If your site is not secure, then really think hard if you want to take the risk.

The two-legged pests are not the only thing to consider.

Foxes are increasingly a problem in urban areas. Luckily they can be defended against but you need to bear them in mind when keeping poultry.

Will your livestock be a nuisance?

Free-range hens are wonderful but you won't be popular if they free range onto someone else's plot and eat his prize brassicas! If houses surround your site, you won't be popular if you keep a cockerel either. Most people don't take happily to cock crow at first light. Luckily you don't need to keep a cockerel with hens to have eggs, unless you want fertile eggs, of course.

Keeping animals involves keeping food for them and this can be a magnet for rats. You need to consider where you will store the food and what measures you will take to prevent vermin becoming a nuisance.

Bees are a wonderful boon to the gardener, not only producing honey, beeswax, etc, but also pollinating plants. Can you keep them safely and securely so that they do not present a danger? Remember that many people bring their children onto allotment sites and happily let them roam.

One question I was asked about was the danger of avian flu from keeping hens. You may need to explain that the real risk is minimal but it is hard arguing with media hype and hysteria.

What if you are not there?

The final thing to consider before launching into livestock on a plot is what provision you can make for them if you are not there. Asking a neighbour to pop in and feed the cat when you are away is one thing but getting somebody to go down to the allotment and look after the hens twice a day is something else, even with free eggs as an incentive.

Do you have the time? You can leave a plot to its own devices for a few days with no harm done but animals require visiting at least every day – including Christmas Day. Do think this one through carefully and be honest with yourself. Discuss it with your family as well; what happens if you fall ill?

Having gone through all the negatives and decided you can keep some livestock, then next you need to consider what to keep.

I'll ignore large animals like pigs, goats and horses. Although I've seen them on a site, I don't really think they're that suitable for allotments as a rule and you need some specialist knowledge. The main livestock kept on allotments are poultry and bees.

Bees on the Plot

Fig. 9. Beehive.

As I said, the first consideration is safety. Assuming you can site the hive so it can be secured to prevent curious young children from gaining access, you need to consider that the bees will be flying back and forth to it.

There is a relatively easy answer to the flight path problem: surround the area of the hive with a fence or hedge about 6 feet (1.8 metres) high. The bees will leave the hive and fly high, above the heads of your fellow plotholders. This also provides shelter for the hive.

It's obviously beyond the scope of this book to go into the ins and outs of keeping bees. A visit to your local bookshop or library is called for and you should also contact a local beekeeper for some hands-on experience and guidance before jumping in with both feet. The British Beekeepers' Association (see page 249) will be able to help and put you in touch with local beekeepers and associations.

Poultry on the Plot

Fig. 10. Poultry house and run.

There's an awful lot to be said for keeping some poultry on the allotment. For a start, those bolted lettuces and cabbages are perfectly acceptable green food for hens. Not to mention that they love eating those slugs. Anything that gets rid of slugs is a friend of mine.

Their waste product is what we call fertilizer. As a general rule, poultry droppings are too strong to use directly on the plants but, being full of nitrogen, they make a great activator for compost heaps. Or drop some into a barrel of water to make a rich liquid feed.

Once again, covering everything about keeping hens or ducks is beyond the scope of this book but there are a few things worth mentioning. Neither chickens nor ducks are hard to keep and both provide eggs and possibly meat if you are actually able to kill them.

There is no need to go out and buy a purpose made ark or house for hundreds of pounds, you can convert an old shed easily enough or knock one together yourself. There are plans available to buy or take a look at what others do and make a few notes – that allotment recycling philosophy again.

One item that is good for both hen and plotholder is a movable cage to allow your birds the freedom to wander but to keep them from heading to the plot next door. When you have harvested a patch, the hens will happily scratch around and clean up, devouring any slugs and pests as they go.

Since you'll be leaving them on their own, your cage should be fox proof. This will also keep out any curious dogs or cats. Don't trust chicken wire; this is chicken proof but a fox will just bite through it. You should use weldmesh, which is easily available and much more robust. It will actually stiffen your cage so you don't need to use more than 2" x 1" (5cm x 2.5cm) wood for the bars. Make sure you use enough staples to hold it firmly. It only needs to be a couple of feet high as your birds won't be flying around.

Now foxes are clever beasts. They will dig a tunnel to get into your cage or tip it over if they can. Burying the wire side is not practical for a moveable cage but if you make a 'skirt', extending the wire horizontally for about 18 inches to 2 feet (45cm to 60cm) from the base, the fox will usually give up but, in any case, be unable to get at your birds before you come back to put them to bed. Just use some old-fashioned tent pegs or similar to hold the cage to the ground firmly in case Mr Fox gets his nose under and pushes it up.

Do provide cover over the top part of the cage, even a piece of tarpaulin laid on will suffice. In summer it provides shade for the birds and in winter shelter from the rain; also hens, being descended from jungle floor living birds, feel much more comfortable with somewhere to hide from those swooping eagles.

Ducks are not kept as much as hens although some breeds are remarkably productive of eggs. Duck eggs are larger than hens' eggs and make the richest omelettes and scrambled eggs, as well as being perfect for cake making due to their high fat content. However, admittedly they are not to everyone's taste.

Ducks don't actually need a pond but they do need access to water (as well as drinking water) for washing and preening. A large bucket or a baby bath filled with water will suffice although some breeds are more demanding than others.

With both ducks and hens, you need to provide feed above the green waste from the plot, which is more of a treat than a staple. A plastic dustbin with a firm-fitting lid kept in a rat-proof shed is ideal for storing on the site.

Hens and ducks are the most common poultry found on allotments but you could also keep guinea fowl, geese or turkeys on a plot.

12

TOOLS, EQUIPMENT
AND TECHNIQUES

There is a bewildering array of tools, gadgets and gizmos available to the gardener. You name it, somebody has thought about it and sells it. Being a man, I'm not immune to buying gadgets (boys do love their toys), but what is actually useful and what ends up left on the shelf?

You don't really need that many tools, so when you start out concentrate on buying good quality basic tools and leave any fancy equipment until you know exactly what you what to grow and how.

Before spending money on new tools, check the adverts in your local newspaper for secondhand ones or offer to buy them from plotholders moving off the site. Remember: a well made tool will last longer than a lifetime.

The Spade

First, you need a digging spade. This will also double as a shovel. A shovel is a spade where the sides and top are upturned to form a container and prevent spillage. Shovels are used for moving quantities of loose material like sand or gravel and not for digging. Whilst you can use a spade as a shovel (the extra material held by the shovel shortens the task of moving a pile of sand, for example), you cannot use a shovel as a digging spade.

Stainless steel spades, which slip through clay soils easily, are available, but an ordinary spade is sufficient. The most important thing is to get the handle height right. People are taller nowadays than they used to be; a longer handle makes the spade easier to use for them and gives better leverage.

A border spade has a smaller blade and is much easier to use if you don't have the strength to handle a full sized spade with a chunk of soil on the blade. It is therefore particularly useful for women. I myself have used a border spade when I was digging a trench through very solid clay. I found the full size spade too hard to push in and lift up but was able to complete the job with a border spade.

I also recommend those spades that are turned at the top of the blade to provide a flat surface to press on. Such spades are useful if you have a heavy soil since a sharp-topped spade wears your boots and the pressure can become uncomfortable.

Before buying a spade, check that you are comfortable with the height, that the blade and shaft are sound and that they are firmly fixed to each other. There are two types of handle: the basic 'T' handle and the 'D' or 'Y' handle. Many gardeners prefer the 'D' style but you should choose the one that is most comfortable for you.

The Fork

Just as with the spade, a comfortable handle height is critical with your fork. It is also important that the tines are strong. If you can bend them, then in no time at all they will be bent by stones in the ground and become useless. A smaller border fork is useful as a second tool when working in close confines even if you can handle the full size fork.

The potato fork is a variant of the standard fork. It has flat rather than square section blades and is designed to go into the soil easily and lift potatoes that will not fall through the reduced space between the tines. I have a potato fork and I don't think the advantages make it worth buying as the little potatoes slip through anyway.

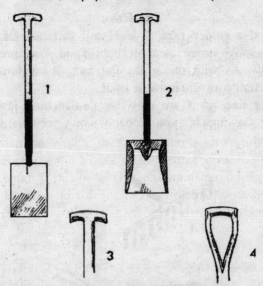

Fig. 11a. Types of spades and handles.
(1) Digging spade.   (2) Shovel with wide blade and raised edges.
(3) 'T' handle.   (4) 'D' or 'Y' handle.

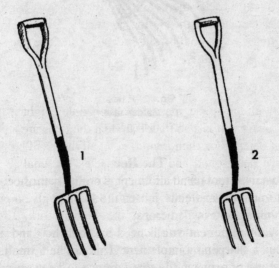

Fig. 11b. Forks.
(1) Digging fork.
(2) Border or 'ladies' fork.

The Rake

You need a garden rake to level soil surfaces, rake down lumps, remove stones, clear off rubbish and, sometimes, draw out drills. As with the spade and fork, it needs a strong construction with a reasonable shaft.

Spring tine rakes are used for de-thatching lawns and clearing mowings but you probably won't need one for your allotment.

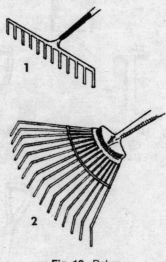

Fig. 12. Rakes.
(1) Garden rake.
(2) Sprung rake.

The Hoe

The most used tool on an allotment is probably the hoe. You'll need it to cut down weeds, loosen the soil and give a preliminary thinning to crowded crops.

For your allotment you'll need a Dutch hoe and a draw hoe, plus a sharpening implement. This can be a small sharpening stone or a metal file that you use to keep an edge on the blade. A sharp hoe is a joy to use but a blunt hoe is hard work.

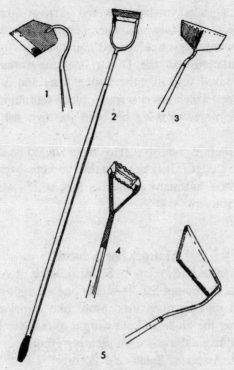

Fig. 13. Hoes. (1) Draw hoe.
(2) Dutch hoe with plastic grip.
(3) Flat weeding push hoe.
(4) Push-pull weeding hoe.
(5) Swoe.

Use a draw hoe by pulling it towards you and chopping into the weeds. It is also very useful for drawing a drill when sowing seeds or planting potatoes.

Use a Dutch hoe by pushing the blade just under the soil surface, thereby cutting the weeds away from their roots. To stop it digging in or planing over the weeds, hold the hoe so that the blade is level to the ground. With practice and by employing a back and forth motion, you can control positioning very accurately and cover quite large areas in a short time. I tend to stop and sharpen the blade about every 15 minutes. So that you can see what ground you have covered and to avoid walking on the hoed plot, work forwards when cutting larger weeds, and work backwards when hoeing seedlings.

Two variations on the Dutch hoe are a flat weeding push hoe (used just like the Dutch hoe) and a push-pull weeding hoe (which has a serrated blade that remains in the soil all the time, working on both the forward and back strokes).

Finally, there is the Swoe. This is an angled head hoe with three cutting edges. It is not popular, perhaps because of its unusual shape, but many gardeners love it. It's worth trying one to see if it suits you.

Mattocks or Azadas

A mattock (also known by its Spanish name of Azada) is a broad blade on a stout handle rather like a larger scale draw hoe. When digging, it is used more like a pickaxe than a spade, lifting the blade and allowing it to fall into the soil. It is also used like a draw hoe for clearing ground.

In South America, Spain and Portugal it is the standard gardening tool. It is another one of those tools that some users love whereas others find it of no more use than the other more usual tools available in the UK. Try before you buy if you can.

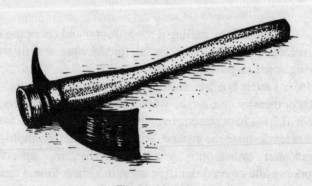

Fig. 14. Mattock.

Hand Tools

As with your other tools, make sure you get quality hand tools. That bargain trowel for 50p or £1 probably won't last you a month.

The following four hand tools are really useful:

A **hand trowel** for digging holes. This acts as your miniature spade. You can also get very narrow trowels which are great when working between close-planted crops.

A **hand fork** for loosening and breaking up the soil just like its larger version.

An **onion hoe** for weeding close to plants and in raised beds is also very useful. However, these are becoming harder to find.

Finally, a **double hoe** where one side is a blade for hoeing and drawing drills, with three tines on the other side for cultivating. I actually find this the most useful hand tool in the shed, replacing all of the above hand tools except for the trowel.

Wolf manufacture an inter-changeable range of tool heads that can be attached to different handles, which means you can use a cultivator as both a hand tool and as a full tool. If you have a combination of raised beds and normal soil, these can be an economical solution to buying quality tools. If you have security concerns on your site, another benefit is that you can take the tool heads home of an evening and thieves are unlikely to know what to make of the handles on their own.

Special hand tools such as the Easi-Grip range are also available for those with mobility problems, due to arthritis, etc. The handle is at 90 degrees to the tool, which means the force line passes in a straight line through the wrist and arm.

The Lite Lift range provides full sized tools for older gardeners or those suffering from back, neck or arm problems. They're very light – you can balance them on one finger – and ergonomically shaped, with an additional handle that can be positioned for optimum control.

Fig. 15. Wolf interchangeable cultivator head.

Bow Saw, Loppers and Secateurs

A pair of long-handled lopping shears and a bow saw are invaluable if you have fruit trees to prune or overhanging trees and bushes. However, just buy the cheapest ones you can find unless you need to use them frequently. With secateurs for pruning, the most important thing is comfort. Look at the handle carefully and try squeezing it frequently. We have an expensive pair that gives blisters and a cheap pair that doesn't.

Pegs and Line

Although this is one of the simplest tools, I think it's essential. You can make your own with two sticks and a length of string. I use bright coloured nylon line so that I can always see it clearly. It provides a guide for digging and for drawing a row. As its cost is negligible it is worthwhile having two or three lines.

Measuring Stick

This is a great aid to sowing and planting which you can make yourself for pennies. Take a length of 2" x 1" (5cm x 2.5cm) wood about 6 feet (1.8 metres) long, and mark out, using an indelible marker or felt tip pen, on one side with a half width line every 6 inches (15cm) and a full width line every foot (30cm). On the other side, mark similarly but with the half width lines every 4 inches (10cm). When sowing or planting, just lay the stick by the row and you have a spacing guide suitable for most plants.

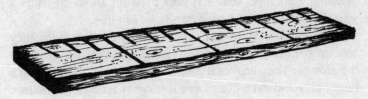

Fig. 16. Measuring stick.

Watering Can

It's worth buying a large watering can to reduce the walking back and forth to the tap or butt. Plastic cans are robust and lightweight, an important consideration since 10 litres of water weighs 10kg. If you get two cans, you can carry one in each hand, halving the walking and balancing the load.

The actual can may be cheap to buy but it's worth spending more on the rose (the spray head). A fine brass rose with fine spray is much better for watering seedlings than a rose with a heavy flow which knocks the seedlings down. When using a fine rose, turn it so it faces upwards and, when you tip the can, the water will flow in a gentle arc, further reducing the force.

You may need a smaller can for the greenhouse (one that is easier to handle when watering seed trays, etc), as well as a long-stemmed can (which is useful for getting water to crops at the back of a border).

Power Tools

I've not come across an allotment site with power points by the plot, although who knows what will happen next. However, some powered machinery is well worthwhile using.

Rotavator

I'm the proud owner of two rotavators, the first being a 30-year-old Merry Tiller. Although that may seem ancient for a machine, remember that it is only used for about 20 hours a year. If it was a car it would hardly be run in.

Although rotavators may appear daunting at first sight, they are easy to use and will save many hours of hard work preparing the ground. They are not a total substitute for digging (with a heavy clay soil even quite large rotavators tend just to bounce over the surface), however they will break the soil up into a fine tilth in short order. I dig over in the winter and use the rotavator to finish breaking the clods in the spring.

If you just rotavate year after year you will create a pan below the cultivation depth, so it is as well to dig over every three to five years in any case.

There's quite a range available, both new and secondhand, anything from small tillers to large walk-behind tractors so the choice can be bewildering. Make sure you select a machine

Fig. 17. A Merry tiller.

that you can handle. A machine with an engine size from 3hp to 6hp is suitable for most people and plots. Some of the larger machines have reverse gears, as well as more than one forward gear which make them easier to use.

As most engines are reliable nowadays, the quality of the tines is of most importance. Check the width of the tines. A narrow width enables you to manoeuvre better but a larger width covers more area in a pass. Avoid weak tines that will bend or may even break.

My other rotavator is a Mantis Tiller. Unlike a full rotavator that breaks up large areas of soil often to a depth of a foot (30cm) or more, a Mantis tiller produces a very fine tilth of soil to a lesser depth, around 8 inches to a foot (20cm–30cm)

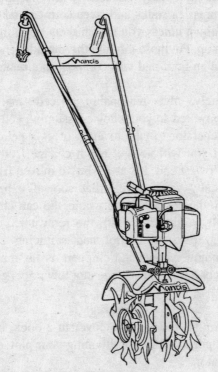

Fig. 18. A Mantis tiller.

maximum. It can even be used as a mechanical hoe, chopping the weeds as the soil is turned.

The Mantis is very lightweight (about 20 lb/9kg), with a tiller width of 8 inches (20cm). It is therefore ideal for growers with raised beds as it can easily be lifted into and out of the bed.

The truth is that you can cultivate a plot without a rotavator but they save an awful lot of time. Because you don't use them that much, they're an ideal piece of equipment to share between two or three plotholders. Just agree beforehand about fuel and servicing costs.

Chippers and Shredders

Shredders are absolutely fantastic when making compost. Things like brassica stalks and sweetcorn can take a year or more to rot down unless you smash them up with a hammer and cut them up. Put those through the shredder and they'll be heating up in an hour and will compost in a matter of a few weeks.

Unfortunately, the reasonably priced machines are electrically powered so your choice, assuming you don't have a portable generator to take to the plot, is a petrol powered machine and you will not get much change from £600 and that's at the lowest end. It's as if you've moved from a car to a lorry. I really can't justify that sort of expense as an individual plotholder but if the whole site can club together then it's well worth it. As with the rotavator, you need to consider who pays for petrol and servicing costs when required. Finding secondhand chippers is far more difficult than rotavators but if you see one at a low price, go for it.

Digging

It may seem a bit too basic to cover in a book, but digging over is an important part of cultivating your plot, even if you have a rotavator.

Unlike raised beds that are never walked on, your moving

around the plot compacts the soil and this makes it difficult for plant roots to penetrate, water to drain and air to get in. Digging loosens and aerates the soil and can increase the depth of topsoil.

If you just dig a hole, you will see the soil changes below a certain depth. This lower subsoil is lifeless and provides little to help the growth of our plants. The topsoil has organic matter, worms and millions of invisible microbes who work tirelessly to help our plants grow. As a general rule, the deeper your topsoil, the better your crops; anything under 18 inches (45cm) will certainly benefit from improvement.

There are two distinct types of digging. Single digging, where you just turn over the top 9 inches (22cm) of the soil, and double digging, which is harder work but increases the depth of topsoil. With a good depth of topsoil established you should only need to double dig about once every five years.

If you have a light sandy soil, then even single digging isn't really necessary. It will be sufficient most years simply to fork over to aerate or run over with a rotavator. A heavy clay, however, needs working to break it up and stop it from becoming either a muddy quagmire in the wet or a concrete yard in the dry.

Digging over is undertaken from late autumn through the winter. The earlier the better, as we want some frost to work on the clods for us. Don't worry about breaking the clods up too much when digging, just upend them and the action of freezing and thawing will break them down into fine particles for you. Then in the spring, a quick going over with the rotavator or a hand cultivator will finish the job, leaving a fine tilth to sow into.

Don't try digging too much at once. Split your plot into manageable sections. My plots are 15 feet (4.5 metres) wide and I find a length of about 8 or 10 feet (3 metres) is quite enough for a session.

Start by marking a trench slightly wider than your spade and half the width you are digging over. Cut into the sides, then dig out the middle, putting the soil on the ground where the other half of the vegetable patch is.

Now you can just keep turning the soil in the empty trench, upending it as you go until you reach the other side, where you repeat the trench cutting exercise but the soil goes into the empty trench.

Back down the plot until you reach the soil you piled up originally which now goes into the empty trench you've created. Fig. 19 should make it obvious.

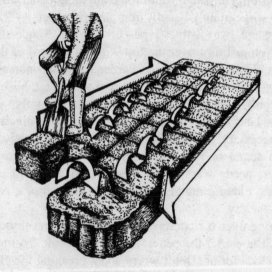

Fig. 19. Digging and rotating.

Double Digging

Essentially we are following the same pattern of working a circle to avoid carting soil about but we take out the soil until we get down to the subsoil. You may need to make your trench double width to get working room to start with.

Avoid mixing the subsoil with the topsoil. Once exposed, use a fork to break up the subsoil, opening it up as you go. This can be really heavy work on heavy clay, so don't try and go to the full depth of the fork; 3–6 inches (8–15cm) is enough, unless you're strong and fit.

Next add organic matter. This could be rotted manure, compost or leafmould. Even fresh leaves will be better than nothing. The more material you can add, the better.

Then the topsoil from the next row goes on top and we repeat until finished.

What happens is that the organic matter gets down into the broken-up subsoil and the worms dive down from the topsoil to feed on the organic matter, breaking up the subsoil further and mixing it all together to create topsoil. Isn't nature wonderful?

If you don't double dig occasionally, but just single dig or especially rotavate each year, you build up a solid pan below and effectively end up with a shallow topsoil.

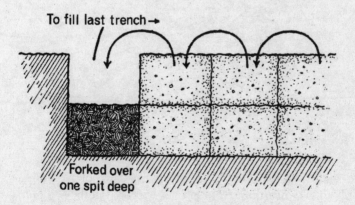

Fig. 20. Double digging.

13

MANURES, FERTILIZERS AND COMPOST

John Seymour, a wonderful proponent of self sufficiency, once said something on the lines of, 'The best way to make compost is to put grass through the guts of a cow,' and there is an awful lot of truth in that.

Your soil is made up of rocks and rock dust mixed with organic matter that we call humus. This humus holds everything together and at the same time stops the rock dust from setting into a solid, cement like mass. It absorbs water, holding it like a sponge and, by keeping the pores of the soil open, allows it to drain so it doesn't become a waterlogged stagnant swamp.

This structure is vital for growing any plant and especially for vegetables which have been bred for their benefit to us rather than their ability to thrive in adverse conditions.

The humus holds nutrients as well as those available to the plant roots from the rocks. In nature much is the result of symbiosis; the whole structure is based on creatures and plants taking in each other's washing so to speak. One bug's waste is another's food supply. Humus provides the home for these billions of bacteria, thousands of microscopic creatures, worms and insects who combine to make growing possible.

So adding humus helps your soil whether it be a heavy clay or light sand, opening one up and holding the other together. It also darkens the soil so helping it to absorb energy from sunlight and so warm up faster in the spring, helping our crops to grow.

Humus is the reason that the purely chemical-based agricultural systems will fail. The soil gradually loses its structure, making it harder and harder for the plant's roots to get into the soil. At the same time, the plants are weakened by lack of micro-nutrients and the absence of symbiotic organisms.

Growing by just chucking on some Growmore fertilizer each spring will work for a while but it is on the same basis as living off credit cards. One day there is a reckoning and the bill has to be paid as the limits are reached.

That's not to say that chemicals have no place in the grower's armoury and this is where I personally part company from the organic growers. Working with nature rather than against nature is obviously sensible but an additional input of nutrients will often make the difference between mediocre crops and a great harvest. Some plants, which have been bred far from their wild forebears, need high levels of nitrogen to live up to their potential; for example, brassicas and sweetcorn. Supplying this just from manures, etc, is often not possible.

The way to add humus to your soil is to add manures, compost and leafmould in large quantities.

Horse and Cow Manure

The home grower might well buy the odd bag of horse manure from a local stables but a bag does not go far on an allotment plot. Ask around – other plotholders will know of a source. Often you will find, especially in a town, a riding stables only too pleased to get rid of their waste problem for free and who will deliver a trailer load to you. Don't complain if they do make a nominal charge for the transport; it's still a tremendous bargain.

In terms of the nutrients in the manure, there's little to choose between horse and cow manure but cow manure is less solid and, if you have a wet plot, then go for horse manure if you can.

You will see throughout this book I refer to 'well rotted manure'. The reason is that fresh manure is a mixture of dung and bedding materials like straw and shavings. Initially the manure has very high nitrogen levels and may well be too high for your plants. The bedding materials, however, need nitrogen to break down. All you need to do is pile the manure somewhere out of the way, cover it with an old tarpaulin or plastic sheet to stop the rain from leaching the nutrients out and leave it for a year. After this there should be no smell and it will become a crumbly dark material full of worms and will be the finest thing you can put on your plot. Some stables will even deliver old manure, which is already well rotted.

As a rule, if you can supply a good barrow load or two per square yard/metre on a third of your plot each year it will be in very good heart.

An Awful Warning!

In 2007 and 2008 many growers noticed crops failing, looking as if they had been sprayed with weedkiller. Eventually it was realized that the cause lay in the manure. What had happened was that the farmers had been using a new selective weedkiller, Aminopyralid, and this was in the manure. The product was sprayed on grassland and killed off the docks and thistles. At the same time it was absorbed by the grass and this in turn was eaten by grazing cattle and horses.

Once in the animal's gut the grass was broken down and the weedkiller was excreted in the urine. The manufacturers had put warnings on the product about using the manure but this was generally ignored.

Once the story broke and the scale of the problem began to dawn, the manufacturer withdrew the product from sale and DEFRA revoked the licence for use. However, on review the manufacturer promised to ensure that users were more careful and the product is now back on sale.

Unfortunately this stuff will be coming through in manure until at least 2012 and probably 2013. That is assuming the farmers returned any stocks they held and stopped using what was a very cost-effective product in 2008.

Due to the nature of modern farming with contractors and so forth, often the suppliers of manure were completely unaware that Aminopyralid was used and in their manure. Just stacking and rotting the manure will not degrade the chemical, even for three years. The only answer is to spread it on the ground and fork or rotavate it into the top 6 inches (15cm) or so. After a month or so, repeat this to break it down further. After about six months the microbes in the soil should have broken it down completely. Of course, your soil is out of action in this period.

There is no simple, reliable and cheap test for this. If you suspect your manure is affected, then mix some fifty/fifty with multi-purpose compost and try raising some tomatoes in that. It's a sad fact that persistent chemicals will linger in the environment and can have unexpected and unfortunate consequences.

Poultry Manure

Birds do not separate their urine from their droppings; it all comes out the same way. Urine actually has a high level of nitrogen so bird muck is very strong – too strong to apply directly to your crops even if aged.

It is, however, brilliant to activate your compost heap. Spread a thin layer every 6 inches (15cm) as you build your heap and it will heat up in short order.

If you know of a turkey farmer in your area, it can be worth calling him as turkeys produce huge amounts of waste. Usually it's mixed with shavings and can be treated as horse manure. We had mountains of the stuff delivered to our site and those who were lucky enough to get it on their plot really saw a big improvement.

If you have rabbits or guinea pigs, their manure is best used as a compost heap activator as well. It's far better than putting the hutch clearings in the bin.

Sheep Manure

If you see someone walking across a field of sheep with a carrier bag and putting sheep droppings into it, I bet you he's a vegetable grower and you don't need to call in a psychiatrist.

Put the droppings into hessian sack and dunk in a barrel of water until the water looks like strong tea. It's one of the finest high-nitrogen liquid feeds you can have.

Dog, Cat and Human Manure

One question I'm frequently asked is if you can use cat and dog manure on your plot. I've even had people who ask about human waste. The answer is simply no. Both dog and cat manures can carry a few parasites and diseases that people can catch. It really isn't worth the risk. Human faeces will contain bacteria and rarely parasites that are specific to people and are consequently far more dangerous. You can have composting toilets but this is specialist and well outside the scope of this book.

Municipal Compost

Many local authorities now run separate green waste collections which reduce landfill. The garden waste is taken to a central point and there put through giant shredders and then properly hot composted with the materials being turned to ensure that everything is heated to kill any diseases. After this they go through a giant sieve and large pieces that made it through the first time go back into the shredder and round again.

The scale of these operations is quite amazing, often taking 100 tonnes of green waste a day to convert into compost. Some of the better councils deliver this for free to allotment sites, sometimes the contractor who processes it sells it and will deliver in bulk loads.

It's well worth finding out about. If nobody on your site has heard about it, try ringing the council and tracking down where the green waste goes.

Comfrey

Fig. 21. Comfrey patch and plant.

A comfrey patch is a real boon to the allotment holder. The plant is grown for its leaves which are harvested to produce a liquid tomato feed, a potato fertilizer and a compost activator.

It's easy to grow and very tolerant so you don't need to worry about it when it is established. It will thrive in partial shade and doesn't mind a boggy patch, so position it in the least valuable part of the plot. A patch of 10 feet x 15 feet (3 metres x 4.5 metres) is about right for a plot.

Rather than just grow any old variety, try to obtain Bocking 14. This was developed by Lawrence D Hills, the founder of the Henry Doubleday Research Association on their trial grounds in Bocking, Essex. It is a sterile clone so it won't set seed and spread like wild comfrey and it has been bred for a high level of nutrients.

Wilted leaves of Bocking 14 actually contain as much nitrogen and phosphorus as farmyard manure but about four times the level of potash, which is why they make a fantastic tomato feed.

You start it off from root cuttings, planting them directly

at a spacing of 2–3 feet (60–90cm) between plants each way in a prepared bed in March, April, May or September. To prepare your bed, just dig it over deeply, removing any perennial weeds as you go and breaking up the subsoil. Comfrey roots will go deep so it does no harm to help them get started.

Once it has grown away and produced its attractive purple flowers, take your first cut with a pair of shears, just cutting the leaves about 6 inches (15cm) above ground level.

Don't buy more than the minimum quantity of root cuttings to start as it's really easy to propagate comfrey from root cuttings. Once you have a plant established, plunge a spade into the centre and lever up some of the root. Cut this half of the plant up top to bottom to make more root cuttings. I potted these up in multi-purpose compost in 3 inch (8cm) pots to measure the success rate. From half a plant I potted 26 root cuttings and every one of them took.

When handling comfrey, wear gloves. The leaves have small hairs on them which can be irritating. When the leaves have wilted, the hairs collapse.

When winter arrives, the comfrey will die back, so after the last cut of the year hoe between the plants and give them a nitrogen-rich feed. This helps them establish well and pays them back for their hard work during the year.

Comfrey is a very strong plant; you can even put raw poultry manure around the plants without harm. The flip side of this is that getting rid of a comfrey patch is no easy task. You will probably have to resort to a systemic weedkiller, so do think carefully about the position before planting.

Once properly established in the second year, you can then take four or five decent cuts a year.

Comfrey is great for making your own organic tomato feed: comfrey tea is as good as almost anything you can buy and it's quite easy to make. Take a cut and allow the leaves to wilt for a day, then stuff into a hessian sack or a couple of old pillowcases.

Place the sack into a water butt with a lid and leave for

about six weeks. You can then draw off tomato feed as you like. It's also great for potatoes and any potash-loving plant.

The reason you put the leaves into a sack is that, if you don't, the bits of comfrey will block the tap and you have to get it out of the barrel with a bucket. The lid is required as the stench is awful as it rots down. Not only will every fly for miles around head for it, anyone downwind will be moaning about the smell. Once your feed is used, pop the contents of the sack onto the compost heap.

Nettle Tea

Nettles are a difficult weed to deal with but, by using the comfrey tea method described above, you can produce a worthwhile liquid fertilizer and be confident that the nettles are dead before they are added to the compost heap. The only drawback is that this liquid can become quite smelly.

By taking a number of cuts during the year from a large patch of nettles, you will weaken the nettles over time and in the end kill them off, helping you to bring the land into productive use.

Green Manures

The concept of green manures is that instead of leaving ground bare you grow a crop to hold or even to add to the nutrients in the soil and then dig it in to add humus. Many of the green manures are great if you're a farmer with a plough to turn them under when ready, but they are really hard work for the allotment holder who needs to dig them under properly with his spade.

Mustard is useful as a follow-on to potatoes as it confuses the eelworms that can be a pest. Unfortunately, mustard is a brassica so using it on a plot with club-root is not advisable, since it will increase the problem for your brassicas.

Field beans are often recommended as an over-wintering crop, as being legumes they add to available nitrogen, which tends to leach quite quickly from the soil. However, broad beans do the same and are a palatable crop. Over-wintering green manures are of value on light soils but, with heavy soils, the annual dig is more valuable.

For filling in spaces between a crop and that annual dig, dwarf French beans are useful. The seed is cheap and sometimes you can be lucky and get a late crop.

Annual ryegrass or clover sown in the autumn is a useful over-wintering green manure. The clovers also fix nitrogen but grazing rye is exceptionally hard work to turn over in the spring.

Leafmould

Fig. 22. Leafmould bin.

Leafmould does not add much in the way of nutrients to the soil, the trees having taken those back into themselves before shedding them for the winter. It does add humus to the soil though and improves it that way.

Often the local authority can be persuaded to dump their road sweepings on the site for the benefit of the plotholders. There's usually a fair bit of grit in with them, which is good for opening up clay soils, but sadly there's usually a lot of litter that needs to be picked out as you go along. I have to wonder what we are leaving for future generations when I turn up a sweet wrapper that's been under the soil for years and is still in perfect condition.

Anyway, you don't compost the leaves and there is no benefit in adding activators. Just pile them together and leave nature to it for a year or two. To stop them blowing about, construct a cage from wire netting. This can just be four posts driven into the soil with wire netting attached.

If you bury leaves as part of your double digging, you'll find that a 6 inch (15cm) compressed layer will just be a thin dark line (about ½ inch/1cm) in the soil next year. So, you always need more than you think to do any real good.

You can spread leaves over the soil and the worms will take some down, leaving the rest to dig in come the spring. This works well on a light soil but holds far too much water for heavy clays.

Compost

I'm always a bit in awe of compost; you take your rubbish and convert it into a wonderful, nutritious plant food and soil improver – one of nature's miracles. I've seen all sorts of methods for making it and have read of many more but it's really quite simple in my opinion.

Without getting bogged down in carbon/nitrogen ratios and so forth, what goes into the compost is all your green waste, kitchen waste, weeds and something to fuel the process. Shredded paper can go in as can ripped up newspaper and cardboard as long as you don't add too much at a time.

Don't add any meat products, which will attract rats and flies, and soon stink. Nor should you add perennial weed roots like docks, dandelions and nettles. These have a nasty habit of re-growing in the heap but if you drop them into a bucket or barrel of water for three weeks they will drown and can then go in to rot down.

If you have club-root on your plot, do not add brassica roots or you will help spread the curse. Either burn them or dispose of in the bin. Many people caution against adding blighted potato haulm as well but I don't think it does any harm as blight is mainly spread by airborne spores.

Save up your materials until you have enough to make a pile and then, using a pallet constructed heap as described on page 64, put in the first layer. If you have things like brassica stems or sweetcorn stalks, bash them with a hammer to break them down a bit and add them first, making the base of the heap.

The idea is that the stems will help get some airflow under the heap. In a way we're building a slow acting bonfire and air helps the microbes to burn the waste. It's not vital but it does help get things going.

If you've access to a shredder on the site, use it. The composting process will take a quarter of the usual time with shredded materials.

On top of your first layer, which should be about 6 inches (15cm) deep, put an activator. If you have poultry, a thin layer of their manure is ideal, or some fresh horse manure, but otherwise some dried blood or sulphate of ammonia sprinkled on, just a tablespoonful or so, will do the job of providing extra nitrogen to get things going.

Another way to provide an activator is to save some of your urine, perhaps a bottle in the shed, and mix 1:5 with water and sprinkle that on to dampen the heap. Urine is sterile when it leaves the body and presents no health hazard and contains high levels of nitrogen in the form of urea.

Now add your next layer of 'waste' but on top of this put some garden lime. Just add enough to lighten the surface, rather like with icing sugar on a cake. This will stop the compost from becoming acid and sour, which the microbes and worms don't like.

Now just keep building the heap, layer on layer, alternating lime and activator until the materials are used up. If it towers over the top, don't worry because it will halve in size over the next week.

On the top of the heap put some old carpet or sheeting to stop it from getting too wet and to help keep the heat in.

Ideally the heap should heat up to around 60° Celsius to kill any weed seeds. They have been known to catch fire when too dry, although that's very rare. Check the heap isn't too dry especially when building in high summer. Just add some water if need be to make it damp.

After it has heated up and cooled again, fork it into the next bin mixing outside to inside. The heap may well re-heat which is good. When it cools down, the worms move in. You'll notice lots of small red worms. These are brandling worms and they'll eat their way through your heap, like a huge herd of miniature cows with tiny guts.

Properly made compost should be dark, smell sweet and nothing should be recognizable from the source materials. If things haven't quite worked and some parts aren't properly rotted down, just put them through the cycle again.

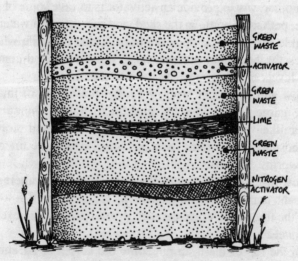

GREEN WASTE
ACTIVATOR
GREEN WASTE
LIME
GREEN WASTE
NITROGEN ACTIVATOR

Fig. 23. Compost layers.

Fertilizer

We demand an awful lot from our plots. Each year we take the crops away to feed ourselves and with them the nutrients that have gone into producing them. You don't get something for nothing and if you don't put anything back into your soil after a few years it will be exhausted and production will plummet.

Compost and manure are great, not only adding the basic nutrients but also the micro-nutrients, the vitamins of the vegetable world, but often we just can't obtain or produce enough to provide the optimum levels for our crops. This is where the fertilizer comes in.

The three main elements needed by plants are Nitrogen (N), Phosphorus (P) and Potassium (K), which is more commonly known as Potash. Very simply put, plants need: nitrogen for the leaves, phosphorus for the roots and potash for the fruit.

Just like we need vitamins, plants also need micro-nutrients and trace elements such as magnesium to thrive.

Fertilizers will have on the label a description of the contents, prominently showing the amount of NPK as a ratio. Growmore, which was originally known as National Growmore and made available by the Government as an aid to growers in the Second World War, is 7:7:7.

The organic version of this is Fish, Blood and Bone which also contains the main elements at 5:5:5. I prefer this generally because the nitrogen is usually released over a slightly longer period.

You can buy straight fertilizers which only contain one element: sulphate of ammonia which is 20 per cent nitrogen; prilled urea which is 40 per cent nitrogen; and organic dried blood with 20 per cent nitrogen, although this is becoming harder to find. Pelleted chicken manure is high in nitrogen and trace elements. Because they're pelleted, they release their nutrients over a period rather than in a rush which is more useful.

Pure bonemeal or hoof and horn are useful where you want to provide a stock of nutrients for a plant such as a fruit bush over a few years and encourage root development.

Osmocote is slow release inorganic fertilizer which is packed into small pellets that release the nutrients over six months. It is useful for plants like leeks with long growing periods.

If you're buying a tomato fertilizer rather than making your own it's worth paying extra for one with a selection of micronutrients especially as magnesium deficiency often occurs with tomatoes.

Wood ash is a natural source of potash, but do be careful. Trees and bush cuttings and untreated timber ashes are fine but avoid using ashes from mixed burnings with plastic and treated timbers as they can be contaminated with a range of unpleasant chemicals. Store in an airtight tin or bag until required.

Don't buy your fertilizer in silly small packets from the DIY stores. If your allotment site doesn't have a shop, then find an old fashioned garden centre that offers fertilizers in 25kg sacks. This will be far cheaper over the season and you won't be tempted to skimp on the feeding. The sort of store that sells in sacks will often pack straight fertilizers themselves and offer them at very competitive prices in 500g or 1kg packs.

Lime

Not strictly a fertilizer, lime is nevertheless vital for your plot's health. If your soil is acid, or 'sour' as the old boys would say, then your plants will find it increasingly hard to absorb their nutrients. So the effect is the same as the soil being exhausted.

As a rule, most of your plants require a pH between 6 and 7, with potatoes preferring 5.5 at one end and the brassicas preferring 7 or even 8. We measure the level of lime in the ground using the pH scale where the lower the number, the more acid the soil is. You can test this with meters or soil test kits but applying lime regularly as part of your rotation should be sufficient to keep the levels right.

Another good indicator of a soil becoming acid is the type of weeds that thrive. Sorrel, creeping buttercup, nettle, dock and mare's tail are all signs that your soil is becoming or is already too acid.

Lime also helps particles bind to each other and form larger particles in a process called flocculation; so adding lime will greatly improve clay soils.

The two main types of lime you can buy for the plot are ordinary agricultural lime made from pulverized limestone or chalk and Dolomite lime which is similar but contains a higher percentage of magnesium. Once again, don't buy fiddling little packets from the DIY store; look for someone supplying 25kg sacks.

Lime is usually applied in the autumn or winter after the digging and is then finally mixed into the soil in the spring cultivation.

How much lime to apply will depend on your soil and how long since it was last applied. To raise the pH from 5.5 to 6.5 add just over 1½ lb per square yard (just under a kilo per square metre) to a clay soil and a bit less for a light or sandy soil. On my clay I add about 2 lb per square yard every three years, plus a little extra for the brassicas as I go along. That's about three sacks each year for a normal 10 rod plot.

14

VEGETABLES

Rather than listing in alphabetical order the various vegetables you can grow on an allotment, I think it makes sense to look at them in their families since they will have similar requirements and be susceptible to the same problems and diseases. For example, all brassicas, being leafy vegetables, require lots of nitrogen and share a dislike of acid soils. It's also helpful when planning your rotation to have the same crops listed together.

The main groups are:

- The brassicas (the cabbage family)
- The alliums (the onion family)
- The root crops (carrots, parsnips, etc)
- The cucurbits (squash, pumpkins, courgettes and cucumbers)
- The legumes (all the beans and peas)
- Potatoes, although just one vegetable, should be thought of as a group since they normally take up anything from a fifth to a third of the space on the plot each year
- Permanent crops that will be in the same bed for many years and so fall outside of rotations
- All the rest, the crops that should be moved each year but can be mixed with the others or treated as a separate group, again depending on your rotation plan

THE BRASSICAS

The brassica family includes cabbages, kale and cauliflowers, Brussels sprouts, broccoli and calabrese, as well as swedes, turnips, radish and mustard.

It is one of the most important families on the plot because its members can provide a fresh staple on any day of the year.

Brassicas are usually leaf vegetables and need plenty of nitrogen to fuel that growth. They all share a love of lime along with a constant supply of water which is best served from ground rich in humus. They are less tolerant than many other crops and it can be difficult to provide everything they require. Nevertheless, if you succeed, they are well worth growing.

The ideal brassica bed needs both nitrogen and humus which can be provided by adding manure in autumn. First, dig over the soil. Then add a barrow load of manure per square yard/metre to the land. Some of the best brassica growers add twice that amount of manure, so add more if you wish.

Leave the manure over the winter to allow the worms to take some down into the soil. In the early spring, fork over the top 6 inches (15cm) of the soil to mix the manure in or run over with a rotavator and leave to settle for a week.

Adding the manure makes the soil more acid and, of course, brassicas don't like an acid soil. So test the pH to measure the acidity of the soil, if possible, and add the appropriate amount of lime to take the level up to 7.0.

It won't matter if it goes a little above 7.0 so, if you can't carry out a test, in the spring just add about 2 lb of lime per square yard (a kilogram per square metre) on a clay soil, with about half that on a sandy soil, and leave this to weather in for a couple of weeks.

Never add lime and manure at the same time because they react together and there's no benefit. By adding manure in the autumn and lime in the spring, sufficient time will have elapsed to prevent any adverse reaction.

Your brassica bed is now nearly perfect but they are greedy and will benefit from your adding 2 oz per square yard (60g per square metre) of a general purpose fertilizer such as Growmore or fish, blood and bone before planting out.

Most failures with brassicas are caused by lack of nutrition so, if you cannot provide loads of manure, add extra fertilizer. Because they demand high nitrogen levels, an additional handful per square yard/metre of pelleted chicken manure will really help them. This is a high nitrogen fertilizer but releases over a month or so, which is ideal.

Brassica Pests and Problems
Club-root

Fig. 24. Brassica roots affected by club-root.

Club-root is a serious disease that affects brassicas. It is caused by a soil-borne organism, *Plasmodiophora brassicae*. The organism produces cysts that remain in the soil until a suitable host is available to infect, starting the cycle again. The cysts can live for eight or nine years so normal rotations are of little use in eliminating the problem.

It is spread so easily: simply walking from an infected area onto a clean patch of land will infect the soil. It can also travel on plants, so if you aren't sure that brassica seedlings offered to you are clean of the disease, do not accept them.

Plasmodiophora brassicae infects 300 species of crucifers (the family brassicas belong to) including weeds. So, once in the soil, even if the plot does not grow brassicas and is well tended, the disease can effectively remain a problem for many years, with weeds continuing the infection cycle.

Symptoms of Club-root

The first indication of club-root is when the plants wilt, especially in dry weather. The plants fail to develop well and often don't develop a crop. If you examine the roots, you will notice swellings and roots that look knobbly, like advanced arthritis. This is the origin of the old colloquial name of 'fingers and toes' for club-root.

Chemical controls are no longer available to gardeners, but there are now some resistant varieties of brassica on the market, with more being developed. Check the seed catalogues for the latest information. The club-root resistant cabbage Kilaxy (Suttons or Dobies seeds) is an excellent variety even if you don't have club-root. There is also Kilaton from Thompson & Morgan who also offer the cauliflower Clapton. There is a resistant swede available from Suttons: Invitation. Swedes, being in the ground for a long time, are very susceptible to club-root so this is a blessing for the grower with an afflicted plot.

Coping with Club-root

Once you have club-root on your plot I'm afraid you are stuck with it. However, you can continue to grow ordinary, non-resistant brassicas successfully if you cultivate them carefully.

To achieve this you must practise good hygiene. When your brassicas are finished, carefully remove all the roots. Do not compost them but either treat as household waste or incinerate. As the affected family includes radishes and mustard, do not use a mustard green manure and make sure you promptly remove radishes that have grown too large and woody and do not compost them. This will reduce the club-root in the soil.

Start your brassicas off in modules using bought-in composts to which a small amount of lime has been added. Then pot into 3 inch (7.5cm) pots and then into at least 5 inch (12.5cm) pots before planting out. (See page 113.) This encourages the development of a good root system prior to infection.

Club-root thrives best in acid, wet soils so dig your brassica bed well and add grit if necessary to keep the soil free draining. Increase the pH to 7.5 or even to 8.5 by adding lime. Before planting, dig a hole at least one foot (30cm) deep and in diameter and then dust with lime to whiten the soil in the hole. Fill the hole with bought-in multi-purpose compost and then plant in this.

This method has been proven to work and it enables good quality crops to grow – even prize-winning cauliflowers.

You may read in old gardening books about putting rhubarb into the planting hole as a cure for club-root. I'm sorry to say that a number of trials of this have shown that it doesn't help.

Cabbage Root Fly

The cabbage root fly is a serious pest affecting most brassicas including cabbages, cauliflowers, broccoli, calabrese, Brussels sprouts, kale, swedes and turnips. It is caused by the fly's maggots eating the roots of brassicas.

Affected plants tend to wilt and droop initially, showing a blueish tinge later as if nutrient deficient. Young plants die although older plants may well survive. Cabbages often fail to heart and cauliflowers form a tiny head. To confirm it is the cabbage root fly, you need to examine the plant roots and look for tunnels and/or white maggots eating the roots, which blacken and die.

In April and May, with the advent of warmer weather, the first generation of flies emerges from pupae of the latest generation of the previous summer, which have over-wintered in the soil. The female flies lay their eggs close by the stems of the brassicas. These then turn into maggots that make their way into the stem and roots, creating tunnels where they feed.

After about three weeks the maggot is fully grown and leaves the damaged plant behind, moving a short distance into the soil and it becomes a small brown pupa, about half an inch (1cm) long.

A week or so later, another generation emerges and flies off in search of more of the cabbage family to cause the grower problems. This means that, unlike the carrot root fly with defined danger periods, **the cabbage root fly is a problem all through the season.**

Starting plants in modules and pots can help as a stronger root system is developed before the attack, and earthing up affected plants may enable them to produce more roots to compensate for damage.

There is no chemical insecticide answer available to the home gardener so we must rely on organic prevention methods. For stemmed brassicas (cabbages, cauliflowers, broccoli, etc) the best method is to use a disc or square of barrier material. You can buy these or easily make your own by cutting a piece of carpet underlay about 6 inches (15cm) square, cutting a line to the centre and placing it around the stem of the plant. You may need to peg this to stop it blowing off. It is time consuming but it is effective.

To keep the fly away from turnips and swedes, the best way is to grow them under tents of horticultural fleece.

Digging over in the autumn and winter will expose the pupae to the birds, which will help reduce the problem for next season.

Butterflies and Caterpillars

The butterflies are not actually a problem but their caterpillars are. Eggs are laid, usually under the leaf, which hatch out the caterpillars that eat the crop. Worst affected are cabbages and cauliflowers but all leaf brassicas can suffer. Even swedes can have their leaves reduced to skeletons in a bad year.

You can usually deal with them easily, without resorting to chemicals or biological controls. If you check regularly under the leaves for clusters of eggs, you will see small (approximately 2mm) yellow or white spheres which can be washed off easily or crushed with your finger.

If you miss a batch, pick off the caterpillars by hand and dispose of them away from the plant. However, they do seem to manage to hide, so re-check frequently. Most years butterflies are not too much of a problem but some years they can be a really bad, locust-like problem. The best bet then is to resort to an insecticidal spray or a nematode-based biological control spray.

The best preventative for caterpillars is to grow plants under fleece or butterfly netting. Do not expect this to stop them all; it's amazing how one always manages to get under your defences.

Flea Beetle

This pest is worst on radishes but can affect turnips and swedes as well. It is a small beetle that jumps when disturbed, hence the name 'flea beetle'. The beetle eats holes in the leaves which weaken the plant, since with less leaf area to produce food for the plant it cannot grow so well.

You can spray with a pesticide but you could try an alternative strategy from Bob Flowerdew. Coat one side of a piece of cardboard with treacle and wave the card just above the affected plant, brushing the topmost edges of the leaves. The beetle jumps onto the treacle and sticks there. The card can then be fed to chickens who will pick off the flea beetles. Even if you do not have chickens, it is still worth it to avoid using an insecticide.

Cabbage Whitefly

These small white flies suck the sap of the plant through the leaves. Great clouds of them may fly up when the leaves are disturbed. They don't cause too much harm and are easily handled by either washing with a jet of water or an insecticidal soap. Insecticidal soap does not contain an insecticide as such, just fatty acids that block the breathing holes of the pest.

Mealy Aphids

These are grey-green aphids that form colonies on the leaves and stems in the summer. They can cause a serious check to growth and need to be addressed. Ladybirds will eat the mealy aphids or you can squash them by hand or treat with insecticidal soap. They over-winter on brassica stumps so do not leave these in the ground after harvest.

Pigeons and Birds

Pigeons are serious pests, especially in winter when their food sources are scarce. The only real answer is to net the crop to stop them from getting to the leaves. Do ensure that the net is supported so that the weight of a fat pigeon cannot bend it onto the leaves and allow it to feed.

You can buy various bird scarers or make your own. I have seen pigeons sitting on CDs placed as a bird scarer, perching on a scarecrow and they have taken a tray of seedlings from our garden where three, admittedly elderly, cats live. Nets are the only answer I know that works.

Slugs and Snails

Like many other crops, brassicas suffer from slugs and snails so take the usual precautions. See page 25.

My Method for Sprouts, Broccoli, Calabrese, Cabbages, Cauliflowers, Kale and Romanesco

Traditionally all of these crops are started in a seed bed and later transplanted to their final growing spots. This method does work but the plants are vulnerable to pest damage. One hungry pigeon under the net or a couple of hungry slugs and the bed can be devastated overnight.

The simple answer is to start these in a seed tray divided into 15 modules. Just fill the modules with a good quality commercial multi-purpose compost with a little extra lime added. By a little lime, I mean about a tablespoonful to a 6 inch (15cm) plant pot full, mixed in well. You don't need to fill every module, if you don't want to grow too many plants. I will often start a tray with 6 cauliflower and 6 cabbage; labelled of course, so I will know which is which.

After germination, thin to one seedling per module and, when they are big enough to handle, usually two or three weeks after sowing, transfer from the modules to pots. I use square 3 inch (7.5cm) pots so the whole module can be dropped in on top of some compost without any root disturbance or damage.

By planting a little low in the pot, more compost can be trickled in round the seedling, which will encourage the development of a good rootball. Now it is important not to let the plants get potbound so, if you are delayed in planting out, transfer them to larger pots. It's easy enough to check the root system: just turn upside down, allowing the plant to come between your fingers which form a plate to stop the compost from falling out, and lift the pot. If the white roots go around and around, then it is pot bound. Move on to a larger pot or plant out, but gently tease the roots out to the sides so they do not continue the endless circle.

When you plant them out, do firm them in well and water. Sprouts, in particular, can suffer from wind rock where the fine root hairs that extract nutrients from the soil are damaged and a firm soil helps keep the plant stable.

The beauty of this method is that you can get the plants going in a protected environment such as a greenhouse, coldframe or a cloche.

Broccoli, Calabrese and Romanesco

Broccoli and calabrese are different crops, despite the supermarkets confusing the public by calling both by either name. To distinguish them in your own mind, just remember that broccoli is an over-wintered crop whereas calabrese produces its crop the same year before winter and is not hardy. Both are brassicas and the general brassica growing instructions apply.

Broccoli

Fig. 25. Broccoli.

Broccoli consists of Purple Sprouting and White Sprouting, with the early varieties being ready first. Generally you sow in spring and plant out in early summer for a crop in February/March through to May. The spears are removed from the plants and turn green on cooking. They should be freshly picked for best flavour. Steaming tends to retain the flavour and texture better than boiling.

The average seed packet contains enough for 200 plants. Although the average family probably needs two or three plants, the seeds will store for up to four years.

There have been a number of studies that suggest that broccoli and calabrese can help protect you from cancer. Broccoli contains a chemical called sulphoraphane which helps neutralize cancer-causing substances found in the gut and can help against colon cancer – one of the biggest cancer killers in the UK.

Broccoli also contains a compound that helps boost production of BRCA proteins. These are helpful against some forms of cancer, including breast, ovarian and prostate cancers.

Because they are standing through the winter, a sheltered site is best and earthing up around the stems to 4 inches (10cm) will help keep the plant stable and prevent wind rock. On windy plots, consider staking to keep them steady.

Broccoli is a slow-growing crop and not exceptionally hungry but improved results can be achieved by giving a liquid feed, high in nitrogen, in the spring as the heads begin to form or some pelleted chicken manure.

Sprouting Broccoli Claret F1 is exceptional. It has a vigorous habit so you need fewer plants to produce the same yield as normal types. It performs well even on poorer soils and is an RHS 'Award of Garden Merit' winner.

Calabrese

Fig. 26. Calabrese.

This has a milder flavour which many, including me, prefer. It's also an easier crop to grow. Sowing in early spring, under glass, and planting out in June and July provides a crop from August through October.

Calabrese doesn't like having its roots disturbed, so starting in modules then moving to pots will enable it to be grown on before planting out and won't cause root disturbance.

With some varieties, cutting the spears and leaving the plant in the ground will result in a second flush – a free extra crop, albeit smaller than the first.

Belstar can be successfully sown from April to June and will crop through the autumn. It keeps in good condition for a long time, producing plenty of side shoots once the centre head is cut. It's an RHA 'Award of Garden Merit' winner and available from Thompson & Morgan. However, my favourite variety is Chevalier (available from the Organic Gardening Catalogue). It starts cropping in September and then produces a good secondary crop after the prime head is cut.

Romanesco

Fig. 27. Romanesco.

This can be described as a green cauliflower, although it's often called calabrese. It is a sort of cross between the two, producing large pyramid-shaped heads. It has a taste and texture exceeding the finest broccoli. To appreciate the flavour it should be cooked and served individually with melted butter.

Romanesco broccoli was first documented in Italy (as *broccolo romanesco*) in the sixteenth century. It is sometimes called broccoflower, but that name is also applied to green-curded cauliflower cultivars. Confusing, isn't it, this growing business!

Start off in modules, usually around May time, and don't allow them to be checked by becoming potbound so pot on early until planting out in their final position.

The usual spacing suggested is between 18 inches and 2 feet (45–60cm) each way between plants depending on variety but I would suggest that, as they are large plants, larger than cauliflowers or calabrese, they really need at least 2 feet

(60cm) each way between plants and will benefit from more room than that. Because they grow quite tall, you need to keep this in mind when netting.

They are about as difficult to grow as cauliflowers and really do need careful cultivation to produce well. However, the taste is worth it and we found they went exceptionally well in homemade piccalilli.

Romanesco can be difficult to find in seed catalogues, not because it isn't stocked but because the seed manufacturers don't seem to know where to list it. Sometimes it's in with broccoli or calabrese and sometimes it gets thrown in with the cauliflowers. Perhaps it's time they listed it for itself.

Brussels Sprouts

Fig. 28. Brussels sprouts.

Cooked properly, Brussels sprouts are delicious and they can be enjoyed fresh from September through February. It's just a shame that they have a bad reputation, having been ruined so often by overboiling on Christmas Day.

To cook them, just clean and remove any loose outer leaves, then drop into water at a rolling boil for two or three minutes. Remove and drain well, then gently fry in butter with plenty of black pepper for a few minutes. They won't bear any resemblance to that soggy vegetable traditionally suffered with Christmas lunch.

The sprout packs a lot into a small space. If you strip the leaves from one sprout and spread them on a table, you'll be surprised how much leaf is crammed in there.

Started off in March and April, they are usually planted out in May and June where they will sit until required, even through to March. Make sure you allow plenty of space for them: most varieties need 30 inches (75cm) between plants.

They really benefit from an extra feed in August or September to produce well, since they are in the ground so long and put so much into each sprout. A good handful of pelleted chicken manure scattered around each plant is ideal.

In early autumn as the sprouts begin to form, draw some earth a few centimetres up around the stem or mulch with garden compost to help stabilize the plant as well. The sprout is a tall plant and will catch the wind. Wind rock moves the roots, breaking the tiny root hairs that take water and food into the plant and so causes lower yields. To help stop this, plant in a sheltered spot and stake tall varieties.

The most common fault with sprouts is blown sprouts. This is where they start to open up rather than forming a tight head. It is caused by wind rocking and lack of nutrients. To stop the problem, remove any blown sprouts and feed with a liquid fertilizer high in nitrogen. This will help the sprouts further up the plant to develop properly. I use sulphate of ammonia mixed with water, about a dessertspoonful per plant in half a gallon (4.5 litres) of water. The organic equivalent would be to scatter about the same amount of dried blood around the base of the plant.

Sprouts left too long on the plant will blow anyway so you will continually need to remove them. Gluts can be frozen. Just blanch for two or three minutes beforehand and remember when you defrost them that they are effectively three-quarter cooked.

Once you have stripped the sprouts from the plant, the top can be removed and used as a small cabbage – a bonus crop.

Older varieties often tend to be more susceptible to blowing than the modern F1 hybrid varieties. However, these F1 varieties have been developed more for the farmer than for the garden grower. They therefore produce over a short period, which is great for picking in one go to supply the shops for the Christmas rush, but for the home grower an extended cropper is preferable.

Each plant should produce around a couple of pounds (about a kilogram) so limit the number of plants to a sensible level: for a couple, six plants will be more than sufficient.

Pest and disease problems are the same as with other brassicas but do remember to protect with netting as there are few edible crops available for the pigeons in winter.

My personal favourite variety is Wellington, an F1 hybrid that is a late-maturing heavy cropper and holds well. It is available from Suttons Seeds. You can also try red varieties such as Red Delicious (Suttons) or Falstaff (Thompson & Morgan). Falstaff matures over a long period and has a milder, nuttier flavour than standard green types.

Cabbages

Properly cooked, the cabbage is a delicious vegetable and surprisingly contains nearly twice the vitamin C of an apple or orange and four times that of a potato, making it a very healthy part of our diet. Unfortunately, many people's childhood memories are of cabbage being an over-cooked, soggy mess.

If you choose the correct varieties you can arrange to provide fresh cabbage throughout the year but don't grow too many. Just 12 cabbages in a year will be more than enough for most families.

The big problem is that the seed suppliers happily put 100 or more seeds into the packet, so we sow far too many and then end up with huge gluts. Luckily the seeds will keep if stored well for five years or even more.

Another problem with cabbages is that you can end up, if you're lucky, with some pretty big specimens. Rather than growing normal cabbage, consider growing smaller varieties like Minicole or Hispi. These can be spaced more closely than most varieties and produce a smaller head, ideal for one meal.

The cabbage comes in three waves: spring, summer and winter. Varieties are described by their cutting period not their sowing times.

The spring cabbages are sown in July and August for planting out in September and October to be ready in April and May.

The summer cabbages are sown in late winter/early spring (sown under glass in February and March and outside in April), and planted out from late April through June providing a crop from July right through October.

The winter cabbages are also sown in April and May, planting out in July but cropping from November to February.

The green cabbages come in conical, somewhat loose-leaved types and tight balls called drum head, as well as the savoy cabbages recognizable by their crinkled leaves.

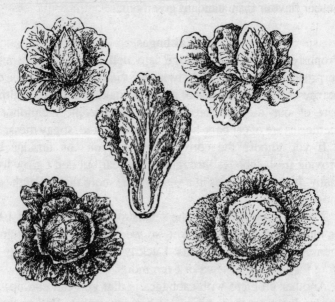

Fig. 29. Cabbages.

Red cabbage is often used as a pickling cabbage but it is a flavourful addition when grated into a salad and can be cooked just as the green cabbages.

Cultivation is as for brassicas generally and spacing will vary between varieties. Harvest as needed but cabbage will store quite well if kept cool until required. Drum head winter cabbages can be cut in November and stored right through to spring. Cut off the stem and remove outer leaves where any slugs may be hiding. Keep cool and dark. When you harvest spring and summer cabbages, cut the stem about 2 inches (5cm) from the ground and make a cross in the top, about half an inch (1cm) deep. This will result in the plant forming four small heads giving you a free secondary crop.

Chinese Cabbage

Sometimes sold as 'Chinese leaves' or pak-choi, these cabbages look more like a lettuce than the traditional cabbage. Unlike ordinary cabbages, they are sown in place and are not transplanted. Sowing varies depending on the variety, but is usually in July or August which provides a crop from these fast-growing plants in October. Sow at 4 inch (10cm) spacing in rows a foot (30cm) apart. Thin to a foot (30cm) apart in the row.

Fig. 30. Chinese cabbage.

Cauliflowers

Fig. 31. Cauliflower.

It's very satisfying to produce a large, white cauliflower with tight white curds, especially as cauliflowers aren't the easiest of the brassica family to grow.

Make sure they establish good roots and don't allow them to get potbound otherwise the plant will form its curds early, resulting in a small cauliflower. The same will happen if the plant isn't firm which means the root hairs which absorb the nutrients from the soil become broken.

We love the taste of the cauliflower but unfortunately so do the pests. Caterpillars eat the leaves and also get into the curd itself, while slugs love to climb the stem to eat away in the sheltered centre, leaving brown trails where they have munched their way across the surface. Cauliflowers are more vulnerable to those pests and the cabbage root fly than any other brassica.

To protect against pests for a good crop, plant properly in rich, firm soil. If too much sunlight gets onto the head, it will go slightly yellow and off colour. To prevent this, bend some of the inner leaves over the head to shade it. If you leave the cauliflower too long after the head has formed, then the curds continue to grow and come apart. So harvest the cauliflower as soon as it is ready. As some varieties will stand longer than others, check your seed catalogue for those recommended as holding well.

A cauliflower keeps well in the fridge if wrapped in cling film and put into the salad drawer or it can be frozen. However, do not over blanch or it goes mushy when defrosted.

Recently yellow and purple varieties of cauliflower have become available. The Purple Graffiti variety is particularly striking and retains its colour when cooked. The flavour is not, unfortunately, quite as good as the normal white varieties.

Cauliflowers are usually ready for cutting from March to November but it is possible to have one cut nearly every day of the year. There are three types: summer varieties which are started in late winter to be ready as early as June or July; autumn varieties ready for October and November; and the winter varieties that are very slow to mature, taking 40 to even 50 weeks to mature from March through to June.

My favourite variety is Pavilion, an F1 Australian variety that crops well and holds well in the ground. Galleon, maturing in April or May, also does well on my plot, as does Mayflower which is started in January under glass and can produce a crop in May. It has an excellent flavour.

Kale

Fig. 32. Kale.

Kale (also known as borecole) is one of the easiest and hardiest brassicas to grow. It will produce on poorer soils than any of the others in the cabbage tribe and is even tolerant of club-root to some degree. Curly kales are also attractive in their own right so you might expect it to be grown on every allotment. However, kale is an acquired taste and nowadays when fresh vegetables can be bought in supermarkets every day of the year, whatever the season, people are less forgiving of acquired tastes even in the 'hungry gap' when the winter crops are finishing and the spring crops yet to arrive.

The taste is much improved if you harvest young leaves rather than old, tough ones and cook it properly. Kale is a very good source of vitamins A, C, K and folate and provides 50 per cent of the daily requirement in a single 3 oz (80g) portion, so it's worth developing a taste for it.

Try steaming and then serving with a knob of butter and black pepper rather than boiling. Like the Brussels sprout, kale suffers from a reputation more due to the cooking than the actual flavour of the crop.

Started in May and planted out in July, it comes into production late in the year, November or December, going right the way through March. Even in deep winter, you can brush the snow off and get a fresh vegetable.

Kale comes in curly leaf and plain leaf varieties; the curly leaved types are smaller and more tender than their plain leaved cousins so they are the best ones to try initially. Redbor F1 has good winter hardiness and excellent tolerance to pests and diseases, along with flavoursome purple-red curly leaves.

Kohlrabi

Kohlrabi is popular in Europe but still uncommon in Britain. The taste is a cross between a turnip and a cabbage, with the name actually derived from the German Khol ('cabbage') and Rabi ('turnip'). It is well worth the price of a packet of seeds to try this unusual crop.

It is not so demanding of the soil as the swedes and turnips despite being a brassica, but it is still vulnerable to club-root and cabbage root fly.

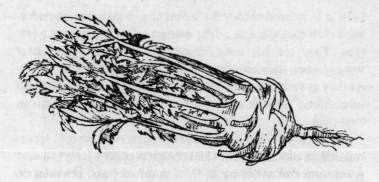

Fig. 33. Kohlrabi.

Successively sow directly in the ground in late April onwards at half an inch (1cm) deep in rows one foot (30cm) apart, thinning to 6 inches (15cm) apart in the row for a crop from late July through to December. Harvest the ball-shaped roots when they are about 3 inches (8cm) across and use immediately. Unlike swedes and turnips they are not a storing crop.

Turnips

Fig. 34. Turnip.

There are now available modern hybrid varieties that are delicious grated raw into a salad or as a welcome side dish.

Bear in mind that they are a brassica so take into consideration club-root when deciding where to sow. Turnips are a fast crop. They are harvested in just six to eight weeks after sowing when they are the size of a golf ball or a little larger. As they grow on, they become less tender and flavoursome so successional sowing every two weeks will provide crops at their peak.

Sow thinly half to three quarters of an inch deep (1–2cm) and thin to around 4 inches (10cm) apart either in rows spaced at one foot (30cm) or equidistant in raised beds. Do keep on top of the thinning or you'll end up with a crowded bunch and be unable to thin without damaging the one you want to grow on.

Sowing can start as early as late February under cloche and run through to August. Maincrop varieties that are sown in July and August require a larger spacing: 10 inches (25cm), to allow the larger root to develop for harvesting in November and December. However, the maincrop turnip is arguably less well flavoured and is inferior in minerals and vitamins to the swede, so you may consider it only worthwhile growing early turnips.

Apart from club-root, turnips are vulnerable to cabbage root fly so you may need to cover with fleece as a barrier. Water them well in dry weather or the result will be cracked roots and a woody texture.

Purple Top Milan has distinctive flat-topped roots, white with purple crown. It is quick maturing, useful in frames and under cloches but my favourite is Snowball, a first-class white, globe turnip.

Turnip tops are edible although I must admit I'm not keen; try them for yourself.

Swedes

Swedes are very similar to turnips. Despite being totally different from cabbages, they are still part of the brassica family and so club-root will cause trouble if you have this on

Fig. 35. Swede.

your plot. Cabbage root fly can also be a problem, so cover with fleece to offer some protection. The flea beetle is the other real concern.

Swedes are a slow growing vegetable, taking 20–26 weeks to reach maturity. They are hardy and best left in the ground over winter until required. Although they can be lifted and stored as other root crops, they are at their best within a week of picking.

For best results, the soil should be light and the humus rich with a pH around neutral. Like other brassicas, swedes do not like an acid soil.

They are not a particularly hungry crop but they will benefit from 2 oz per square yard (50g per square metre) of general purpose fertilizer like fish, blood and bone or Growmore applied a couple of weeks before sowing.

Sow thinly in May and June half an inch (1cm) deep in rows 16 inches (40cm) apart, thinning out in stages until the plants are around 8 inches (20cm) apart. To avoid woody texture and split skins, keep watered in dry periods. Start harvesting in November. Leave in the ground, slowly growing, lifting as required through to March.

Often used in soups and stews, swedes also work well as a mashed vegetable. Cut into cubes and boil for 30 minutes, drain and mash with butter, cream and pepper. To give some zing, you can also add a little powdered ginger or nutmeg. As swedes can be a little sloppy, try mixing fifty/fifty with mashed potatoes.

The best variety to grow is Brora a fast growing variety having attractive deep purple skins with bitter-free, creamy-yellow flesh which makes it the ideal kitchen swede. It has outstanding winter hardiness and the foliage has good resistance to powdery mildew. It's readily available.

If you have club-root on your plot, then grow Swede Invitation available from Suttons. Not only does it have resistance to club-root, Invitation is also resistant to powdery mildew. Both these varieties have won the RHS 'Award of Garden Merit'.

Radish

Fig. 36. Radish.

The normal salad radish is ideal for getting children interested and enthused in gardening as it's one of the fastest and easiest crops to grow. Radishes can be ready in as little as 18 days from sowing.

As they develop so quickly, they are not bothered by club-root. However, slugs nibble the root, and flea beetles also attack them.

The radish is very much a crop to fit in as it suits you, because of its speed in growing. Where there is a small space sow a pinch of seed thinly – about an inch apart (2.5cm) is ideal – and rake in or cover with half an inch (1cm) of soil. They should develop, as long as there is sufficient water.

They very quickly go woody once grown and then go to seed, so sow weekly in the salad season to ensure a continuous supply. It doesn't matter if they go over as the seed is cheap. Simply compost them and harvest the ones sown the week after. In hot summers they benefit from some shade and can be grown in the shadow of other crops.

The most well known variety, French Breakfast, is white at the tip and red at the crown. There are many other available salad varieties which can be grown.

Asian Radishes or Mooli

Although we think of radish as a summer salad crop, there are winter varieties, Japanese types or mooli radishes. These grow much larger with roots up to a foot long. Since they are in the ground much longer, the soil needs more preparation as for other root crops and club-root becomes a consideration.

The Asian radishes are sown directly, usually about half an inch (1cm) deep, spaced around 4 inches (10cm) apart in rows 1 inch (2.5cm) apart. Most of these types are sown in May through July as earlier sowings will tend to bolt.

They are ready in around eight weeks and will often hold for a few weeks in the ground before harvesting.

Large winter radishes are sown later, usually in late summer, and should be treated as parsnips. Leave them in the ground until required, protecting with straw or fleece in frosty weather to enable them to be harvested if the ground should be frozen.

THE ALLIUMS

The alliums or onion family are a major staple in our diet, not just as a foodstuff but for the flavour they add to a meal. Like most vegetables, they like a soil that is rich in humus but not one that is freshly manured. They don't like an acid soil either, so check the pH level, and lime if necessary to take it up to around 6.5. We'll start with onion.

Onions

Fig. 37. Onion – with onion sets on the left.

For the beginner, the easiest way to grow onions is from sets (which are immature bulbs whose growth has been stopped) planted directly into the ground. The sets have a head start on seed sown onions so they get off quickly, are more disease resistant, avoid the onion fly, crop better in poorer soils and will usually provide a crop even if they go in a little later than they should.

Plant sets in March and April fat-end down so that the tip is just above soil level. Plant them 6 inches (15cm) apart each way or spaced at 4 inches (10cm) in rows 8–12 inches (20–30cm) apart. If you plant them closer, you'll produce smaller bulbs. However, unless you are trying to grow huge onions, there's no point spacing more than 6 inches (15cm) apart. As large sets are more prone to bolting do not discard small sets in the pack in favour of them.

Scrape a small hole or a drill to plant in, put the set in, then backfill the soil. Never simply push the set into the soil, especially a heavier soil, as this can damage the root plate and kill the set. Also don't plant too deeply or the crop will probably develop a thick neck and not store well. Ideally the soil should come about a third to half way up the set when planted.

Birds like to pull sets out of the soil so it's advisable to use netting or even cloching until the sets are established.

Because of postage costs, sets are quite expensive when bought by mail order so your choice will depend more on what is available in your allotment shop or garden centre. Bolting, where the onion shoots up a flower head which reduces bulb size and spoils it for keeping, is more common in sets than seed sown onions. To overcome this you can pay a little more for heat treated sets that do not bolt as often.

For an early crop you can plant Japanese onion sets in mid-September to early November to provide a crop for June (a good month), or you can sow before the spring-planted crop arrives. Unfortunately, these don't keep too well but they'll see you through until the spring-planted crop arrives at the end of summer. You can grow autumn onions from seed but I'd stick to sets for these.

Once planted, just keep the weeds down and water in dry weather. Do be careful weeding, I lose more onions to my own hoe than the birds. Once the onions have swollen to harvest size, stop watering. They don't need a lot at this stage and too much water will encourage rot and reduce their keeping quality.

You can pull at any point for using straightaway but, if you want to store onions, wait until the foliage is starting to bend over of its own accord. Old books talk about bending the foliage over – do not do this because it damages the neck causing problems in storage.

To lift the bulbs, gently lever under them with a fork and then dry them out for storage. Ideally place them on some sort of rack outdoors where air can flow all around them for a couple of weeks. If the weather is really wet, they'll need some sort of cover, but the odd shower will not cause any harm. Be careful if you dry onions in a greenhouse. If it gets really hot, they will start to cook and then they won't store.

Once they have dried out, string them up or put them into nets and hang in a cool, dark place. Check the base of the bulbs occasionally for rot starting and remove those bulbs to prevent it spreading.

Onions from Seed
Growing onions from seed is harder than sets but you have the benefit of a much wider choice of varieties, and seeds are far cheaper than sets. Onions are sensitive to day length so they are one crop that is not forgiving if you're late in sowing.

Direct Sowing Method
Sow as thinly as possible in rows about 9 inches (22cm) apart, just under the surface. Thin out to the final spacing when they germinate and are about 4 inches (10cm) high. Just as with carrots, this thinning process releases the scent of the onions and, like a guided missile, the onion fly's scent-based radar will guide it to the crop.

My Module Method
You can sow directly but much better results will come from starting off under glass in modules, 15 to a seed tray, in multi-purpose compost at a temperature between 10–15°C in late February to early March. If you have a heated propagator, especially a thermostatically controlled one, germination will be good.

Move out of the greenhouse into a cold frame and harden off before planting out, spaced as for the sets, usually in April. The beauty of this method is that the onions can be held if the weather is bad until you are ready to plant.

What onions to grow will depend on what your conditions are like and what sort of flavour you are looking for. Our favourites are Ailsa Craig, often described as a show variety although I don't grow for show, and Red Baron, which is an excellent red onion.

For pickling, the accepted onion is Paris Silverskin (a little mild for us), or Brown Pickling SY 300. Personally I prefer to close space Ailsa Craig and have a really flavoursome pickled onion.

Onion Problems

Rust, smut mildew and white tip (where the leaves go white from the tip down the stem) all affect onions. Spraying with seaweed fertilizer may help prevent spread by increasing the plant's resistance as there are no available chemical treatments. White rot (where a white fungus grows on the base of the bulb and kills the plant) is serious and there is no treatment at all. To try to prevent it, avoid growing onions on the same spot for eight years or grow them in large containers or raised beds with bought-in compost. White rot is the club-root of onions, as it is easily spread and difficult to cope with.

The onion fly, where small maggots, 5–10mm long eat the base of the bulb, is the main pest. If this is a common problem in your area, grow from sets or try keeping under fleece or cloche until well established.

Bolting, where the plant sends up a flower shoot, is a fairly common problem. Cut off this flower stem when seen and use those onions first as they will not store well.

Shallots

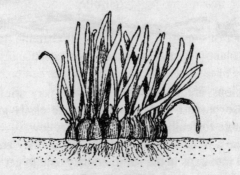

Fig. 38. Shallots.

Shallots, being the 'gourmet onion' are prized for their flavour but the big benefit, to my mind, is that they store really well. Nine months is common and a year if kept in good conditions so they fill any gap when the stored onions have gone over.

Normally shallots are grown from sets which are actually just a single shallot, although you can get shallot seed. Prepare the soil as for onions and plant the sets about 8 inches (20cm) or a little more each way. You need to plant early; any time from late December onwards is good. Once again, watch out for the birds, and net or fleece if need be.

As they grow, each shallot planted will split into a ring of bulbs. They are subject to the same problems as onions, with a tendency to bolt in hot summers but generally they are easy enough to grow. They are harvested as a clump with the individual bulbs in a ring. There is no need to split them apart until you come to use them.

Spring Onions

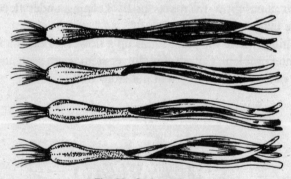

Fig. 39. Spring onions.

Spring onions are a popular crop and very useful. Salad onions, also properly called scallions, are easily grown and can substitute for bulb onions if stocks are low.

They like a rich, well drained soil but, as they are a useful crop to fill into gaps in the summer, they tend to get what they are given. I recommend giving some general purpose fertilizer a week before and raking the soil into a fine tilth before sowing them.

They are generally grown in rows 6 inches (15cm) apart but can more easily just be thinly scattered in a patch and either raked in or covered with three-quarters of an inch (1.5cm) of fine soil.

For a continuous supply, successively sow each week or two from early March. Late sowings in August, September and a fine October will provide an early spring crop. Use a winter hardy variety for late sowings. White Lisbon is the best known variety but look for White Lisbon Winter Hardy for the over-winter sowing.

Red spring onions are available as well and I'd recommend North Holland Blood Red. This has the benefit that you can sow a patch, removing as required, and any left will just bulb up.

They do not need a great depth of soil and a winter crop can even be grown in the greenhouse in an ordinary seed tray filled with compost.

There are few problems with spring onions as long as the soil can provide enough nutrition.

Garlic

Fig. 40. Garlic.

Garlic is quite an easy crop to grow, if you get the right variety. Don't simply buy a garlic bulb from a supermarket to plant out. It will be a foreign variety, bred for warmer climates than ours and probably won't produce a decent crop for you.

Garlic comes in two types: hard neck or Rocambole garlic and soft neck. Some people prefer the flavour of the hard neck varieties but they do not store as well as the soft necked types, which can be platted into strings to hang in the shed until required.

Elephant garlic is actually a perennial leek, and has a much milder flavour. Its cloves split up when it is dried, so elephant garlic does not store for very long.

My favourite garlic is Solent Wight, a soft neck variety that produces well with a fine flavour. Some varieties do best planted in November whereas others will produce a crop from an early spring planting; just check the merchant's description.

It likes a sunny spot but does not need a rich soil, preferring one that has not had manure in the preceding year. Plant by dibbing holes around 8 inches (20cm) apart each way or a little less, around 4 inches (10cm) deep. Break the seed bulb up into individual cloves and drop these into the holes flat-end down. Fill the hole with soil or, better still, some fine multi-purpose compost. Larger cloves produce larger garlic bulbs. If space is limited, don't bother planting very small cloves.

Garlic doesn't do well in a waterlogged heavy soil so, if you suffer with this, dib your hole a little deeper and drop some grit and sand into the base to ensure good drainage before dropping the clove in.

Alternatively, start the garlic off in 4 inch (10cm) pots in a coldframe in November, then plant out in the spring just after the leaves have appeared.

Keep weed free but otherwise do nothing unless the spring and summer are dry, in which case water.

Harvest the bulbs when the leaves turn yellow in midsummer, using a fork to dig them up carefully. Don't leave them too long or the bulbs will split into separate cloves under the ground.

Before storing, allow to dry off for a week or so. Wet or fresh garlic is prized by many chefs and you can use immediately as that. When fresh, the flavour is much milder, and roasted wet garlic makes a wonderful side dish.

Leeks

Fig. 41. Leeks

Last but not least in the allium family is the leek. This is quite an easy vegetable to grow and really useful as it is available throughout the winter. Leeks can make a useful substitute for onions in many recipes and young leeks, pencil thin, are delicious in stir fries.

I've tried a number of methods with leeks and the one that works best and most reliably is to start them by sowing thinly into compost in 9 inch (22cm) or larger pots, preferably under glass, in March.

Once the leek, looking very like a spring onion, has reached the thickness of a pencil and about 6 inches (15cm) high, it can be planted out, usually in June and July. If the roots have tangled in the pot, soak in a bucket of water for half an hour and then gently wash the leeks apart.

Of course, you can start them in a seed bed or modules, but the above method has never failed me.

The long white stem of the leek is mainly caused by blanching (that is, excluding the light), so they are planted in holes. Take an old spade handle or similar and push this some 6 inches (15cm) deep into the soil, spacing between 6 and 8 inches (15–20cm) apart each way. Drop the leek into the hole and water well to settle it in. Soil will naturally drop into the hole but, because it isn't compacted, it allows the leek to swell.

Then just ensure that the crop is watered in dry weather and keep it free of weeds. By the end of summer the leeks will have filled the hole. If you wish to increase the blanched length, you can gently earth up around them. However, this does risk soil getting between the layers, and can add an unpleasant crunch to your meal. So an alternative is to collar it with a toilet roll or kitchen roll cardboard inner tube. Cut the tube lengthways so that it can be fitted and hold it on with an elastic band or similar tie.

Extra seedlings left at planting can be used as a substitute for spring onions in stir fries. When planted out you can pull alternate leeks from the row, leaving those left to grow on.

Old books used to advise trimming the roots and tops of the leaves before transplanting. This has now been shown to be counter productive and proof that not all the old-fashioned methods are sound.

Some varieties mature more quickly than others and some will stand for longer through the winter. Therefore sow two or three varieties if you really like leeks and want the longest season. The seeds store for three years in the right conditions.

Leeks grow best in a soil which is rich in humus and nutrients but they are less demanding than onions. They do not like a waterlogged soil which can cause rotting. Rust, which is a fungal disease, named after the reddish rust that appears on the leaves, is the only disease that affects them. There is now no approved chemical control so buy rust resistant varieties like Porbella.

THE ROOT CROPS

Usually the root crops are considered a separate rotation group, although they may, under strict classification, belong to different families. The importance of the root crops is that they can be stored to provide sustenance when fresh vegetables are unavailable.

As turnips and swedes are brassicas, they are considered with them. This leaves us with carrots, beetroot, parsnips, salsify and scorzonera. Jerusalem artichokes, although a root crop, tend to have a permanent placing as once planted they are quite hard to get rid of, springing up again from the odd missed tuber, and therefore they are considered separately.

None of the root crops likes a soil freshly manured. This will cause them to fork, developing into those weird shapes that used to be on TV programmes like *That's Life!* in years gone by. The ideal growing medium for the carrots, parsnips, salsify and scorzonera is a deep sandy soil; so, if you have a clay soil, you can add gritty sand to lighten it or a light compost. Root crops do exceptionally well in raised beds if you can provide them with a compost/sand mixture. Although they don't like fresh manure, they do need nutrients, and applying a balanced fertilizer like fish, blood and bone or Growmore at a couple of ounces per square yard (50g per square metre) a week or two before sowing will provide that.

With all the root crops, except for celeriac, sow directly because transplanting or modules is going to fail 90 per cent of the time.

Beetroot

Breeders have perfected beetroot over many years making modern varieties easy to grow and producing consistent results with a little care. The older varieties of globe beetroot

Fig. 42. Beetroot

had a tendency to develop white rings inside but with modern varieties this just doesn't happen.

Beetroots are usually a deep red colour but yellow and white varieties are now available.

Unusually, beetroot seeds are actually a cluster of seeds in one package: thinning is thus nearly always required unless you buy pelleted seed or a variety which is a monogerm, i.e. one seed per package.

The earliest sowings can suffer from bolting so choose varieties such as Boltardy. The main sowing season starts in late April and runs through to July but you can sow under cloche as early as mid March.

Sow directly 1 inch (2–3cm) deep, at a spacing of 4 inches (10cm), in rows a foot (30cm) apart, thinning to one plant per station. Avoid acid soils and ensure a good level of humus, although they aren't too particular about the soil.

Once sown, keep the weeds off and ensure they get sufficient water. Dryness will cause low yields of a woody texture and cracked roots. Pull alternate roots when they reach the size of a golf ball, leaving the rest to grow on a little.

Leave the later June sown crops to mature fully and lift them in October and store as a winter crop just as you do with carrots and parsnips.

Beetroot are now generally an easy, trouble-free crop, with

modern bolt-resistant varieties having solved the problem of bolting.

The globe shaped beetroot is best known today, but there are cylindrical varieties that store well and provide slices of equal diameter which are helpful for cooks.

Long varieties, very much a root crop, are available. These require a deep sandy soil to perform really well. They produce a larger crop from a given area but tend to be more popular with show exhibitors than gardeners who grow for food.

Unlike the other roots, beetroot will benefit from additional nitrogen as they produce quite a bit of foliage; so a scattering of pelleted chicken manure will help get a good crop.

There are a number of fancy beetroot available in different colours but for me the only varieties worth growing are Detroit or Boltardy. Of the two, Boltardy is the winner.

Carrots

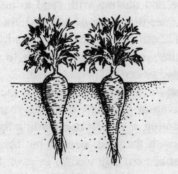

Fig. 43. Carrots.

The carrot is one of our most popular vegetables but it can be a little tricky to grow, especially in heavy soils. Although you will only ever see orange carrots in the greengrocer's shop, you can grow a range of different coloured carrots, including a deep purple variety, Healthmaster, which provides a third more beta carotene than any other carrot.

Carrots come in various shapes: small, round carrots

through short cylindrical ('stump rooted') to long rooted varieties more suited to show growers than table growers. Some develop quickly and can be eaten fresh in around 10–12 weeks from sowing, whereas others, the maincrop varieties, take around 16 weeks to mature and can be stored for use over the winter in damp sand or peat.

The most notable early varieties, Amsterdam Forcing and Early Nantes, are ideal for an early planting in a greenhouse border or under cloche.

Carrots grow best in a sandy soil but, if you don't have that, grow stump rooted varieties where the root is more of a cylinder than a long cone.

You can grow carrots traditionally in rows, allowing 6 inches (15cm) between rows and, depending on the variety, around 4 inches (10cm) apart in the row after the final thinning. Or you can use the area method, which is ideal for early varieties and raised beds. It involves scattering the seed over the surface and dusting with sand to hold the seeds in place. When the seedlings can be handled, thin out to around an inch or two (2.5cm–5cm) apart. Thin again after six weeks when the thinnings will be large enough to make a tender addition to a salad or cooked with a meal.

The carrot root fly, as described below, is the main problem. Otherwise cultivation involves ensuring there is sufficient water and preventing weeds from crowding the crop. Hoeing is not possible with the area method but the density of the foliage should shade out any weeds. In rows be very careful with the hoe; hand weeding is recommended.

You can harvest from as early as mid-May from a greenhouse border through to November. The carrots are best harvested when ready as leaving them in the ground after they are mature encourages slugs to damage them.

Carrots can be stored in damp sand or peat in a frost free shed or frozen in battens. If the carrot is damaged, it is unlikely to store well so freeze it instead.

Carrot Root Fly

The carrot fly affects carrots and parsnips and even celery. The damage is caused by the fly's maggots killing seedlings and tunnelling just under the skin of more mature plants, leaving brown tunnels behind. Parsnips left in the ground through to January can be ruined as the maggots continue to feed, causing more damage.

The flies produce two generations in a year and are active in April/May and July/August. You can try sowing outside of those times (in February, March, June, September and October) but they can still cause damage.

The fly, which is attracted by the smell of carrots, is most active in the day so it's best to carry out thinning (which bruises foliage and releases the scent) late in the day to avoid their notice. Inter-planting with stronger smelling onions is supposed to confuse the fly but doesn't always work.

It's recommended that you erect a vertical barrier to keep the fly off since the fly tends to fly near the ground. Surround the carrot bed by some sort of solid fence at least 2½ feet (75cm) high but not more than 3 feet (1 metre) wide. This is fairly effective, but not 100 per cent. Growing your carrots high in containers like half barrels above the 2 foot (60cm) level can also help by keeping your crop out of reach.

Parsnips

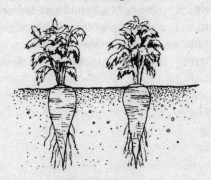

Fig. 44. Parsnips.

Sow in March or April and you'll produce a good crop with good germination rates. If you sow in February (as many recommend) the soil is often cold and wet, and the germination rate will be poor. As the flavour of parsnips is improved by a few good frosts, there is little benefit to an early crop.

Use parsnip seed when you open the packet and discard any left over as the seed does not store. Sow them thinly in rows 1 foot (30cm) apart, about half an inch (1cm) deep and thin to around 6 inches (15cm) apart. Germination can be spotty but you can try station sowing a small pinch of seeds each 6 inches (15cm) and then thin to one seedling. Do not overcrowd the plants, as the foliage grows quite large and you'll end up with very small parsnips.

Weeding and watering in a dry summer are all you need to do until you lift the crop after the first few frosts. Parsnips can be left in the ground over winter but if the ground is frozen they are hard to harvest. To keep the ground workable, mulch with straw. Otherwise store in a dark shed as for other root crops.

They will start to re-grow if left in the ground beyond February, using the stored energy in the root. In mild winters they can start this earlier so it's best to complete harvesting in January.

Carrot root fly (see previous page) can attack them and slugs can cause minor damage to the crown (top of the root).

A canker, which creates a blackened area towards the crown and rots the root, is a major problem. Lack of lime, an irregular water supply and manure in the soil seem to cause this. To avoid this, grow resistant varieties like Avonresister or Gladiator.

Salsify and Scorzonera

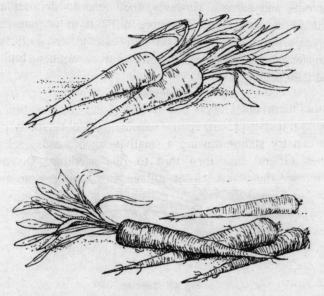

Fig. 45. Salsify and Scorzonera

These root crops, which resemble parsnips, but with a thinner root, are rarely seen in the shops despite their flavour being considered far superior to parsnips. Salsify is often called the 'vegetable oyster' because of its subtle flavour, while scorzonera is similar in flavour but has a black skinned root.

They require a good depth of light soil and do best in deep raised beds and large containers.

Sow three seeds per position directly into the soil in late April, early May at 6 inch (15cm) spacing, half an inch (1cm) deep, thinning out to one plant per station. Weed carefully by hand because the crown is easily damaged; don't use the hoe.

Water in dry weather and harvest from mid-October. They can stay in the ground through to February or even March although it's difficult to harvest in frozen ground since the foot-long roots are quite fragile.

It's easier to harvest in November and store them as for parsnips and carrots. However, they tend to dry out and wrinkle in store. They are more difficult to prepare than parsnips, but scalding makes the skin easier to scrape off, then you steam or boil until tender. Some chefs recommend boiling and then peeling.

Celeriac

Fig. 46. Celeriac.

Also known as turnip root celery, this is more popular in Europe than Britain, although it is becoming more common here. It is a demanding crop, which needs to be started in heat in March, then planted out in manure-rich, fertile soil in a sunny spot in late May, spaced a foot (30cm) apart in 18 inch (45cm) rows.

As it grows, you need continually to remove side shoots to expose the crown and then earth up in September. You must keep the crop weed free and regularly watered, taking precautions against slugs and carrot fly.

Harvest the white, knobbly ball about 4–5 inches (10–12cm) in diameter in November. Peel it thickly and grate into salads or use in cubes in stews where it adds a celery like flavour. Celeriac can be left in the ground and lifted as required or stored as other root crops such as carrots and parsnips.

If you like celery then give celeriac a try, otherwise forget it. Monarch is the favoured variety by celeriac fans.

Jerusalem Artichokes

Last and least, in my opinion, is the Jerusalem artichoke. It is noted for causing flatulence, giving it its nickname of 'fartichoke'. The flavour is described as smoky nuts and honey and

Fig. 47. Jerusalem artichokes.

it has become quite a gourmet dish. However, it's not to everyone's taste so try a few meals with it first to see how everyone likes it before growing it on the allotment.

Its saving grace is that it is really easy to grow and crop, producing foliage between 6 and 8 feet (2–2.5 metres) high which can make a useful shade for a greenhouse. The stems are quite fragile, though, so in windy locations give them support with stakes and string.

Jerusalem artichokes are grown in the same spot each year, for if you miss a tuber it will grow like a volunteer potato, so prepare the ground well with plenty of manure which you can top up as a mulch in winter.

In early spring, plant individual tubers about 18 inches (45cm) apart, around 4–5 inches (10–12cm) deep, and the shoots will appear in a few weeks. If you have more than one row, allow 30 inches (75cm) between rows. When they reach about a foot (30cm) high, earth up a little as for potatoes.

When the foliage changes colour in the autumn, cut it down to about a foot (30cm) above the ground as a marker. Then leave them in the ground to dig as required. You don't need many seed tubers as they are quite a productive crop (6 lb/3kg from one plant is a typical yield). You can save your own tubers to plant in subsequent years.

The best variety is Fuseau, which is less knobbly and so easier for the cook.

THE CUCURBITS

An easy way to remember this name – 'bits of cucumber'! However, the cucurbits are not just the cucumbers; squash, marrows, courgettes and pumpkins are all members of the same family

They're all quite greedy feeders so some preparation will pay dividends. For all of them, except greenhouse grown cucumbers, the method is much the same. Start by digging a hole, anything up to a couple of feet square and about a foot deep (60cm x 30cm). Into the hole put some good compost or well rotted manure and replace the soil, mixed with more of the same on the top, creating a little hillock.

You can sow the seeds directly into the mound, usually using a jam jar or half a clear pop bottle as a mini cloche, for none of them likes to get going in the cold. It is easier to start them under glass in a 3 inch (8cm) pot and plant out later though. The seeds are all flat, oval-shaped and should be planted sideways rather than flat in the soil to stop water sitting on them and causing them to rot off.

Once started, to keep the cropping going well, some tomato feed as the season progresses will be of benefit.

One problem they all share is a susceptibility to powdery mildew, which appears as a white or grey dust on the foliage and gradually kills the plant. It is a fungal disease that thrives in humid conditions, a little like potato blight. The conventional method of control was fungicidal sprays or organically some bicarbonate of soda mixed with a sticking agent like soft soap. However, researchers have discovered a cheap and effective control using milk.

Take skimmed milk and mix 1 part milk to 4 parts water by volume or half an ounce of milk powder to 1½ pints of water. Spray onto the leaves at the first sign of attack and the disease is checked.

You can use full fat milk but the fats in this tend to get a bit smelly after a while, hence the recommendation for skimmed milk, which is just as effective.

Cucumbers

Fig. 48. Cucumbers

Don't confuse home grown, especially outdoor grown cucumbers, with those green tubes of water in the supermarket of the same name. Yours will actually have flavour.

The outdoor or ridge cucumber does well most years in this country. My favourite variety is Burpless Tasty Green. Unlike shop cucumbers, these have small spikes on the fruit so you need to peel before eating but they really excel in flavour.

Sow mid-March in 3 inch (8cm) pots on a windowsill at home or under glass if you can keep them warm. Then plant out once they're a few inches high in your mound. You should train the foliage up netting or, as I do, onto an old pallet to keep the fruits off the ground away from the slugs and other pests. Do keep them cloched as they start because they hate the cold.

Once the main shoot has developed about six or eight leaves, pinch it out. This will encourage side shoots, increasing the yield no end.

One oddity of the cucumber is that it needs a fair amount of water but hates having the base of the stem wet, which can just rot off and kill the plant. Water well around the mound in dry weather.

Harvest your first fruits when they're just ready; leaving them on too long can slow or even stop the plant making more fruits.

If you have a greenhouse, you can grow cucumbers in there as well. The greenhouse varieties crop earlier than outdoor varieties, but to get that earlier crop you need to be able to maintain temperature if a late cold spell arrives. In the past, you needed to remove male flowers from the greenhouse cucumbers to avoid a bitter flavour in the fruits but that's not necessary now that the breeders have produced all-female F1 hybrids. However, the all-female varieties tend to need a warmer greenhouse to perform well.

After sowing in mid-March, plant them into the greenhouse border, or into large pots or into growbags when large enough. They start fruit production in June, usually running through the summer until October.

Allow plenty of room and prepare your frame for them to grow up in good time. Once the plant is all over the house, it's a bit late.

My favourite greenhouse variety is one favoured by show growers called Carmen but the seeds are pretty expensive. Luckily they will last up to seven years if stored well, so sow one and give it 10 days to germinate before sowing a second if it fails.

If planting in a border, water via a bottomless pot sunk into the soil next to the plant or draw a trench around the plant and water that. They really do hate a wet stem as I said above.

Cucumber tends to be a glut crop, one or two plants being sufficient for the average family but often fruits arrive all at once. They will keep for some time in the fridge but cannot be frozen. One storage method is to salt them but this is only moderately successful. We've made large batches of cucumber and potato soup and frozen that to store the summer crop for winter.

Controlling greenfly is quite important as cucumbers are susceptible to cucumber mosaic virus, which is passed by aphids. Feeding is important too: treat as tomatoes and feed when the fruits have begun forming.

Courgettes and Marrows

Fig. 49. Courgettes.

I used to follow the spacing instructions for both courgettes and marrows as given by the seed merchants but my experience is that they do better given more space, at least 2½ feet (75cm) and preferably 3 feet (90cm) between plants. This allows plenty of air space which reduces the mildew problem later in the year.

A courgette is simply an immature marrow so if you leave a courgette on the plant it will grow on to become a marrow. However, different varieties have been developed for each use and so usually just leaving a courgette to develop will produce a very inferior marrow.

It's best to harvest small, cylindrical varieties of courgette when they are around just 4 inches (10cm) long. If you wish, you can even cook the flowers in batter. Yellow varieties are available, as are ball-shaped ones instead of the cylinder shapes.

If you pick regularly and shelter with large cloches at the end, the plant will continue to crop and the season will be extended, giving fruit from June right through October.

In poor weather when pollinating insects may not be about, courgettes may fail to set but F1 hybrids are available that will set fruit without pollination. Don't sow the entire packet of seeds as they have a good germination rate. As two plants will probably be more than sufficient for the average family, sow four seeds at most and discard the weaker two. If you are trying a number of varieties, then one plant of each will be enough. However, start two plants to provide a reserve in case of failure. The seeds have a life expectancy of six years so save the rest of the packet for the following years.

Cultivate marrows in the same way as courgettes but leave the fruits on to develop and limit them to a maximum of four fruits per plant. Like squashes, allow the skins to harden at the end of the season, then the marrow will store well for a few months, preferably on a slatted shelf which allows airflow all round, or string it up in a net bag or even in an old pair of tights.

Unlike the courgette, the marrow's skin is not eaten, being too tough and the seeds are removed. Marrow can be served in the traditional stuffed marrow dishes, in chutneys and, because of its mild flavour, as a bulking agent in jams.

Marrows and courgettes are usually trouble free, apart from slugs, but they are susceptible to cucumber mosaic virus and mildew. The milk treatment works on them outdoors as well.

Pumpkins and Squashes

Pumpkins come in various sizes from the gigantic to the size of a football while squashes can be ball shaped or any type of strange looking fruit.

Both need plenty of food and water, plus some good weather. Started in pots in April or directly sown and planted out in May under cloche, they produce the fruit for summer and autumn.

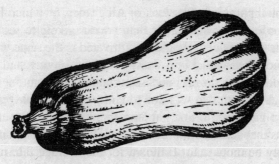

Fig. 50. Butternut squash.

The standard butternut squash is a consistent, reliable cropper and one of the best in terms of flavour. The vegetable spaghetti varieties are also popular with cooks. Summer custard squashes are very similar to courgettes in flavour although their shape – scallop edged discs – is very different.

The bush varieties of summer squash can be extremely prolific; one plant per variety is enough for a household and often some friends as well. The butternut squashes require a lot of space. I think they're best spaced with at least 4 feet (120cm) and preferably 6 feet (180cm) between them and other plants. I've tried allowing them to grow into a stand of sweetcorn to make the best use of space but it was a failure. The shade of the sweetcorn held the squash back.

As the foliage grows, just train it into a spiral pattern from the centre. Once you have six fruits developing, remove any additional small fruits and flowers to concentrate the energy of the plant into the forming fruits.

When the fruits of the winter-storing varieties are mature, remove from the plant, cutting the stalk an inch or so from the fruit. Place somewhere sheltered and sunny to allow the skin to harden off and then store in a cool, dark place. A slatted shelf is best, allowing airflow all round, or string up in a net bag or old pair of tights. Storage times vary but pumpkins will keep until Christmas and butternut squash can last into February or even longer.

Normal pumpkins like Jack of All Trades, by which I mean edible ones somewhat larger than you are likely to see in the shops for Halloween, should be cultivated in the same way but held back to around 3 or 4 fruits per plant. Having said that, I have managed a dozen good sized pumpkins from one plant, although in truth that was due to luck rather than judgement.

The biggest pest to worry about is the slug, while mice and rats can, on rare occasions, nibble the fruit. Do watch out for children pinching a pumpkin for Halloween. That happened to me one year and now I take them home to ripen. However, the youngsters couldn't steal my giant pumpkin. I had to get help to lift it into the wheelbarrow to take it home, so they had no chance.

Generally squashes and pumpkins are a very trouble-free crop, but if it's a wet summer watch out for mildew and use the milk treatment mentioned on page 149.

Giant Pumpkin

Fig. 51. Giant pumpkin.

A lot of allotment sites and village shows have a giant pumpkin competition and it is actually quite easy to grow a pumpkin that you'll need help to lift. Don't be afraid to give it a go, if only to show the old hands on the plot that the newbie may know a thing or two, after all!

Make your planting mound at least 2 feet (60cm) each way; there's nothing wrong with it being bigger if you have the energy. Add a good couple of ounces of general fertilizer as well. Make sure you've plenty of room for your monster to develop in. Ten feet (3 metres) between the pumpkin and other crops should do it.

Pick the right seed. I found Dill's Atlantic Giant wonderful but Hundredweight and Mammoth have equally good reputations. Sow into a large pot (a 9 inch/22cm one is fine), to get it off to a flying start under cover.

Once one small fruit has started to form, pinch off any other fruits as they form and commence weekly feeding with liquid tomato fertilizer. Put a strong, good pallet under the pumpkin. This will ensure air gets under it and stops it from rotting on the ground.

Real giant pumpkin enthusiasts use all sorts of magic fertilizer mixtures but this strategy will produce a pumpkin guaranteed to impress.

THE LEGUMES

Legumes are the bean family, which includes peas. They have the highest protein level of the vegetables and have been a staple food for six thousand years.

They share one amazing ability in that they help to produce some of their own fertilizer. They have developed root nodules in which symbiotic bacteria called rhizobia live and these fix nitrogen from the air, the N in NPK fertilizer. Because of this, they are an important crop in the rotation, especially for organic growers or anyone seeking to minimize their inputs into the soil.

Legumes like a humus-rich soil and prefer a pH around 6.5 or over. Although they produce nitrogen, they still need some fertilizer. Most will benefit from additional potash, so if you have some wood ash available, a couple of pounds per square yard (a kilo per square metre) will be beneficial or 2 oz (50g) of sulphate of potash applied before planting. Otherwise a couple of ounces per square yard (50g per square metre) of general fertilizer like fish, blood and bone or Growmore should ensure they get enough nutrients.

If you start your beans in pots to plant out later, you will find you can improve germination rates by mixing some soil (about a fifth by volume) which has grown beans the previous year into the compost.

Broad Beans

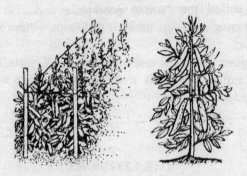

Fig. 52. Broad beans.

Broad beans are a fairly easy crop to grow. As with all the legumes they will benefit from extra potash, especially as it helps to prevent a disease called chocolate spot.

The beans come in three main types: longpods (which can be nearly 16 inches/40cm long with 8–10 beans per pod); Windsor (which are shorter and fatter with 4–7 beans per pod); and dwarf varieties (that grow just 12–18 inches/30–45cm high, half as much as the others). Depending on variety, beans are generally green or white but this does not seem to affect flavour although some claim that the Windsor varieties taste the best. A reddish bean, Red Epicure, is also available. This has an exceptional distinctive flavour. If steamed it retains the red colour, but if boiled it turns a yellowish colour.

Broad beans can be sown in both winter and spring. The winter sowing, in late October and November, should result in the earliest crop in June. However, especially in a wet winter, losses can be high, with seeds rotting in the ground, even when cloched to start. All the broad beans are hardy but some varieties, such as Aquadulce, are more suitable than others for winter sowing. In a bad winter or spring it makes little difference to cropping time what variety you use and the spring sown beans will catch up. These can go in as early as late February under cloche or as late as early May to provide a cropping period from June to October.

Early spring sowings are best made in 3 inch (8cm) pots under glass or in the cool greenhouse for planting out around three weeks later. If sowing direct, it is well to sow a few in pots anyway to plug holes in the row. Autumn sowings and mid-spring sowings can just go directly into the ground.

Generally, beans are spaced in a row 8 inches (20cm) apart, with another row 8 inches (20cm) away, staggering the plants so they will provide support to each other. These double rows are spaced 2 feet (60cm) apart to allow access for picking. In windy areas you will need to provide support by means of wires strung on the outside of the double rows.

Blackflies are a big problem for broad beans on the growing tips in the summer. Although they do not seem to cause much, if any, harm to the crop, to get rid of them snip off the top 6 inches (15cm) of the plant and dispose of it with the blackflies.

Dwarf French Beans

French beans are very easy to grow and provide a gourmet crop. The majority are best eaten as pods but with some it's best to allow them to develop as haricot (dried) beans. There are many varieties available: flat pods, pencil pods in shape, and yellow and purple pods, as well as the more usual green ones. The yellow waxy pod varieties have a particularly good flavour but, unfortunately, tend not to freeze well,

Fig. 53. Dwarf French bean plant in crop.

unlike the green podded ones. The tipi varieties are good in
that the beans appear above the foliage, making them easy
to harvest.

Sowing is usually direct and can be started under cloche
in late March and early April. However, as they are not hardy,
better results will come from a May sowing. You must
protect from late frosts. Generally they are sown 2 inches
(5cm) deep, 4 inches (10cm) apart in rows 18 inches (45cm)
apart.

Start cropping as early as July. Successional sowing will
provide crops through to the first frosts in October. If you pick
continually, it encourages the formation of another flush of
beans, while feeding with a liquid tomato fertilizer will keep
production going.

To grow haricot (dried) beans, leave the pods on the plant
to swell and the pods begin to dry. Remove the pods and hang
indoors to dry until the pods are brittle and begin to split. Shell
the beans and dry further on a rack, then store in an airtight
container. If you prefer, you can uproot the entire plant and
hang this upside down to dry rather than individual pods. In
a poor summer when the haricots are not thoroughly dried,
just freeze them, as any damp will cause moulds to grow in
store.

Runner and Climbing Beans

Fig. 54. Runner beans.

Every allotment site seems to have its rows of runner beans. It is a very productive crop which can lead to waste as the family often tires of eating the beans well before the plant finishes. However, they do freeze well.

As well as our runner beans, you can grow climbing French beans which are more productive per square foot of plot space than their dwarf cousins. The climbing borlotti beans will provide pounds of high quality haricots from a small space as well.

The traditional growing method was to use a row of sticks or bamboo canes at 9 inch (22cm) spacing in a double row, 18 inches (45cm) apart, angled to meet at the top with a horizontal support.

An easier method than constructing the traditional row of canes is to insert 8 foot (2.4m) bamboo canes or wooden poles at 9 inch (22cm) spacing in a circle tied at the top to form a wigwam. You can even get a plastic circle to hold the canes which is easier than tying at the top.

If you have a light soil which doesn't hold water well, then a row above a bean trench is the best method. Started in winter, the bean trench should be about a foot (30cm) deep and a spade blade in width. Line it with sheets of newspaper and add the contents of the kitchen waste bin, covering with soil to stop vermin. By May this will have reduced well and ensures that water is held available for the season. Often permanent supports are erected with metal poles which avoids the chore of erecting bamboo canes each year. However, this practice encourages the build up of fungal disease – many gardeners have discovered to their cost that beans should be rotated.

As runner beans are not hardy, a late frost will destroy your plants. Therefore the best method is to start off in pots under glass in early May and plant out when the risk of frost is past in June. You can sow direct, at a depth of 2 inches (5cm), by the base of the poles. If a late frost does arrive, protect overnight with fleece or even newspapers. In the worst case of losing the first sowing, don't despair because a late sowing in June will still produce a respectable crop.

When the plants reach the top of the poles, pinch out the growing tip to encourage bushier growth. Once the pods start to form, harvest them young and tender or leave to grow longer. If you want large beans for eating, then look for varieties described as 'stringless'. Some varieties such as Enorma tend to produce larger pods.

If you find you have a bigger crop of beans than you want, leave the pods to swell and harvest the beans inside. These are good in stews and you can also save some seed for next year.

Peas

Fig. 55. Peas.

Last, but definitely not least in the legumes, are the peas. Although we tend to treat them with contempt as a vegetable, they are a valuable source of riboflavin, vitamin B6, magnesium, phosphorus and potassium, and a very good source of dietary fibre, vitamin A, vitamin C, vitamin K, thiamine, iron and manganese. Raw peas, by the way, contain four times as much vitamin C than cooked peas, so adding them to a salad is great way to eat healthily.

Since their sweetness comes from natural sugars which are converted to starch when picked, the sweetest peas are the freshest. If you eat them raw, straight from the pod on the plot, you will be amazed just how sweet they are.

The pea is very popular and there are many varieties.

The wrinkled varieties (also known as marrowfat peas) are so called because when dried they are, in fact, wrinkled. They tend not to be hardy but are more popular than other types as they produce heavier crops.

These are further sub-divided by the height they grow (dwarf varieties at 18 inches to 2 feet/45–60cm; and tall varieties at up to 6 feet/2 metres) and how quickly they develop.

The first earlies take around 11 weeks to start cropping, second earlies 13–14 weeks and the maincrop 15–16 weeks, a bit like potatoes really.

The round varieties (which are smooth when dried) are more hardy. They are all first earlies and are usually sown as a first crop when frost still threatens. However, they can be sown at the end of the year to provide a last, quick crop before the cold weather properly sets in. You can sow some round varieties in October/November with a view to a very early crop the following year but, as with winter sown broad beans, failure rates can be high and early spring sown under cloche will often catch up anyway.

Mangetout peas are also called eat all, Chinese peas, snap peas or sugar peas. With these, the whole pod is eaten. They should be picked young before the peas swell.

Petits Pois are specially bred small and very sweet peas. They are not simply ordinary peas cropped small. They are a gourmet's delight and worth growing despite not being the most productive.

For the earliest crop, cloche a week before sowing direct in late February to early March. You could also start an early crop in the greenhouse by filling a length of roof guttering with compost and sowing into that. When the shoots appear, draw a trench outside and very carefully slide the content of the gutter into the trench. However, this method is unlikely to be any more successful than sowing under cloche and it is difficult to transfer to the soil.

Normally peas are sown in a shallow trench about 6 inches (15cm) wide and 1 inch (2.5cm) deep. Drop the peas into the trench about 4 inches (10cm) apart in two staggered rows. You can sow a second 'double row', spaced the expected height of the crop from the first.

With the dwarf varieties in rows, the usual method is to use pea sticks. These are usually the twigs left from pruning bushes, etc, and are inserted into the trench at sowing time to provide a structure for the peas to climb and keep their pods off the soil.

With tall varieties, insert firm stakes at 36 inches (90cm) or less intervals and attach pea netting right by the row. This must be soundly constructed as once a mass of foliage has climbed this net it acts as a sail and catches the wind.

Another method is to stake on the outside of the row every 4 feet (120cm) or so and to run twine along the row 6 inches (15cm) above the ground.

If the soil is in good heart you don't need to provide extra feed, but if you have spare liquid comfrey fertilizer available it is beneficial to give a feed when the pods begin to form.

Harvest from the bottom as peas develop upwards. Leaving mature pods on the plant will stop new pods from forming, as with runner beans, so pick little and often. A glut of peas is easily frozen, the sooner after picking the better. You can home dry peas to store them. In fact, in Britain peas were always eaten as dried peas in stews, etc, before the seventeenth century when somebody had the bright idea of trying them fresh.

Peas are not a troublesome crop but they are attractive to birds and mice when sown. Sowing under cloche will keep the birds off. Some people recommend laying spiky gorse clippings or holly leaves over the peas when sown before drawing the soil over in an attempt to thwart the mice.

The pea moth can be a problem in some areas. It lays its eggs at flowering time, producing nasty little maggots in the peas. To keep it off, use fleece. It is active mid-May to mid-June so sow early and late to avoid the pest. It is easy to spot: if you are processing a large number of peas for freezing, drop them into cold water before blanching and you will see them as floaters.

POTATOES

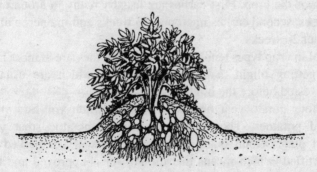

Fig. 56. Potatoes.

The potato is probably the most under-rated vegetable we eat. At best it's been a boring filler on the side of the plate but home grown potatoes are a mouthwatering vegetable in their own right. When you taste your own potatoes, you will not believe they are the same vegetable as those bought from the shop.

They are a carbohydrate food but they also provide a good source of vitamin C with around 15mg per 100g. Although this is one vitamin reduced by cooking and potatoes are always eaten cooked, they actually give us a good proportion of this important vitamin in our diet.

There is a huge range of varieties available to the allotment potato grower; literally over 400 types are fairly easily obtained. You may be surprised to hear that you can even buy blue potatoes like Edzell Blue, not just reds and whites, boilers or chippers.

Your choice of what to grow will depend on what you like and what grows well in your locality. Most seed catalogues will describe the flavour and whether a variety makes a good mash or roast, etc. For varieties that grow in your locality, ask around on your site. If others enjoy success with certain varieties, you are likely to do the same.

The main potato terms you will hear, that may confuse, are first early, second early and maincrop. These merely refer to the amount of time the potato takes from planting to production of the crop. First earlies are usually ready in around ten weeks, second earlies in around 13 weeks and maincrop after about 20 weeks.

Maincrop types tend to store better but they are at more risk of getting blight than the faster types, which are usually harvested before the blight periods begin.

Your potato year begins in January when you buy your seed potatoes. These are just ordinary potatoes that you will plant. Good quality seed potatoes will be marked as 'certified' which means that the grower is approved and the stock is free of disease. They should be about the size of a hen's egg, free from damage, not shrivelled, and not sprouting.

There is some evidence that larger seed potatoes produce better crops while very small seed potatoes definitely fail to crop well.

Do not buy potatoes from the supermarket and try to plant

those. They will probably have been treated to prevent sprouting and disease.

Due to delivery costs, seed potatoes are expensive to buy by mail order but often your allotment shop, if you have one, will sell them in small quantities whilst many garden centres only sell in larger bags of 2.5kg or 3kg. If you want to try a number of varieties, then see if you can split your purchase with some other plotholders. Otherwise you will end up growing enough potatoes to feed an army and have no room for anything else.

A 2.5kg bag of seed potatoes is enough for about four 10 foot rows and these will produce between 40 lb and 80 lb of crop and use about 100 square feet of your plot. If you try five varieties, you will quickly fill half of the allotment! So try smaller quantities of different types.

For the earliest crop, you could choose a variety like Swift or Rocket but I prefer the flavour of the old variety Arran Pilot, even if it does take a week or two longer to crop. Winston is highly regarded and, although it is technically a first early, you can leave it to grow on producing quite large potatoes.

When we come onto the second earlies, Kestrel is an excellent flavoured potato with a white skin and purple eyes. Charlotte is a great salad potato and our favourite speciality potato is Anya. This is a cross between Desiree and Pink Fir Apple, quite knobbly, so not one to peel. Scrubbed and boiled it has a distinctive nutty flavour.

When we come to the maincrop we're always in danger of being struck by blight. Valor produces excellent flavoured chippers and has some blight resistance but the most blight resistant varieties are the new Sarpo (pronounced Sharpo) types. At the time of writing there are a number of varieties in trial and you can buy Sarpo Mira and Sarpo Axona. Mira has very dense flesh and this seems to deter slugs who just can't get in too far. They store really well and, because of the denseness, are great in dishes like Potatoes Dauphinoise or in stews as they don't break up. They mash well and bake well but I don't rate them as a roaster or chipper.

Chitting Potatoes

Fig. 57. Tray of chitting potatoes.

This means that when you get your seed potatoes home you put them in a cool but frost-free place where they get some light but not direct sunlight. A north-facing window is ideal in a frost-free shed but we use an unheated spare bedroom.

The potatoes then grow short stubby shoots, which will get them off to a fast start when planted out. Some people suggest rubbing off all but three shoots to help get larger potatoes with the maincrops, but I've not found a lot of difference and prefer to have a spare shoot or three in case of damage whilst planting.

Planting Out

You need to watch the weather as frost can damage the crop. Usually mid-March is about the right time to plant your earlies and a few weeks later to plant the maincrop. If after planting, the leaves (also called haulm) start to show through and frost threatens, you need to protect the plants. Do this by pulling earth over the haulm from the side or covering with fleece.

If you have a greenhouse or a good coldframe, it's well worth growing a few earlies in pots or black plastic potato bags. Just put some commercial multi-purpose compost into a 9 inch (22cm) pot and put one seed potato in. When the weather warms, bring it out in the day and eventually all the time. You'll have the earliest potatoes on the plot unless the weather is really freezing in February.

However, if you leave them in the warm all the time, they seem to produce a lot of haulm but few tubers.

Potatoes will benefit from some tomato fertilizer after about six weeks.

You will often hear that potatoes are good for clearing or breaking new ground. Unfortunately, this is untrue. What is true is that the cultivation they require is good for breaking new ground, although they do shade out the majority of weeds once established.

Your ground should have been well dug over and broken into a reasonable tilth. This is where a rotavator really makes light work of a hard job on heavy ground. This is a good time to incorporate some well rotted farmyard manure. A barrow load over a couple of square yards is about right, but don't be afraid to use more if you have it.

Unlike most vegetables that like their soil to be just slightly acid or neutral, potatoes prefer their soil to be somewhat acid with a pH as low as 5.5. Do not lime the soil the year before planting as limey soil encourages scab.

To plant, you can just make a hole with a trowel and pop the seed potato in or you can draw a trench (take a draw hoe and scrape a trench) and place the potatoes in it. You want it to be about 4 inches (10cm) deep. You then pull the soil back from the sides to cover the potatoes.

If you have a comfrey patch, get a cut of comfrey leaves, allow to wilt for a day and just place them on the bottom of your trench. Comfrey will quickly rot down to provide fertilizer and it is almost a perfect feed for potatoes as well as tomatoes.

Plant your first and second early potatoes about a foot (30cm) apart, in rows about 2 feet (60cm) apart. As the maincrop is the heaviest cropper, it needs a bit more space, so plant them about 18 inches (45cm) apart, in rows 30 inches (90cm) apart.

Draw the earth from the sides of your rows over the plants as they grow. The potato tubers (the actual potato you eat) tend to grow towards the surface and if light gets to them they go green. The green part of the tuber contains an alkaloid called solanine, which is poisonous, so you don't want to eat green potatoes as they will upset your stomach. Potatoes are part of the same family as deadly nightshade! Don't let that worry you though.

'Earthing up', as this is called, will cover these tubers and increase your crop. It doesn't hurt the plants or slow down their growth but it kills off any weeds that have sprouted.

Potatoes are greedy feeders, so it helps to give them some more fertilizer after a month or so when the plants are established. You can use specifically formulated potato fertilizer or a general organic fertilizer such as fish, blood and bone. Good results can also be had from using a liquid comfrey feed because the liquid is immediately available to the plant.

When the potatoes are established and the haulm is beginning to touch its neighbours, they will benefit from some extra nitrogen. A handful of pelleted chicken manure per yard of row is ideal.

Water them well in dry weather. They produce a lot of crop and need their water. If the water supply is irregular, the yield will be reduced and the potatoes can be cracked and split from uneven growth.

Usually the appearance of flowers is a sign that the tubers are forming under the soil. You'll notice with maincrops particularly that they can form small apple-like seedpods. These are not edible or of any value, except to professional potato breeders, so ignore them. I have heard that removing these as they start to form increases the yield but I've not noticed any difference from doing so.

With the first earlies, harvest one plant at a time as required until they start to get too big and then just dig them all up. They'll store for quite some time. With the maincrops it can be beneficial to cut the haulm off a few weeks before harvesting to allow the skins to harden, although I do not think it makes a great difference.

You can buy a special potato fork to help harvest. It has flat tines so the theory is that it holds the potatoes and lets the soil through. Of course, the tiddlers just fall through. However, I do find a long handled potato fork useful as it gives the leverage to lift without too much effort.

Approach from the side, giving enough room so you don't spear your potatoes. I'm afraid there is a law that the best potato on any plant you harvest will be the one the fork hits.

Try to be thorough, get down on your knees if need be and make sure none is left behind. These travellers, as they are known, will harbour disease in the soil and try to grow on next year, so becoming a weed. You'll always miss a few, I'm afraid.

Harvest as early in the day as you can and preferably on a sunny day. That way you can leave them in the sun for a few hours on a sack to dry and further harden the skins for storage.

Storing Potatoes

After they've dried off, brush off any excess soil and check for damage. Sometimes it is hard to tell as a little hole on the surface can indicate a network of tunnels and even a live slug hiding in the potato so check as carefully as you can.

Any forked, slugged or suspect potatoes should be put to one side and used as quickly as possible.

Unlike other root crops, potatoes should preferably be stored above 5° Celsius as below that the starch turns into sugars, which can give them a sweet taste. The optimum temperature range is between 5 and 10° Celsius.

The most important point when storing potatoes is to exclude light. Prolonged exposure to light will cause greening of the potato. Green potatoes are poisonous, remember.

You can store potatoes in paper sacks but leave the neck slightly open to allow excess moisture to escape. For this reason, do not use plastic bags under any circumstances. The best container is a hessian sack. You can buy these quite easily and many potato suppliers sell them as well. They last a few years and can be washed if you have had some blighted potatoes in store the previous year.

After you have had the potatoes in store for a month or so, wait for a fine day and empty the bags out. Re-check for developing rots and don't be surprised if you find the odd slug or two you missed first time. I pop a few slug pellets into the sack with my potatoes to catch any emerging slugs.

If storing in a shed or garage, keep an eye on the weather. You do not want the potatoes to freeze so throw some cover over the sacks or consider some heating in really cold weather. If they do freeze, they may rot in store and will develop a strange, sweet taste. Bring them into the warm a week before eating and that taste goes away.

If you find some green on your potatoes before you store them, don't worry as keeping them in the dark will usually make it go away.

Potato Problems

Split potatoes at harvest time indicate that their water supply has been interrupted when developing, so in dry weather do water if you can. They've a lot of foliage to lose water through and they need it to develop the tubers properly.

Particularly if you're breaking grassland into growing land or the allotment has been overgrown with grass, then you're going to have a major problem with wireworm. These are the larvae of the click beetle, and a grassy plot could harbour half a million of the beasts. They are only about half an inch (1cm) long but they eat into the potatoes leaving tunnels behind.

If you must plant into ground that was grassed, you could try burying some cut, eating potatoes to distract them but it's not very effective, I'm afraid. However, if you sow some agricultural mustard as a green manure, they will eat their fill of this and change into the beetles and fly away to bother somebody else. It's a good idea regularly to follow on your potatoes with a mustard green manure to keep the numbers down.

Potato Blight

Potato blight is caused by a fungus *Phytophthora infestans*. This can also infect other members of the potato family, *Solanaceae*, such as tomatoes. It spreads through the air and develops when the weather conditions are warm and humid – as in the British summer, as we laughingly call it.

You can predict when it is likely to occur using Smith Periods. A 'Smith period' is a 48-hour period in which the minimum temperature is 10° Celsius or more and the relative humidity exceeds 90 per cent for at least 11 hours during the first 24 hours and for at least 11 hours again during the final 24 hours. However, any period of warm, humid weather increases blight risk.

The first thing you may notice are brown freckles on the leaves or sections of leaves with brown patches and a sort of yellowish border spreading from the brown patch. In a severe attack you may walk onto your patch to find all the potato foliage a rotting mass.

Tubers (the actual potato) affected by potato blight can be recognized by dark patches on the skin. Cutting the potato in half will reveal brownish rot, spreading down from the skin. Later the entire potato will turn into a soggy, foul-smelling mass. Once you smell it, you cannot mistake it for anything else.

Potato blight fungus is generally killed by cold weather, although there are some rare resistant crossbred strains that over-winter. Otherwise, the disease reservoir is infected tubers in the ground or your sack. Wherever it comes from, it can travel miles on the wind and there is little you can do if the weather is right.

There is a range of chemical treatments available to farmers but gardeners are more limited. The traditional spray was Bordeaux mixture. This isn't such a good idea as it contains copper and is hardly good for your diet although it is organically approved. Inorganic Dithane 945 is good as long as it is applied before blight has hold or better still as a preventative.

Once blight is well established there is little you can do to stop it. The best bet is to cut off the foliage and burn if possible. Those dustbin style incinerators are good for this as they hold in the heat and ensure all the spores are gone. Composting isn't so good but, since the spores are airborne, I doubt that hot composting generates much more risk than there is in the air anyway.

Leave the tubers under the ground for a couple of weeks before harvesting and the spores that are on the soil surface will be mostly dead, reducing tuber infection. In really bad years, when summer is more of a monsoon season, wash the potatoes off before drying for storage. Check after a week and again after a month, for the blight will spread from one tuber to the whole sack really quickly.

Generally the first early varieties miss the blight, although the variety Orla is quite resistant. Second earlies do get blight in exceptionally bad years. Cosmos, Nadine and Nicola are blight resistant. I rather like Nadine for flavour as well.

For the maincrop, I'd always grow Sarpo either Mira or Axona to ensure at least some crop. The varieties listed below have some resistance but have not as much as Sarpo.

- Cara
- Golden Wonder
- Record
- Sante
- Kondor
- Lady Balfour
- Valor
- Picasso
- Kerrs Pink
- Romano
- Symfonia
- Verity
- Pentland Dell
- Pentland Squire

The taste of the potato is not just a product of the variety; the type of soil and growing conditions will have an effect. I may enjoy one variety but it can taste quite different when grown on your soil.

Because of the water content and flesh structure, different potatoes cook differently. Some fry well, making great chips (or crisps – Golden Wonder is a potato variety), some boil well and some mash well. Waxy potatoes are better for salads than floury potatoes.

The tables below should give you some help on what to grow for what purpose. I have not covered all the varieties available but I think I've got the main ones that are readily available from both garden centres and specialist suppliers. You may find one variety appears in two or more sections as some potatoes are more multi-purpose than others.

Best Potatoes for Boiling

First Earlies   All first earlies boil well

Second Earlies	Anya	Marfona
	Cosmos	Maris Peer
	Edzell Blue	Nadine
	Estima	Saxon
	Kestrel	Wilja

Main Crop	Ambo	Maris Piper
	Arran Victory	Maxine
	Cara	Pentland Squire
	Celine	Picasso
	Desiree	Pink Fir Apple
	Harmony	Romano
	King Edward	Sarpo Mira
	Kondor	Stemster

Best Potatoes for Baking

First Earlies	Arran Pilot	Red Duke of York
	Duke of York	Rocket
	Epicure	Swift
	Foremost	Vanessa
	Pentland Javelin	Winston
Second Earlies	Cosmos	Maris Peer
	Edzell Blue	Nadine
	Estima	Saxon
	Kestrel	Wilja
	Marfona	
Main Crop	Ambo	Maris Piper
	Arran Victory	Maxine
	Cara	Pentland Squire
	Celine	Picasso
	Desiree	Pink Fir Apple
	Harmony	Romano
	King Edward	Sarpo Mira
	Kondor	Stemster

Best Potatoes for Roasting

First Earlies	Accent	Ulster Chieftain
	Swift	
Second Earlies	Catriona	Mona Lisa
	Cosmos	Osprey
	Edzell Blue	Wilja
	Kestrel	
Main Crop	Arran Victory	Maxine
	Cara	Picasso
	Celine	Remarka
	Desiree	Romano
	Dunbar Standard	Sante
	King Edward	Stemster
	Kondor	Valor
	Maris Piper	

Best Potatoes for Chipping

First Earlies	Accent	Swift
	International Kidney	Winston
	Premiere	
Second Earlies	Kestrel	Saxon
	Nadine	Yukon Gold
Main Crop	Cara	King Edward
	Celine	Majestic
	Desiree	Maris Piper
	Dunbar Standard	Pentland Dell
	Golden Wonder	Stemster
	Kerrs Pink	Valor

Best Potatoes for Mashing

First Earlies
Accent
Epicure
Winston

Second Earlies
Cosmos
Kestrel
Merlin
Nadine
Osprey
Wilja

Main Crop
Arran Victory
Desiree
Harmony
Kerrs Pink
King Edward
Majestic
Maris Piper
Maxine
Pentland Crown
Remarka
Sante
Sarpo Mira
Stemster

Best Potatoes for Salads

First Earlies
Amandine
Anoe (Claire)
Belle de Fontenay
BF15
Cherie
Duke of York
International
  Kidney
Pomfine
Red Duke of York
Rosabelle
Swift
Ulster Chieftain

Second Earlies
Altesse
Anya
Carlingford
Charlotte
Franceline
Juliette
Linzer Delikatess
Maris Piper
Nicola
Roseval
Wilja

Main Crop
Pink Fir Apple
Ratte
Pompadour
Sarpo Miras

THE PERMANENT CROPS

Although most vegetables should be moved around year on year as part of your crop rotation, there are a couple that remain in the same bed for their life. When you do replant, it's a good idea to move them to another place though.

The Jerusalem artichokes, which I've covered as a root crop, are effectively permanent. Because of the tall foliage do consider carefully where you plant them. The little tuber doesn't seem like much when you drop it in the ground but by the summer it is towering eight feet high and shading whatever is near.

Asparagus

Fig. 58. Asparagus.

Asparagus is a wonderful crop, absolutely delicious, but it does take time to establish and become productive. Because of this time and the cost of crowns to start the crop, if you expect to be moving within five years, I would not bother with it. Traditionally grown on a mounded ridge, they are an ideal crop for a well prepared and constructed raised bed.

Asparagus likes a sandy soil so if you have a heavy clay soil, add a fair amount of compost and some gritty sand to the soil. This crop is going to be producing for 20 years, so it is worth the initial investment in preparation.

You can start asparagus from seed but it is more usual to buy one-year-old crowns. They're not cheap but, as I said, they're going to be producing for 20 years so it's worth spending on a good variety. You can obtain a purple asparagus (Stewarts Purple) which is sweeter than the green varieties and has less fibre. Gijnlim is a heavy cropping, green variety that has performed well in European trials.

The crowns are planted 12–18 inches (30–45cm) apart in April in a 12 inch (30cm) wide trench about 8 inches (20cm) deep, slightly mounded in the centre so the roots slope downwards and out. In a standard raised bed, 4 feet (1.2 metres) wide, the trench goes down the centre. Cover with fine riddled (sieved) soil to about 2 inches (5cm) above the top of the crown and then fill to the surface as the plant grows.

Keep the bed weed-free, water as required but don't let it get too wet and don't take a crop in the first year. The plants are shallow so don't hoe deep; in a raised bed it's best to hand weed. The spears turn into foliage to feed the plant. In autumn when the fern-like foliage begins to yellow, cut it off a couple of inches above ground level.

In the spring. draw up a ridge over the plant centre about 4 inches (10cm) high and add a balanced fertilizer like fish, blood and bone or Growmore or mulch with compost. The spears start to appear in early May. They are so tempting that you won't be able to resist taking them, but just take a few and leave the rest to develop.

When the spears are about 4 inches (10cm) high above the ground, cut them with a sharp knife some 3 inches (7.5cm) below the ground. The real season starts in mid-May and runs through June when you must show restraint and stop cutting. In the second year just take 6 or 8 spears per plant, double that in the third year and expect about 20–25 spears per plant for the rest of its life.

If a late frost strikes in May, it will damage the crop so cover with fleece. Otherwise slugs are the main pest and rust can be a problem in wet years. If rust strikes, remove the affected shoots. The asparagus beetle is rarely a problem to home growers. They are small with orange markings on their 7mm-long bodies and will attack foliage and spears. Use an approved insecticide if available.

Over cropping asparagus in the early years causes weakened plants and spindly spears. It is hard to resist the urge to overcrop in the first years, but your restraint will be rewarded.

Globe Artichokes

Fig. 59. Globe artichoke.

These are a fantastic plant, seen all too rarely on allotments, which is a shame especially as they need a lot of room and so don't get into many gardens either.

They look more like a decorative thistle about 4 feet (1.2 metres) tall than a vegetable crop, with silvery leaves stretching 2 to 3 feet (60–75cm) to either side, so they need to be spaced well.

They can be started from seed, but it is tricky and the usual method is to grow from rooted offsets planted in early to mid spring with the head just above soil level.

In the first year keep it weed-free and water when dry. It is quite greedy and will benefit from mulching with well rotted manure or compost and a liquid feed every couple of weeks.

Small heads will start to develop in the first year. You should cut these off and discard them to reserve strength for the next year. In the late autumn cut off the foliage and mulch the crowns to protect them for the winter.

You can pile leaves or straw over the crown, using

wire netting to keep it in place, and cover this with plastic sheeting to keep it dry or use some doubled up fleece to keep it snug.

When the plant starts to grow again in early spring, remove the covering. After they start to produce heads in July or possibly June, feed them. First remove the main stem head (which is called the king head) and then remove the secondary heads as they are developed. Do not allow them to develop more than six heads in this second year but in later years you can get up to 12 heads per plant. Once cut, reduce the stem by half.

The plants will be productive for around four to six years but you can harvest rooted suckers (offsets) and so grow more plants. Select from your best plants and you will improve your strain over time.

ALL THE REST

These don't quite fit in our orderly rotation plans, isn't nature cruel? However, avoid growing in the same soil two years in a row and fit them in as best you can.

Leaf Beet or Chards

'What's in a name? That which we call a rose, by any other name would smell as sweet' said Juliet in Shakespeare's play. It's a good job he picked roses as the beets are really confusing. Swiss Chard, Ruby Chard, Beet Leaf, Seakale, Perpetual Spinach, Spinach Beet are all variants on the same theme.

Some are fairly boring to look at and some are a riot of colour, rivalling any foliage plant in the ornamental garden. There's a large range of varieties available but the most stunning visually would have to be Bright Lights for my money although I think Rhubarb Chard pips it for flavour.

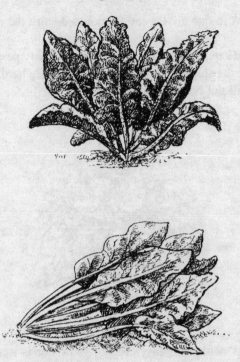

Fig. 60. Ruby chard and sea kale or silver beet (Swiss chard).

They're an easy vegetable to grow, just sow thinly in April through to the end of June in good soil, preferably manured the preceding winter. They will be in the ground for over a year but half a row is all you will need.

Once they're up, thin to one plant every 8 inches (20cm) and keep weed-free and watered in dry weather. Harvesting can start in August and will provide leaves right through to the following June by which time the plants will be getting tired and can come up, freeing the soil for another crop. Move your beet leaf bed round the plot, sowing in a different place each spring.

Don't harvest all the leaves in one go, just take a few outer leaves of each plant, preferably fairly young so cropping the whole row in one go. Be careful not to disturb the roots when cropping.

They are remarkably trouble free as the only pests to cause worry are the slugs. They're also exceptionally hardy so a cold winter will not bother them at all.

True Spinach

Fig. 61. Spinach.

Spinach is neither an easy crop to grow nor is it as exciting to the eye as the chards but I think it has a far finer flavour. Spinach is very much a 'love it or hate it' vegetable. If you love it, it is worth persevering and growing the true spinach.

The problem with spinach is that it runs to seed easily and it is temperature sensitive. It will not even germinate in a very hot summer, preferring cool weather, and tends to bolt in the sunshine.

The two main types are summer and winter spinach. With summer spinach, try growing a row in the shade of a tall crop of peas or sweetcorn and you may avoid the bolting.

Spinach needs a good rich soil with plenty of available nitrogen to power the leaf growth and also plenty of water. It grows best on ground recently manured; alternatively scatter a few handfuls of pelleted chicken manure around.

Successively sow summer spinach in April and May,

winter spinach in August and September. Both are thinly sown about an inch (2.5cm) deep in rows a foot (30cm) apart thinning to 4 inches (10cm) apart as soon as they show. When they have developed a little, remove every other plant for use in the kitchen.

Once well developed, pick young leaves from the outside of the plant as required. With summer spinach you can take up to half the leaves at one time but be more gentle with winter spinach. Spinach must be used immediately as it does not store, although cooked spinach will freeze well for later use. A seemingly large number of leaves will reduce in the pan to quite a small amount, so you'll need to pick far more than you realize the first time.

I'd suggest growing either Tetona or Spokane, both are F1 hybrids that are slow to bolt and resist mildew, which can be a problem with spinach.

Celery

Fig. 62. Celery.

I must admit I loathe the taste of celery. Even in small amounts in a stew I can taste it and there's no way I could eat a stick of it with cream cheese, as my wife loves to do. Luckily, on my allotment there are others who like it and put the effort in to grow it so we're both happy. This is one of the beauties of an allotment, you can all help each other. There's often someone with a glut of something offering it around and spare plants to be had when someone realizes that they don't need 20 cabbage plants. I've lost my runner beans to a surprise frost and immediately been given new plants to replace them by another plotholder.

The old trench method of growing celery was exceptionally demanding and a test of skill. It needed two people, one to hold the leaves together and one to shovel soil to blanch the celery. Modern self-blanching varieties are still demanding but far easier than that, and blanching with brown paper or cardboard tied around the plant is preferred now to trenching.

Celery needs a rich soil to grow well so loads of manure or compost in the soil is a must for success, pretty much like a brassica but you don't need to make the pH too high, 6 to 6.5 is fine. The manure is not just for the nitrogen, which it needs, but also to hold water because celery is a thirsty crop as well. The week before planting out, apply a couple of ounces per square yard of general fertilizer and the same of pelleted chicken manure for the extra nitrogen.

Plant in a block around 8 inches (20cm) between plants so they cover each other. You may need to insert straw between plants, to help the blanching process, and wrap the outer plants in the block.

The self-blanching varieties are less stringy and finer flavoured than the old trenching varieties but are not hardy so will be finished by the arrival of hard winter frosts.

Alternatively, plant a little further apart and then wrap the lower leaves with cardboard or brown paper tied with string. If they grow above your wrapping, just wrap another cylinder around higher up, always leaving the top leaves open though.

The slug is the biggest pest problem; it particularly likes celery. Slug damage can also cause a bacterial disease, celery heart rot, to take hold. This ruins the plant by turning the centre into a brown slimy mess.

Celery fly can occasionally be a problem. It burrows into the leaves causing blisters to appear on them. There is no real treatment but it's sensible to avoid planting next to parsnips which can be affected by the same bug.

Bolting can also be a problem. In addition, the plants must not be allowed to dry out in good weather, so water daily in hot spells. You'll be surprised how much water they need: a couple of gallons per square yard per day in hot weather.

Best varieties (so I am told) are Tango F1, Victoria F1 and Galaxy which is an early variety you can also grow in polytunnels for a really early crop.

Lettuce and Salad Leaves

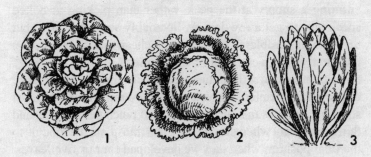

Fig. 63. Lettuce.
(1) Butterhead. (2) Crisp heart. (3) Cos.

Because we associate lettuce and salads with summer, we think of it as a warm weather crop yet surprisingly it is anything but. Lettuce prefers cool weather and germination becomes difficult in temperatures above 25° Celsius. Hot weather also makes your lettuce decide it's time to set seed and so it bolts. Some lettuce varieties are remarkably hardy, Arctic King and Winter Density being the best known of the autumn sown varieties to provide winter and spring salads.

My personal favourite is Little Gem, a small cos variety. One lettuce is ideal for a two-person salad or you can use two when you're feeding more (pretty obvious really!). Larger varieties can be a problem in that home-grown lettuce doesn't store well in the fridge, which makes you wonder what they do to the commercial varieties that do seem to keep well for a few days.

You can get around this problem by pulling the plant with roots on to take home, using what you want and putting the roots into a vase of water in a cool place. The lettuce will remain fresh and crisp for three days or more.

Another route is to grow loose leaved varieties like lollo rosso where you just cut off the leaves you want for a meal at a time rather than harvest the whole plant at once.

Lettuce is a crop that tends to develop quickly, reach perfection and then bolts, so rather than planting dozens at a time, it is far better to start a few off each week or two, thereby ensuring a supply at the peak, rather than picking at bolted specimens to get a few leaves. Invariably some will bolt, but that's no big problem. The seeds are cheap and, at worst, you recycle them into compost or chicken feed.

You can sow directly, lettuce doesn't like the root disturbance of being transplanted, but you can get around this as well. Just sow into modules in a seed tray, a small pinch per module, and thin to one plant when they're up. Then transplant the module to the final position when they've developed four or five leaves. By sowing a few every week you can have a continual supply at the peak of perfection and minimize waste.

This also helps avoid the scourge of the lettuce seedlings: slugs and birds.

If you're sowing in high summer and we're lucky enough to have hot weather, sow in the afternoon and water with cold mains water. The reason is that the germination process will start some hours later in the cool of the night.

Lettuce does not require too much from the soil, but nitrogen is useful to fuel all the leaf growth so pelleted chicken manure or an artificial nitrogen source like sulphate of ammonia will help it grow.

It's an ideal crop for tucking into odd spaces as it develops on the plot. Being fast growing in the summer, it will intercrop well between slower growing brassicas and, in hot summers, the shade of the edge of the sweetcorn patch also helps prevent bolting, making use of the space between the plants.

You can buy seed mixtures from many suppliers based on cut and come again mixed salads containing a selection of different leaves, including peppery rocket to add zing to the mix. With these, you simply scatter the seed on a patch and leave it to grow. After six to eight weeks or so, cut off the leaves an inch (2.5cm) above the ground with a pair of scissors and you have a ready-made mixed salad. Sow three or four patches two weeks apart to ensure you always have a salad mix available, cutting round them in a circle.

There's quite a range of alternative salad plants you can grow throughout the year, purslanes, rocket, land cress, mustard, lambs lettuce and corn salad to name the principals. Personally I would suggest that a cut and come again mix is far easier for the ordinary gardener.

Sweetcorn

Fig. 64. Sweetcorn.

Just 30 years ago any gardening magazine would give dire warnings about the difficulties of growing sweetcorn in the British climate north of Watford. Now the breeder's art and increasingly warm, if wet, summers means that the farmers' fields are filled with corn in the north and gardeners can succeed with sweetcorn almost anywhere in the British Isles.

Originally a south American crop it does like some good hot weather to give of its best but I've never failed with it even in bad years. It is actually a grass and is quite unusual in that it grows at night rather than in daylight, being geared for the equal day and night length near the equator.

The trick with sweetcorn is to get it started in good time and get it going before the long days and short nights of mid-year. Working against this is the fact that it needs to be warm for the seeds to germinate. You can sow directly and cover each position with a cloche but, the further north you are, your chances of the soil warming enough early enough are reduced.

The best varieties tend to be F1 hybrids whose seeds are more expensive to buy, so to get the maximum number germinated it is well worth chitting the seeds. In the base of a shallow container, lay a sheet of damp kitchen paper, place the seeds on the paper and cover with another sheet of damp paper. Put the lid on the container and place in a warm (around 20° Celsius) dark place. An airing cupboard is ideal. Check carefully after three days to see if any have sprouted, then check daily after that. Generally they will all sprout within a day or two of each other.

As soon as they start to sprout, you must quickly pot them up. You can use 3½ inch (9cm) pots or root trainers, peat pots or old toilet roll inners. Dib a hole about 1–1½ inches (3cm) deep with your finger and drop into multi-purpose compost. Water in with tepid water, not cold to avoid shocking the seeds. Root trainers are deep modules that open up to enable easy planting and are excellent for plants that have long roots that do not like disturbance.

You can also save toilet roll inner tubes and fill these with compost as a pot. When the tube is planted out, it rots away in the soil. Some people have no problems with this method but the cardboard inner tubes dry out easily so check daily and spray the tubes with water to prevent this. Re-usable plastic pots are an easier option in my opinion.

Keep the pots reasonably warm. They need not be kept quite as warm as the seeds but you want them kept over 10° Celsius. Cover with fleece in cold weather, particularly overnight. When the pots have been started, pre-warm the soil by putting up a cloche or covering the soil with fleece where you intend to plant. It is time to plant out when the plants are nearly 4 inches (10cm) high as the roots will be pushing at the other end.

Make a hole a couple of inches (5cm) deeper than your pot and plant into that, filling to the same level so the plant is in a little depression in the soil. Cover with a cloche and leave this on until the plant is pushing it off of its own accord.

Sprinkle a little dried blood or sulphate of ammonia around each plant to provide a nitrogen boost and get them away quickly, unless your soil is very rich having been manured the preceding winter.

A good couple of ounces of general purpose fertilizer per square yard a week before planting out will also help and I like to give a handful of pelleted chicken manure per plant as the cloches come off.

To encourage additional root growth to power the plant, when the plants reach a height of 2 feet (60cm) or so, draw soil up to the stem, filling in the depression and a little above.

Often I look around our allotment site and see spindly weak plants that rarely amount to much or crop well. The two main reasons for this are over-crowding and under-feeding. For decent corn, you must allow plenty of room. Sweetcorn should be planted in a block to help it pollinate rather than in rows but you must space it at least 18 inches (45cm) and preferably 2 foot (60cm) apart each way.

To produce the corn on the cob, which are actually the seeds of the plant, they need to be fertilized. The male flowers at the top of the plant scatter pollen down to the female flowers, which are the tassels hanging off the developing cobs. That's why we block plant rather than use rows.

Crowding is counter-productive. Although the individual plants look lonely to start with, they'll soon fill the space and reward you with a good crop. The space around the sides of your sweetcorn block can be quite useful for growing some lettuce which doesn't like it too hot and will benefit from the shade. You can also interplant the outside rows with dwarf French beans, which should get enough light to be productive. Inside the block is too shaded for anything, except the weeds of course.

You only need to hoe once or twice until June when a liquid feed will help boost the cob production. Comfrey feed is ideal but a general purpose liquid fertilizer will be fine.

Harvest when the tassels that hang from the cobs turn brown. It can be a fine line between under-ripe and over, when it goes hard.

My method is quite fussy but it never fails to produce a good crop with a high germination rate from expensive seed.

The price of seeds may be high, but the varieties available now are far better than in the old days. Super-sweet are, as the name suggests, incredibly sweet while tender-sweet are less chewy in texture. Lark F1 is an excellent variety but Sundance F1 is better for freezing and is more reliable if you live in the north.

The sooner you use sweetcorn after picking, the better, but it will keep well in the fridge, still in its wrapping of leaves, for a week. Once picked, the sugars begin to convert to starch, thus losing the sweet taste. When freezing, try to freeze on the day you pick for best results.

One warning: if you grow two varieties side by side, then you can get cross-pollination and inferior cobs. Ideally you want the two varieties about 8 yards (7 metres) apart. It is worth checking with your neighbours where they are growing their sweetcorn or arranging to grow the same variety.

Tomatoes

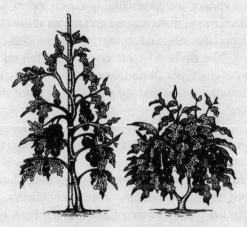

Fig. 65. Bush and cordon tomatoes.

The tomato is one of the most popular crops for the home grower and with good reason. The taste of a tomato, sun warmed and vine ripened compared with shop bought specimens from the chiller cabinet is like that of vintage wine in comparison to plonk.

In the shops you are unlikely to find more than half a dozen varieties but as a grower you have a choice of hundreds. The shop varieties are grown to travel and store well but you don't need to worry about that. Your concerns are taste, cropping and suitability for your area.

This huge range does present a problem for the grower in that you are spoilt for choice. My advice is to grow some bankers, that is, dependable known varieties you can bank on, each year and to try a couple of new ones. Six or possibly eight types will be more than enough.

Some tomatoes are bred for outdoor growing, some just for greenhouse growing and others will serve for both. They come in sizes from cherry to the giant marmande types, like Big Boy, and in different shapes from the round varieties to the plum shaped. In colour they range from bright yellow, through orange to the familiar red and then to tomatoes so dark they're almost black. One variety we rather like is Green Zebra which has medium sized round fruits that are green with yellow stripes.

Apart from the size and colour, tomatoes come in three main types. The first and most common is the tall *indeterminate or cordon* types. With these, the side shoots will grow out, sub-dividing and producing a giant bush if not stopped by pinching out.

The second is the *bush or determinate* type of tomato where the side branches develop naturally, forming a bush that stops itself eventually. No pinching out of the side shoots is required.

The third type is the *dwarf* variety – very small bush plants, often grown in hanging baskets or small containers.

Grow cordon types in a greenhouse as the bush types take up too much space. Tomatoes do well in a polytunnel but the higher light level in a greenhouse brings the crop on faster and helps in ripening.

Growing tomatoes outdoors in Britain is always risky, just like the famous British summer. They need warmth and sunlight to crop well but even if those are available there is the problem that they are susceptible to blight, just like potatoes.

Outdoor tomatoes still need to be started indoors to have a long enough growing season to produce any sort of crop. Usually mid-March is right for outdoor tomatoes but the greenhouse varieties can be started a couple of weeks earlier. Sow them thinly in a shallow pot on a windowsill or in a propagator and, when large enough, transplant into a 3 inch (8cm) pot of multi-purpose compost. If you dib the hole so that the soil level is about halfway up the seedling, it will encourage it to produce more roots.

If you look closely at the base of the stem of a tomato you will see fine hairs and these all have the capability to become roots. Whenever you transplant, plant deeply to cover these, that will ensure that all those new roots will develop and work for you, pumping nutrients to produce tomatoes, which is what we want.

Pick the most sheltered sunny spot on your plot and dig the

soil over well, adding plenty of compost or well rotted manure. If possible, try and construct some sort of windbreak around the area. Fleece on polypipe hoops will work as a temporary greenhouse, at least until the plants grow too large. At a minimum, cloche until they are established. If you can keep some sort of cover over them all through the growing season, it will also help no end in stopping the blight from getting the plants. Blight arrives on the wind and needs damp foliage to gain a foothold. If you keep the foliage dry, you greatly improve your chances of not getting it.

Do not plant out before the risk of frost has passed, usually June; move them up to larger pots if need be because the weather is bad. For cordon varieties, put a stout stake or cane in for each plant. Bush varieties, like Plum Roma, will trail over the ground and here weed suppressant matting under the plants will help keep the crop from harm. Between each plant sink a bottomless pot or large bottle through the matting to water and feed through.

Slugs are a real problem with bush tomatoes, so take action to control them as the season goes along.

Fig. 66. Removal of side shoot from tomato.

With the cordon types, tie them to the cane loosely with twine each foot as they grow and pinch out the side shoots. I'm told by the professional tomato growers that ripping or pinching off side shoots does less damage to the plant than cutting them off. It doesn't feel right but they know what they're doing and think it reduces infection risk.

This business of taking off the side shoots often seems to confuse the novice, but it's not that complicated. The plant is trying to produce lots of stems and foliage but we want lots of fruit so we concentrate its energy into that by taking the side shoots out, leaving one main stem. Off that stem you will get the leaves and fruit bearing stalks, which we call a truss. The side shoots start in the joint between the leaf and the main stem. The earlier you pull these off, the better, so no energy is wasted. Sometimes a truss will go on to try and form a new stem and should be cut off after the fruits.

Once the fruits start to form, it is time to start feeding the plants. Either a commercial feed as per the instructions or home-made comfrey liquid. We get an awful lot from a tomato plant and we really need to feed them enough to keep them cropping.

In a hot, dry summer water daily if possible. You probably need to give a couple of litres per cordon plant and for bush varieties three times that may be needed.

It is critical to keep tomatoes watered regularly. In hot sunny weather they may well need double the amount of water to a cloudy day, so ensure that you have not just wet the surface of the compost. Irregular watering will cause the fruits to split and develop blossom end rot where the base of the fruit turns black and rots.

Once the cordon varieties have developed four trusses, five in a glorious heatwave summer, pinch out the growing tip of the plant. This concentrates energy into the fruit. If you just leave them to develop more trusses, you will get a lot of immature fruit but fewer ripe developed fruit at the end of the season.

The bush varieties do not need much attention. Just keep the slugs away and remove any excess foliage towards the end of the season so the fruit gets plenty of light to help it ripen.

Once the weather turns cold, there is little point in leaving the plants. You can try freeing the stems of cordons from the cane and laying them down onto straw then cloching or fleecing but I think you're best to call it a day and bring the green fruits in.

Green tomatoes aren't wasted anyway. Apart from making them into chutney, they can be stored. Just pop them into a tray in a cool, dark place and they'll keep for quite a while. When you want to ripen them, bring them into the warm and put a ripe banana with them. The ethylene gas produced by the banana will cause them to ripen quite quickly.

If you have a greenhouse, you have a much better chance with tomatoes. Because it's warmer you can start them off a few weeks earlier and keep them going longer at the other end so producing a larger crop per plant. Unless you have a huge greenhouse or polytunnel, you're best staying with cordons. Allow them to go to six or seven trusses of fruit before stopping the plant.

Do resist the urge to overcrowd. They look so lonely when you plant them out initially but when they're overcrowded it reduces airflow and encourages fungal disease. In a wide border, plant out in a zigzag pattern to make best use of the space.

With greenhouse growing, whitefly can become a problem. One way to deter them is to grow marigolds between the plants. It does work; I assume they don't like the scent. Some varieties work better than others. Thompson & Morgan actually sell Marigold Tomato Growing Secret especially for this. It makes the greenhouse look rather pretty as well.

Although you can grow in pots or growbags in a greenhouse, I much prefer to grow in the border soil. The reason is that with a garden greenhouse it is just a minute's work to go up to water but when you have to travel round to a plot you may find you've missed a day or two. Life does have a nasty habit of getting in the way of allotmenting at times!

A border will hold much more water under the surface than a pot or growbag thereby giving you that leeway when needed. Although old books talked about damping down a greenhouse by throwing water around to increase humidity, this practice encourages fungal problems. If you insert bottles neck down into the compost by each plant and water into them you keep the border soil drier. This avoids the humidity problem and, incidentally, helps stop weed growth in the borders.

A fairly common problem with tomatoes is a magnesium deficiency due to the high feeding rate, locking out this micronutrient needed for utilization of nitrogen. The lower leaves will begin to yellow and this yellowing then moves up the plant. Treatment is really easy. Buy some Epsom salts from the chemist and mix 30g per litre of warm water. Allow to cool and spray the plants every couple of days, adding about 10g per plant into the water when watering.

Smokers should take care, particularly with greenhouse tomatoes. Tobacco often contains a virus that tomatoes can catch. Wash your hands after a smoke before handling your tomatoes, especially side shooting. If you're unsure whether it is an incurable viral infection or a deficiency problem, try the Epsom salts cure anyway. It will not do any harm.

Sometimes you will find the leaves have curled on the plants. This is nothing to worry about and tends to happen as the nights get cooler. As I said earlier, it is critical not to let your tomatoes dry out. Water them regularly to prevent blossom end rot.

Like most plants you should avoid growing the tomatoes in the same spot year after year. With a greenhouse border, take off the top 6 inches (15cm) of the soil and replace with fresh compost. Outside, if you have just one perfect place for them, plant next to where they grew the year before and add plenty of compost to the soil.

I mentioned the wide range of tomatoes available. What you grow will depend on your tastes and your area. We love Sungold, a yellow/orange F1 hybrid of incredible sweetness that will perform well in the greenhouse or outdoors. They're so sweet that the biggest pest is children who can strip a plant in minutes.

For a bottling/sauce tomato we find Plum Roma the best. It's a prolific cropping bush variety and usually does well outdoors. San Marzano is reputed to have a better flavour but we found it cropped later and was caught by the end of the season giving a very poor crop. Perhaps it would do better in the south.

If you like a large tomato, try Beefeater, which we found superior to Big Boy. For a standard tomato Ailsa Craig is well worth growing for the exceptional flavour even if it is prone to greenback, a condition where the top of the tomato remains hard and refuses to ripen. More reliable, but not quite as tasty is Alicante, and Cedrico seems to be an excellent tomato for the table as well as the show bench.

Do try some heirloom or heritage varieties, by which they mean old varieties that have survived down the years. Green Zebra with its green and yellow stripes may look a little unusual but the tartness goes really well in a salad.

If you grow in a particularly cold area then try Sub Artic Plenty. It was developed by the US Air Force of all people in 1940 to supply their forces stationed in Greenland with fresh tomatoes. It's a bush variety, quite a heavy cropper and very early, producing small sweet fruit in just 55 days. It's not hardy, so it will not take a frost but it will thrive when other varieties won't. I'm told it's also possible to get a very late crop with them by starting a plant in July/August and planting in a tunnel or greenhouse.

Another method of gaining a later crop is to plant on a few side shoots from any cordon variety. Allow them to grow to about 6 inches (15cm) and then remove from the parent and put them 1–2 inches (2.5–5cm) deep into a 3 inch (8cm) pot of damp multi-purpose compost. Use a small stake to keep the plant stable. Sometimes you can get a really good late crop, sometimes not but it hasn't cost you a penny to try.

One variety I would urge you not to grow is Moneymaker. Tasteless and watery, it amazes me it's still popular when so many really wonderful tomatoes can be grown.

Peppers

Fig. 67. Sweet peppers.

Peppers, or capsicums to give them their proper botanical name, are really not an outdoors crop in the UK. Unlike tomatoes, where you at least have a chance of an outdoor crop, peppers need it too warm for too long to be viable except possibly, in a good year, in the far south of England.

If you don't have a greenhouse you will need to construct some form of shelter, perhaps one of those temporary plastic greenhouses they sell cheaply in the bargain shops or something built from scrap and polythene.

Whether you are growing sweet salad peppers or blisteringly hot chilli peppers, cultivation is basically the same except I have noticed that some chilli peppers actually fruit better before the end of the season if grown in pots rather than the ground. I assume the plant is reacting to the lack of nutrition in the pot by attempting to reproduce and so producing the fruit.

Sow under heat in late February and March. When large enough to handle, move the seedlings along to 3 inch (8cm) pots and later from there to a 6 inch (15cm) pot before planting into their final home. They do well in the border of the greenhouse or in large 9 inch (22cm) pots under cover but they are sensitive to cold and you must keep them warm throughout.

When the flowers appear, mist spray with water to encourage the fruit to set and deter the red spider mite At this time also start feeding just as for tomatoes. When the fruits are the right size for the variety they are edible and can be taken. All the fruits are green initially. Coloured varieties change to red or yellow over the next week or so on the plant but the flavour does not change. Chilli peppers do not get any hotter as they change colour

Like tomatoes, peppers can suffer blossom end rot if they are watered irregularly. Otherwise the main pests are red spider mite and aphids. Effective biological controls for both are available.

We find that just one hot chilli plant provides more than we need for a year. They're easily dried just by stringing and hanging them in a dry, warm place in the kitchen. Do be careful with chillies when preparing them. Wash your hands thoroughly after handling because if you touch your eyes you will be in agony. Seriously.

With sweet peppers, it depends how much you like them. They will freeze well to use in cooked meals so I grow about six plants. My favourite variety is Gypsy F1 for a sweet pepper and habenero for a hot.

Aubergine

Fig. 68. Aubergine.

Once again, I'd have to say this is a greenhouse crop despite the seed merchants claims for some varieties that you can grow them on a patio. Cultivate in the same way as the peppers but be aware they seem to attract whitefly and aphid problems.

The stems can be a bit prickly and irritating so you may like to wear gloves when handling the plant.

There's quite a wide range of different colours and fruit sizes available but, being traditionalists, we grow Black Beauty which seems fairly reliable and is the dark purple to black aubergine you find in the shops.

15

FRUIT

Although allotments are temporary, in the sense you rent them from year to year, if you're going to be on the same plot for five years or more it is well worth investing in a fruit section. I say 'investing' because fruit requires quite a lot at the start and the return comes over the years.

Most allotment sites will not allow you to plant trees, a policy I agree with. A tree takes up a lot of space, shades everything under and to the south of it and will probably be there long after the plotholder who planted it has gone.

However, most will allow cordons or espaliers for tree fruit which are varieties grown on dwarfing rootstocks so they don't get too large and take over the site. You may have to undertake a little negotiation with the site manager first though. It's always best to discuss your plans beforehand and avoid presenting a fait accompli which will get people's backs up.

When buying your fruit bushes or canes, please remember they are going to be there for a number of years. It is well worth spending some time looking through the nurseryman's catalogues and paying extra for a quality plant of a named variety. Often you will find currant bushes very cheaply in discount supermarkets. I love a bargain, but my experience is that it takes a couple of years to discover you have wasted your time growing either an inferior variety or one developed for commercial growers with different requirements from the home grower.

After deciding what you want to grow, you should have some idea of the space required and where the permanent fruit beds are to go. Your biggest problem with all soft fruit is going to be the birds. Unprotected they can be stripped bare in a day and I'm quite convinced birds watch each other, so if one finds your bushes, his pals will not be far behind.

The Fruit Cage

The easiest solution to the bird problem is to plant within a fruit cage. You can buy fruit cages in kit form constructed with an aluminium or steel framework over which nylon netting is laid or you can cheaply construct your own.

The frame doesn't have to be particularly strong and ordinary 2" x 1" (5cm x 2.5cm) timber will be adequate as your construction material. Because you will need a fair

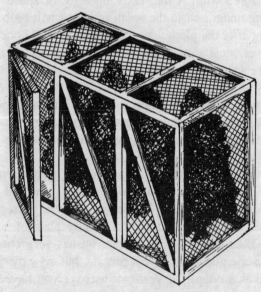

Fig. 69. Fruit cage.

amount, it will pay you to obtain your wood from a timber or builders' merchant rather than a DIY store. Most will deliver locally for free as well. Ask what the standard lengths supplied are and you can then work out your cutting list for the minimum waste.

It is worth buying treated timber, which is impregnated with preservative, and additionally painting with a preservative like Cuprinol and soaking the ends that will be in the ground to maximize the life of your cage (see page 65).

It's far easier to work in a cage in which you can stand up otherwise a few hours pruning will leave you bent over with an aching back. So the height of your cage will depend on your height to some extent. Six feet is fine for me but if you are tall, then you may want a little more.

Your uprights will be 18 inches or so in the ground to provide stability, so a length of 7 feet 6 inches for the uprights is ideal but 8 feet is a standard length so you may as well have a bit more headroom.

Before you actually begin construction, clear your fruit bed thoroughly of any perennial weeds and level the ground. Preparation is everything in building as in growing. Take your time, this is going to be here for many years and a few extra hours now will be forgotten in a year's time, never mind ten years'.

The uprights want to be spaced about 8 feet (2.4 metres) apart with an upright to either side of the door. Don't forget you will need a door to get in and out! Dig a hole around 20 inches to 2 feet (50cm–60cm) deep and put some gravel into the base. This will ensure good drainage and you will not have standing water on your post rotting it. If you can borrow a post borer, a 6 inch (15cm) width one is ideal; it will make short work of this job but it's not worth buying one unless you have a fencing job to do as well.

Tamp some sand and gravel in around the post, ensuring it is vertical. Don't trust your eyes for this, use a spirit level and don't forget to check both directions, forward and back, side to side.

Put your top bars on as you go and fix angle braces from bottom corner to top, which will hold the vertical posts stable. Add some stretchers across the roof and the job is nearly done, just the door to construct. You'll find some galvanized metal angle brackets useful in the corners for fixing and a battery powered drill/screwdriver will save a lot of time.

Having constructed your framework, all you need to do is fix the netting on. The ideal size is 0.75 inch (20mm) mesh as birds can get through smaller spaces than you expect. Staple frequently, keeping the net taut.

Do be aware that snow is quite heavy and you may need to take the roof netting off or be willing to knock snow off in a cold winter. There is another advantage to removing the roof netting for the winter when there's no fruit for the birds to steal: those birds will become allies in the cage, eating the pupae of raspberry beetles and other pests. A gentle forking over of the surface, just a couple of inches deep, will help them find their winter food and reduce our summer problems.

Having built your cage it's now time to stock it, so we'll look at the soft fruits, starting with the berries. The blackberries, raspberries and hybrid berries are similar in that they are grown tied to wires as described below.

Before you plant any of the berries, mix 2 lb per square yard (900g per square metre) of hoof and horn meal or bonemeal into the top foot (30cm) of soil in the planting area. This will provide a long-lasting slow-release source of nitrogen to get your plants off to a good start.

Blackberries and Hybrid Berries

Blackberries and hybrid berries if just left to their own devices will produce a tangled mass of brambles in short order, so we tie the shoots to wires. This keeps them neat and easy to crop as well as enabling us selectively to prune the plant to

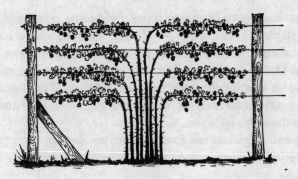

Fig. 70. Blackberry.

maximize production. It also ensures airflow around the fruit, helping to prevent mould growth.

Before we plant we'll construct the frame on which they'll grow for many years to come, so it's well worth spending some effort now to avoid having to repeat the exercise in a few years' time.

This frame method is also used for raspberries. You will need two stout posts, one for either end, and possibly an intermediate post if you are stringing your wires over 8 feet (2.4 metres) in length. Eight feet (2.4 metre) fence posts are ideal. Soak the base in preservative and give the rest of the post three good coats with a brush. You'll also need two pieces of scrap wood about a foot (30cm) long and 3–6 inches (8–15cm) wide – old floorboard is ideal. Soak this and nail to make a cross on each face on the base, as in Fig. 71 overleaf. The idea is that the pressure of the soil will stop the strained wires from pulling the posts inward.

As with the fruit cage, some gravel in the base will stop standing water from rotting the post. Drill one post and fix wire straining bolts, easily available from DIY stores. The first one should be about 3 feet (90cm) above ground level and 1 foot (30cm) apart after that to the top of the post. The top of the post should be about 6 feet (1.8 metres) above ground level.

With the posts fixed straight and vertical, wrap your wire

around one post a couple of times, twist to fix with pliers and then staple the wire to the post firmly. Take the wire across to the straining bolt and tighten. If the wires are being run over 8 feet (2.4 metres), you may find another post in the middle useful for keeping the wires separate and level. It isn't actually taking any strain so 2" x 1" (5cm x 2.5cm) is fine; run the wires through vine eyes.

Instead of galvanized fencing wire, you can get some pretty strong nylon wires but do watch out with nylon wire – one careless snip!

The wild blackberry is a pretty vigorous plant, as any allotmenteer clearing a plot of brambles will attest, and it grows amazingly well even on poor soil. Your cultivated berry with prepared fertile soil will do even better. You will usually need a 12 foot (3.6 metre) run of wire and 15 feet (4.5 metres) is advised for some of the most vigorous varieties. However, you can try Loch Ness, a compact variety only requiring a 6 foot (180cm) run or Oregon Thornless requiring 8 foot (2.4 metres) and avoiding those thorns.

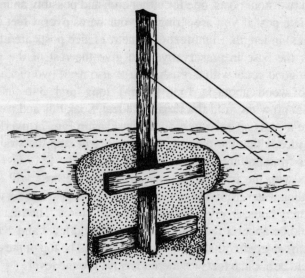

Fig. 71. Post and wire fruit support.

Cultivated blackberries are often larger than their wild cousins and crop more. Ken Muir recounts an allotment holder getting 163 lb of fruit from one blackberry Fantasia, which is noted for its large fruits about the size of a 50p coin. I presume the gentleman is opening a jam factory!

You can buy bare rooted plants which are best planted in November or December. You can plant all through the winter to March but in a cold winter the plants may not establish or even die. Having prepared the soil as above, plant shallowly, spreading the roots carefully. It can help to soak the roots in a bucket of water for a few hours before planting as well.

Alternatively, you can obtain container grown plants and these can be planted at any time of year. After planting, shorten the canes to about 9 inches (22cm). The fruit develops on one-year-old canes and the easiest method is to allow these to grow to one side. The next year's growth is trained up the other side and, after fruiting, the first side is cut off at ground level. Next year the new canes grow up that side so the fruiting side alternates year on year.

There are various other methods of training the canes but they are harder to keep up with and my experience is that you can end up with tangled masses far too easily so the above method is the one I stick with.

Hybrid Berries

There are quite a number of blackberry like fruits you can grow, although many of them offer little advantage over our blackberries. The four below are the ones I would consider.

Tayberries

The tayberry is a cross between a blackberry and a raspberry, developed by the Scottish Crop Research Institute. It is a good cropper and has large red berries that could be mistaken for a large raspberry but a different, sweeter taste. The only drawback with tayberries is that they are not as hardy as blackberries and the further north you live, the risk of losing them in a harsh winter increases.

Loganberries

Loganberries are similar to raspberries in looks and size but more acid in flavour. Not a berry I find palatable raw but it works well in a jam, its tartness counter-acting the sugar in the jam.

Boysenberries

Looking like a large raspberry-shaped blackberry, these are noted for a similar flavour to the wild blackberry.

Japanese Wineberries

These are a lovely flavoured but small berry, looking like red brambles. Not actually a hybrid, they are a true separate species.

Raspberries

Fig. 72. Raspberries.

Although we still use the training wires, raspberries are cultivated a little differently from the blackberries. To start with, raspberries are not very tolerant of waterlogged heavy soils. They love a sandy soil as long as it has plenty of humus. If you have a heavy clay soil, it's well worth digging a trench where you are intending to plant and adding grit and sand to improve drainage. Alternatively, a narrow raised bed, around 2 feet (60cm) wide, will keep their feet out of the water.

Although they don't like being waterlogged, they do need quite a lot of water in the summer when growing and producing fruit.

You can buy bare rooted canes for winter planting of blackberries or container grown plants for summer planting. Container grown tend to be easier to get going than bare rooted but if ordering by mail order, delivery costs are increased. Either way, don't plant too deeply. You should aim to plant the same depth as they were originally grown, which you will see on the stem.

With bare rooted, soak the roots in a bucket of water for a couple of hours before planting and spread the roots carefully before gently firming the soil around them.

They will benefit from a couple of ounces (60g) of general purpose fertilizer per plant mixed into the soil at planting time. Once planted, cut back the cane if necessary to just above a bud, about 1 foot (30cm) high.

They always look a bit lonely when planted but resist the urge to plant much closer than 16 inches (40cm) apart. If you are planting two rows, you want 6 feet (1.8 metres) between them, or between them and a row of blackberries. It always seems too far apart until you are harvesting in the summer when you'll see why the space is required.

Cultivation is easy enough. Keep the weeds down but do be careful not to damage the roots as raspberries are shallow rooting plants. In March give them a couple of ounces (60g) of general fertilizer per plant scattered down the row and mulch with about an inch (2.5cm) of compost or some cut and chopped comfrey leaves mixed with lawn mowings. This helps suppress weeds and provides some welcome potash. Ensure they have enough water in summer and that's about it, apart from pruning.

If you notice any suckers developing, individual canes

growing a little distance from the mother plant, cut these out with secateurs just below ground level. If your stock is good and healthy, get as much root with them as you can and you have a new plant for free.

Raspberries are pretty trouble free but they can get viral infections, which are spread by aphids. If you burn prunings, assuming you're allowed to have a fire on your plot, then it will help keep them disease free. Scatter the ashes back along the rows.

Grown from good, clean stock, you can expect about 10 years' productive life but once viral disease takes hold, as it always seems to do in the end, grub up the row and burn them. Replant new stock in a different position where raspberries have not grown before.

Raspberries come in a range of colours from yellow through pink to dark red, and your choice will depend on what flavour you like. Personally, I do not find the yellow varieties as flavoursome as the red ones, but tastes differ.

Just to confuse you, raspberries also split into summer fruiting and late autumn fruiting varieties. The autumn varieties bear fruit on this year's canes but summer fruits develop on last year's canes. Summer varieties produce more fruit from the run, a 6 foot (1.8 metre) run will produce around 8 lb (3.5kg) but you'd probably only get 3 lb (1.3kg) from the same run with autumn varieties.

My favourite summer varieties of raspberry are Malling Jewel and Malling Admiral but I've heard very good reports about a new variety called Tulameen which is supposed to have large tasty berries produced over a long period for raspberries.

For autumn varieties I would suggest Autumn Bliss. As always, check what's on the market before buying because new varieties are always being developed.

Autumn varieties are really simple to prune. In February cut the lot down to ground level and then just tie the new canes in as they grow, allowing 3 or 4 inches (8–10cm) apart between the canes. You can't go wrong.

Summer varieties are a little more work, but you get a lot

more out of them. After you've finished picking, cut the fruited canes down to ground level. The new canes need to be tied in now to produce next year's crop. Do not leave it too long or you will be wondering which is which! In the spring, tip prune your growing canes back to a healthy bud about 6 inches (15cm) above the top supporting wire.

Blackcurrants

Fig. 73. Blackcurrants.

I doubt that there is anyone in Britain who does not know that blackcurrants are full of vitamin C thanks to Ribena adverts, but just in case I'll say it again. They contain about six times more than limes that our sailors used to take to sea to ward off the vitamin C deficiency disease of scurvy and about 30 times more than apples.

Unfortunately, cooking tends to reduce the amount of vitamin C so cooked blackcurrants may only contain four times the vitamin C of the raw lime but they're not a very palatable raw berry. I must admit to some bias here. I'm sticking with my story that blackcurrant jam is a health food.

Ben Sarek is an excellent variety but does suffer from the problem that it crops so heavily, the weight of the currants can break the branches and so you need to prop them in good years. New varieties Ben Connan and Ben Hope are being well spoken of. The more northerly you are, the more important to go for a frost resistant variety to ensure consistent cropping.

Blackcurrants are really greedy feeders so prepare the ground well with a good amount of well rotted manure if available. Under the planting hole, mix a couple of pounds of hoof and horn meal or, if you can't get that, bonemeal into the soil to release slowly and help the bushes establish.

Make your hole large enough to spread the roots comfortably and plant at the same depth as the nursery did. With bare rooted stock, planting should be in winter when the plant is dormant but container grown stock can go in at any time. Allow at least 4 feet (1.2 metres) between plants, a little more with some varieties. Your nurseryman should be able to advise.

After planting, prune hard to just a few inches (6cm) above the soil. After a couple of years you will need to prune each winter. Take out any weak or damaged branches and crossovers so you have an open bush. Shoots older than four years can be cut out to make room for the younger, more productive shoots.

In the spring, give each bush about 4 oz (100g) of general fertilizer and a good mulch of compost or rotted manure. In June and July when the fruits are forming and swelling, a mulch with comfrey or liquid feeding with tomato feed will help the crop no end.

There are pests and problems that can affect blackcurrants but usually they're trouble free until they start to reach the end of their life after about ten years.

Jostaberries

Jostaberries are a blackcurrant/gooseberry cross, resulting in what looks like an exceptionally large blackcurrant but with a different flavour from either of its parents. Cultivation is just as for the blackcurrant.

Red and White Currants

White currants are just a colour variant on the red, so cultivation is exactly the same. Perhaps the most popular variety of redcurrant is Jonkheer Van Tets which crops early but I would grow Rovada. It's a later cropper, which makes it less vulnerable to bad weather in the early spring, exceptionally well flavoured and a heavy cropper. Five pounds (2.2kg) is quite usual from an established bush of Rovada.

Prepare the ground, cultivate and space in the same way as for blackcurrants but the pruning method is different. You can grow these in a cordon, attached to wires, either with a single or double main stem or as an espalier. Usually they're just grown as bushes though.

In the first winter after planting you cut the main stems back to about half their length just above an outward facing bud. If you've any shoots below about 4 inches (10cm) high on the main stem, cut these off flush to the stem.

The fruit arrives on spurs off the main stems, so from the second year on pruning is rather like that of an apple tree, admittedly a very small apple tree. Shorten main branches by about a third, cutting just above an outward facing bud. Then cut back to the first bud any side shoots growing in towards the centre or downwards or crossing over other branches. We're trying to get an open centred bush which will be easy to strip come harvest time and allow plenty of sunshine in. Side shoots left can then be shortened by half, once again cutting just above a bud pointing outwards.

Harvesting is easy; just remove the berries in clusters when ripe.

Gooseberries

There was a time when the gooseberry was the most widely grown and popular fruit for the home grower. The French even referred to it as 'The English Fruit' and back in the nineteenth century there were 170 gooseberry clubs where the members competed to grow the heaviest and most perfect fruits. The Egton Bridge Old Gooseberry Show in North Yorkshire continues to this day after more than 200 years.

Nowadays they are not so popular, perhaps because to describe the taste as 'tart' is an understatement. Yet if you add cream and sugar, the taste is superb. For the jam maker,

Fig. 74. Half standard gooseberry.

they also have the benefit of a really high pectin content – no setting problems.

The other drawback to growing gooseberries is the wicked thorns. Even wearing thick gloves, they'll often get you. So the pruning, which is carried out just as for the redcurrants, tends to get 'forgotten' and after a couple of years a tangled mass results through which the weeds happily grow.

There is an answer: the half standard bush. Here the main plant is grown on a stem, raising the body a couple of feet above the ground. This makes the weeding easy and safe, as well as enabling you to grow an under crop of strawberries if you wish. Pruning is easier and so less likely to be left for another day.

At one time there were dozens of varieties available but as the popularity has dwindled so has the number available. Invicta is a good standard, offering a green berry that's a good all-rounder. Whinham's Industry is the one to consider for a red variety.

Blueberries and Bilberries

Fig. 75. Blueberries.

Blueberry muffins, bilberry pie with ice cream – how can you
not grow them?

Most fruits like a soil that is slightly acid to neutral 6–7 pH.
These moorland plants, however, like an ericaceous (acid) soil
with a pH more towards 5. It can be quite difficult to manage
a separate area of soil. Lime, which makes the soil less acid,
tends to creep from one area to another.

You can grow these in large pots but then you have the
problem of frequent watering and the more vigorous varieties
will be held back by pot growing. You could construct a small
raised bed or, if you have some of those cheap blue barrels
that seem to find there way onto allotment sites, cut one into
three bottomless sections and use them as raised beds.

The easiest route is to invest in some commercial ericaceous
compost to fill them. Thereafter feed with an ericaceous
fertilizer each spring or make your own up by mixing 1 part
sulphate of ammonia, 1 part sulphate of potash with 3 parts by
weight bonemeal and apply at 5 oz per square yard. Don't water
with mains water; use rainwater which does not contain lime.
Otherwise treat very much like your blackcurrants.

Many varieties of blueberries do not crop well on their own,
requiring another plant of another variety to do well but you
can get self-fertile varieties like Sunshine Blue and Top Hat.

Cropping is slow to get going with blueberries but after five years you can expect 5 lb (2.2kg) of fruit per bush.

Strawberries

Fig. 76. Strawberries.

Although we still need to defend against birds, the strawberry is not usually grown in the fruit cage because it moves around the plot. The strawberry is a short lived plant, after the third year of fruiting you need to replace the plants and preferably grow in a different position to avoid building up problems in the soil.

To keep the birds off when the strawberries are fruiting, you will need to net them and to keep your net raised enough so the birds don't just stand on it to eat. One easy way is to use short bamboo canes with old milk containers over them and drape the net over quite tightly.

There are two main types of strawberries: the normal that crop over a short period, usually around three weeks; and the perpetual that produce flushes of fruit over the whole season.

Some varieties will crop early and others late, some are ideal for eating fresh and some for jam, so having a number of varieties is required to cover all your needs. However, it can get very confusing growing a number of varieties as all the plants look much the same.

You can start from seed but it's far easier and faster to fruit from plants. Your local DIY store is unlikely to sell anything apart from the commercial variety Elsanta. They're not a bad strawberry but if you go to a specialist nursery you could try Pegasus instead, which are just as productive but easier for organic growers as they're resistant to botrytis. For a perpetual try Flamenco and for jam making try Tenira.

They like their soil slightly acid and are not a very hungry crop although they will benefit from 1 lb per square yard of bonemeal prior to planting to give them a slowly released source of nitrogen.

They are usually started from plants rather than seed, planting out in March or April. Normally planted with 8 inches to a foot (20cm–30cm) between plants, you need to be careful how you plant. They need to have the growing point just above the surface and the roots shallowly spread just under the soil. Make a shallow wide hole, then mound up the soil into an inverted 'V' mound in the centre just below soil level. Place the plant on the mound and spread the roots down the sides.

Strawberries propagate naturally from runners. These are shoots that form small plants along their length. In the first year after planting, remove all runners as soon as you notice them. From your second and third year plants, you can allow the odd runner to develop. Use a piece of wire (coat hanger wire is ideal), bent into a 'V' to clip the plantlet on the runner down into a small pot of compost. Cut the runner before the next plantlet. Luckily, strawberries are really easy to propagate so each year you can replace your oldest stock without the expense of buying new plants or seeds.

The biggest problems with strawberries are mould, rot and slugs. To stop mould and rot, keep the fruits off the ground by mulching under with straw or planting through weed suppressant fabric.

At the end of the season, the plants die back and this is time to clean them up. A trim, just above ground level, with shears will remove foliage, and any pests hiding within will be moved or exposed to the birds. Often gardeners in the old days would set fire to the straw, burning off the dead foliage and pests in one operation.

Strawberry plants are hardy, but their fruits are not. The season can be extended at both ends by using cloches. Commercially, strawberries are grown in polytunnels in the UK to provide the longest growing season.

Rhubarb

Fig. 77. Rhubarb, with forcing pot.

Believe it or not, I've actually seen grown men becoming irate with each other discussing the subject of whether rhubarb is a fruit or a vegetable. I believe it's technically a fruit, if only on the basis that this is how it is used, but whatever it may be in theory, it's in the fruit section in this book.

Despite what you may have heard, the leaves are perfectly safe to compost although they shouldn't be eaten as they contain oxalic acid. The leaves can be shredded and boiled in water for half an hour (1 lb to 2 pints/500g to a litre of water) to make an insecticidal spray for aphids and spider mites but, unfortunately, it is not true that dropping a piece of rhubarb into the planting hole will prevent club-root from affecting brassicas.

Most allotments will have a rhubarb patch, often sadly neglected at the furthest end of the plot and well past its best but don't be too quick to discard it. As winter begins, the leaves will die away and now is your chance. Dig the old roots up and split them vertically with a spade into sections about 8 inches (20cm) across. Leave them on the surface somewhere and ignore them until late February or early March.

In the meantime prepare your new rhubarb bed. They're going to be there for a long time, possibly ten years, so it's worth the effort. You want a good depth, at least 2 feet (60cm), of good topsoil with plenty of organic matter. It needs plenty of nitrogen to fuel the leaf growth so adding rotted manure will be helpful.

If you haven't any rhubarb on the plot, you can start rhubarb from seed but it takes longer to produce fruit and often doesn't result in plants true to type so it is better to start from plants, which are known as 'crowns'. If you are buying new stock, Timperly Early is an excellent old variety and Champagne is well thought of. Both are suitable for forcing as well.

You plant the crowns just an inch (2.5cm) under the surface about 3 feet (90cm) apart each way in March. They don't need much care after that, apart from weeding and feeding. In late autumn, when the leaves die down, mulch them with compost or preferably rotted manure. Then in February, just as they start growing again, give a handful of general purpose fertilizer like fish, blood and bone per plant.

Do not harvest any sticks in the first year after planting. Instead allow the plants to establish well. In the second year only take a few sticks per plant, but each year after that you can remove all but a few sticks.

Forcing rhubarb produces the sweetest crop and one so tender that it doesn't need peeling before cooking. Simply place a large container (like a black plastic dustbin) over a plant as soon as it starts growing. The extra warmth promotes growth which means that, after about four weeks in the dark, a crop of pale sweet sticks can be taken.

Don't crop again for at least a year, or preferably two years. You will exhaust and kill the plant if you keep forcing it year after year.

Different varieties of rhubarb will crop best at different times so if you plant a range of varieties you'll have a crop right from April through to August.

You can get crown rot and honey fungus in rhubarb, although generally it's a trouble-free crop. However, both these diseases are incurable, so you will need to dig up and burn any plants so afflicted and then plant new stock as far away from them on the plot as possible.

Kiwi Fruit (Chinese Gooseberries)

Fig. 78. Kiwi fruit.

The ideal place to grow Kiwi fruit is in a sheltered walled garden in the south of England. They don't like frost in spring and they don't like a cold wind either, so if you don't have a sunny, sheltered plot then my advice is not to bother.

However, if you do want to give them a try, you'll need a tall trellis or wire fence about 15 feet (4.5 metres) long to grow them on. To describe them as rampant is an understatement. Plenty of manure or compost is needed to fuel the growth, of course.

The best bet is to grow Hayward but this is not self-fertile so you will need to grow a male plant, Tomouri, along with it to get the fruit to set. Pollination is usually carried out by hand in the UK, yet another task for the busy allotmenteer. Remove a flower from the male plant and mate it to the female by rubbing the centres together. After about six females are fertilized, a new male flower will be needed.

Grapes

Not so long ago grapes were exclusively a greenhouse crop in the UK but now with warmer years there are commercial vineyards as far north as Leeds, and Champagne producers looking at buying up land in Kent.

They're still not a reliable crop for the amateur. If you're looking at making your own wine from your own grapes, then be prepared for some sober years.

There's a huge range of varieties available and picking varieties for different types of wine is well beyond the scope of this book. However, Dornfelder has a good reputation both as a wine making grape and as a dessert grape.

It's best to consult a reputable nurseryman when purchasing who can suggest varieties fit for your purpose, area and method of growing.

The easiest way to start is with a pot-grown plant, which you plant out in late February or early March in well cultivated and rich soil but vines really don't like water-logging so a well drained soil is required. Having said that, I have seen grapes growing on heavy clay albeit not too productively.

If you have a greenhouse you'll increase the range of varieties you can grow and have more chance of a decent crop. Because the grape enjoys a cold break in the winter and needs a good root run, plant outside the house and train the stem to the inside via a small hole. Provide plenty of ventilation when greenhouse growing or you will have a problem with mildew, especially as the fruits develop and ripen.

Most hobby allotment growers will be growing one vine, whether in a greenhouse tied to wire or up a framework or pergola. Yes, pergolas on allotments! Basically just prune the side shoots back to about five leaves in the summer and keep the bunches down to about one every foot (30cm) of the main vine. Grapevines can get out of control very easily, so keep an eye on them or they'll take over a greenhouse in short order.

In the winter, cut the leader back to about half its length and in the spring give it a good couple of handfuls of general fertilizer around the roots.

Apples and Pears

Fig. 79. Espaliers.

As I said elsewhere, many allotments do not allow fruit trees as such but some will allow them if they are grown on dwarfing rootstocks. Fruit trees are usually grown by grafting the fruiting stock onto a rootstock that controls how vigorous the whole tree will be.

There are all sorts of training methods: cordons where the tree is kept pruned to a single stem tied to wire; espaliers where the tree is developed with the side shoots tied to wires; stepovers where the tree is allowed to grow up about a foot high and then developed sideways – hence the name. Dwarf pyramids and bush, the list goes on.

As well as all those training methods, some require a tree of another variety to pollinate and set fruit, some actually require three varieties to fruit successfully.

Once again, different varieties will be more suitable for different conditions and locations. Obviously we have cookers and eaters, but some will store better than others and different types are ready at different times.

There really is too much to cover in detail in this book but, once again, a knowledgeable nurseryman should be able to give you advice and provide the correct trees for your growing system.

16

SOWING AND HARVESTING CHART

This chart applies to the UK but there can be large variations between areas. Generally the south is earlier than the north. Each year is different as well. The art is to judge when the time is right for your area and the weather. Not easy!!

Vegetable Sowing and Harvesting Chart

	Jan	Feb	Mar	Apr	May	Jun	Jul	Aug	Sep	Oct	Nov	Dec
Aubergine[1]	I	I						H	H	H		
Bean, Broad[2]		O	O			H	H	H	H	O	O	
Bean, French Climbing				IO	O	SH	SH	H	H	H		
Bean, Dwarf French				I	O	O	SH	H	H	H		
Bean, Runner				I	IO	O	SH	H	H	H		
Beetroot			O	O	O	SH	SH	H	H	H		
Beet Leaf Spinach[3]				O	O	O	SH	SH	SH	SH		
Broccoli, Autumn		I	O	O			H	H	H			
Broccoli, Spring[4]			SH	SH						H	H	H
Brussels Sprouts			O	O	O			H	H	SH	H	H
Cabbage, Chinese						O	O	SH	SH	H	H	H
Cabbage, Summer			I	I	I		H	H	H	H		
Cabbage, Winter				O	O	O	H	O		H	H	H
Cabbage, Spring[4]				H	H		O	O	O			
Calabrese			O	O	O	O	O	H	H	H		
Carrot		O	O	O	SH	SH	SH	H	H	H		
Cauliflower, Summer			O	O	O	O		H	H	H		
Cauliflower, Winter					O	O		O	H	H	H	H
Cauliflower, Spring[4]					H	H	O	O	O			
Capsicum (Pepper)			I	I	I		H	H	H	H		
Courgette			I	I	I		H	H	H			
Cucumber, Indoor		I	I	I	I		H	H	H			
Cucumber, Outdoor				I	I	H	H	H	H			
Leek	H	H	O	O					H	H	H	H
Lettuce		I	I	SH	SH	SH	H	H	H	H	H	H
Marrow			I	I	O	O	H	H	H	H		

Vegetable Sowing and Harvesting Chart (contd.)

	Jan	Feb	Mar	Apr	May	Jun	Jul	Aug	Sep	Oct	Nov	Dec
Onion, Spring			O	O	SH	SH	SH	SH	SH	H	H	
Onion (Seed)	I	I					H	H	H			
Onion (Set) and Shallot	I	I	O				H	H	H	O		
Onion (Japanese Sets)[2,4]							H		O	O		
Parsnip	H	SH	O	O		H			H	H	H	H
Peas			O	O	SH	SH	H	H	H			
Pepper			I	I	I		H	H	H	H		
Pumpkin			I	I					H	H	H	
Radish			O	O	SH	SH	SH	SH	SH	H		
Rocket			O	O	SH	SH	SH	SH	H	H		
Spinach			O	O	SH	SH	H	H	H	H		
Squash			I	I	I			H	H	H		
Swede	H	H			O	O	O		H		H	H
Sweetcorn				I	I			H	H			
Tomato[1]	I	I	I	I			H	H	H	H		
Turnip			O	O	SH	SH	SH	H	H			

Key to Chart

I Sow indoors or under cover such as a cloche   **O** Sow outdoors   **IO** Sow indoors/outdoors

SH Sow outdoors/harvest   **H** Harvest

1. I never have much joy with starting aubergines and tomatoes too early – the seedlings tend to get very leggy due to low light levels.

2. You can sow some varieties (like Aquadulce) in October and November to get an early start. My own experience is that there is little gain in time but a high risk of loss due to weather.

3. Also known as perpetual spinach.   4. Crops the following year.

17

SAVING YOUR OWN SEED

Allotmenteers are a thrifty bunch: we reuse and recycle wherever we can. When it comes to our seeds, why buy what nature will provide for free? In theory, anything we grow can be propagated by ourselves; after all, the seed merchants get their stock from somewhere.

In practice it isn't quite that simple, unfortunately. When you buy your seeds, you will notice many of them are described as F1 or F1 hybrid. Years back, the plant breeders noticed that if you crossed two strains of a plant sometimes the offspring would have the best of both and be more vigorous than the parents. This phenomenon of the child being more vigorous is actually referred to as 'hybrid vigour'. F1 stands for Filial 1 by the way; the first crossing of two strains.

The downside of F1 hybrids is that the new strain does not breed true. If you try to save seeds for the next year from an F1 it may, if not sterile, be like one of its parents or neither. However it develops, it will not be as good as its F1 parent.

Because these hybrids have to be grown fresh each year and can often involve hand-pollination, they are more expensive than ordinary or open pollinated seed. You pay for the quality and you can't breed your own on an allotment.

Even the open pollinated seeds are not always that easy. Many brassicas will easily cross with each other; cabbages with cauliflowers or sprouts with kale, for example. It just goes to show how close they are to each other. To stop this, you would need either to grow the plants far from other members of the same family (which is well nigh impossible on an allotment) or isolate them from any pollinating insects. The seeds are cheap anyway, amazingly so when you think of this isolation problem, so not really worth the effort that would be involved for the plotholder.

Carrots are another crop that suffer the same problem as are parsnips, but there are some plants where it is possible to save seed and not just save some money but you can develop your own strain.

If you've ever gone to a vegetable show and seen the fantastic giant onions and leeks, etc, you will realize that the growers really know what they're doing. What you might not have realized is that they develop their own seed strains. It's quite a simple theory: if you grow from your best specimen, then the offspring will be good. Then from those offspring, select the best again and repeat for a number of generations. That's why you will see that specialist seed merchants who supply showmen advertise 'selected seed'.

The variety will be a known type but selected seed is quite different. At one time the seed merchants would all select for various characteristics but they would re-name the variety. This resulted in a bewildering number of types, many of which were quite similar, and so the EU kindly decided that these different but similar types were confusing the consumer and that legislation was required.

To sell seeds, the variety must be included on a National List or the EU Common Catalogue and to get on the list they must be distinct (ruling out selected strains as separate varieties) and meet laid down quality standards as to viability, etc.

All this costs an awful lot of money so the effect was that many varieties didn't make it onto the list and were lost. The HDRA (now Garden Organic) formed a Heritage Seed Library where some members, known as Seed Guardians, grow and save seeds that are made available to other members as well as being saved for posterity (see Further Information and Contacts).

Reducing the number of varieties generally available also increases the risk of crops being wiped out by disease. The Irish potato famine that was caused by blight wiping out the crop could possibly have been lessened if not averted if only they had been growing a number of varieties where some would have been at least partially blight resistant. Nobody can predict what diseases are going to hit in the future, but the wider the range, the greater the chance of a resistant gene being in one plant.

You don't need to be a show grower to want to develop your own seed strain. You will notice that one plant in a row does particularly well, despite them all being from the same packet of seeds. Perhaps that one does well on your soil or in the micro-climate of your site. Whatever the reason, that is the plant to save seeds from. The rule is: only save seeds from the best.

Beans and Peas

These are probably the easiest crop for seed saving. They're generally self-pollinating and so will come true, i.e. the offspring will be like the parent. Try to avoid growing two varieties next to each other though; a spacing of around 6 feet (1.8 metres) should be sufficient.

This applies to runner beans, French beans and all types of peas.

As you harvest, keep an eye for the best plant. Perhaps this is the one with the most beans or the straightest runners, or whatever you want to select for. Don't harvest from this plant, just leave it for as long as possible until the pods are bone dry and paper thin. The beans should rattle in the pod.

If it's a damp year, uproot the plant and hang it upside down in a cool, dark place with plenty of airflow. For runner beans, strip the oldest and store them on slatted shelves.

Once thoroughly dry, pod the beans keeping a close eye for insect damage. Spread them on a table and discard any that look abnormal. Watch out for tiny holes; if there is a bug in there, it may crawl out and attack the rest of the crop in storage.

Put the beans or peas into a paper envelope marked with the variety and date. Don't store in plastic bags as they encourage condensation which encourages mould. Keep in a cool, dark place and they should remain viable for three years.

Lettuce

Lettuce, being self-pollinating, will come true even if growing different varieties near to each other. Normally we complain about lettuce bolting but that is the plant going to seed, so if you have a bolted plant you can make use of it.

A single lettuce can produce many thousands of seeds; one plant will be more than enough for you. The seeds do not all ripen at once, typically they change to a darker colour when ripe. Just collect them by shaking the seed head over a paper bag each week until you have enough.

Dry them on a sheet of paper for a week before storing in an envelope. If the germination rate seems poor, try putting the seed into a refrigerator for a couple of days to fool them they've been through winter.

Cucumber

Cucumbers are insect-pollinated and will cross with other varieties so your own crop may well not come true – perhaps you'll develop a new variety! It's safest to work with one variety in a greenhouse.

Allow one or two fruits to remain on the plant and fatten as well as turn yellow, which should be for about six weeks after you would normally harvest. Cut the cucumber lengthways and scoop out the seeds and pulp into a jar of water. Stir two or three times a day for a few days and the viable seeds will sink to bottom.

Drain off the water, reserving the seeds. Rinse them until clean and allow to dry for a week or two on paper. Pack in envelopes and see what grows next year.

Tomatoes

Tomatoes, being self-pollinating, usually come true, although sometimes one will be insect-pollinated and surprise you. To be certain, you should avoid two varieties by each other. They are remarkably easy and were noted for growing by sewage works, having arrived with the effluent and survived being eaten.

Take a fully ripe tomato, scoop the seeds into a jar of water, and leave at room temperature for a few days, stirring a couple of times a day to stop mould growing. The viable seeds will sink to the bottom. Drain off the water, then wash the seeds and dry on a sheet of newspaper for a week or so. You will find that the seeds tend to stick to the paper so if you space them when you place them on there, you can then cut the paper into strips and just sow like a seed tape. Being a small seed, they are difficult to handle and this method makes life easy next season.

Peppers

Peppers are ridiculously easy. Just let one, either chilli or sweet, ripen fully. It may look a little tired and shrivelled for eating at this point. Cut open and scrape out the seeds. Allow to dry for two weeks and put into an envelope for next year. They are self-pollinating although, like the tomatoes, some could be insect-pollinated and you should just grow one variety in a greenhouse to be certain of them coming true.

Squash and Pumpkins

The only problem with saving squash and pumpkin seeds is cross-pollination if you're growing more than one variety. This can be very difficult to control on an allotment but doesn't seem to be a major problem.

Just wait until you are ready to eat the fruit, take out the seeds and wash the pulp off and dry them for a week or two. Job done!

Leeks

Fig. 80. Leek with umbrel.

Leeks are biennials, which means that they take two years to make seeds. They are insect-pollinated but cross-pollination is not a problem unless someone nearby is also growing for seeds and their leeks flower at the same time.

Being very hardy, just leave the best specimens in the ground over winter and harvest the rest. The next year the leek will throw up a central stalk and develop a seed head, called an umbel. Once this is mature, just cut it off and place in a paper bag to dry thoroughly. When properly dry, rub the head to get the seeds free, and next year's stock is in the bag.

The leek may well develop some bulblets around the base in the spring; these can be removed and planted on as well. The leek is popular amongst the showing fraternity but they tend to do it a bit differently. Remember they're often growing in polytunnels with protected conditions.

The leek is dug up at the end of winter and the outer leaves removed to clean interior ones. It's trimmed back to about 10 inches (25cm) high and then replanted in good compost and allowed to grow on, throwing up a seedhead. Next the seedhead is shaved, removing the seeds. After about three weeks, tiny leeks develop on the seedhead. These are called grasses and are planted on and grown as for seed sown leeks. Because this is vegetative propagation, each leek grass is a clone of the parent plant and cross-pollination is not an issue.

Onions

Onions are another favourite of the show growers and again are biennials. Unless you are growing under cover, cross-pollination is likely to be a problem. Harvest your seed onions carefully so as not to damage the roots in the autumn and store in a cool place.

Replant in the spring and the onion will throw up a seedhead which you treat just like a leek except you cannot use the vegetative method.

Onion sets are small, immature bulbs. Unless they are especially heat treated they tend to bolt, throwing up a seed head. Larger sets are more likely to do this, which should make sense now you know how they are propagated.

Buying Seeds

One of the joys of gardening is settling down on a dark December night with the seed catalogues and deciding what varieties to grow next year. Usually you end up with a list of seeds long enough to fill the entire allotment site! Then the hard part is deciding which of the seven varieties of cucumber you actually want to grow most.

Before you place your order, do check what you have in stock. The seed merchants tend to pack far more than you will use in a year. I'm looking at a packet of 900 lettuce seeds as I write. Even if only half of them germinate, that's enough to keep us going for a few years.

Most seeds will store for a number of years as long as you keep them properly. The three main points are to keep the seeds cool, but not frozen, dark and to exclude air. Reseal the little silver foil packets by folding over and then place the seeds in an airtight tin or plastic storage box. Ideally you would keep them in the fridge but anywhere cool will have to suffice in most households.

The chart opposite will give you some guidance on lifespan but seeds can really surprise you by being viable well beyond what is expected. You will see there is usually a 'sow by' date on the packet. Just like food manufacturers with their 'use by' dates, seed merchants are cautious.

Even when past their best, you'll find that some of the seeds will germinate, although the percentage falls year on year. You can test the viability of stored seeds by chitting. To chit, your seeds need to think they've been sown, so take a piece of kitchen roll and dampen it. Onto the damp kitchen roll put a number of seeds (20 is good if you have a lot), and place into a plastic bag or Tupperware type container. Put into somewhere dark and warm, such as an airing cupboard or a closed cupboard in an occupied room.

Check the seeds to see which have sprouted – if they fail, you haven't wasted time and effort planting them. The table opposite gives the average germination time for each seed, so you know how long to wait before declaring a failure. Often they germinate well before the average time, so check frequently.

Seed Life Chart		
Seed	**Expected Life (Years)**	**Avg Days to Germination**
Beans, Broad	2	21
Beans, French	2	14
Beans, Runner	2	14
Beetroot	5	13
Spinach Beet, Chards	5	13
Broccoli	5	8
Cabbage	5	8
Carrot	3	16
Cauliflower	5	8
Cucumber	7	9
Kale	4	8
Kohlrabi	4	7
Leek	3	14
Lettuce	4	7
Marrow & Courgettes	6	7
Onion	4	14
Parsley	2	10
Parsnip	1	17
Peas	2	10
Radish	4	6
Salsify	2	12
Spinach	2	11
Swede	2	8
Sweetcorn	3	9
Tomato	3	7
Turnip	2	8

GLOSSARY

Some of the more common gardening terms you might come across.

Allium   The Latin name of the onion family which includes onion, shallot, garlic, chives and leek.

Blanch   To deprive a plant of light to produce a tender growth as with chicory, celery and leeks.

Blight   A fungal disease, usually of potatoes and tomatoes.

Bolt   When a plant prematurely produces flowers or seeds at the expense of the edible crop. Most often affects onions and lettuce.

Bordeaux Mixture   A mixture of copper sulphate and slaked lime used to control blight in potatoes and tomatoes.

Brassica   General term for members of the cabbage family from the Latin *Brassicaceae*.

**Chitting
(of potatoes)**

Allowing the seed potatoes to form shoots prior to planting – see Potatoes, page 166.

**Chitting
(of seeds)**

Germinating seeds before sowing – see Sweetcorn, page 188. Also useful for establishing viability and germination rate of seeds.

Cloche

Any kind of (transparent) low-lying temporary shelter for use on open ground.

Club-root

Serious soil-borne fungal disease affecting all brassicas – see Club-root, page 107.

Coldframe

A low, glass-covered structure to provide sheltered growing conditions – see Cold-frames, page 56.

Compost

Term used for a growing medium produced by the decomposition of organic matter. Also commercial composts which include other materials such as peat or fibre, minerals and fertilizers, etc.

**Crop
Rotation**

Moving crops around to avoid the build-up of pests and disease and to best utilize available nutrients – see Crop Rotation, page 46.

Cucurbit

The plant family that includes cucumbers, marrows, squashes, pumpkins and courgettes.

Cultivar

A variety or type of plant; for example, Sungold and Gardener's Delight are cultivars of tomatoes.

Damping Down   Raising the humidity in a greenhouse by watering the floors and/or staging. Tends to lower the temperature and reduce water loss from plants.

Damping Off Death of seedlings due to overly wet, crowded or poorly ventilated conditions.

Derris   An insecticide of plant origin and so technically organic. It is non-poisonous to warm-blooded animals but deadly to virtually all fish and insects (including beneficial ones) The licence for use expires in 2009 and will no longer be available after that.

Double Digging   A method of deeply digging over land, incorporating organic matter to increase the depth of topsoil, improve drainage and fertility – see Double Digging, page 86.

Earthing Up Process of drawing up loose earth around the stems or even over the foliage (especially potatoes) of plants to improve the crop and/or protect against frost.

Eelworm   Tiny transparent worm which adversely affects yields and/or quality of several plant varieties, notably potato and onion.

Flea Beetle Insect pest that mainly damages radish, swedes, turnip and Chinese cabbage.

Fleece   Horticultural fleece is a lightweight, translucent cloth that allows water to pass through and is used to provide shelter to plants and protection from pests.

Forcing Process of making a plant grow in the dark to produce a tender leaf or fruit as with rhubarb.

Germinate Not all seeds are viable, those that develop are said to germinate. Also the process of growing a seedling from a seed.

Germination Rate The number of viable seeds that develop against the total number of seeds.

Gone Over Term used when a crop has gone past its optimum harvest point.

Green Manure A crop grown to retain and provide nutrients and organic matter in the soil to improve fertility – see Green Manures, page 96.

Hardy A plant which is tolerant of frosts/winter conditions in the area in which it is being grown.

Haulm The stems and foliage of a plant, usually used in regard to potatoes.

Heel In Method of holding a plant in the soil for later use.

Heritage Variety Old variety of plant, usually harder to obtain than modern varieties but often with fine flavour.

Legume The bean family of plants noted for the ability to fix nitrogen from the air.

Module Section or cell of an insert put into a seed tray to divide it up into separate pots.

Mulch   To place a layer of material on the surface of the soil. Usually to provide nutrients or prevent water loss or inhibit weed growth.

Offset   A short lateral shoot by which certain plants are propagated – see Globe Artichokes, page 179.

Pinch Out   The action of removing the growing tip of a shoot, to produce a more bushy plant, also known as **stopping**. Also the removal of small side shoots by using the end of the finger and thumb to pinch the stem until it is separated from the main stem.

Pole   Ancient British measurement of distance or area equivalent to a perch or **rod**, often still used in referring to allotments.

Pot On, Pot Along   The action of placing a seedling into a pot and of moving a plant from one pot to a larger pot as it grows.

Riddle   Basically a coarse sieve made of plastic or metal to sift compost and soil.

Rod   Sometimes called Square Rod, ancient British measurement of land area equivalent to 30.25 square yards or 25.29 square metres. A rod is equivalent to a pole.

Rust   Describes different fungal diseases by the appearance of orange patches that look like rust. Often affects alliums, especially leeks and comfrey.

Seed Potato Small potato used to start the new crop – see Potatoes, page 165.

Set Usually as in 'onion set', a small immature bulb which has been raised from seed before having development stopped by the grower. The resulting bulb is then *set* the following spring so as to complete its growth in one season.

Spacing The distance required between plants to maximize the crop and efficiently use the space.

Station Sowing Sowing of seeds in their final position. Usually two or more seeds are sown and then only the strongest seedling is allowed to grow on.

Stop or Stopping See Pinch Out.

Successional Sowing Method of sowing crops at intervals, usually every fortnight or three weeks, to provide crops ready to harvest over a period rather than in one go.

Tender Describes a plant which is not tolerant of frosts or even cold weather in the area in which it is being grown. Typically requiring a greenhouse or coldframe.

Thinning, Thin Out Removal of seedlings or small plants to permit others space to develop to their full potential. Because seeds may not all germinate, we sow more than required then thin out to the required spacing.

Transplant   To re-plant, usually, into final cropping position.

Truss   Used mostly with tomatoes to refer to the cluster of fruits on a stem. Vine tomatoes in a shop are more properly called a truss of tomatoes.

Tuber   The thickened portion of a root such as the actual potato in a potato plant.

Volunteer   A plant growing in the wrong place after self-seeding or re-growth of a missed tuber when lifting (main culprits are potatoes and Jerusalem artichokes).

White Rot   A serious disease of onion, shallot, leek, garlic and chives. It is soil-borne, very persistent, and can lie dormant for up to fifteen years.

Wireworm   Small worm pest mainly of potatoes, particularly troublesome when the ground is recently converted from grassland.

FURTHER INFORMATION AND CONTACTS

My Website

As well as growing and writing, I run the largest website on allotment growing. There's information on growing, of course, along with sections on keeping poultry, recipes, storing and preserving food and a large chat area where members (free to join) swap advice and chat about gardening. Do pop over and see us online: www.allotment.org.uk

You may also like my book *Vegetable Growing Month by Month*. Although I hope this book will stand alone, I do cover more general areas of vegetable growing in there.

Organizations

Garden Organic was formerly known as the Henry Doubleday Research Organisation and was founded by Lawrence D Hills in 1954. He named it after a nineteenth century Quaker smallholder who introduced Russian comfrey into Britain, and Lawrence Hills spent much of his life researching, breeding and popularizing comfrey. It is now the premier organic gardening charity in the UK with demonstration gardens, magazines and a range of research and advisory roles.

Garden Organic
Garden Organic Ryton
Coventry
Warwickshire
CV8 3LG
www.gardenorganic.org.uk

The National Vegetable Society was formed in 1960 with the aim of helping kitchen gardeners in the growing of their vegetables. The society trains and examines judges for vegetable shows, and provides lecturers and advice to members on vegetable growing. These are seriously knowledgeable people who welcome and help new growers.

The National Vegetable Society
c/o National Secretary
Mr D S Thornton FNVS
36 The Ridings
Ockbrook
Derby
DE72 3SF
www.nvsuk.org.uk

The National Society of Allotment and Leisure Gardeners Limited aims to protect, promote and preserve allotment gardening. They provide a discounted seed scheme, insurance, magazine and advice and guidance.

National Society of Allotment & Leisure Gardeners Ltd
O'Dell House
Hunters Road
Corby
Northamptonshire
NN17 5JE
www.nsalg.org.uk

I doubt there is anyone in Britain who has not heard of the RHS if only for the famous Chelsea Flower Show. Founded in 1804 it is the largest horticultural association in the UK with a Royal Charter, no less.

The Royal Horticultural Society
80 Vincent Square
London
SW1P 2PE
www.rhs.org.uk

The British Beekeepers' Association will be able to help and put you in touch with local beekeepers and associations.

British Beekeepers' Association
The National Beekeeping Centre
National Agricultural Centre
Stoneleigh Park
Warwickshire
CV8 2LG
www.britishbee.org.uk

Mail Order Garden Equipment Suppliers
Although the DIY shops and garden centres can supply most requirements, for more specialist equipment a mail order supplier with a wider range of products is invaluable.

Two Wests & Elliott Ltd
Unit 4, Carrwood Road
Sheepbridge Industrial Estate
Chesterfield
Derbyshire
S41 9RH
www.twowests.co.uk

Harrod Horticultural
Pinbush Road
Lowestoft
Suffolk
NR33 7NL
www.harrodhorticultural.com

MANTIS UK Limited (for the Mantis Tillers)
Orchard House
Hempshaw Lane
Stockport
Cheshire
SK1 4LH
www.mantis-uk.co.uk

Wolf Garden Division
E P Barrus Limited
Launton Road
Bicester
Oxfordshire
OX26 4UR
www.wolf-garten.co.uk

Some UK Seed Suppliers

There are a lot of reputable seed merchants in Britain and it would probably take a whole book to list them all, but these should get you started. They'll all send a catalogue on request.

Thompson & Morgan
Poplar Lane
Ipswich
Suffolk
IP8 3BU
www.thompson-morgan.com

Suttons Seeds
Woodview Road
Paignton
Devon
TQ4 7NG
www.suttons.co.uk

Dobies Seeds
Long Road
Paignton
Devon
TQ4 7SX
www.dobies.co.uk

Specialist Vegetable Seed Suppliers

These supply extremely high quality seed, often from selected strains, and are used by the show growers as well as ordinary kitchen gardeners.

Medwyns of Anglesey
Llanor
Ffordd Hen Ysgol
Llanfairpwllgwyngyll
Anglesey
LL61 5RZ
www.medwynsofanglesey.co.uk

Select Seeds
58 Bentinck Road
Shuttlewood
Chesterfield
S44 6RQ
www.selectseeds.co.uk

Specialist Fruit Nursery

I'm listing Ken Muir as they have been supplying certified stock since 1965, have won 12 RHS Chelsea Gold Medals and provide a free advisory service as well as a good catalogue.

Ken Muir Ltd
Rectory Road
Weeley Heath
Clacton-on-Sea
Essex
CO16 9BJ
www.kenmuir.co.uk

INDEX

The main entry for each fruit/vegetable is in **bold**.

253

Index

255

Also by John Harrison

VEGETABLE GROWING MONTH BY MONTH

John takes you through the vegetable year and shows you when you should sow your seeds, dig your plot and harvest your crops.

- Choose appropriate vegetables for your soil
- Select the right position so that they flourish
- Make your own compost and organic fertilizers
- Use the best methods for pest control
- Extend the season with cloches and cold frames

'Forget about any glossy pictures, what's in this book is solid words of advice, written in plain-to-understand English from a grower who's had frustrating years of experience behind him in trying to grow nutritious vegetables, whilst at the same time running a business and raising a family. Everyone will benefit from this book and I found the glossary at the back, which explains gardening terminology in a way that everyone will understand, to be extremely useful. It will certainly have a place on my extensive gardening bookshelf.'

Medwyn Williams, Chairman of the National Vegetable Society and member of the Fruit and Vegetable Committee of the Royal Horticultural Society

the Secrets of Love

Rosie Rushton

Piccadilly Press • London

For everyone who finds the true meaning of love
– and has the courage to live it.

First published in Great Britain in 2005
by Piccadilly Press Ltd,
5 Castle Road, London NW1 8PR
www.piccadillypress.co.uk

A catalogue record for this book is available from the British Library

ISBN: 978 1 85340 774 1 (paperback)

7 9 10 8

Printed in the UK by CPI Bookmarque, Croydon, CR0 4TD
Cover illustration by Susan Hellard.
Cover design by Fielding Design.
Text design by Textype Typesetters. Set in Goudy.

Alloy Entertainment
151 West 26th Street
New York, New York 10014

A tried and true secret of love:

If a woman doubts as to whether she should accept a man or not, she certainly ought to refuse him. If she can hesitate as to Yes, she ought to say No, directly.
– Jane Austen

PROLOGUE

*I*T WASN'T LONG AGO that photographs of the Dashwood sisters' ancestors – yellow with age, the occasional school picture of Ellie, Abby and Georgie tucked into the edge of the frame – hung along the long winding staircase at Holly House, the Dashwood family's home for generations. There were other photos, too – an aerial shot of the Holly House grounds, the girls' father at the ribbon-cutting of one of his many businesses, their mother in her wedding dress, a toothless Georgie on her first bike, Abby as Juliet at the local theatre, Ellie winning a spelling bee.

But that was then. *Before.* Before the divorce and the terrible day that changed everything for ever. And now, the pictures all lay packed away somewhere, too full of memories to find a place in the Dashwood girls' new home.

All, that is, except one: a portrait of their family – Dad, Mum, seventeen-year-old Ellie, sixteen-year-old Abby, and thirteen-year-old Georgie – painted long after the last time they'd all been together. The Dashwoods had never posed for the painting; they couldn't have even if they'd wanted to.

Now it hung in their new hallway – miles away from the old Holly House stairway – and the girls realised that this was the way they wanted to remember their family. After all, it had taken a year for the Dashwood sisters – Ellie, Abby, and Georgie – to discover the secret of love, and now that they'd found it, they weren't about to let it go.

❧ SECRET NUMBER 1 ❧

Sometimes a broken heart beats louder than all the whole hearts combined.

HI BABE! R U ON 4 2NITE? CROWD GOING 2 CLUB XS 8PM. B GR8 2 C U. XX {1}

Abby Dashwood let out a squeal of delight, dropping her mobile phone on her bed and dancing around in her bare feet.

'This is it,' she announced to Manderley, her somewhat overweight ginger cat, who was eyeing her critically from the chintz-covered window seat. 'I just know this is it!'

She grabbed the phone and began stabbing madly at the keys.

SURE I'LL B THE –

No, that sounded like she was desperate to see him. Which of course she was but it wouldn't be smart to let him know that.

WILL C IF I CAN MAKE IT.

Should she put a kiss or not? Yes. No. Did the message sound too offhand? She held down the delete key.

SURE I'LL BE THERE. XX

After another moment of deliberation, Abby held the

phone away from her, closed her eyes, and pressed the send button. Then she bent down, lifted the corner of her mattress and pulled out her purple diary – the one no one knew about. She had a scarlet one that held boring stuff, like dental appointments and reminders about homework, and acted as a decoy if her inquisitive sisters or over-anxious mother found it. But the purple diary held her secret, most intimate thoughts – stuff that her totally unromantic family would have mocked.

Today at 8.58, she wrote, *my dreams came true. Fergus Mortimer wants me, desires me, yearns to be with me . . .* OK, maybe that was a tad over the top, but she'd read somewhere that if you send out positive vibes to the universe, it gives you exactly what you want.

'Abby, for the last time, will you please hurry up? It's nearly nine o'clock!' Her mother's shrill voice wafted up the stairs.

'OK, OK, I'm coming!' Abby hollered.

She kissed the page, and rammed the diary back under the mattress. Nine o'clock. In less than twelve hours, she'd be with him. Of course, there were a few minor obstacles to overcome in the meantime – like that she wasn't allowed out late during term, that her mother would die a thousand deaths if she knew her sixteen-year-old daughter was planning to venture anywhere near Club XS, never mind inside it, and that she had to find a watertight alibi that wouldn't land her in trouble like the last time. But somehow she would do it. She had to. Her future happiness depended on it.

She slipped her feet into her new silver wedges, grabbed her bag and crossed to the dressing table mirror, sticking a large green flower clip into her flame-coloured curls.

She blew a kiss at her reflection, and assessed her capri-clad bottom before deciding they were way too last year. She unzipped her trousers, hurling them on to the floor as she yanked garment after garment out of her wardrobe, all the while wishing she had the same bean-pole figure as her sister Ellie. She cringed when she heard her mother's voice coming from downstairs again.

'Abigail, Ellie's getting the car out right now and you will be in it within the next three minutes or else! This is your sister's day, remember?'

Abby groaned inwardly as she wriggled her bottom {3} into a pair of black satin trousers. Another complication. Mum would expect her and Ellie to have supper at home, eat birthday cake, make a fuss of Georgie. Her mother was big on the happy family bit, especially after everything that had happened. Abby let herself wish, for only a second, that things could go back to the way they used to be.

ARE YOU DARING? IN SEARCH OF AN
ADRENALINE RUSH?
WELL, NOW YOU'VE GOT IT!
TWO HEART-STOPPING SESSIONS OF
ZORBING – SPHERING – CALL IT WHAT YOU WILL!
IT'S THE NEWEST, FASTEST THRILL ON EARTH
AND IT'S YOURS
WITH LOVE FROM
Tom

'This is just the coolest present!' Georgie exclaimed,

leaning on the garden gate and clutching the voucher in her hand.

'You really like it? You're not just saying that?' he asked, running slightly muddy fingers through his unruly blond hair.

'Course not,' Georgie assured him, flicking her ponytail over her shoulder. 'It's awesome!'

That was the best thing about Tom – unlike her own totally boring, completely predictable family, he was on her wavelength. He always had been, ever since she'd wriggled through the gap in the stone wall separating their houses and demanded that he let her have a go with his new bow and arrow. That was several years ago, when he told her that six-year-olds couldn't shoot arrows, and she'd have to wait until she was eight and a half like him. Georgie, who'd never taken no for an answer in her life and had no intention of starting then, wrestled him to the ground with the moves she'd learned at Kiddies' Karate. He told her she was quite OK for a girl, she spat on her hand and then helped him up with her sticky palm, and that had been that – they'd been best mates ever since.

'Georgie, I've got a confession to make. I didn't pay for it – my cousin Josh works at SportsExtreme and he fixed it up for me.'

'Who cares, as long as we get to do it?' Georgie grinned. She knew her sisters thought she was too old for tomboy activities but she didn't care. Pushing the boundaries was her thing – not dressing up and worrying about what other people thought.

'Get to do what, dear?' Julia, Georgie's mother asked,

panting slightly as she reached them. 'Oh, another birthday card! How sweet of you, Tom dear. Do let's see, Georgie!'

She reached out and took the envelope from Georgie's hand.

'Mum, I . . .'

Her mother perched her new Calvin Klein spectacles on the end of her nose, read the florescent orange card and frowned.

'Zorbing? Sphering? What is . . .' She turned the card over to where there was a diagram of a person rolling down a hill inside a ball. 'Georgie, you can't!'

Tom suddenly found something of enormous interest under his left thumbnail.

'Isn't that just the coolest thing, Mum?' Georgie smiled. 'And it's totally safe, honestly.'

'You're trying to tell me that strapping yourself inside an inflatable ball and rolling down a hill at high speed is safe? And besides, why would you want to?'

Georgie counted silently to ten in her head and took a deep breath. It was a trick their father had taught them to do when they were little that all three sisters had taken to heart.

'It's an experience, Mum, an adrenaline rush. Tom and me are going to do it together.'

'Tom and I,' her mother corrected her. Even the shock of her youngest daughter going zorbing could not dampen her passion for good grammar. She eyed Tom suspiciously.

'Does your mother know about this?' she asked, glancing over the garden wall as if hoping that Mrs Eastment would appear and put a stop to the whole idea.

Georgie cringed with embarrassment. What kind of a question was that to ask a fifteen-year-old boy?

'Oh, sure,' Tom said. He grinned, hooking his thumbs through his jeans belt. 'My cousin runs it.'

Julia swallowed hard and fixed a bright smile on her lips. 'Really? How fascinating. Well, I suppose . . .' The sound of a car engine firing-up inside the garage put an end to her musings.

'Ellie, no! Stop this minute! What are you doing?' She ran across the gravel drive towards the garage, her ample breasts bobbing up and down in alarm.

'Georgie,' she called over her shoulder. 'Come. Car – now!' When distraught, Julia tended to wind down to monosyllables.

'What's keeping her?' Ellie leaned on the horn of her bright red Fiat Uno and sighed impatiently. 'She's been getting ready for the last hour.' She zapped down the window and peered up at Abby's bedroom window.

'Mum, go and get her – we'll miss the train if she doesn't get a move on,' Georgie complained, climbing into back of the car. 'Ellie drives so slowly . . .'

'So I should hope!' their mother said sharply, clicking her seat belt in place even though the car was stationary. 'She's still a learner driver, remember?'

'Not for much longer,' Ellie said grinning, unzipping her bomber jacket and hurling it on to the back seat. 'Four weeks and three days, and these L-plates can go out the window.'

'Don't you be so sure, young lady,' her mother teased, touching up her lipstick in the rear view mirror. 'Not if . . .'

'Here she is!' Georgie interrupted, as the studded oak front door of the half-timbered house banged shut and her sister crunched down the gravel drive. 'Come on, Abby, what kept you so long?'

Abby hitched her bag up on to her shoulder and clambered into the back seat of the car beside Georgie amid a cloud of L'Eau d'Issay.

'Couldn't find my new lavender mascara,' she replied. 'And then my lip liner smudged and . . .'

'Abby, for heaven's sake,' Ellie interrupted, dropping the sun visor to cancel out the glare from the distant ocean. 'We're going to London for the day, not parading down a catwalk.'

'Whatever,' Abby retorted, clicking her seat belt in place. 'Some of us like to look our best even if it is only our kid sister's birthday.'

'Even if the little sister looks like she's about to go on a protest march,' interjected Julia, glancing in the rear view mirror at her youngest daughter. 'Georgie, couldn't you have worn something a little smarter? Ellie and Abby manage to . . .'

'Mum, these are dead cool combats, OK?' Georgie stressed, ramming her baseball cap more firmly on her head. 'Anyway, it's my birthday and I can do what I like.'

'Ellie!' Julia Dashwood cried, grabbing on to the dashboard as the car lurched forward. 'Gentle on the clutch!'

'Sorry,' Ellie apologised, to the car as much as to her mother. She shouldn't be taking out her frustration with her family on Fenella the Fiat.

'And not so much of the little sister routine,' protested

Georgie, digging Abby in the ribs. 'I'm thirteen today, remember?'

'Sorry,' said Abby sweetly. 'I keep forgetting. I mean, when I was thirteen, I'd already started dating . . .'

'You started dating at nursery school,' Ellie muttered under her breath.

'Will you concentrate on your driving?' her mother shouted. 'You nearly took the branches off that bush!'

Ellie drove slowly down the long rhododendron-lined driveway. 'OK, we're on our way,' she chanted, trying to lighten everyone's mood.

'See you, house, at the end of the day!' they all chorused and then giggled in a slightly embarrassed way. It was a feeble tradition but one they could never quite break. It had started when Abby was two and insisted on saying goodbye to everything before she went out – the cats scattered about the house, the doves in the dovecote on the back lawn, the stone cherub on the fountain, and of course, the house. Abby had been sure that Holly House had a heart, and so she had always told it she would be back. The habit had stuck and now none of them wanted to be the first to break it.

'I wish the weather would warm up,' Abby said. 'Then we could mow the tennis court and put the nets up. I want to get some practice in.'

'You what? You don't even like tennis,' Ellie protested, slowing to a halt and pressing the remote control that opened the wrought iron gates to the road. The traffic was already building as tourists sped along the coast road to enjoy the delights of Brighton on a spring Saturday.

'She does now,' Georgie intervened. 'She's in love.'

'She's permanently in love,' Ellie retorted, zapping the gates closed behind her, 'but it doesn't usually involve her moving any faster than a slow amble.'

'It's Fergus Mortimer,' Georgie informed her. 'He's a tennis whiz and Abby fancies him.'

'I don't!' Abby snapped.

'You do so,' Georgie countered calmly. 'You wrote *Fergus 4 Abby* on your homework notebook and all over your biology folder.'

'All of Abby's books are covered with love notes,' Ellie commented. 'So what's so special about this Fergus?'

'Will you three just stop all this chattering!' their mother exploded. 'My nerves go through enough with Ellie's driving without listening to all your nonsense.'

Ellie bit her lip to stop herself replying. She knew quite well why her mother was on edge, and it had nothing to do with Ellie's ability behind the wheel. It was the fact that the girls were off to see their father. And Pandora.

'So where have you asked Dad to take us this year, Georgie?' Ellie heard Abby ask from the back seat as she pulled into the outside lane. 'Not another safari park, I trust. Remember when Mum screamed because that buffalo stuck its tongue out at her?'

If Ellie hadn't been driving, she would have turned round and thumped her sister. How tactless could she get? Mum wouldn't need any reminders that this time last year, she and Dad were still together. Just.

Twelve months ago – just fifty-two weeks – they hadn't had a clue. Dad had, of course. All the time they'd been at the safari park, with him laughing and joking and taking photographs, he'd known he was going to leave them. And by the time the pictures were developed, he had.

'I've grown out of safari parks,' Georgie retorted sharply and Ellie guessed she was watching the same mental-movie in her mind as well. 'This year it's going to be the London Dungeon first, then lunch at Piggy Passions, and a ride on the London Eye.'

'Sounds like a fun day,' her mother said.

Ellie caught the wistful note in her mum's voice.

'Why don't you come too, Mum,' Georgie cried, leaning forward as far as her seat belt would allow and tapping Julia on the shoulder. 'It would be just like old times.'

'Georgie!' Ellie hissed. 'Shut up.'

She knew Georgie meant well, but the hard fact was that nothing would ever be like old times again.

'That's sweet of you darling,' her mother said calmly. 'But I don't think Pandora would relish my company, do you?'

She sounded amused, but Ellie could see the way she was clenching and unclenching her hands in her lap.

'But Mum, that's the whole point. Pandora won't be there,' Georgie insisted.

'Georgie, of course she will,' her mother retorted sharply, flicking a stray hair from her shoulder. 'Your father and Pandora are joined at the hip. With superglue.'

It was almost a relief to Ellie to hear the note of acerbity in her mother's voice. There were times when she seemed to be almost too dignified to be true.

'Mum, I promise . . .' Georgie began.

'Georgina, leave it, OK?' Their mother only ever used

their full names when she was about to explode and it never failed to stop them in their tracks.

'Which way?' Ellie asked her mother. 'North Street or along the sea front?'

'North Street,' her mother replied. 'You need practice in traffic.'

Ellie took a deep breath and manoeuvered her way past the Royal Pavilion, with its Indian-style turrets and enthusiastic clusters of Japanese tourists waving guide-books, past the carpet gardens, and into her favourite area of town. Not that she dared to take her eyes off the road long enough to soak up the buzzy, Bohemian sidestreets of North Laines with its artists' studios, funky nightclubs and tiny shops selling vintage clothing. The narrow streets were a challenge to even the most experienced driver, and Ellie found herself holding her breath as if that would help the car squeeze past the pavement cafés with their tables spilling on to the road.

'Well done, dear,' her mother said as Ellie turned into the station forecourt. 'Pull up over there and give me the car keys.'

'Will you be OK, Mum?' Ellie whispered, grabbing her jacket as her sisters piled out of the car.

'OK?' Julia replied brightly, leaning across to give her a hug. 'I'll be fine. I've got those rose bushes to prune, then I'm having lunch with Fran at the new organic bistro down by the marina – Fresh and Fancy, I think it's called . . .'

'Come on!' Georgie interrupted, hopping from one foot to another and grabbing Ellie's arm. 'The train goes in ten minutes.'

'Before you go,' their mother said hesitantly. 'You will give my love to – well, remember me to your father, won't you? Tell him the daffodils are all out and those cowslips he planted . . .'

Her voice petered out and she gave a brief wave, before firing the engine and driving off, narrowly missing a couple of seagulls pecking for scraps at the kerbside. Ellie, Abby and Georgie just watched her go.

✄ SECRET NUMBER 2 ✄

There really is no accounting for taste.

'IT MAKES ME SO ANGRY!' Abby yelled. They were {13} halfway across the crowded station concourse when she swung round to face Ellie. 'Why didn't she fight more for him? I mean, you can tell she still loves him to bits. Why did she let him go?'

Abby's voice rose to a crescendo and a couple of pigeons stopped pecking round a rubbish bin and flew into the air in front of them.

'Abby, for goodness' sake,' Ellie began, conscious of the glances of the other passengers hurrying for the London train. 'Don't start all that again. It's over – and besides, there was nothing Mum could have done about it. It wasn't her fault that Dad fell in love with Pandora.'

'Pandora seduced him, you mean! All those come-hither looks and giant silicone boobs!' Abby stormed, stomping into the first free carriage. 'And of course she could have done something about it. If she'd been more – oh, I don't know – more stylish, more sexy, more in your face . . .'

'Look, Abby, I wish Mum was here, I wish she and Dad were still together, I wish we were just a normal family like before, but we're not and – '

'Stop it. Shut up and stop it right now!' Georgie's face was scarlet as she stomped down the gangway to the first row of vacant seats. 'It's my birthday and I don't want anything to spoil it, OK? Can't we just spend the day with Dad and pretend . . .'

'What? Pretend he'll be coming home with us, pretend nothing's changed?' Abby mocked, slinging her bag on to the overhead luggage rack and slumping into a window seat.

{14} 'Abby, don't,' Ellie said slipping into her usual role of mediator. 'Georgie's bound to feel a bit upset.'

'Upset? I'm not upset!' Georgie stuck out her chin and bit her lip, which was a sure sign that she was.

'Anyway,' Ellie went on calmly, 'I guess Georgie's right. We've got Dad to ourselves for the whole day, so . . .'

'Hardly.' Abby sniffed. 'Pandora, queen of all bird-brains, will be there.'

'Oh no she won't,' Georgie declared smugly.

'Face it, Georgie, she will,' Ellie agreed, peering at her reflection in the train window and musing for the tenth time that day on whether to get her shoulder-length hair cut really short.

'No. She. Won't.' Georgie articulated each word as if talking to a pair of morons.

Ellie eyed her sister closely. 'Georgie,' she asked, as the train pulled out of the station. 'What exactly do you know that we don't?'

'Just that I'm a genius,' she said, giggling. 'Why do you think I chose the London Dungeon, Piggy Passions and the London Eye for my birthday?'

Abby shrugged and stood up to grab a bottle of Evian water from her bag. 'Because you are a hugely strange individual?' she suggested mischievously, unscrewing the cap and taking a large swig.

Georgie pulled a face. 'I chose them because no way will Pandora want to be a part of it. She's a total wimp when it comes to ghosts and ghouls – remember how she almost fainted watching *The Sixth Sense*? And she can't stand heights . . .'

'And she won't eat anything that's not fat-free, gluten-free and grown in organic soil on a south-facing slope of the Andes!' finished Ellie, bursting out laughing as the train gathered speed. 'Georgie – you're brilliant!'

'This is true.' Georgie grinned, scrabbling in her rucksack. 'Want a crisp?'

'Dear me,' teased Abby, 'what would Pandora say? A *crisp*?'

'Don't you realise,' chimed in Ellie, mimicking Pandora's shrill tones, 'that mass produced products loaded with salt and fat can wreak havoc with one's arteries, not to mention destroy the complexion and introduce toxins to the bloodstream?' Ellie giggled and reverted to her normal voice. 'Give me a handful!'

Georgie tossed the bag of crisps on to Ellie's lap.

'Hot in here, isn't it?' Abby said, unzipping her cream leather jacket and flinging it on the spare seat beside her. 'I'll have some too.'

'Abby! That's my new top you're wearing! How dare –'

Ellie's outburst came to an abrupt end as she choked on the crisps she had just stuffed into her mouth.

Her sister ran her hands admiringly across her chest. 'Looks good on me, doesn't it?' Abby said with a grin. 'At least I fill it out!'

Even over the sound of her own coughing and the rattling of the train, Ellie could hear the titters of the two boys sitting across the aisle. Abby's chest was hardly something you could overlook at the best of times; in Ellie's new black and scarlet tube-top it was totally in your face.

'I haven't even –' Ellie leaned across, grabbed the bottle of water on Abby's lap and took a swig in an attempt to regain the power of speech '– worn it yet!'

'I know.' Abby grinned. 'It's been hanging in your wardrobe for weeks, so I thought it deserved an airing.'

'That is so rude of you!' Ellie hissed under her breath. 'I was saving it for – '

'For what?' Abby demanded as the train plunged into the darkness of Clayton Tunnel. 'You haven't been clubbing in ages, and you could count the number of parties you've been to on the fingers of one hand. I don't even know why you bought it in the first place.'

'Because I am – I *was* – going to wear it to Verity's party next week,' Ellie lied. In truth, she wouldn't have dared leave the house in it; she only bought it on impulse one day when Abby had been nagging at her to loosen up a bit. It'd looked cool in the shop, and the assistant told her it enhanced her nearly non-existent chest (though she didn't say it in those words, of course). Ellie glared at Abby, but her sister had already fished a magazine from her bag and was deeply engrossed in an article about snagging the perfect guy. Typical.

'Good magazine?' Ellie touched Abby's knee a few minutes later.

Abby smiled a little and nodded. That was so Ellie – always the first to make the peace after a row, always desperate to keep everyone happy. Sometimes Abby wished she could be more like her elder sister; it must be cool never to be so angry that you felt like your guts were going to burst all over the floor, never so miserable that you couldn't eat, speak or sleep. But if Ellie never plummeted emotionally, she never flew, either. Seventeen years and three months and she'd never been seriously in love. And as far as Abby was concerned, that was majorly tragic.

The trouble was, Abby mused, staring out of the train window at the encroaching suburbs, Ellie lacked passion. She'd had a couple of boyfriends and apparently had snogged one of them in a fairly hands-on kind of way, but she was always so detached about them. You never caught Ellie writing 'E ♥ F' all over her French folder, or skipping lacrosse practice to slip through the back hedge of the playground and chat up the guys from Bishop Radford College next door. You never found her sobbing in a corner because a guy had ignored her at a party.

Even when Dad left to live with that little piece of lowlife, Plastic Pandora, Ellie had been all buttoned up and controlled about it. Georgie had cried and fallen behind in class and got chubby from eating too much chocolate and cake; Abby had shouted and ranted at her father, thrown up a few times (stress frequently caused

{17}

Abby to vomit) and bought her father a whole load of books written by psychologists about how tough divorce is on kids; Mum had sobbed for weeks. But Ellie had just sighed a lot and cooked the meals because their mum was falling apart and having migraines. In the end that had turned out to be a good thing since Ellie's cooking was so gross that Georgie dropped a bit of the cakeweight and eventually their mother rallied enough to drive them to The Old Mill for supper rather than stomach another one of her meals.

'We're here!' Georgie's elbow driving into Abby's ribs broke her reverie as the train pulled into Victoria Station. 'Come on. Quickly. Dad will be waiting!' Georgie was already scampering toward the train exit.

Abby stuffed her magazine back in her bag and stood up, irritated to find her stomach lurching in nervous anticipation. She hoped Georgie was right, and that Pandora wouldn't be standing at the barrier, her arm woven through Dad's, calling him Maxi Boy, as if Max wasn't a perfectly acceptable name.

So Abby did what she always did in times of emotional crisis – pretend it was a movie and she was the acclaimed and idolised star. Just thinking about it made her feel better: *tragic, deserted child of millionaire leaves train, her eyes searching the platform as the wind catches her hair.*

'There he is!' Georgie cried. 'Hi, Dad!'

The pathos of the beautiful scene playing in Abby's head was shattered by the comic sight of their father, standing at the turnstile, hands in the air, waving one of those 'Happy Birthday' banners you stick on the wall at parties. He was chanting, 'Here they come, here they come, here they come,' like a drunken football hooligan.

'Dad!' Georgie hurtled down the few remaining meters of the platform and flung herself into her father's open arms.

Her father grinned, threw back his head and burst into somewhat discordant song. 'Happy birthday to you, happy birthday to you . . .' he warbled, totally oblivious to the smirks of passersby. Abby caught a whiff of pungent aftershave as she caught up with her sister.

'Dad, you're totally mad!' Abby planted a kiss on her father's cheek, love for her dotty father welling up inside her. Her father gave her a hug and Abby noticed that his hands were shaking.

'Not mad, just so pleased to see you all,' Max said, pulling away from Abby and hugging Ellie. 'Hi sweetie. Congratulations on your French prize – what a triumph! And runner up in the public speaking – is there no end to your talents?'

For a moment, Abby was overcome with jealousy. There she was, struggling to cram for her GCSEs, struggling to pass, while everything Ellie touched seemed to turn to gold.

'Thanks, Dad,' she heard Ellie say. 'But it's Abby you should be congratulating – she was an absolute star as Juliet.'

The jealousy vanished in an instant, and Abby impulsively squeezed Ellie's hand. Drama was her thing; she was good and she knew it. Which was just as well really, since she had every intention of becoming the best thing on the West End stage since Dame Maggie Smith.

'I wish I could have been there, kiddo,' Max said, 'but as I said at the time, Pandy had one of her heads . . .'

'I didn't know she had several,' Abby murmured. 'How unusual!'

Max threw her a sideways glance. 'Abby . . .' He cleared his throat and sighed.

'Shall we get a taxi, Dad? To the Dungeon?' Ellie poked Abby in the ribs and gave her a look.

'Good idea!' Max said, his good spirits returning in an instant as he steered them across the crowded concourse to the line of black cabs waiting outside. 'And then we'll have lunch – I've booked a window table at Piggy P's.'

'Ace!' Georgie grinned. 'Can't wait.'

'Isn't Pandora coming, Dad?' Abby asked, winking at Georgie.

'Afraid not,' Max replied. 'Thing is, she's got such a delicate stomach, bless her. Besides, the big wheel would get her vertigo going.'

Georgie gave Abby and Ellie the thumbs up sign behind their dad's back.

'But don't worry,' he went on, 'you'll see her when we go back to the apartment later.'

'Go back?' Abby gasped. There was no way she could go tearing across London to her dad's flat when she had to be back in Brighton by seven thirty to get to the club.

'I don't think we can do that,' she began.

'Nonsense!' cried her father. 'You couldn't come to London and not see our amazing new apartment, could you?'

'Watch me,' Abby muttered.

'Besides, I've got presents for Georgie,' Max added, 'but they are too heavy for me to hike around town all day! So we'll go back for them later.'

Oh, clever one, Dad, thought Abby wryly, as they clambered into the taxi. No way can we wriggle out of it now.

'Tooley Street, please – London Dungeon,' Max instructed the driver before turning back to his girls. 'Well now, isn't this fun? What did you get for your birthday, Georgie?'

'Sound system, mirror shades, baseball boots . . .' Georgie began.

Abby stared out of the taxi window. No way was socialising with Pandora going to wreck her chances with Fergus. She had to make sure they were home by eight at the latest. She *had* to.

'Wow, I'm stuffed!' Ellie leaned back in her chair, rubbing her tummy. 'That was a scrummy lunch. Thanks, Dad.'

'The biggest meal I've had in a long time,' her father said with a grin. He stood up and fished in his back pocket for his wallet.

'You do look thinner,' Georgie ventured, as her father beckoned to the waiter.

'Great, isn't it?' Max replied. 'Don't you think I'm looking good?'

To Ellie's embarrassment, he stood up and twirled round, right in front of the neighbouring diners.

'Yeah, great,' Ellie muttered hurriedly, even though she didn't mean it. She'd been looking at him all through lunch. His hair, which a month ago had been streaked with grey, was now a solid mahogany blob on top of his head and his face looked gaunt and drawn.

'Pandy's put me on a fitness regime,' he told them, handing his credit card to the head waiter. 'No wheat, no dairy, lots of bean sprouts – and plenty of exercise.'

That, thought Ellie, groaning inwardly, accounted for

the trainers he was sporting with his jeans. They were so not Dad – he had always prided himself on his Italian loafers and highly polished English brogues.

'Pandy thinks that it's very . . .' Max began, only to stop in mid-sentence as the waiter returned to the table, his forehead puckered in a frown.

'I'm sorry, sir, but your credit card has been declined.'

'Rejected?' Max frowned, as he stuffed his Mastercard back into his wallet. 'Can't imagine why. Not to worry, try this one.' He slapped his Visa card into the waiter's hand. 'Better get a move on, girls,' he gabbled. 'I've booked the London Eye for three o'clock.'

He hustled them towards the door, tossing Abby's bag at her and shooing them with both hands.

'You three go out and hail a taxi,' he told them. 'I'll be with you in a couple of minutes.'

Abby and Georgie scuffled out to the street first, and Ellie's hand was on the doorknob when she heard the waiter's voice.

'I'm sorry, sir, but that card has also been declined. I must ask you to pay in cash or with a guaranteed personal cheque.'

Ellie hung back as her father fumbled in his breast pocket and pulled out his chequebook.

'Is everything OK, Dad?' she asked anxiously.

Her father laughed. 'Of course it is, sweetheart,' he assured her. 'Trouble is, you transfer funds from offshore accounts to pay bills and what happens? The idiots mess up the transactions. Nothing to worry about.'

Ellie sighed with relief. 'That's OK, then,' she said, slipping her arm through his. 'Let's hit the big wheel!'

* * *

They were queuing for the London Eye when Abby whipped her mobile mobile from her pocket.

'I won't be a minute, Dad,' she said, edging away. 'Just got to make a quick call, OK?

'Is that a new phone?' he queried, eyeing the tiny psychedelic-patterned phone in Abby's hand.

'Great, isn't it?' she enthused. 'Mum got it for me after I did Juliet – it's a WAP. It does a whole load of stuff. You can send photos round the world, do e-mails, play games . . .'

'And send the bill for the whole damn lot to your father, I suppose?'

Abby's mouth dropped open.

'But then again, why not?' he ranted. 'After all, I'm the bottomless pit of money, aren't I? Never mind the stock market crash, never mind falling interest rates. Good old Max, he'll sign the cheques, never a murmur . . .'

'But Dad,' Abby burst out, her heart thumping in her chest as she realised that half the people in the queue were staring at her father. 'You agreed – I mean, you've always paid our phone bills and you never said . . .'

Her father took a deep breath. 'Course I have, love,' he said, nodding. 'And it's a great phone. I was only teasing you, silly. You've got to learn to take a joke.'

Abby sighed with relief and began punching the keys.

'Do you have to do it now, Abby?' Ellie protested. 'What's so important?'

Abby pretended not to hear. She was certainly not about to tell Ellie her master plan. It was far, *far* too good to risk sharing with her sister.

{23}

❧ SECRET NUMBER 3 ❧

*Love is a bit like a doodle by Van Gogh – your lopsided
circle could be a masterpiece to someone else.*

{24}   'HERE WE ARE!' Max cried as the lift juddered to a halt on
the fifteenth floor of Wapping Heights, one of the most
luxurious and exclusive buildings in London. 'Just wait
till you see the flat. It'll blow your mind!'

Georgie sighed inwardly. Whenever Dad started to
use what he thought was cool jargon, she got an ache
deep down in her chest, a bit like the homesick feeling
she'd had on Brownie camp when she was eight.

'Pandora angel, we're back!' He ushered the girls
through the tiny entrance lobby and into the huge
sitting room. 'Ta-da! What do you think?'

'Good grief, it's like an operating theatre!' The words
were out before Georgie had time to stop them, but it
didn't matter – Dad clearly didn't hear her. At that
moment, Pandora came running across the clinically
pristine room, and hurled herself into Max's arms. She
was wearing a pink and white lace dress with a fluffy
cardigan and Perspex sandals and looked, Georgie
thought, like a mobile meringue.

'Give your Pandy a kissy, then!'

Georgie's heart lurched, and she turned away. All the time they had been having lunch or fooling about at the shops, she had been able to pretend that nothing had really changed. She had even kidded herself that because Dad so clearly loved having them around, he'd wake up one morning very soon and come to his senses, tell Pandora that it had all been a huge mistake, pack his bags and come home to Holly House. But now, watching as Pandora wrapped herself around Max like a boa constrictor about to suffocate its prey, she was forced to acknowledge that a happy ending didn't look likely.

'Missed you, missed you, MISSED YOU!' Dad chanted, enveloping Pandora in a bear-like hug. He kissed the top of her bottle blond hair.

'Missed yooooo too, gor-jus!' Pandora puckered her scarlet lips and made ridiculous kissing noises.

Abby nudged Georgie. 'I think I'm going to vomit,' she muttered in her ear.

'Make sure you do it all over her then,' Georgie whispered back, giving her hand a quick squeeze.

'So what do you think?' Max finally managed to put three centimetres between himself and Pandora's enormous silicone-enhanced chest, and waved an arm airily round the flat.

'It's very, um, white, isn't it?' Georgie remarked, gazing at the painted floorboards, bare walls and billowing voiles at every window.

'And empty,' added Ellie, perching awkwardly on the arm of a white leather sofa. She then leaped to her feet as Pandora threw her a warning look. 'Where are all your pictures and stuff?'

'We don't do "stuff" any more, do we Maxi?' Pandora explained, flicking her immaculately-manicured hand over the area where Ellie's bottom had dared to touch the sofa. She had the kind of high-pitched voice that sounded like a tape being played at the wrong speed. 'It's all about de-cluttering your surroundings, throwing out anything that doesn't enhance, uplift and embrace your soul and spirit.'

'So why hasn't she been chucked out, then?' Georgie hissed at Ellie.

'We've gone for the minimalist look, haven't we, Maxi darling?' Pandora twittered. 'Just a few eye-catching features.'

She waved a hand to indicate a vase containing one orchid (white), a few candles (white) and a large floor cushion that had the audacity to carry a splash of pink across one corner.

'My nephew Blake is very arty, bless him. He helped me to capture the very essence of me in this place – purity, light and freedom of spirit.'

With more than a touch of rampant insanity, thought Georgie.

'Oh, speak of the devil!' Pandora giggled as the front door opened and a gangly, sandy-haired guy in paint spattered jeans and cowboy boots struggled with a port-folio case and a huge camera bag. It occurred to Georgie that he looked rather too normal to be related to Pandora.

'Blake, just in time!' Max boomed. 'Meet my girls. Ellie, Abby and Georgie.'

'Hey,' Blake raised a hand and promptly dropped his portfolio case.

'Careful, Blake!' Pandora urged. 'You'll chip the wood floor. Go and put that stuff away – you know I can't stand mess. And change your clothes – you look like a tramp.'

Tell her to stuff it, thought Georgie savagely. Put paint on her stupid white walls, and see how she takes that! Sadly, Blake just nodded at Pandora and ambled out of the room.

'You never mentioned that you had someone staying,' Ellie said to her father, as Pandora began anxiously rubbing invisible marks off the varnished floorboards. She wasn't sure quite why it mattered that this Blake was staying there, but it did.

'Didn't I?' Max murmured vaguely. 'He's with us for a few weeks – he's got some problems at home . . .'

'Max!' Pandora threw her father a warning glance.

Poor Blake, Ellie thought. Maybe that accounted for the rather dreamy, faraway look in those extraordinary grey-green eyes?

'Dad?' Abby asked, walking back toward her dad after checking on the invisible marks that Pandora was scrubbing at. 'Where are all those things you brought from Holly House? I don't see any of them here.'

She's right, thought Georgie. She glanced quickly around, searching for his collection of antique Toby jugs that they used to tease him about so much, the fading sepia photographs of Dashwoods of long ago parading in long dresses in the garden of Holly House, the lopsided head of Mum that he'd made when he first started sculpting. Come to think of it, thought Georgie, where was his potter's wheel, his kiln, all that gear that used to live in the old summerhouse behind the vegetable garden?

'You haven't chucked them, have you?' Ellie asked.

'No, darling, of course not, I – ' Max didn't have the chance to finish his sentence before Pandora cut in.

'I had to be firm with him, silly old sausage,' she tittered. 'We don't want the junk from an old life cluttering up our new one, do we?' She didn't give anyone the chance to answer. 'But then I thought, no Pandora dear, you're being a real meanie . . .'

'Clearly the first worthwhile thought to have crossed your mind this millennium,' Georgie quietly muttered and received a sharp nudge from Ellie.

'. . . so we've turned the third bedroom into a little hidey hole for your father, haven't we, babe?'

Max nodded. 'Come and look,' he invited them, striding across the room and throwing open a door. 'Sweetheart, I expect the girls would like a drink.'

'Sure,' Pandora said and nodded, as she patted the odd stray hair back into place on top of Max's head. 'What would you like – elderflower pressé, gentian and lime flower cordial, or wheat grass juice?'

'Um, could I just have a cup of tea?' Abby asked.

'Mango, mint or camomile with spiced apple?'

'Just regular tea?' Abby queried. 'You know, in a tea bag. From India? Normal?'

'Sorry!' Pandora shook her head. 'We don't do regular – too much tannin. It's so bad for the joints.'

'Elderflower will be fine,' Ellie intervened, desperate to avoid any more snide remarks from either of her sisters. 'Georgie? Abby?'

'I suppose,' Abby said with a sigh, pulling her mobile

phone from her bag and flicking open the cover.

'I suppose,' muttered Georgie, not because she didn't like elderflower – she did – but because she saw no reason to give in to Pandora's ridiculous fetishes.

Pandora nodded triumphantly, and tottered across the room to the kitchen. Georgie glimpsed a mass of gleaming stainless steel and an array of chrome and leather bar stools. It didn't look as if anyone had ever so much as eaten in there, let alone cooked.

'So you see,' Max was saying, beckoning them into his den, 'it's got everything important in it. Here are my photos of you three . . .'

Aren't we important enough to be in the sitting {29} room? thought Georgie, peering into her dad's den. At least it looked as if a human being occasionally sat down in it. And it wasn't white.

'. . . and look, I've got my old desk, my CDs and the paperweight Abby made at infant school and all my Holly House pictures.'

Georgie gazed at the cluster of familiar photos on the pale gold walls. There was the one taken for Granny and Grandad's golden wedding when she was only five, the aerial shot of the house and gardens that Mum had done for his fortieth birthday and her favourite, the one of all five of them with Bridie, their old flat-coat retriever in front of the Christmas tree. Bridie was dead now, and George was convinced that the old dog had died of a broken heart after Max left them all.

'What about your potter's wheel and stuff?' Ellie butted in. 'That's not here.'

'No, I agreed to put it down in the caretaker's store

room, just until I find a little studio somewhere. Pandora's not keen on. . .'

'Speaking of wheels,' Pandora interrupted, appearing at Ellie's elbow with a tray. 'How was the Eye?'

'Round,' muttered Georgie. She looked across at Abby, expecting a thumbs up for quick-wittedness, but her sister was standing by the window, fiddling with her mobile phone. 'Oh, Dad, by the way, Mum sends you loads of love.'

OK, so she knew Abby had told Max that within the first few minutes of seeing him, but when she saw Pandora's pale face flush a livid purple, she knew it had been worth repeating.

'The wheel was great, thank you,' Ellie muttered. 'So, Dad, you're not going to give up sculpting, are you? I mean, you love it so much.'

'Sculpting?' Blake reappeared in the doorway in clean jeans and a rugby shirt. He threw Max an admiring glance. 'Max, you never told me you were into that type of thing. Can I see some of your stuff?'

'Well, I . . .' Max hesitated and Georgie couldn't help smiling to herself. Blake was in for a disappointment. Dad's skill at sculpture didn't quite match his enthusiasm; half the door stops at Holly House had started out as his attempts at Greek goddesses or birdbaths surrounded by overweight cherubs.

'He has no time for all that now, do you, Maxi Boy?' Pandora put the tray on the glass-topped coffee table and ran a hand over his shoulder, removing two stray hairs. 'Our life is so full, what with t'ai chi on Mondays and Thursdays, and our shamanism sessions and of course, the daily runs . . .'

'Runs?' Georgie and Ellie gasped in unison. 'Dad, *you* run?'

Even Abby stopped whispering into her phone and stared at him in astonishment. Georgie did her best to stifle her giggles.

Max nodded proudly, tapping his tummy.

'Now then,' Pandora announced, retreating into the kitchen again. 'Do sit down. I've made a cake for Georgie.'

For a moment, Georgie felt hugely guilty. She's been thinking nothing but horrid thoughts about Pandora since they arrived and now here was, carrying a plate with an enormous cake.

'That's really kind, Pandora,' Georgie said and was rewarded with a quick hug from her father.

'Looks scrumptious,' he enthused. 'Can I have a slice?'

'I'll let you have the teeniest bit, honey, because it's gluten free and I've used soya instead of milk, and carob instead of chocolate, but remember to take it off your calorie allowance for today, won't you?'

If her father hadn't at that moment been rummaging in a drawer and pulling out two parcels wrapped in florescent pink paper, Georgie would have been tempted to tell Pandora that calorie counting was for dweebs with no self esteem, but she didn't want to break the moment.

'Happy birthday, Georgie darling!' Her father slapped two hearty kisses on her cheeks and handed her the parcels.

Georgie ripped the paper off the first package and threw it on the floor. Immediately Pandora was at her side with a black rubbish bag.

'Dad, that's ace!' She turned her brand new skateboard over in her hands, spinning the wheels and running her hand over the deck. 'I've always wanted an Alien Workshop board! Wait till Tom sees this!' She dropped it on the floor and stepped on the board.

'No!' Pandora's cry of alarm ended in a high-pitched screech. 'Not in here, for heaven's sake! You'll scratch the floor.'

'Sorry,' Georgie said, flicking the board with her toe and deftly catching it in one hand. Blake caught her eye and winked.

'Why don't you blow out your candles?' Blake suggested to Georgie. 'Oh, sorry. Candle, singular.' He eyed the pink and white striped candle in the centre of the cake solemnly.

'It's organic,' Pandora murmured.

'The candle or the cake?' Blake enquired, and received a withering look from his aunt. Perhaps, thought Georgie, he's not that wet after all.

Georgie blew out the candle and Pandora began placing tiny slices of cake on to paper plates.

'Open the other present!' Abby urged, glancing at her watch. 'I really think we ought to get going soon.'

'Oh, chill out,' Georgie muttered, ripping the paper from the second parcel. 'Wow!'

Her mouth fell open and she gazed awestruck at the digital camera in her hands.

'I thought you could take a whole load of pictures of all the things you get up to, and then e-mail them to me,' her dad said. 'Come to think of it, get your sisters to snap you on the skateboard – action stuff, of course!'

'I'll start practising right now.' She grinned, flicking through the instruction manual. 'Give me five minutes.'

'We haven't got five minutes,' Abby protested, biting into her slice of cake.' If wedungoshaysunim . . .'

'Pardon?' Ellie eyed her sister in confusion.

'I shed, if wedongoshaysun . . .' Abby gave up, stuck a finger in her mouth and dislodged a lump of glutinous slop from her upper jaw. Pandora thrust a paper napkin under Abby's chin.

Georgie, who had just taken a bite from her slice of cake too, understood the problem. The cake – if you could call it that – was disgusting; it had the consistency of play dough and the flavour of prunes mixed with liquorice. No way could she eat it.

'Don't you like it?' Pandora looked hurt.

'Mmm, much too good to hurry,' Georgie said with a smile. She dumped her plate on the floor and stood in front of it. 'OK, I'm ready! Dad, you go over there by Abby and Ellie, you sit in front, OK?'

Abby sighed and moved towards her father. Ellie took no notice. She was deep in conversation with Blake.

'Ellie!' ordered Georgie. 'Over there.' She gestured towards the mock fireplace and held the camera to her eye.

'Wait for me!' Pandora dabbed at her mouth with a paper napkin and sidled over to Max, slipping her arm through his and gazing up at him with doe eyes.

Georgie bit her tongue. She didn't want the princess of plastic in the picture but she could hardly say so. Reluctantly, she took the picture.

'Hey,' she said peering at the screen and vowing to

{33}

delete it when Pandora wasn't looking. 'Not bad. Now just Dad on his own . . .'

'No, no,' Pandora chirped. 'Take one of all of us, out on the balcony. After all, I'm your new stepmother, aren't I? All one happy family together – that's what your Dad wants, isn't it, Maxi Boy?'

She grabbed Max by the arm and dragged him over to the balcony door, sliding it open and beckoning to Georgie and her sisters to follow.

'And you too Blake!' she ordered.

Blake shook his head. 'No way,' he said. 'I don't mind taking the shots but you're not getting me in the frame, that's for sure.' He glanced at his watch. 'Anyway, I'm out of here,' he said. 'Life class starts in half an hour.'

'Life?' gulped Ellie. 'Isn't that . . . ?'

'Nudes,' said Max, laughing. 'Sure, but when you're planning on being the next Salvador Dali . . .'

'Not nudes, actually,' Blake burst in hastily, his cheeks flushing. 'And Dali's not my thing.'

'What is?' asked Ellie.

'Well, to be honest . . .'

'Excuse me,' interjected Pandora, walking towards the french doors and gesturing to everyone to follow. 'We're supposed to be taking photographs, not discussing your little hobbies. Now then, aren't the views wonderful?' She gazed out over the rooftops to the River Thames where a couple of barges were chugging slowly upstream past the ranks of cargo ships moored on the wharves. 'Now, if you just take a shot of me pointing to the horizon, with everyone crowding round me . . .'

Georgie had an overwhelming desire to push Pandora

over the edge and watch her plummet to the street below. Instead, she kicked the plate of revolting cake under the sofa, and grinned with satisfaction as a smear of carob icing stained the pristine leather. Blake gave her the thumbs up sign as he headed for the door, which Georgie considered fairly decent considering he'd probably end up getting the blame for the mess.

Georgie stomped out on to the balcony. Abby was glowering at her, tapping her hand on the balcony rail and sighing; Ellie was gazing into space, smiling the sort of sickly smile that covers up a distinct desire to scream obscenities.

'No, no,' Pandora shrieked as Georgie took the shot. 'My profile's better this way – take one more.' She turned and smiled up at Max, puckering her lips in a silly, girly fashion.

'I want one of my Dad on his . . .' Georgie began again, shoving her father back into the sitting room and blocking Pandora's way. At that moment Abby's phone shrilled and she grabbed it like a drowning man seizing a lifebelt.

'Hello, yes? Oh my God, no!' Her sister clamped a hand to her mouth and dropped into the nearest chair. 'Is it bad? I can't bear it.' Her bottom lip quivered and she bit it.

'Abby, what is it? What's happened?' Ellie demanded anxiously. 'What's wrong?'

Abby ignored her, eyes wide with horror. 'He did? He does? I'm coming – I'm coming right now, OK? Bye!'

She stuffed her phone back in her pocket and leaped to her feet.

'I've got to go,' she gasped, clamping her hand to her mouth and stifling a sob. 'You all stay – I'll get a taxi – I . . .'

'Darling what on earth is it?' Max asked, an arm round Abby's shoulder. 'What's happened?'

'It's Marcus.' Abby stifled a sob. 'There's been an accident. He's in the hospital and his mum and dad are abroad on holiday and he keeps asking for me and I've got to go because – '

'Of course you must go!' Her father was already scooping Georgie's skateboard into a carrier bag. 'Pandora angel, phone for a mini cab, will you?' He paused and turned to Georgie. 'Who is Marcus?' he mouthed at her. 'Boyfriend?'

'Mmm,' Georgie murmured non-committally. After all, it didn't seem the right time to tell him that Abby had broken up with Marcus – her boyfriend of precisely nine weeks – over a month ago under less than friendly circumstances.

'Don't cry, Abby,' Ellie was saying, hugging her sister and scooping up all their shopping bags. 'I'll come with you. You don't have to do this on your own.'

Abby looked at her sister in alarm. 'No, I don't want you to. I mean, we can't both desert Georgie on her birthday, can we? I'll get a taxi from the station, you tell Mum what's happened.'

'We'll talk about it on the train,' Ellie said, patting her hand.

'There's nothing to talk about!' For a moment, Abby's eyes flashed with anger. 'I mean, honestly, I'll be fine.'

'I want to take a picture of Dad before we go,' Georgie half-whined. 'Dad, stand over by the – '

'Georgie, not now,' her dad insisted. 'Abby's upset – we must get going. You can take my picture any time.'

'Yes, but . . .'

'I've got a meeting in Hove a week on Friday. I thought I'd pop along and take you out to supper afterwards.' He smiled at his three daughters. 'We'll combine it with a photo shoot, OK?'

'OK,' Georgie said, grinning. 'I'll be an expert by then.'

'When you've quite finished,' Abby butted in. 'I've got to get the train or I'll be late – I mean, Marcus will think I'm not coming.'

That's when it clicked. How could she be late? Georgie thought. People lying prone on hospital beds weren't about to whiz off into the night. Abby was plotting something – Georgie was certain.

She didn't know just what her sister was up to as yet, but with a bit of luck, and a bit of gentle blackmail, there just might be something in it for her.

'Ellie, wake up, we're nearly there.'

Ellie's eyes flew open as Georgie nudged her in the ribs.

'You've been asleep all the way from London,' Abby said accusingly, grabbing her bag from the overhead rack.

Ellie rubbed her hand over her aching temples. She hadn't slept, she had simply closed her eyes in order to think. About Dad, and Pandora, and the new flat.

And that guy Blake.

Dad had never invited them to stay with him – not at the old flat or the new one. But then, Blake had problems and judging by the look on Pandora's face, pretty awful ones at that. After all, thought Ellie, they must be bad if he's willing to spend days on end with Pandora. Root canal work would be preferable.

'Frankly, I don't know how you could just nod off after everything that's happened,' Abby persisted.

Immediately Ellie felt a pang of guilt. 'Oh, you mean, Marcus? I'm sorry, Abby, you must be feeling . . .'

'Marcus? No – well, I mean, yes of course Marcus,' Abby stammered, slipping her arms into her jacket. 'But what about Dad and – ?'

'So you noticed it too?' Ellie felt a wave of relief wash over her. 'Didn't he look dreadful?'

'Slightly deficient on the fashion front, I admit,' Abby said with a grin. 'That shirt . . .'

'No, not that. I mean, he was so jumpy. I reckon . . .'

She stopped. No, it was too crazy. She was just letting her imagination run away with her. Dad just seemed off because of the weight loss. Nothing more.

'You reckon what?' Abby asked.

'Oh, just that he seemed a bit stressed, that's all,' Ellie improvised hastily. After all, he *had* seemed stressed. For some reason Ellie couldn't get the scene in the restaurant where Dad's card was rejected out of her mind, and she wasn't certain that Dad had seemed as though he was joking about Abby's mobile phone, at all. Then again, Ellie was known as a worrywart.

'Huh,' muttered Abby. 'I'd be flipping stressed, too, if I was living in that flat. Wall to wall bland. How could he bear to swap Holly House for that soulless box?'

She's right, thought Ellie. Holly House had meant the world to Dad. His parents, his grandparents and even his great-grandparents had lived there; there were stories and memories in every corner of the eighteenth-century house that years ago had stood alone on a hilltop overlooking Brighton, its front windows gazing over the rooftops all the way to the English channel and its rear ones looking out over the rolling sweep of the South Downs. Over the years the expanding town had encroached on the house but even now, almost overtaken as it was by a mish-mash of redbrick Victorian villas, mock Tudor semis and squat post-war bungalows, it retained its spacious, set-apart atmosphere.

'No one's going to get their hands on Dashwood land, that's what your grandad used to say,' Dad would tell them, recalling the story of how their grandfather had refused to sell of the land to property developers. 'We've got it all – sea air, space and the sound of birds to wake us in the morning.'

Of course, Ellie and her sisters used to raise their eyebrows, tap their foreheads and mutter about galloping senility and gross sentimentality – but Dad would just smile and tell them that there were some things in life that were sacrosanct and Holly House was one of them.

Well, he doesn't think that any more, does he? Ellie thought bitterly, as the train lurched forward and crawled into the station. One come-hither giggle from Pandora and he just upped and walked away from the house – and from them. How could he endure being cooped up in a high-rise without a blade of grass in sight and pretend to love every minute of it?

'I've just had a thought,' Ellie burst out as the train juddered to a halt in the station. 'Maybe Dad . . .'

Stop it, she admonished herself fiercely. OK, so she'd spotted a few letters on his desk with the words 'Final demand' in red letters, but that didn't mean anything. Dad's memory was never good at the best of times.

'Hurry up,' Abby was urging her, jumping from the train, grabbing her arm and pulling her down the crowded platform. 'I've got to grab a cab.'

'There's no need to get a taxi,' Ellie insisted, fishing her mobile phone out of her bag. 'Mum's coming to pick us up as soon as we've phoned her – she'll drop you off.'

'No!' Abby burst out, hitching her bag over her shoulder. 'I mean, I just need to get there, you know what I mean? That train journey seemed to take for ever . . .'

Ellie nodded. She guessed that despite all her protestations to the contrary, Abby still had a bit of a thing going for Marcus. 'OK, but before you go, ring Mum will you? My reception's terrible here.'

'I haven't got time.' Abby quickened her pace as they crossed the concourse towards the taxi rank.

'Give me your phone, I'll do it,' Georgie offered, falling in step beside her. 'I left mine at home.'

Abby tossed the phone at her sister and joined the queue, tapping her foot impatiently as the row of taxis edged forward. Georgie flipped back the cover and began scrolling through the menu.

'Hurry up!' Abby urged, as an empty taxi pulled up beside them. 'Just speed dial. It's number two!'

Ellie touched Abby's arm as Georgie punched the numbers. 'You're sure you don't want me to come with you? I mean, what if he's really badly hurt – you're not that good with blood and stuff.'

'I'll be fine,' Abby assured her. 'I mean, the hospital said it wasn't critical.' She clambered into the taxi.

'Where to, love?' the driver asked, pausing to slurp coffee from a paper cup.

'The Sussex County Hospital,' Ellie told him. 'Which wing, Abby?'

'Wing? Oh, North, I think,' she gabbled.

'There isn't a North wing,' Georgie cut in. 'It's East, West and New.'

'New, that's it,' stammered Abby. 'I knew it began with N.'

The taxi driver quaffed the last of his coffee, tossed the cup into the nearby litter bin and clicked the switch on the fare meter.

'You'll ring us when you need picking up, won't you, Abby?' Ellie called to her sister as the taxi began edging away from the curb.

Abby nodded as the cab inched forward. 'But it might be quite late,' she called back at them. 'You know, if Marcus is . . .' Her voice was drowned out by the sound of the taxi's engine.

Ellie waved and turned to Georgie. 'Poor thing,' she said, sighing. 'I reckon she's in for a tough evening, don't you?'

Georgie muttered under her breath, something that sounded like 'Hardly.'

'What did you say?' Ellie demanded.

'Hard,' Georgie replied, nodding gravely. 'Very, very hard.'

But even Ellie could see that Georgie knew something she didn't.

❧ SECRET NUMBER 4 ❧

*Very few things are worth taking a risk for – love, family,
and the prospect of a first kiss.*

{42}SHE'D DONE IT! Abby was here, at Club XS – the newest, trendiest club in town. And she was on the dance floor with Fergus. OK, so it had taken nearly two hours before he'd asked her to dance but that was only because Melissa Peck, who was in the year above Abby and who everyone knew was a total slag, kept dragging him off and he was too nice to tell her where to go. But Abby had seen him glance in her direction every few minutes, and the more great shapes she'd thrown on the dance floor the more he'd watched. The best bit had been the look on Melissa's face when Abby had shimmied past them and Fergus had grabbed Abby's arm and sidled up next her.

That one moment made it all worthwhile – bribing Phoebe to phone her at Dad's place and pretend to be the hospital receptionist; the battle to get past the bouncers by pretending she'd left her ID in her mate's pocket, and he was inside; the pangs of conscience about inventing Marcus's accident and the gnawing worry that

Mum would find out the truth and she'd be grounded for eternity. None of that mattered now – she and Fergus were really connecting, and Abby knew full well that besides the fact that he was unbelievably hot, hooking up with an older guy from Bishop Radford was going to make her more popular than ever. When Abby glanced over Fergus's shoulder to see her friend Phoebe (who had legs up to her armpits and was no stranger herself to snagging hot, older guys), watching her with envy, it confirmed how worth it this whole episode had been.

When she'd called Phoebe that afternoon to beg her to call and give the fake news about Marcus, she'd insisted on coming along.

'What are you going to tell your Mum?' Abby had asked.

'The truth, of course,' Phoebe had replied. 'She doesn't care what I do these days – as long as she's got the house to herself and that nerd Vernon.'

Abby sighed. Sometimes she thought life would be a lot easier if she had a laid-back, passion-seeking mother who cultivated men the way her mum cultivated freesias and hollyhocks.

Remembering Phoebe's words, Abby felt a pang of conscience. If Mum knew what she was doing she would go ballistic. But she didn't, Abby reminded herself, and in a little while, she would kiss Fergus goodbye, grab a cab, go home and give them the good news that Marcus wasn't half as badly injured as she'd thought, and that would be that.

'Cool club,' she whispered into Fergus' neck as a slow song ended, and she tried to ignore the blisters on her feet from walking round London in her silver wedges. She ran her tongue over her top lip, the way that *Hot Lips* magazine said was a dead sexy turn on.

'Are you thirsty?' Fergus asked, slipping his arm round her shoulder and guiding her towards the bar, which had tropical fish swimming under the glass topped counter and stools in the shape of giant sea shells. 'What can I get you?'

'You can get me a fruit punch!' Melissa appeared at Fergus's left elbow, thrusting her chest in his direction. 'The *passion*fruit variety.'

The way she put all the stress on the word 'passion' made Abby want to claw her eyes out. Or vomit. Either one, really.

'And then we'd better make tracks, yeah?' Melissa asked.

Abby's stomach lurched as Melissa nuzzled up to Fergus and gazed at him with her round, irritatingly pretty eyes.

'You're not leaving, surely?' Abby gasped. 'I mean, it's only – oh cripes, it's nearly ten thirty!'

'Bit late for you, is it, little one?' Melissa smirked at her condescendingly. 'Time you were tucked up in bed?'

'Now *there's* a good idea . . .' Fergus's witty innuendo was cut short when Melissa's kitten heel engaged with his left foot.

'To make tracks, I mean,' he added, laughing hastily. 'Coming, Abby? We're going to The Lighthouse – you know, over at Shoreham Harbour. They've got a dusk till dawn rave going on!'

Abby's heart sank. There was no way she could go. It was one thing to pull the wool over Mum's eyes for a couple of hours, but to dash ten miles down the coast for an all-nighter was out of the question. But then again, if she didn't go, Melissa would get her claws well and truly into Fergus, and she wouldn't stand a chance. She had to think of something, some way to keep Mum in the dark and get a few more hours to make Fergus fall hopelessly in love with her . . .

And she had to do it in about ten seconds flat.

'Mum, you can't do this – Abby will kill me!' Georgie jumped in front of her mother and attempted to block her way to the front door. 'Please, Mum!'

'What do you expect me to do?' Julia Dashwood {45} demanded, slipping her arms into her cashmere jacket and grabbing her car keys. 'Sit around here while my daughter is prancing around in that dreadful, seedy club?'

'Mum, it's not that bad,' Ellie interrupted half-heartedly. 'I mean, she is sixteen, after all.'

'And if Abby finds out that it was me that told you about the phone, I'll be dead meat,' Georgie pleaded.

'By the time I've dealt with her, she won't be in any position to criticise anyone!' Julia stormed. 'It's not just the club – although heaven knows, that's bad enough – it's the lies. And when I think of Marcus's poor mother . . .' She shook her head as words failed her.

'But – ' Georgie started.

'Georgina, leave it!' Her mother pushed her out of the way and wrenched open the front door. A rush of cool night air sent a shiver down Georgie's spine. 'Ellie, you come with me. Georgie, stay here, get ready for bed and if Abby gets back, phone me, got it?'

The front door slammed and Georgie heard the car engine firing up and the scrunch of gravel as Julia and Ellie roared off down the drive.

She ambled through to the sitting room and began idly flicking through the pile of birthday cards still lying on the walnut coffee table. Why hadn't she kept her mouth shut? Come to think of it, why had she grabbed Abby's phone in the first place and offered to ring Mum? If she hadn't done that, she would never have scrolled through the Calls Received menu and seen that it wasn't the hospital who had phoned Abby, but Phoebe Spicer.

Not that she had had any intention of dropping Abby in it – not at first. She'd reckoned that keeping quiet about those two being together deserved a ticket to the movies or enough cash for at least one session at the Snow Dome. But within minutes of getting home, things had got out of hand.

'What sort of accident? How bad is he? When did it happen?' Julia's questions came thick and fast.

Georgie shrugged. 'I don't know,' she said. 'Abby didn't say.'

'She just said,' Ellie interrupted, 'that his parents were abroad and he was asking for her.' That's when things got a bit sticky.

'Abroad?' Julia queried. 'Nonsense. I saw Madeleine only yesterday at the hairdresser's. That woman is so grey, it's untrue. And the wrinkles!' She patted her own immaculate golden blond bob, and sighed. 'You must have misheard. I must phone her at once to see if we can help in any way.'

'No!' Georgie blurted out. 'I mean, she's probably at

the hospital, and besides, maybe she was having her hair done to get ready for going on holiday and . . .'

'You could be right,' her mother mused and for a moment, Georgie thought the moment had passed. 'Then again, if they're not there, they won't answer the phone, will they? And at least if I leave a message, they will know we're all thinking of them.'

Georgie winced, remembering what had happened next – the phone call to Marcus's mother who had screamed into the phone and nearly fainted from shock until, by some stroke of good fortune, Marcus had sauntered through the front door, large as life and without a scratch on him. The Spanish Inquisition that followed as soon as Julia hung up the phone had left Georgie with no option but to come clean about the call from Phoebe Spicer.

After calling Phoebe's mum and giving her an earful about responsible parenting, Julia slammed the phone down and stormed into the sitting room, her normally pale skin flushed.

'She's at Club XS!' She had made it sound as if Abby was at that very moment drinking cocktails with the leader of the local Mafia. And with that, she and Ellie had taken off in the car, leaving Georgie to sit and imagine how angry Abby would be when she found out.

The music was pumping through the club when Abby first noticed the crowd parting. Fergus was standing just in front of her, waiting for her to say whether or not she could come to the rave and Melissa was staring at him with her big stupid eyes. Abby was about to tell him, that yes, of course she'd join him – no way was she about to let Melissa get her slimy paws on Fergus without a fight – when she heard it. When she heard *her*.

'Abigail! Out! Now!'

It can't be, thought Abby. She closed her eyes for a second, willing her mother's crystal tones to fade alongside the music. Instead, they got louder.

'I mean it, Abigail!'

For a moment, Abby stood rooted to her spot on the dancefloor, her mind racing as she stared disbelieving at her mother who was standing, arms akimbo, in the middle of the crowd, the flashes from the strobe lighting making her look like a resurrected ghost.

How did she know where to come? Who told her? Abby's thoughts were spinning around her, in rhythm to the music.

'I said it was past your bedtime, didn't I?' Melissa jeered, nestling up to Fergus. 'Anyway, we're off. Ciao!'

As she dragged Fergus towards the door, Abby prayed that he would turn and at least give her a wave, or grin at her, or acknowledge her presence somehow.

But he didn't. Melissa pulled him through the door, and if Abby was going to be completely honest about the whole thing, it didn't really look like he minded.

Please God, Abby murmured silently in her head, let me die right now, OK? She could feel her face burning with the shame of it all as her mother grabbed her arm, and Abby caught Pheobe's eye.

'Bad luck!' Phoebe mouthed and put her hand to her ear, mimicking a phone before ducking behind one of the gaping onlookers.

Julia dragged Abby toward the exit, pulling her through a sea of mocking faces. That's when she spotted Ellie, lurking in the doorway.

'What are you grinning at?' Abby snapped at her sister, although in truth Ellie wasn't even smiling. 'Enjoying the role of little Miss Perfect yet again, are you?'

The moment she'd said the words, she felt guilty. It wasn't Ellie's fault that they shared a mother who was still locked in the Stone Age.

'I tried to get her to stay in the car,' Ellie whispered apologetically, as their mother stomped out on to the pavement, pushing a couple of people lighting up cigarettes out of the way in her frustration. 'I tried to come in a get you alone, but she wouldn't have it.'

'How did she find out?' Abby began, only to find herself being shoved unceremoniously into the back of the car with a curt, 'Seat belt! Now!'

'I found out,' her mother interjected, 'by phoning Marcus's mother to commiserate over his supposed accident.' She spat the words out and released the clutch with such ferocity that the car lurched forward like a kangaroo on speed.

'Oh no – was she – did she . . . ?' Abby stammered.

'Have a heart attack? Collapse with fright? Almost – till Marcus showed up. That's when Georgie told me the truth.'

'Georgie?' Abby glanced at Ellie. 'How did she know anything?'

'Phone,' muttered Ellie. 'She scrolled through and – '

'The devious brat!' Abby sputtered, but she knew full well that faced with Mum in overdrive, anyone would have come clean.

'She didn't mean – ' Ellie started.

'Never mind, it doesn't matter now,' Abby said dejectedly.

'Oh, doesn't it?' her mother snapped. 'I think it matters a great deal. You are grounded. For a month.'

Ellie gasped. Surely her mum couldn't be that harsh?

'It doesn't matter,' Abby said, shrugging. 'After tonight no one will ever ask me out again. I'm a laughing stock, an outcast, a social pariah and Fergus . . .'

She'd been doing so well. But the thought of Fergus, who by now was probably speeding to Shoreham with Melissa's head on his shoulder, finished her. She did

what she'd been fighting against for the last ten minutes.

She burst into tears.

✄ SECRET NUMBER 5 ✄

Even mums have hearts.

'I'LL JUST TAKE THIS UP TO ABBY.'

Ellie looked up from the *Sunday Times* the following morning and smiled to herself as her mother piled hot croissants and fruit on to a breakfast tray.

'She's forgiven then, is she?' Ellie asked, opening a kitchen drawer to find a pen for the crossword.

'No – yes – oh, I don't know!' Julia sounded exasperated and defeated at one and the same time. 'Maybe I was a bit over the top . . .'

Just a tad, Ellie thought, but decided that silence was the best option.

'It's just that, it's so hard, being a single parent . . .'

Ellie bit her tongue and counted silently to ten. Then she repeated the exercise, in German. It was all very well for her mum to moan about Abby being a drama queen, but it was pretty clear where she got it from. Her mother talked as if she was living in a high-rise on social security, rather than enjoying a five-bedroom house on an acre of beautiful gardens, with an ex-husband who paid all the bills.

Ellie swallowed. With all the drama of the previous evening, her worries about Dad had been pushed aside. But now an image of him swam before her eyes, as clear as if he was standing in front of her, leaning against the oven like he used to – bum warming, he'd called it.

'Dad looked really tired yesterday,' she ventured, as her mother poured a glass of apple juice and balanced it on the tray.

'Really?' her mother replied curtly, pulling off her Laura Ashley apron and flinging it over the back of a chair. 'I guess keeping up with someone just out of nappies would do that to you.'

'What's for lunch?' Ellie cut in, determined not to let her mother move toward the self-pitying spiral that she could feel sneaking up on them.

'Roast chicken. Did you say tired, though?' Julia added anxiously.

'Pardon?'

'Dad – you said he was tired – I mean, not ill or anything?'

'No, he's fine,' she reassured her mother, sorry now that she had brought it up. 'Although I did think. . .'

'Right, well, it's eleven o'clock,' Julia interupted Ellie. Perhaps she wasn't much in the mood for self-pity today either. 'Surely that girl can't still be asleep? Mind you, all that throwing up last night must have worn her out. I hope she hasn't caught a bug at that awful XS place.'

Ellie raised her eyebrows. 'Mum, you know full well that Abby throws up the moment she doesn't get her own way,' she snapped. 'She's done it all her life.'

'Right, well, I'm going up.' Julia pushed past Ellie,

kicking open the kitchen door with her foot.

Ellie shut the drawer she was searching in for a pen and opened another. As she scrabbled among the chaos for something to write with, she found a letter. And even though it wasn't in Ellie's nature to read what wasn't hers (except for an occasional peek in Abby's scarlet diary to see of she was still just blubbering on about dentist appointments and homework assignments), something about the note caught her eye.

Ellie began reading out loud, which was something she always did when she was nervous.

'Dear Mrs Dashwood,
Since we have received no reply to our several items of corre-
spondence with yourself, and since the balance outstanding on
your Visa card is now well in excess of your credit limit . . .'

'Mum!' Ellie turned but her mother was already halfway up the stairs. She took a deep breath and read on.

'. . . we must ask you to return your card immediately and to
settle your account within seven days. In the event that you
do not cooperate, we will have no option but to issue a court
order for reclamation of outstanding . . .'

'Oh my God, Mum!' Ellie shouted. 'Mum, come here!'

There was no reply. Ellie ran up the stairs two at a time, the letter clutched in her hand, and sped along the landing towards Abby's room.

The low murmur of voices stopped her in her tracks. Abby's bedroom door was closed, but Ellie could tell that Abby was crying, and Mum was making the sort of soothing noises that she used when they were tiny and fell over and got gravel in their knees. Ellie slumped down on the top stair to wait and began chewing her thumbnail.

A court order! It made Mum sound like some sort of criminal. What was Mum thinking about? Ellie had seen that the outstanding balance was over nine thousand pounds. Sums like that didn't accumulate overnight, not even with Mum's spending ability. Besides, her mother said she sent all the bills to Dad and he paid them. But clearly he wasn't paying them any more.

Ellie wheeled round as Abby's door opened and her mum came out, looking slightly flushed.

'Mum, I need to talk to you,' Ellie began and then hesitated when her mother held up her hand.

'No more talking until I've had a strong cup of tea,' she declared.

Ellie followed her mother down the stairs and into the kitchen. 'Is Abby OK?' she asked.

Her mother turned the tap and filled the kettle. 'I suppose.' She sighed. 'We've declared a truce, put it that way. She will never, ever go anywhere without telling me, and I'll try to lighten up a bit about curfews and clubs.' She shuddered on the final word as if the mere thought of such places was more than she could bear. 'And she will spend every evening studying – heaven knows she needs to. I know she's deferred her exams for a year, but those mock results were dire. She needs to pull her socks up right now if she wants to do well in the real thing . . .'

'Mum,' Ellie ventured, before her mother could get carried away over Abby's lack of academic prowess. 'I found this.'

'What's that, dear?' Her mother flicked the switch on the kettle and threw a couple of tea bags into the teapot.

'It's from the credit card company,' Ellie replied. 'It says that you owe them a load of money and –'

'Elinor! Since when has it been appropriate for you to read my private correspondence?'

Ellie tried to bite her tongue but it didn't work. 'Since you started filing it in the kitchen cutlery drawer,' she retorted. 'Mum, this is important.'

Her mother frowned. 'Give it to me,' she demanded, snatching the letter and scanning her eyes across it. 'Oh, I've dealt with that.' She tossed the letter on to the table. Ellie sighed with relief.

'Thank goodness,' she murmured. 'So, you paid it?'

'Well, of course I didn't pay it,' she laughed. 'Your father did. You know he looks after all that sort of stuff.'

Ellie took a deep breath. 'And he's really cleared it? All of it?'

'Of course, darling,' her mother assured her, but Ellie didn't feel so reassured.

❧ SECRET NUMBER 6 ❧

There's nothing like a bit of competition to make you want something (or someone) more than you probably should.

ST ETHELREDA'S SCHOOL had stood high on the cliffs overlooking the English Channel for nearly three hundred years, its red brick façade and octagonal bell tower visible for miles along the coast. Surrounded by rolling sports fields, all-weather tennis courts and two lacrosse pitches, the exterior still bore the air of the stately home it had once been – although Mrs Eveline Passmore, the headmistress (a woman of large buttocks and little humour, whose upper lip had never seen the effects of depilatory cream) was apt to comment that the behaviour of some her girls must cause the ghosts of past lords of the manor to turn in their graves.

All three Dashwood sisters loved St Ethelreda's, although for totally different reasons. For Ellie, it was the vast library, with its floor to ceiling shelves, oak-panelled recesses and huge bay windows, a place where she could lose herself in books without anyone interrupting; for Georgie, it was the sports hall, the swimming pool, the playing fields – anything, in fact, that gave her a break from studying by being outdoors, smelling the sea air; for Abby, the best thing about St Ethelreda's, apart from the purpose-built theatre and Dramatic Arts Centre, was its proximity to Bishop Radford College; she had chosen CAD as one of her GCSE options for the simple reason that the computer room windows overlooked the college playing fields where the neighbouring boys' school practised rugby.

Sadly, drooling and swooning had not, Abby reflected the following Friday, featured very highly in her week. For one thing, it hadn't stop raining for the last three days and all outdoor sports had been cancelled. For another, Melissa had arrived at school on Monday morning, arm in arm with two of her snooty mates, and made a beeline for Abby.

'Abigail! Out! Now!' Melissa had jeered in a voice which, had Abby not felt so totally humiliated, she would have had to admit was an exact replica of her mother's strident tones in the nightclub.

'Like Fergus said, little girls shouldn't play big girls' games,' Melissa added, as the bell rang for registration.

'Fergus said that?' The words were out before Abby could stop herself.

'Along with other things,' Melissa reported. 'Oh, and just one other thing. Fergus and me – we're an item. So just back off, baby face.'

While Abby had howled her eyes out, Phoebe had reasoned that she should be looking on the bright side.

'I mean, look at it this way,' Phoebe had pleaded, stuffing paper tissues into Abby's hand. 'If Melissa didn't see you as a threat, she wouldn't have bothered warning you to back off. Stands to reason – Fergus fancies you and Melissa's dead worried.'

Abby had clung on to that hope all week, even on Tuesday when Melissa flashed a friendship bracelet under her nose ('At least it's not a ring,' Phoebe pointed out), and Wednesday when she saw Fergus dropping Melissa off at the school gates in his MG Midget ('Not just Melissa,' Phoebe reminded her. 'Chrissie and Justine as well'). She bombarded Ellie, who was in Melissa's class, with questions about what she was saying, how she was looking, whether Fergus rang her on her mobile in the lunch hour, but as usual Ellie was useless.

On Thursday, Melissa was not at school. Abby's mood swung from joyful anticipation of dire tragedy ('Maybe she's got some terrible illness and will be housebound for weeks!') to sheer dread ('Perhaps she and Fergus have eloped'). When Abby ate, she felt sick; when she slept, she dreamed of Fergus jeering at her, one arm round Melissa; she couldn't concentrate in class and already had a detention for failing to hand in homework on time.

Then, in the school-dining hall, just at the very moment Abby pushed her plate of vegetable lasagne towards Phoebe, Ellie came over to their table.

'Why are you looking so miserable?' Ellie asked, slinging her purple and gold blazer over her shoulder and grinning at her sister. 'The sun's out, the afternoon football game is on . . .'

'It's pretty bloody obvious why I'm miserable,' Abby retorted. 'Not that you'd understand, since the only thing to turn you on is some boring old Day Car book.'

'Descartes,' Ellie corrected her, making a big show of inspecting her fingernails. 'I just thought that you'd be pretty chuffed – you know, with all that's happened with Melissa and – '

'What? What's happened?' Abby jumped to her feet. 'Tell me.'

'I don't know all the details, of course . . .'

'Never mind details, just talk! Talk!' Abby demanded.

'Melissa was crying in French, and I asked why, and she said – well, I don't remember exactly what she said, but it was something like – '

'Get on with it, Ellie!'

'Well, Melissa told me to get lost, and according to Verity, Fergus dumped her last night. Something about her being self-centred and always wanting her own way.'

'Yes! Yes!' Abby punched the air in delight. 'Did she say anything else?'

'No – oh, just that apparently Fergus is rugby mad, and the rumour is that Melissa refuses to do the girlfriend on the touchline bit because she hates getting cold.'

'That's it! Oh my God, that's it!' Abby flung her arms round her sister's neck and hugged her. 'Ellie, you a star! You've just given me my life back.'

'Abby, you can't do this,' Phoebe urged her at the end of the afternoon as they headed for the locker room to change out of their sports kit. 'You've got detention, remember?'

'I know, and I'll do the detention,' Abby assured her.

'All you have to do is buy some time for me.'

'Why me?'

'Because you're my friend, because you love me, and because this is one of those crucial, life changing moments when my whole destiny hangs in the balance.'

'OK, OK, I get the message,' Phoebe said with a sigh, opening her locker and stuffing her lacrosse cleats inside. 'What do I have to do?'

'You just go and tell Mrs Gourlay that I've gone to the nurse's office. Say I've got period pains.'

'You used that one last week and the week before,' Phoebe reminded her. 'There's only so many periods you can have in one month.'

'Fine, say I look really pale and faint, and you're worried that I've got mental burnout, OK?'

'Like she's really going to swallow that one,' teased Phoebe, slamming the locker door shut. 'And what if she comes looking for you? It's not worth the risk.'

'Of course it's worth the risk,' Abby told her, glancing at her watch. 'Fergus has got rugby training, right?'

'So?'

'So all I have to do is be there, look enthusiastic, clap when he gets a goal . . .'

'They don't *get goals*,' Phoebe said, laughing. 'They *score a try*.'

'Whatever,' snapped Abby. 'I'll stay just long enough for him to see that I'm the sort of girlfriend he needs and then I'll scoot back to the detention room, apologise, clutch my stomach pitifully and do detention. Simple!'

Abby grabbed her blazer, threw it round her shoulders

and fumbled in the pocket for her lip gloss. 'How do I look? Is my hair OK? Should I put eyeliner on?'

Phoebe gave her a friendly shove. 'Just go,' she ordered. 'Before I change my mind.'

Abby grinned, and pushed her way through the clusters of girls thronging around the students' exit. She ran across the quadrangle towards the playing fields, her heart pounding in anticipation of seeing Fergus. But as she reached school driveway, she saw something that almost sent her into immediate cardiac arrest.

Her mother's silver BMW was swinging through the school gates and screeching to a halt outside the main entrance, sending showers of gravel in all directions.

'I don't believe this,' Abby swore under her breath. What on earth was her mother doing here? Ellie couldn't be in trouble and Georgie –

Of course – Georgie. She was going off with Tom and his mum that evening, down to Dorset for the Zorbing day tomorrow. They were going to spend the night at Tom's grandmother's and Mum had arranged to fetch her and drop her over at Tom's after school.

The coast was clear. Over the fence she could see the Bishop Radford rugby squad doing their warm-up exercises at the far side of the games field. Any minute now, they'd run round the perimeter of the field to warm up, and she'd be there, and Fergus would see the look of enthusiasm and devotion on her face.

As Abby tucked her trousers into her socks so as not to catch them on the fence, she knew that as soon as Fergus saw her, he would know that she was the one.

* * *

'Mum, couldn't you have waited in the car park like every other parent?' Georgie charged up to her mother, who was sitting in one of the high-backed oak chairs outside the headmistress's study. 'It's dead embarrassing when you hover around like I'm some eight-year-old kid.'

She stopped dead as Julia turned to face her. Her mum looked as if she had seen a ghost, and her hand, clutching a sheaf of papers, was shaking.

'Georgie, go and get in the car,' she told her. 'I have to see Mrs Passmore.'

'Why?' Georgie gasped. 'You haven't seen my report card yet and if it's about that acid burn on the lab floor, I can explain.'

A faint smile crossed her mum's face and faded as fast as it had come. 'It's not about you,' she said, sighing. 'It's just business.'

'What business?' Georgie asked.

'It's got nothing to do with you,' her mother snapped. 'I just intend to tell that woman precisely what I think – ' But Julia's tirade was interrupted when the office door swung open and Mrs Passmore was on the other side. 'Oh, Mrs Passmore! There you are.'

Mrs Dashwood leaped to her feet and the head-mistress, clad from head to foot in black velveteen and looking a tad less friendly than the Ice Queen, boomed, 'Come in, come in. So glad you finally saw fit to drop by.'

The door closed firmly behind them. Georgie looked quickly over her shoulder and then edged towards the door, straining to make sense of the low murmurs inside.

'. . . a silly mistake?'

'. . . hardly, there has been no cheque for nearly five months . . .'

'. . . perhaps lost in the system . . . ?'

'. . . my staff never lose anything . . . Mr Dashwood is not answering calls . . .'

'. . . running multinational conglomerates takes time, Mrs Passmore . . .'

Georgie was just beginning to make a bit of sense of the conversation when a hand landed on her shoulder. Georgie wheeled round, half-hearted excuses already forming in her head.

'Oh, it's you!' She sighed with relief, as Ellie pulled her away from the door. 'Mum's in there with Mrs P. I was trying to listen till you came along.'

'What have you done this time?' Ellie asked with a grin. 'Not skateboarding in the staff car park again, surely?'

'No,' she retorted. 'And the scratch on Mrs P's car wasn't even visible to the naked eye. Anyway, they're not talking about me – for once.'

Ellie frowned. 'So what's going on?'

'Couldn't hear much – something about cheques. I hope they hurry up, though. I'm supposed to be leave for Dorset any minute. Hang on, I think they're coming. Scoot!'

They flew along the corridor and were halfway down the stairs to the students' exit by the time the study door opened.

'I will see that this is sorted by Monday, Mrs Passmore,' Georgie heard her mother trill. 'And please, in future, just remember that my ex-husband is a force to be reckoned with in the City.'

'Go, girl!' Georgie whispered. 'It's time someone put that old cow in her place.'

Ellie simply sighed and said nothing.

'It's so cool being me, can't you see being me . . .'

'Oh Abby,' Ellie said as her sister flew into the kitchen and perched on one of the huge milk churns that served as stools.

'. . . is the funkiest way to be-ee-ee. He saw me!'

'Who saw you?' Ellie said, ripping the top off a pot of yogurt.

'Fergus. He looked at me twice in the first five minutes of rugby practice, and I swear that when they all got into that huddle thing . . .'

'I assume you mean a scrum?'

'Yeah, that – well he kind of burst out of it, and stared at me straight in the face, kind of with yearning, you know? I think I've cracked it!'

'Cracked what?' Her mother burst into the room. 'Don't tell me you've broken another lacrosse stick. You really are . . .'

'No, Mum – I was talking about my maths homework.'

She's a quick thinker, I'll give her that, thought Ellie, winking at Abby.

'Well, as you've cracked it,' Julia murmured sweetly, taking a spoon of yogurt from Ellie's carton, 'shouldn't you go and write it all down? Before you forget how to do it?'

'Sure!' Abby was clearly in a very good mood. *'It's so cool being me, can't you see . . .'*

She danced out of the kitchen, blowing kisses with both hands, movie star style, as she kicked the door shut behind her.

As Abby hopped up the stairs, the phone in the hall shrilled.

'That might be your father,' Julia gasped. 'I left a message on his answering machine. Stir the sauce, Ellie.'

Her mother dashed into the hall and grabbed the phone, and the image of Pandora's nephew Blake flashed in Ellie's mind. How could someone so interesting – never mind handsome – be related to that twit Pandora? Must be by marriage, Ellie decided.

'Hello? Oh, Georgie, it's you. No darling, no of course I'm not disappointed, I'm thrilled – are you safely there? Lovely!'

'Now do be careful . . .' Ellie mouthed to their cat Manderley who was eyeing the half empty yogurt pot hopefully. 'Make sure . . .'

'Now do be careful,' her mother's voice resounded from the hall. 'Make sure you follow all the safety instructions and if you change your mind . . . no, well I know you won't but if you do . . .'

Ellie put the pot on the floor and Manderley stuck a pink tongue gratefully into its depths. From upstairs came the thud-thud of Agro Rampant's latest hit, punctuated with Abby's slightly discordant singing.

'Georgie's arrived in Dorset,' her mother said, coming back into the room and closing the door. 'I'm not happy about this Zorbing, you know.'

'She'll be fine, Mum,' Ellie assured her. 'At least she's not bungee jumping.'

'Of course, it's all down to the divorce, you know,' Julia muttered through gritted teeth. 'She's going off the rails – kids from broken homes do that, it's a proven statistic.'

'Mum! Georgie is not going off the rails, she's been a daredevil all her life. You can hardly blame Dad – I mean, I know you're worried about the school fees.'

'I am not worried,' her mother declared. 'I just want your father to give that opinionated Mrs Passmore a piece of his mind! Trying to say he hasn't paid the fees. As if.'

'Yes, but what if she's right?'

'Don't be ridiculous, Ellie,' her mother retorted. 'You know full well your father's primary concern is for you three girls. He'd use his last penny to see you right.'

'I know, Mum,' Ellie nodded.

'Anyway,' Julia continued, grabbing her waxed jacket, 'I'm going down the garden to pick some mint. Pass me the torch, will you? Does your sister have to have that racket blaring quite so loudly?' Julia flicked on the torch and stomped out of the back door, muttering under her breath.

The door had hardly slammed behind her, when the telephone in the hallway shrilled again.

'Mum . . .' Ellie began and then stopped. No point in calling her mother until she knew it was Dad, and besides, Ellie did hope to have a word with him. She ran to the hall and grabbed the phone.

'Hello? Ellie Dashwood speaking – who? Blake!' For some inexplicable reason, her heart lurched. 'Sorry I can't hear . . . hang on.'

She covered the mouthpiece and yelled up the stairs. 'Abby, turn it down – I'm on the phone!'

Realising that it was pointless to try to make herself heard over the din, she grabbed the handset and darted through to the den. Sticking a finger in her left ear, she tried again.

'Sorry, I'm back. Total chaos over here – my sister . . .' She knew she was babbling but somehow her tongue appeared to have taken on a life of its own. 'Anyway, how's things your end? How's the painting . . .'

But Blake interrupted her before she could go on. 'Ellie,' he said quietly, 'Are you sitting down?'

That was the last thing she'd hear before her life changed for ever.

She'd read in books about people's blood running cold but she had always thought it was just poetic licence. Perching on the arm of the old armchair that had been her father's favourite, she knew it actually happened.

'When? Where? But . . . Oh God. You mean . . . Yes, at once. OK. Bye.'

She let the phone fall from her hand, her heart racing and nausea rising in her throat. Her hands were shaking and when she stood up, her legs felt as if they were about to buckle underneath her.

Keep calm, she told herself firmly, taking a deep breath. Tell Mum. Get Abby. You've got to keep calm. It'll be OK – it's going to be fine.

She repeated the words, mantra like, as she ran down the hall, through the kitchen and out the back door into the garden.

'Mum!' she yelled. 'Mum, come here!'

Through the dusk, she could make out the pinpoint of light as her mother emerged from the herb garden, waving the torch. Ellie ran across the lawn towards her.

'It's Dad . . .' Ellie began.

'About time too,' Julia said. 'Thank heaven for that – I'll just take my boots off and – '

'No, Mum,' Ellie cried, grabbing her arm. 'Dad's not on the phone. He's in the hospital. He's had a heart attack.'

Even in the dark, Ellie could see the colour drain from her mother's face.

'Mum, Blake rang. The hospital asked him to. They say we've got to go. Now. They say' – her voice shook and she could feel the bile rising in her throat – 'they say it's critical. Mum, I think Dad's dying.'

❧ SECRET NUMBER 7 ❧

Nothing hurts more than a heart broken without warning.

'I'M SCARED.' Abby closed her eyes and tried to breathe {69}
deeply as her mother manoeuvered the car through the
barriers of the Chelsea and Westminster Hospital car
park.

'It'll be OK, though, won't it?' she said for the fifth
time in as many minutes. 'I mean, they can do heaps for
heart problems these days, can't they? Pacemakers and
bypass surgery and stuff.'

'Of course they can,' her mother replied confidently,
ramming the brakes and switching off the engine.

The knots in Abby's stomach tightened and the palms
of her hands felt cold and sweaty at the same time. She
hated hospitals at the best of times. Everything about
them scared her: the awful smell of disinfectant mixed
with unspeakable secretions, the sight of people lying on
trolleys groaning in pain, and the way those wretched
fluorescent lights made even the healthiest visitor look
like the walking dead. Once, when Georgie had taken a
tumble –

'Georgie!' Abby gasped. 'We haven't told Georgie.'

'Until we know more, there's no point,' her mother reasoned. 'She'd be asleep now anyway, and she's got this treat tomorrow. Ellie and I agreed she can come up and see Dad on Sunday.'

A familiar stab of jealousy pierced through Abby's anxiety. 'Oh Ellie and you agreed, did you? Well I don't agree. What if Sunday's too late – what if Dad's . . .' She stopped. What was she saying? Dad would be fine. He *had* to be fine. 'I didn't mean – it's just that . . .'

Ellie reached out and touched her hand. 'It's OK,' she whispered. 'We'll call Georgie in the morning.'

Abby clutched Ellie's hand. Her sister could be an awful pain and a goody-goody, but she was brilliant in a crisis.

'You two had better get going.' Julia released her seat belt and switched on the interior light.

'But Mum, you're coming too, surely?' Abby gasped.

'I can't come.' Her mother's voice was calm but firm. 'Pandora . . .'

'To hell with Pandora!' Abby burst out. 'This isn't about Pandora – it's about Dad. We're his family, not that slag.'

'She's his wife, Abby – she's the one he chose to be with.'

Abby saw her mother's lip tremble as she turned away. 'Oh Mum, don't feel like that,' she pleaded. 'He's ill, he'll be scared, he'll want you, I know he will.'

'You have to be there, Mum,' Ellie pleaded. 'For all our sakes.'

To the girls' relief, Julia nodded slowly, sighed and opened the car door.

'I'll come as far as the ward,' she said, putting an arm round both of them for a quick hug. 'Tell you what, we'll find a hotel and then you'll be able to visit him again in the morning. What do you say to that?'

Abby's heart lifted slightly. 'The Gore? Can we stay there? That is such a cool place!'

She caught her sister's eye and guilt washed over her. 'Sorry,' she whispered. 'Sorry.'

None of them spoke as they walked down the corridor, the clatter of their heels breaking the late evening silence.

'Please, God, let him be OK,' Ellie prayed quietly, fingering the cross and chain around her neck, the one her Dad had given her when she was confirmed. 'I'll do anything as long as you make Dad well. Please. Please.'

{71}

'This is it.' Her mum pointed to double doors marked CCU. She read, *Press green button for admittance*. Ellie pressed.

'Yes?' A voice echoed through the speaker unit at the side of the door.

'We've come to see our father, Max Dashwood,' Ellie stammered, moving closer to the speaker.

'Ah. Right. Just a minute.'

They waited, the silence broken only by the sound of Abby gnawing at her fingernails. The door opened and the staff nurse smiled at them.

'Come in,' she said. 'I'm Roxanne – now, if you'd just like to wait in here . . .'

She pointed to a door marked 'Relatives' Room'. 'We'd really like to see our Dad,' Ellie said. 'We've driven all the way from Sussex.'

'I'll only keep you a moment,' Roxanne said, opening the door and ushering them in. 'Can I get you a tea? Coffee? No?' She turned to go, just as a tall, broad-shouldered guy in a white coat stepped quietly into the room.

'I'm Dr Nisbet and I'm looking after Max.' His voice was soft, with a pronounced Scottish lilt.

'How is he?' Ellie demanded.

'You're his daughters?' the doctor queried, looking from Ellie to Abby and back again.

Ellie nodded.

'And you are . . . ?' He turned to Julia.

'She's his wife,' Abby said. 'Come on . . .'

'I'm his ex-wife. I'm here because the girls need me.'

Ellie's heart went out to her mum. She knew that Julia was here because there was nowhere else on earth she would be; she had never stopped loving Max, and Ellie could see it on her brave face more now than even the days after he'd left when she'd cried and sputtered on about how they'd first met.

'Of course, if Pandora – if the new Mrs Dashwood doesn't want – ' Julia began edging towards the door.

'Mrs Dashwood is taking a bit of time out – having a meal downstairs in the cafeteria,' the doctor said.

'Cow! How could she eat at a time like this?' Abby protested.

The doctor raised his left eyebrow a fraction of a millimetre. 'I do have to warn you that your father is a very sick man,' he went on gently. 'Very sick indeed. You'll see a lot of wires, and machines and we have had to catheterise him, so – '

'It's OK,' Ellie burst in. 'We understand.' She didn't want explanations. She wanted to see her dad.

Dr Nisbet nodded and stood back to let them through the door. Ellie snatched Abby's hand and held on to it tightly, the way she used to when they rode roller coasters.

'In here,' he said, gesturing with his arm.

Ellie took a deep breath and they followed him into the room, past a couple of old men wheezing on day beds, and over to a curtained cubicle. The doctor pulled back the curtains, and nothing, not all the words he had said, not all the episodes of *Medic Man* or *Hospital Alert*, could have prepared them for what they saw.

Their father lay prone on the bed, his face grey, his lips tinged with blue. He looked somehow much smaller without his clothes. The skin of his neck lay in folds against the pristine white of the hospital gown, his mouth was half open, a thin tube resting between his lips. Behind his head, a monitor bleeped.

{73}

'Oh, Max, my love . . .' Julia burst.

The lump in Ellie's throat doubled as her mother moved from behind them to the bedside and tenderly took one of Max's limp hands. Beside her, Abby was stifling sobs.

'He will be OK, won't he?' Ellie murmured as the doctor moved to one side.

'We will do everything in our power,' the doctor reassured her. Raising his voice, he moved towards Max. 'Not giving up yet, are we, old chap?' he said, smiling at Ellie. 'He's not conscious, but he can probably hear everything at some level. Just chat to him normally. And sound positive, OK?'

Ellie nodded, swallowing hard.

'Now you stay with him and I'll just send a nurse along to check his obs. Observation, blood pressure . . .'

'I know.' Ellie smiled. 'I watch *The Surgeons.*' She squeezed Abby's hand. 'Come on, Abby, you heard what the doctor said. We've got to talk to Dad, be normal.'

'Hi, Dad,' Abby muttered. 'Are you OK? Well, no obviously you're not, but . . .' She faltered. 'I can't do this. I'm going to be sick.' She clamped a hand to her mouth and flew out of the room.

Julia went to follow Abby but first she leaned over Max, and brushed her lips briefly against his forehead.

Ellie noticed that tiny beads of perspiration dotted his brow like dew on grass in the early morning. Was that right? Was that meant to happen?

'Mum, is he . . . ?'

'I'll be back in a minute, Ellie,' Julia said, closing the door behind her. 'Just keep talking to him.'

Ellie pulled a canvas chair up to the side of the bed and gingerly touched her dad's hand. 'Hi, Dad, it's Ellie,' she began. 'Georgie's gone Zorbing with Tom, otherwise she'd be here too. She'll come on Sunday though, tell you all about it.' She faltered. She'd never talked to an inert body before. 'She's dead excited about it – not that I'd want to roll down some vertical hill in a big plastic ball, but you know Georgie – never happy unless she's risking life and limb on some death-defying stunt!' Was that a movement? Did his eyelids flicker? 'Dad?'

Her eyes strayed to the monitor above the bed, the wavy lines going up and down, up and down, up and –

Then they stopped. A straight line on the screen. No wavy bits. An alarm blared.

'No! Help, someone, help!'

She heard a voice screaming. Footsteps running.

Then the doctor's strident tones, 'He's in VF! Call the CRASH team!'

'Dad, Dad! No, Dad!' someone was shouting. They shouldn't shout, Ellie thought. Not in a hospital.

An arm round her shoulder, a voice in her ear. 'Best you wait outside. . . Doing all we can . . .'

And then the doctor's voice, urgent and demanding: 'Quickly, everyone, we're losing him.'

Ellie sat motionless, staring at the wall in front of her. A picture of a pond with ducks and a windmill; a few notices about bring and buy sales in aid of the nurses' home refurbishment and the kidney dialysis unit; a phone number for bereavement counselling . . . She snapped her eyes away as the door opened.

{75}

'Mum?' She jumped to her feet and then sank back in the chair. 'Oh, it's you, Pandora.'

Pandora burst into the room, threw her bag on to the nearest chair and began pacing the room. 'You're here? How come . . .? I was going to phone later but . . .'

'Blake phoned,' Ellie mumbled. 'He said . . .' Before she could finish, Pandora gabbled on.

'God, this place is so incompetent!' She began drumming her long, French-manicured fingernails on the window ledge. 'Of course, I'm having Max moved – we'll go private.'

'Pandora, have they told you what's happening?' Ellie burst in, her voice wavering.

'What's happening is that some trumped up nurse – probably not even fully qualified for all I know – tells me

I can't go in and see him because, well, I don't know why! Why they can't talk in plain English and – ' She stopped in mid flow as the door opened and Ellie's mum burst in, closely followed by a pale-faced Abby, clutching a plastic tumbler of water.

'What's going on?' Julia demanded before seeing Pandora. 'They wouldn't let us back in – oh, Pandora. How are you?'

'How do you bloody think I am?' Pandora stormed. 'I haven't had any sleep, the cafeteria serves a load of junk food – do you know, they didn't even have camomile tea and they call themselves a hospital. I've had to send Blake home for some proper food and . . .'

'I hardly think that matters right now,' Julia retorted, looking more baffled than angry.

'No, you're right, of course.' Pandora looked abashed. 'I'm so worried, I can't think straight. Sorry.'

'So what happened exactly?' Julia asked gently.

'He just collapsed. I mean, it all happened so fast. We were out jogging and he sort of keeled over and – '

'Jogging? And that was your idea, I suppose?' Abby stormed, chucking the plastic cup into the rubbish bin. 'You stupid – '

'Abby, enough!' Julia snapped, as Roxanne, the staff nurse, came into the room.

Julia turned to face her. 'Can you throw some light on just what is going on?'

The nurse touched her arm gently. 'The thing is,' she began, 'your husband's had . . .'

'He is *my* husband, not hers!' Pandora snapped. 'Can't you even get that right?'

'Sorry, I wasn't told.' Roxanne let her gaze go round to each of them. 'The thing is, Mr Dashwood's had a bit of a setback. The doctor will come by in a minute to talk to you.'

'What do you mean, *setback*?' Julia said with a gasp, but the nurse had already scuttled off. Ellie thought how odd it was that nurses' shoes always squeaked; you wouldn't think that would be allowed in a place like a hospital, would you? So irritating. Then again, she was beginning to realise that the voice screaming earlier had been her own.

'Ellie, what happened?' Her mother shook her arm.

Ellie broke her gaze from the wall. 'I was just sitting there, trying to talk normally and then the machine just stopped. Those wavy lines, they all went straight.'

'You don't mean . . . ?' Julia grabbed the back of the chair to support herself just as the door opened yet again and Dr Nisbet stepped into the room.

And before he spoke, Ellie knew. Before he had said a word, her blood was turning to ice in her veins.

'. . . did all we could . . . heart simply gave out . . . so very sorry.' The doctor's words washed over her, seeming to come from a long way away.

'You mean – you don't mean . . . he's dead?' Her mum's words ended in a sob.

'Dead? Max? He can't be . . .' Pandora clamped her hand to her mouth and turned away. 'Maxi – no, no, no.'

'I'm afraid he died despite all our efforts,' the doctor said. 'His heart really was in a very bad way.'

'NOOOOO!' Abby let out an ear-piercing wail, flew across the room and began beating her fists against Pandora's shaking shoulders. 'You killed him! You killed my dad! I hate you, I hate – '

Pandora staggered, a look of genuine fear on her face. 'It wasn't my fault – I didn't do anything . . .'

Ellie leaped to her feet and in an instant had grabbed Abby by the arms and pulled her away. 'Abby, stop it,' she shouted. 'It's not Pandora's fault . . .'

It's mine, she thought. Mine for telling him about Georgie rolling down a hill in a Zorb. Ellie was suddenly sure the shock had tipped him over the edge.

'It is!' Abby wailed, tossing her head from side to side and fighting Ellie off with her elbows. 'She made him go jogging! If she hadn't made him, he'd be alive now and . . .' Abby's knees crumpled and she sagged to the floor, rocking backwards and forwards, tears streaming down her face.

Julia put her arms round Abby and helped her to a chair. For one awful, fleeting moment, Ellie wanted to shake her sister. As usual, she was taking centre stage – didn't she realise that they were all in this? That they all loved him? Pandora standing there, running her fingers endlessly through her hair, Mum, hands shaking, trying so hard to be strong, and Ellie herself, feeling numb, dead inside, as if she was playing a part in some far-fetched, third-rate TV drama with the sort of plot that everyone knows just can't be real.

'He said he enjoyed the jogging.' Pandora's voice was flat as she turned to face Ellie. 'He said that he wanted to get fit so that we'd have years and years together to . . .' Her voice broke and her shoulders heaved.

Julia went over and touched her hand. 'I'm sure it was nothing to do with jogging,' she said gently. 'You shouldn't blame yourself . . .'

'I don't, actually!' Pandora spun around and faced

Julia, her moment of weakness clearly over. 'I blame you. All those years when you stuffed him full of red meat and cheese and . . .'

'It's not Mum's fault,' Abby screeched. 'You killed his spirit – you made him give up everything he ever loved – you murdered him!'

'How dare you!' Pandora countered, her face dark red. 'He was happier in the one year we were together than he'd ever been with . . .'

'Now, now this isn't going to help any of you, is it?' Dr Nesbit intervened. 'Mr Dashwood was a grown man – what he ate, and how he lived was up to him. His heart was diseased, his arteries all furred up. None of you is to blame.'

'I want to see him.' Ellie was surprised at the strength of her own voice.

'Darling, no, I don't think that's a good idea,' Julia began.

'I want to see him.' She repeated the words slowly and firmly and turned to the doctor. 'Can I do that?'

'Of course,' he said. 'I'll just make sure he's ready.' He slipped out of the room, closing the door quietly behind him.

'He makes it sound like Dad's gone upstairs to change for a dinner party,' Abby said and burst out laughing. The laughter got louder, more shrill, more uncontrolled until she was wailing and hitting her head with her bunched up fists, her whole body shaking.

And suddenly, Ellie couldn't take any more. She walked out of the room. But even then, standing in the corridor, with no one watching, she couldn't cry.

'Miss Dashwood.' Dr Nesbit tapped her shoulder. 'You can come in now.'

Ellie entered, but inside it wasn't Dad. Just a look-alike body, the closed eyelids pale and waxy, the long fingers splayed still and rigid against the white sheet. Dad – the vibrant, bouncy, fun-loving Dad she had known her whole life was gone.

'I love you, Dad,' she whispered. 'I love you so much.' And still the tears wouldn't come.

When she finally left the room, after holding the hand that she couldn't imagine had ever been her dad's, she bumped directly into Blake.

'I'm so sorry. Really. I just don't know what to say,' Blake said, clutching a Marks and Spencer carrier bag. He touched Ellie's arm as she stood, eyes half closed, in the hospital corridor.

'Thanks,' she said, thinking as she said it how utterly stupid the word sounded.

'Are you OK? I mean, can I do anything?'

Ellie shook her head. 'I guess you need to see to Pandora,' she whispered. Get her off our backs, she thought silently. Take her away.

'I'll get her home,' Blake assured her. 'She's the last thing you need to cope with right now.'

As he disappeared towards the Relatives' Room, it occurred to Ellie that he was the first guy she'd met besides her dad who didn't need to have things spelled out in words of one syllable.

Abby's head throbbed. Her face ached. Her eyeballs were burning in their sockets, and her guts were heaving. Dead. Dead. Dad is dead.

Abby lay in the hotel bed as the shriek of ambulances

from the nearby hospital rang through the room, and whispered the words under her breath. How could it be? Only last weekend, he'd been laughing and joking and spoiling them rotten at the shops.

'I love to give my girls a good time!' His words rang in her head.

'No, no, no!' She bolted upright in the bed, bunching her fists and rubbing them violently against her eyes. 'Dad, dad, dad . . .'

'Abby, it's OK! Abby, wake up, it's me, it's Ellie – you're dreaming . . .'

'I'm not dreaming . . . I just want him – I just want him back.'

Ellie held her sister tight, trying to make the comforting noises that their mother had raised them with.

'I hope Pandora drops dead,' Abby said, sobbing. 'Murderer!'

'I know,' Ellie said with a nod, tears beginning to trickle down her cheeks.

Abby looked at her sister, a little shocked at her tears. Ellie could read it on her face.

'He was my dad, too, you know,' Ellie said, the anger rising in her stomach and her voice at the same time. 'Just because you were his favourite, even though I worked my tail off – '

'Ellie, no, stop,' Abby said. 'It was never like that.'

'Well, it was to me,' Ellie said, stifling a sob.

'Come,' was all Abby said. She opened her arms and folded them around her sister. And then, for the first time in as long as she could remember, Ellie wept and wept as though her heart would break.

✖ SECRET NUMBER 8 ✖

There is nothing you should be gentler with than love.
Except possibly newborn kittens.

'OK, ZORBANAUTS! ARE YOU READY?' The SportsExtreme attendant grinned and gave Georgie and Tom a friendly shove into the Zorb.

For an instant, Georgie's stomach lurched as she asked herself just what she was doing inside a gigantic clear plastic inflatable ball poised at the top of a steep ramp on a windy Saturday morning.

'You OK? I mean, you can get out if you don't want to do it,' Tom began.

'Get out? Who do you think I am?' Georgie protested. Get a grip, she told herself firmly.

'OK, here we go now, folks!'

With a jolt, the huge ball launched itself off the ramp and began rolling down the steep down hill. One minute Georgie was staring at the grass, scattered with dandelions and the odd cowslip, the next she was staring up at the sky, the next spinning, seemingly out of control, Tom's grinning face flashing past hers.

'You OK?' Tom shouted above the vibration of the ball.

'Yeah!' she yelled back.

Just then the ball lurched over a ridge, picked up speed and hurtled at breakneck speed towards the bushes at the bottom of the hill. Georgie opened her mouth to speak but the words wouldn't come – a huge rush of air went spiralling down her throat.

And then as suddenly as it had started, the ball came to rest, Georgie hanging upside down, Tom lying next to her, laughing his head off.

'That was totally surreal!' Georgie cried, as the cone-like hole at the side of the ball was opened by a guy wearing a sweatshirt that said *Adrenalin Junkies Inc*. 'Thank you so much, Tom.'

Tom grinned and gestured to the attendant. 'This is the guy you have to thank,' he told her. 'Josh, meet Georgie.'

'Glad to meet you, Georgie. Of course, that was pretty tame really.' He winked at Tom. 'But I guess that was about as much as you could take, being a girl and all.'

'What?' Georgie exploded, all thoughts of growing up shoved to one side. 'I'll have you know I went abseiling down the Seven Sisters cliffs, I've done paragliding and scuba diving and I would have gone potholing only my mother . . .'

'Go on, Josh,' urged Tom, stifling a giggle. 'Tell her before she bursts a blood vessel.' He glanced up the hill, where his mother was running toward them, her hand clutching her chest.

'Quickly! Before my mother gets here!'

Josh laughed. 'How would you like to HydroZorb?' he asked. 'Same as before only we fill the ball with a couple of buckets of water. It's ace – bit like a cross between a roller coaster and a waterfall.'

'Cool!' Georgie burst out. 'But actually, I don't think . . . I mean, how much does it cost?' No way was she going to land Tom's mum with paying out loads of money.

'Free,' Josh laughed. 'We want to take some pictures for our new brochure and the boss thought you two guys would give just the right image.'

'Image of what?' Tom's mother panted up to them. 'Sheer unmitigated stupidity? Total recklessness? Never, ever put me through something like that again!' she gasped.

'It was ace, Mrs Eastment,' Georgie assured her. 'You should try it.'

'I would rather face a den of starving lions,' Tom's mother assured her dryly. 'Here's your camera, Georgie. I took a few great shots, although I don't think you'd better show them to your poor mother. She'd have heart failure.'

'I'm going to e-mail them to Dad,' she said. 'He wants me to keep him updated on everything I do.'

'Brave man,' murmured Tom's mum dryly. 'Now then, how about lunch? There's a nice pizza place just a few miles down the road.'

'We're doing it again,' Tom interjected firmly. 'With water this time.'

Mrs Eastment closed her eyes and groaned. 'Tom, no, my nerves won't stand it.'

'But you're not going to be the one doing it,' Tom protested. 'Come on, Mum, it's not like you to be a wimp. It's usually Georgie's mum who worries.'

Georgie saw the colour flood his face as he realised what he was saying.

'Precisely!' Mrs Eastment responded triumphantly. 'What would Mrs Dashwood say? I can't let her daughter . . .'

'I'll call her,' Georgie said. 'It'll be fine – trust me.'

She scooted a few metres up the hill, made a big show of punching numbers on her mobile, mouthed a few words, and then gave the thumbs up sign to Tom. She had learned something from her sister Abby over the years, that was for sure.

'She's cool about it,' she declared, crossing her fingers behind her back and grinning at Tom's mum. 'So let's go!'

Mrs Eastment sighed and said, 'Well, if you're sure your mother's comfortable with the idea?'

Georgie nodded furiously, trying to quell the rising guilt of her fake phone call.

'This is just the best day ever,' she declared. 'I'll never forget it!'

'I can't go in.' Abby stood on the threshold of Max's flat, tears streaming down her face. 'It'll just remind me of when we were here last week with Dad.'

'Darling, this isn't about us. It's about what Dad would have wanted. Now trust me.' Julia pressed the bell and almost at once the door was opened by a white faced Pandora who took one look at them and burst into tears.

'I can't cope with all this,' she sobbed, sinking into the nearest chair. 'My psyche is all over the place and my aura is fragmenting.'

'Really? Dear me, how painful,' murmured Julia, looking around the flat in obvious amazement. 'Now, can we help in some way? Phone someone?'

'My sister's coming down,' she sniffed. 'And Blake's here, of course. He's just gone out for some herbal tranquillisers.'

'That's good!' Abby could tell that her mother was highly relieved at not having to cope with Pandora for long.

'It's so unfair,' Pandora went on, 'that I should be robbed of him after such a short time . . .'

{86} 'Oh, and you don't think you were unfair to Mum, snatching Dad away from her and treating him like some tame puppy.'

'Enough, Abby,' Julia interrupted. 'This is not the time or the place.'

Pandora sniffed. 'I'm sorry,' she mumbled. 'He was your dad. I'm sorry. I know it's been hard for you all. It's just that I don't know where to begin. There's the funeral to be arranged . . .'

'That's up to us,' Julia said firmly.

'No,' Pandora retorted. 'He was my husband.'

'Indeed he was,' Julia smiled sweetly. 'But in his will he specified that he wanted his funeral at St Peters in Brighton, and his ashes to be scattered over the South Downs.'

'Oh. Well, he was about to make a new will – we were discussing it only a week ago,' Pandora stammered.

'Well, as he didn't, the old one stands, doesn't it?' Julia smiled. 'I'll phone the funeral directors tomorrow. Don't you worry about a thing.'

Abby saw that Ellie was as gobsmacked as she was at her mother's assertiveness. If only Dad could see her now, Abby was sure he'd have a change of heart about her.

Julia picked up her bag, and ushered the girls to the door. 'I'll be in touch about the arrangements,' she said. 'Oh, and do take care of your aura, won't you, my dear?'

They were almost back at Holly House when Julia's mobile phone rang from the depths of her handbag.

'Get that, Ellie – oh, no, leave it. I can't face talking to anyone yet.'

Ellie swallowed hard and slid her hand into her mother's bag, pulling out the phone. 'It's a text message,' she told her. 'From Georgie. Tom's mum will be dropping her off in ten minutes.'

{87}

Her mother bit her lip, and turned toward Ellie. 'When they get here . . . I mean, would you – could you tell her, Ellie? You're better at these things.'

'Mum, I can't,' Ellie protested. 'What could I say? Oh hi, Georgie, how was your weekend? Oh, and by the way, Dad died.'

'No, you're right. It's my job,' Julia said, sighing. 'I'm her mother, after all. And the poor mite's fatherless and . . .'

'You'll be fine at it,' Ellie assured her. 'Abby and I will disappear and then . . .'

'No!' Her mother gasped. 'You must be there – we've got to support one another through all this. There's so much to think about – choosing the coffin, the hymns . . .'

'You were dead cool, the way you dealt with Pandora, Mum,' Abby broke the silence that she'd maintained for almost the entire journey from London. 'About the arrangements and everything.'

Her mother sighed as she drove the car through the gates and up the drive towards the house. 'I was a bit hard, I suppose,' she admitted. 'She did love him after all. I'll make it up to her, though – let her choose the music or something.'

Abby frowned. 'So we can't stop her from coming, then?'

'Don't be ridiculous, Abby,' Ellie protested. 'She has every right to be there.'

'I didn't know murderers were free to roam the countryside at will,' Abby muttered.

Ellie reached into the back seat and squeezed her hand. As her mother manoeuvered the car toward the front door, she stared out of the window. Suddenly, everything she looked at reminded her of her father. The cracked bird bath that he had made when he started sculpting, the leaded-light window by the front door with 'Maximilian Dashwood, 1959' scratched on to it by the young, rebellious Max who had grown up here, the sonic mole traps that he'd insisted would expel wildlife at twenty paces, but never did.

Julia switched off the car engine, but none of them moved. It was as if they all knew that the moment they went inside the house, they would have to face the enormity of it all. It reminded Ellie of the days after Bridie died; none of them could face looking at her empty basket, scattered with her rubber toys, yet none of them had the heart to get rid of it. Facing the house was going to be like one giant Bridie basket.

The drone of a car engine broke their silence.

'Georgie. It's Georgie,' Ellie murmured, as Mrs Eastment's battered Volvo came up the drive. 'What do we do? How do we tell her?'

The car pulled up next to them, the door opened and Georgie leaped out, closely followed by Tom. Julia, Ellie and Abby stumbled out of the car as Georgie came running towards them.

'Mum, it was awesome! Honestly, you've never seen anything like it – there was this huge ball, and it went so fast and I've got some wicked photos to send to Dad and Tom and me are getting our pictures in a brochure and . . . Mum? Mum?'

Julia, tears streaming down her face, enveloped Georgie in a hug.

'Julia dear?' Margie Eastment pressed the lock button on her key chain until the car beeped and came anxiously towards Julia. 'Is something wrong? It wasn't that dangerous, I promise you.'

Ellie stepped forward and touched Georgie's shoulder. 'Georgie, listen. There's something we have to tell you. It's about Dad. He – ' She closed her eyes, as if not seeing Georgie's face might help.

'What about Dad?'

'He had a heart attack on Friday,' Ellie began.

Her mother squatted down and cupped Georgie's face in her hands. 'Georgie darling, Dad died early this morning. I'm so, so sorry.'

It was, thought Ellie, as if the entire universe was

{89}

holding its breath. Like the freeze frame when you zap the pause button to go and get more chocolate. Like those stills they sell you at Disney World, when a moment on a roller coaster is captured for ever, everyone's mouths open or eyes closed, hair flying wildly about.

Then, slowly, the picture moved on. Georgie's eyes widened, her mouth became a wide, round, gaping hole. Tom's mother clamped her hands to her mouth, Tom took two steps backwards, gripping his mum's arm.

And then Georgie screamed.

Georgie didn't know how long it had been since she had run away from the house, or how long she had been up here on the path to the old windmill. The sun was low in the sky, and she had a stitch in her side and her cheeks burned from the constant flow of salty tears. It was as if a dam had burst inside her and everything – tears, memories, guilt – was all spilling out on to the chalky path.

She had run and run for as long as her body would keep going, trying not to think about what her mum and Ellie had said. But it didn't work. Their words kept echoing through Georgie's mind.

'I was there, by the bed, when it happened,' Ellie had told her. 'We'd all been there – talking to him and holding his hand, so he knew he wasn't alone.'

That was the worst bit. They'd all been there and she hadn't. Even Pandora had been there.

'I hate you, I hate you, I hate you!' Georgie's shouts echoed across the cliffs, as she hammered her heels up and down on the scrubby grass, causing a flock of screeching gulls to fly into the air in alarm.

'Hate who?'

A shadow fell across her outstretched legs. Tom jumped off his bike and let it fall to the ground.

'Get away! Get lost!' The words came out as broken sobs. She couldn't let Tom see her like this; one of the main reasons he was her mate was because he said she wasn't a wet fart like most girls he knew. 'I said, leave me alone!'

She turned away, desperate to hide her tears from him. Tom didn't move an inch, which didn't really surprise her, because he never did anything unless he really wanted to – and that was another main reason that he was her mate.

'Want some gum?' he said, pulling a somewhat mangled strip from the pocket of his jeans. 'I bought chocolate as well, but I dropped it and now it's covered with grass.'

Georgie sniffed. 'Dad did that once with an ice lolly and Bridie ate it, stick and all.'

'I'm sorry,' Tom said. 'About your dad. Bloody bad luck.'

'Bad luck? It's not luck, you stupid moron,' she yelled. 'She did it. She killed him – that Pandora cow!'

'I doubt it.' Tom sounded totally unfazed. 'Come on, we're going home.' He bent to pick up his bike.

'What do you mean, you doubt it?' Georgie snapped, wiping her eyes with the back of her hand and staring at him in disbelief. 'And I'm not going anywhere.'

'I doubt that even Pandora would murder her husband in broad daylight on a jogging path in the middle of London,' he reasoned. 'And you are coming home, because your sister said that if I found you, she'd give me five pounds. I've found you and now I want paying.'

To her astonishment, Georgie found herself smiling. 'I'll come if you split it fifty-fifty with me,' she decided.

'Seventy-five, twenty-five,' Tom parried. 'I did the finding, after all.'

'Sixty-forty and that's my final offer,' she said, repeating their long-standing game. Suddenly she gasped and turned to Tom, her eyes filling with tears again. 'How could I do that? How could I be so awful? Dad's dead, and I'm playing dumb games with you?'

For a moment Tom didn't say a word. He kicked at a clod of earth lying on the path and then bit his thumbnail. 'I guess he'd be pleased, in a funny kind of way,' he mumbled after a moment, avoiding Georgie's eye. 'Remember what he used to say?'

'What?' Georgie frowned.

'He said that Ellie is his clever kid, Abby is the feisty one, but you – Georgie – are the tough nut that no one can crack.'

'I don't feel tough,' whispered Georgie. 'I feel small and tired and angry and . . .' She hesitated.

'And what?' Tom asked.

'Nothing,' she said.

'Go on,' he urged. 'You feel small, tired angry and what?'

'Hungry,' said Georgie with a sigh. 'Have you still got that chocolate?'

❧ SECRET NUMBER 9 ❧

Your heart is the one thing no one can take from you – at least not until you decide to give it away.

DASHWOOD. Suddenly in London, MAXIMILIAN FREDERICK, adored husband of Pandora and father of Elinor, Abigail and Georgina. Funeral service will be held at St Peter's Church, Brighton on April 7th at 12 noon followed by cremation at Downs Crematorium, Bear Road, Brighton. All enquiries to T. L. Marchant, Funeral Directors, Montpelier Road, Brighton.

'HOW DARE SHE! THE COW!'

Abby slammed *The Daily Telegraph* down on the kitchen table and stabbed at the death announcement with her finger.

'No way is she getting away with that,' she stormed.

Her mother looked up from the pile of mail in front of her. 'She already has,' she said with a sigh. 'Besides, what's wrong with it?'

'What's wrong with it?' Abby thundered. 'Adored husband of Pandora? And what about you?'

'I'm nothing now.'

'And then she just puts "*father of Elinor, Abigail and Georgina*", like we don't adore or love him at all. Well, I'm not having it!'

'Not having what?' Ellie ambled through the back door with an armful of daffodils, her skin still blotchy from a night of crying. 'Where do you want these, Mum?'

Julia motioned toward the table, weakly, and Ellie settled into a chair. All the days seemed to be merging into one for Ellie. In the daytime, she felt dead inside, like a robot programmed to do the tasks her mother couldn't face. At night, she dreamed. Always the same dream: Dad lying on that bed, white and still and then dissolving until there was nothing left but a tiny damp patch. She would wake to find the pillow wet with tears and she'd sob and sob until her head throbbed too much to sleep.

{94}

'Mr Diplock will be here any minute,' Julia said, breaking Ellie's trance.

'Why is he coming anyway?' Ellie asked. 'I know he's Dad's solicitor but surely he could wait until after the funeral?'

'I don't know,' Julia said. She shrugged. 'Said he had something important to discuss that wouldn't keep.'

'Ellie, read this!' Abby thrust the paper under her sister's nose, and Ellie scanned the announcement. 'Isn't that just the pits?'

Ellie glanced at the notice again and sighed. 'It's awful seeing it in black and white, I guess,' she murmured.

'Not that – what she's put.' She wheeled round to face her mother. 'You said she couldn't do all this stuff.'

'I said she couldn't alter the funeral arrangements,'

her mother corrected her. 'What else she does is up to her. She's his wife – widow – whatever.'

'Well, anyway, the wording on this is all wrong and I'm going to make sure . . .'

At that moment, the front door bell shrilled.

'Oh my goodness, he's here already!' Julia leaped to her feet and scooped up the pile of condolence cards in her arms. 'Abby, let him in. Ellie, do those flowers. Georgie – where's Georgie?'

'With Tom,' Ellie said. 'He's being brilliant – getting her to help him build a skateboard ramp to take her mind off things. Should I get her?'

'No, let her be.' Julia shook her head, slipped off her apron and ran her hands through her hair. 'I'll get rid of Mr Diplock as quickly as I can. There's so much to do and besides, Pandora can deal with all the legal stuff. Get off her bottom for once.'

Abby shot a glance at Ellie and gave her a quick thumbs up sign. It was always easier to cope with Mum when she was in a feisty mood. She just hoped it would last.

'Don't go, Elinor.' Mr Diplock, her father's long-standing solicitor, motioned for Ellie to stay in the room. 'I – er – I think it would be a good idea if the whole family were together to hear what I have to say,' he suggested. 'Just to make sure that you all understand the implications.'

'The implications of what?' Julia sounded distracted. 'I have quite a lot to get through before the funeral on Friday.'

'Exactly,' said the solicitor in a soothing tone. 'So perhaps we could call the other two girls? Make a start.'

As Ellie went in search of Abby and Georgie, it occurred to her that James Diplock looked as drawn and strained as any of them.

By the time she found Abby, who was scribbling away frantically in her diary (which looked, Ellie noted, a bit different than the journal Ellie had peeked in before), and Georgie who was half-heartedly watching Tom knock nails into a piece of wood, her mother and James Diplock had pulled chairs up to the mahogany dining table. There were sheaves of paper spread out its entire length.

'Right,' he began nervously after the girls had sat down. Abby and Ellie perched on the sagging sofa and Georgie, as usual, knelt on the floor. 'As you know, I've been Max's solicitor for some years now and for most of that time, he was happy to follow my directive.'

What does he mean – most of the time? Ellie thought.

'You've been wonderful,' Julia assured him. 'The divorce settlement that you drew up has been a godsend.'

'Yes, well,' James said, coughing. 'There was, however, one thing over which I failed totally to influence him.'

Ellie frowned. 'What is it?'

'A few months ago, business went badly for Max. He'd sunk hundreds of thousands into a couple of new ventures that went base over apex. Moreover, the stock market was plunging and his personal expenses were soaring. His new wife . . .'

'Is a total cow!' interjected Georgie.

'Georgina!' Julia snapped.

James hurried on. 'Anyway, he was getting into fairly

deep financial difficulties.' He took a deep breath. 'So he did something drastic – I begged him not to, but – '

'What did he do?' Ellie demanded. 'Can you get to the point, please?'

'Elinor, your manners,' her mother snapped. Clearly, thought Ellie, her mother was more taken up with the niceties of etiquette than with the drama unfolding in front of them.

'He put Holly House into his new wife's name,' James blurted out. 'He'd already borrowed a couple of hundred thousand by putting the London apartment up as security, and he must have known he'd lose that if things failed to get better.'

Ellie's mind was racing. She wasn't going to be a solicitor for nothing. 'And that means . . .' Ellie began, but the words wouldn't come out.

'It means,' continued James gently, 'that Pandora now owns this house, lock, stock and barrel.'

'Dear God, no!' Julia turned pale and clutched her throat. 'But how – I mean, this house has been in the family for generations.'

Abby gasped. 'You must have got it wrong – Dad would never give Holly House to anyone,' she stammered.

'I'm sure he thought he was putting it into safe hands for you four,' James assured them. 'Keeping it safe and out of the way of his creditors, until things began to look up.'

'But if Mum and Dad own the house together, surely it reverts to her?' Ellie began but James held up his hand.

'That's the problem, Elinor dear,' he said, sighing. 'They didn't. Max owned it outright, which meant that creditors could have seized it, but it also meant that he could sign it over to the new Mrs Dashwood without much fuss.'

Ellie's heart ached as her mother visibly cringed at the term, 'the new Mrs Dashwood'.

'You may recall that many times over the years, long before your – well, your difficulties – I met with you both and suggested it go into joint names.'

'You did?' Julia sounded vague and Ellie had a great desire to shake her.

'Of course, Max kept saying he'd get round to it, but you know what his memory was like. He never did put your name on the property title and that meant he could do whatever he liked with the property without consulting you. I'm sure he meant it only to be a temporary measure, until he got back on his feet.'

Images of the final demands on Max's desk, his outburst about the cost of Abby's phone and the look on his face when his card was rejected at the restaurant, flashed through Ellie's brain as the solicitor turned to Julia.

'Well, exactly!' Julia stood up, colour returning to her cheeks. 'Pandora will realise that. I mean, what would she want with a great barn of a place like this? She's got the flat, after all.'

James paused and ran a finger round his collar. 'Actually, no. She hasn't. She heard yesterday – it's being repossessed to pay your ex-husband's debts. Max had known that for several weeks, but hadn't plucked up the courage to tell Pandora.' He sighed. 'It's as much of a shock to her as it is to you.'

So that was why Dad had been in such a state, Ellie

thought. He knew that everything was lost.

'Of course, originally Max left you all a great deal of money in his will.'

'Oh, well that's all right then.' Julia sighed. 'We can buy the place back.'

'No, it's not all right,' James stressed. 'He may have expressed a wish for you to have his money. But there is no money left, none at all. Just a pile of debts and a dozen or so very angry creditors.'

'We've got nothing?' The hollowness in Abby's voice shook Ellie as much as the news. 'Nothing at all?'

'There are a few things, books, pictures – oh and three pieces of sculpture,' James said brightly. 'I've got them in the car.'

'But the bottom line is that we're broke.' Ellie didn't bother phrasing it as a question; she knew it was the truth.

'Yes, I'm afraid so,' James said softly. 'Of course, I'm sure that, in any other circumstances, the new Mrs Dashwood would want you to remain here at Holly House.'

'You mean she actually – ?' The words stuck in Ellie's throat.

Georgie sprang up from the floor, wild eyed and cheeks flushed. 'She can't throw us out!'

'Of course she can't, Georgie,' Julia interjected. 'Don't be so silly.'

'I'm afraid she can,' the solicitor said firmly, shuffling some papers. 'In view of her strained circumstances, and the imminent repossession of the flat, she is anxious to take possession of the property at the earliest possible convenience.' He flushed and cleared his throat. 'Well, on Thursday to be precise.'

Julia gasped. 'But that's the day before the funeral,' she whispered. 'She can't . . .'

'She won't expect you to leave just yet, of course,' James reported apologetically. 'She's said that you can stay as long as you need to in order to set other arrangements, but she will arrive on Thursday, by dinner time. She asked that I let you know.'

'But we'll have to leave?' Julia asked, the shock in her eyes visible.

'Yes,' James agreed. 'I am so very, very sorry.'

'Can I have this one?' Abby gestured to the largest of the three sculptures that had been blocking the hallway ever since James left the house the day before. 'It speaks to me.'

'It does?' Georgie eyed it with bemusement. 'What is it?'

'A bird,' Abby said. 'See, its beak's open, and it's wings are spread and it's about to take off, into the blue yonder, in search of its destiny.'

'OK, OK,' Georgie said hastily. 'I'll have the little fat cherub thing – it's kind of cute. Even though it hasn't got any legs.'

Ellie sighed. Ever since the solicitor had left and Mum had told them she had a small sum tucked away for a rainy day – though she wasn't sure how much – Ellie had tried to stay hopeful, even though the feeling in the pit of her stomach told her otherwise.

'That leaves the round thing with the hole for me,' she murmured. 'Looks like a giant Polo mint.'

'You've got no soul,' Abby declared, raising her eyebrows. 'Can't you see it represents Life? The hole is the abyss into which we all fall unless we follow our destiny.'

Ellie frowned at her sister. Between Abby's dreamy antics and her mother's unwillingness to deal with the fact that they might very well soon be homeless (with three very odd sculptures in tow, mind you), Ellie felt as though she and Georgie might be the only ones with their heads screwed on properly. Too bad a straight head couldn't get them back their dad, or the rights to their home.

Ellie looked up at Abby then, noticing that she was no longer smiling at her odd sculpture. 'Abby, what's wrong?'

{101}

'What the hell do you think is wrong?' her voice broke.

'Sorry, that was dumb of me,' Ellie agreed. 'Do you want a tissue?'

'I feel so guilty,' Abby ran her hand over a rough patch on the sculpture. 'All that time – I didn't know – if I had, I wouldn't have . . . but I didn't, so I couldn't . . .'

'Abby,' Georgie laughed softly, 'we can't understand a word you're saying. You didn't know what?'

'That Dad was broke,' Abby said, sniffing. 'I just said yes to everything he offered to buy, and he paid our bills, and all the time he couldn't afford it.' She paused and gazed up at her sisters with red-rimmed eyes. 'And it killed him.' She choked on the words.

'Abby, listen,' Ellie ordered. 'Dad chose to spend that money. No one made him. He did it because he loved us so much and he hated to say no to us.'

Georgie took a deep breath, and grabbed both her sisters into a hug.

'What's this?' Julia demanded the following morning, picking the local weekly paper.

> DASHWOOD: Tragically, and without warning, MAXIMILIAN FREDERICK, for twenty years the cherished and loving husband of Julia, and adored father of Ellie, Abby and Georgie. A man of enterprise, humour and passion, his loss will leave emptiness in the lives of many. Funeral to be held tomorrow at St Peter's Church.

'Who put this in the paper?'

'I did.' Abby stuck her chin out defiantly. 'And it's no good you telling me to apologise, because I won't. I'm not sorry because it was the right thing to do.'

'Yes, I know.'

'And just because you . . . Wait, what did you say?'

Her mother smiled. 'I said, yes, it was the right thing to do,' Julia repeated. 'Thank you, darling. It means more than I can say.' She gave Abby a hug. 'Oh – and there is one more thing you could do for me.'

'Anything, Mum,' Abby assured her eagerly. 'What is it?'

'Make sure Pandora gets a copy, will you? Without fail?'

Abby grinned. 'Consider it done,' she promised, picking up the paper.

❧ SECRET NUMBER 10 ❧

Apparently, even wretched cows fall in love.

'PLEASE CAN WE EAT?' Georgie pleaded the following evening. 'It's nearly eight thirty and my stomach thinks my throat's been cut.'

Her mother sighed, opening the door of the oven and peering in for the tenth time in as many minutes. 'If they're not here in ten minutes, we'll eat,' she agreed.

'They?' Ellie looked up from her attempts at German translation. Even Georgie stopped fiddling with her iPod for a minute.

'Oh, didn't I tell you?' Julia looked sheepish and began clattering dishes. 'Pandora phoned a couple of hours ago. She's bringing her nephew Blake – I think you said you met him at Dad's? I'm putting him in Nanny's old room.'

'Blake? He's coming here? To live? With Pandora?' Ellie gasped.

It occurred to Georgie that she didn't look as upset by the idea as she should.

'Oh I don't imagine he'll live here,' Julia said. 'He's just coming down for a while to give Pandora moral support.'

A screech of brakes followed by the sound of barking stopped the conversation and the Dashwoods all looked at each other.

'This is it,' said Ellie. 'I'll go and let them in.'

'I'm coming too,' Julia said. 'Abby, pour the wine. Georgie, take that snarl off your face, if you can manage.'

'I'm not sure I can,' muttered Georgie as she listened to her mum usher Pandora and Blake through the front door.

'You know my girls, of course,' Julia was saying as Pandora, dressed from head to foot in sugar pink leather, entered the kitchen with a sheepish-looking Blake in tow.

'You've got a dog!' Georgie gasped as what appeared to be a badly-woven rug on legs hurled itself against her.

'Yes, sorry,' Blake said nervously. 'I mean, is it OK? I can put him in a kennel, only I haven't had time to organise it.' He grabbed the dog by its collar. 'Down, boy! Behave!'

'He's fine,' Georgie said decisively. 'We love dogs – Dad had . . .' The words caught in her throat.

'What's his name?' Ellie put an arm round her sister.

'Morris,' said Blake, trying to restrain the enthusiastic animal. 'He's a cross between an Old English sheepdog, a Newfoundland and something ugly that we haven't yet identified! Are you sure you don't mind him being here, Mrs Dashwood?'

Julia smiled and shook her head. 'Not at all,' she said. 'He can sleep in the boot room.'

'Great.' Blake smiled. 'He's usually with my parents but they left for a holiday in Barbados this morning, so I'm in charge.' Morris promptly lay down on Pandora's suede boots and panted pathetically. 'Or not, as the case may be,' Blake said, grinning.

'Just keep that awful hound away from me, that's all I ask!' Pandora wrinkled her nose. 'Ghastly creature.'

'Takes one to know one,' muttered Georgie to Abby, as Morris licked her left foot appreciatively.

'This is the kitchen,' Julia butted in unnecessarily, throwing Georgie a warning glance. 'I thought we'd eat in here because it's so cosy. Pandora, do sit down. Supper's ready.' She gestured towards the most comfortable chair. 'Would you like a glass of wine?'

'Terrific,' cried Blake, clearly embarrassed by his aunt. 'Let me help. Pandora – white or red?'

'Neither, thank you,' Pandora shuddered. 'Do you know what alcohol does to the liver?'

{105}

'Probably rather less,' muttered Julia as she began placing plates in front of the guests, 'than I'm about to do to you.'

'What was that, Mum?' Georgie asked with smirk.

'Nothing, nothing at all,' said Julia as she plopped dinner on to Pandora's plate.

'What is this?' Pandora poked at the food in front of her.

'Game pie,' Julia said. 'Locally shot pheasant and partridge with onions and bacon and – '

'I can't eat that!' Pandora shrilled. 'I'm vegetarian. Didn't the girls tell you?' She eyed Ellie, Abby and Georgie as if they had committed a terrible social gaffe.

'We forgot,' Ellie said sharply. 'We were too busy mourning our Dad and arranging a funeral.'

To her credit, Pandora blushed and nodded. 'Yes, well, that's understandable,' she conceded. 'Still, you know now. Oh – and I drink only soya milk, I don't eat anything from a cow . . .'

'Right, makes sense,' Georgie said, and everyone cocked their heads in wonder at Georgie's change in attitude. 'Well, you wouldn't want to eat your own relatives, would you?' added Georgie before Ellie kicked her under the table.

'. . . and I like my tea made with bottled water, not tap water. Too many nasty things get into our homes these days.'

'Tell me about it,' murmured Abby.

Dinner finished up in relative silence, punctuated only by Blake's admirable attempts at small talk and an occasional giggle from Georgie as Morris stuck his wet nose against her leg looking for table droppings.

'I'm sorry to be a pain,' Blake said as they cleared away the supper dishes, 'but I think I should pop out and take Morris for a walk.'

'But it's dark,' Pandora protested. 'And you won't know where to go.'

'I'll come with you, if you like,' Ellie butted in. 'I mean, that is if you don't want to be alone.'

'That would be great.' Blake grinned. 'Only don't you have loads to do for tomorrow?'

Ellie shook her head, 'Nah. The one thing I want to do about tomorrow is forget it's going to happen. A walk is just what I need.'

'Terrific, then,' Blake said, and then asked Morris if he wanted to go for a walk a few times, much to the big dog's excitement.

Ellie opened the door and led them toward the front path, where they stood in silence for a moment, looking out on the town below them.

'It's an amazing view.' Blake gazed out at the moonlit

sea, the floodlit Brighton Pier and thousands of tiny lights twinkling along the sea front. 'And it smells so different from London.' He gulped in deep breaths of the salty air.

'Wait till you see it in daylight,' Ellie enthused. 'There's a wonderful view right across the bay to Worthing.'

'How will you bear to leave? Oh gosh, I'm sorry, that was so tactless.'

'It's fine. I mean, it's something we've all got to get used to,' she said, pausing under a street lamp and pulling her jacket tighter round her body.

'So where will you go?' Blake asked, yanking Morris's lead as the dog attempted to lie down in the middle of a puddle.

'I don't know,' Ellie said shortly. 'I'm afraid we won't be able to stay in Brighton – Mum won't tell me what's what on the money front, and houses here go for a bomb. I don't even know how we're going to pay for school any more, and there are my A levels next year, and . . .' She turned away in embarrassment. What possessed her to talk to a total stranger about such personal stuff? 'I'd better get back,' she said quickly, turning round. 'If you want to walk on . . .'

'No, I'll come too,' Blake said, stopping in the gravel drive for a moment. 'You must hate us.'

'Not you, just Pan – ' Ellie stopped herself. 'Sorry, I didn't mean . . .'

'It's OK,' Blake said stuffing his hands in his pockets. 'She can be a bit much at times, I guess. All her fads about food and stuff.'

'Bizarre,' agreed Ellie.

'The thing is, her parents – that's my grandparents – died out in Africa when she was ten. Her mum was ill with some water-borne disease and there was a car crash while her dad was trying to rush her to hospital.'

'That's awful,' gasped Ellie.

'Ever since then she's been paranoid about hygiene and food and that kind of stuff,' Blake went on, pulling Morris away from his close inspection of a banana skin in the gutter. 'My mum was nineteen at the time and became a kind of proxy mum to Pandora but I don't think she ever got over it.'

'I didn't know,' murmured Ellie, feeling a wave of guilt about all the evil thoughts she'd spent the last year thinking.

'I think she married your dad because she needed a father figure – or at least, that's what mum says,' he went on. 'So you see – oh, look, I'm sorry, this is crazy. You don't want to hear all this.'

'I do,' Ellie insisted, because as long as Blake kept talking she didn't have to think about Dad or the future. 'It helps. I don't know why, but it does. So you two get on well, then?' It struck her that you would have to be a saint to get on with Pandora.

'Not really,' Blake admitted. 'She lived with us after my mum got married and had me, so in some ways she more like a big sister than an aunt. A very irritating big sister, most of the time,' he added.

'So how come you agreed to come down here with her?' Ellie asked

'Because she persuaded your dad to let me stay with

them for a few weeks, and I owe her one,' he admitted. 'If it hadn't been for Max and Pandora, my father and I would have come to serious blows.'

Ellie started. Blake seemed too soft to come to blows with anyone. 'Why?'

'Oh, it's a long story,' he mumbled as they turned into the drive of Holly House. 'You've got enough on your plate without me going on and on.'

'I told you – anything's better than thinking about tomorrow and Dad in that coffin and . . .' Her voice broke and she turned away.

'Well,' said Blake in a matter of fact voice, 'the bottom line is that my father wants me to do law . . .'

'That's cool,' she began, and then stopped since it was clear from the expression on Blake's face that he wasn't keen on the idea.

'He's an international solicitor, Grandpa was a barrister and the whole family expects me to follow suit.'

'So tell him "no",' Ellie replied, 'if that's not what you want.'

Blake gave a short laugh. 'That's what everyone says – everyone who doesn't know my father,' he said. 'No is not a word that my father responds well to.'

'But surely . . .' Ellie stopped as Blake started to shake his head and kick at the gravel driveway.

'Dad's motto is always the same: *He who pays the piper calls the tune*. He holds the purse strings, so he always wins.' Blake scratched at his forehead. 'Sorry – I always babble on when I'm uptight. Anyway, what are you going to do with your life?'

'Go to university, study . . .' For some reason that she

couldn't quite explain, the words stuck in her throat. '. . . Not sure what yet – plenty of time to think about careers later.' Ellie Dashwood, you are a wimp, she told herself angrily – Ellie knew full well that law school was in her future. She fished in the pocket of her jeans for the back door key. 'Anyway, what do you really want to do?' she asked, eager to divert attention away from her future. 'Really, if you could choose?'

'You really want to know?'

'Of course I do.'

'I want to be an artist. Or an illustrator. Oh, anything as long as it involves painting and drawing.' He eyed her closely. 'Go on, laugh.'

But Ellie didn't laugh. To her horror she began to sob. All she could think about was her dad and his wonky sculptures, and that no matter how much her mum wanted to pretend otherwise, nothing was ever going to be the same, again.

❧ SECRET NUMBER 11 ❧

*Love does not die easily – it often grows while
no one is watching.*

'WHAT TIME DO WE HAVE to get changed, Mum?' Georgie asked, pushing her cereal around her bowl on the morning of the funeral, looking from her mum to her two sisters who were all gathered around the table.

Her mother didn't reply. She was staring, spoon halfway to her mouth, at a letter that she had just opened.

'No,' her mother said, breathing heavily. 'No, no, NO!'

The final word was a scream as the spoon clattered to the table, splashing milk and cornflakes over the table as Julia leaped to her feet.

'I can't take any more!' She sobbed, tears streaming down her face. 'What's the point – you try to be brave and hold things together but there's always someone wanting to pull the rug from under you! First Pandora, next this hateful woman . . .'

'Who, Mum? What's happened?' Abby pleaded, her heart thudding.

'Now this!' Julia flung the letter on to the table.

Abby snatched it up and scanned it hastily. 'It's from the headmistress,' Abby said, gasping.

'Read it out,' Ellie ordered, taking a seat.

'Dear Mrs Dashwood,' Abby read in a quavering voice. *'Firstly, please accept the sincere condolences of the board of governors, myself and the senior management team on the death of your husband.*

'Further to our recent conversations, and while sensitive to your loss, I have to write to inform you that, following a meeting of the governors, I must ask you to settle all outstanding school fees within fourteen days of today's date.

'Failure to do so will necessitate the school requesting the removal of Elinor, Abigail and Georgina.

'Yours truly, Eveline Passmore.'

'She can't do that!' Georgie cried out.

'She can,' Ellie said, putting an arm round her mother's shoulders and squelching the desire to point out that she'd seen this coming. 'Don't cry, Mum. It'll be OK, we'll work something out.'

'Like what?' her mother sobbed. 'First the house, now the school – what have we got left?'

Ellie clenched her jaw to stop herself from crying. Even though she'd expected it, Ellie realised that being enrolled at St Ethelreda's was perhaps the only thing left to tie them to Brighton after losing Holly House. And now it looked like they weren't even going to have that.

'We've got each other,' Ellie said resolutely. 'Dad wouldn't want us to go to pieces.'

'You're right, of course.' Julia sniffed and nodded. 'And besides, if I write to Mrs Passmore, reason with her . . .'

'Passmore and reason don't go together,' muttered Abby. 'Trust me. Don't waste your breath.'

'What's going on?' Pandora wafted into the kitchen, dressed in black chiffon and knee-high boots. 'I can't have people falling apart now, I need support.'

'We've got to leave school because there's no money,' Abby said, glaring at her. 'Doesn't that make you feel awful?'

'I left school at sixteen, and it didn't do me any harm,' Pandora declared.

'When you've only got two brain cells, there's not much harm to be done, is there?' muttered Abby.

At the funeral, the girls wept when they saw Pandora sitting in the front row where their Mum should have been. It was practically the only thing any of them could concentrate on – everything else was simply too much.

Georgie sat stoic, tears running down her cheeks, unconsciously picking at her cuticles until they bled. Abby pretended she was Katharine Hepburn in *On Golden Pond*, as she walked slowly and steadily behind the coffin as they left the church – if she'd let herself think of anything else, she was sure she'd crumble to the ground.

And Ellie watched as the family she had always known changed for ever, right in front of her eyes. There would be no more Dad, and the rest of them would be changed for ever without him.

Just keep handing round the canapés and don't think about it, Georgie told herself firmly. Don't think about

Dad locked up in that coffin, don't remember the velvet curtains opening and the coffin sliding through and Dad tumbling into flames and being burnt. Don't think about leaving Holly House and school and . . .

'Come on, I've got something to show you.' Tom firmly removed the plate from her hand, dumped it on the sideboard and grabbed her hand.

'I can't, Mum said I had to be a good hostess and talk to everyone.'

'It was your Mum's idea,' Tom assured her. 'You look like you've seen a ghost . . . Oh, gosh, sorry, that . . .'

'It's OK.' Georgie tried a watery smile, as Tom pulled her through the throng of murmuring guests. 'It's just that I can't imagine Dad gone. I mean, really gone – cinders, ashes . . .'

'So remember him like he was,' Tom told her, grabbing his jacket from the hat stand in the hall and pulling an envelope out from the pocket. 'Go on, look! It's your photos – remember you wanted me to print them off on my photo suite on the computer? Well, this is them!'

Georgie began flipping through the images – Dad and Pandora grinning at the camera; Dad and Pandora on the balcony with Ellie and Abby; Pandora, lips puckered, fawning all over Dad. Pandora – man-stealer, home-wrecker, who even now wasn't talking to the mourners but lying down in a darkened room because she said she needed to be alone with her agony. Alone with her guilt, more like, thought Georgie.

'Georgie, where are you going?' Tom shouted as she pounded up the stairs two at a time and into her bedroom.

She wrenched open drawer after drawer until she found her nail scissors. Then she began. She plunged them into Pandora's grinning face, photo after photo, wishing that she could actually make blood flow from those pallid cheeks. Then she cut the pictures in half, ripping Pandora into tiny fragments till only her Dad's face smiled up at her.

'Georgie, I'm sorry, I didn't mean to upset you.' Her bedroom door flew open and Tom, red faced, burst in. 'Only your mum thought the pictures would be good for you to have. Hey, what are you doing?'

'Getting rid of every trace of that cow,' Georgie said, panting. 'I may not be able to get her out of my house, but no way do I want her in a photo with my dad. Ever.'

{115}

Downstairs, Ellie knew she should be circulating, making polite conversation to all the black-suited business friends of her father, the wrinkled great aunts from Portsmouth with their loud voices and voracious appetites, but she couldn't bring herself to smile or be polite. For now, she just wanted to sit here in the conservatory, with Manderley asleep at her feet and try to make sense of what was happening to their lives.

The latest blow had come just after they'd left the funeral to come back to Holly House for the reception. Julia had taken Ellie aside and confessed that their savings amounted to only thirty thousand pounds. Fine for living on for a bit, but not nearly enough to buy a house, or pay for even a year of the girls' tuition.

'You could get a job, Mum,' Ellie had ventured. 'Apply for a mortgage?'

'A job? Darling, I couldn't,' her mother had said. 'I can't do anything.'

Ellie had bitten her tongue but hours later she was still stewing. Her mum was such a defeatist – heaven knows there were jobs that anyone could do, no matter what experience they had.

'There you are, precious lambkin!'

A bejewelled hand landed with a thud on her left shoulder, and Ellie looked up to see Davina Stretton, her godmother, and her mum's oldest friend.

'You came!' Ellie jumped up and gave her a hug. 'We thought you wouldn't make it.'

'Angel, the traffic! Solid jams all the way from Burnham. I nearly cried – well, I did cry, thinking of you poor lambs going to hell and back at the funeral and me not on hand to succour and support.'

Ellie laughed and then promptly burst into tears. Big wet drops fell from her eyes and Ellie wiped at her thick eyelashes with the heel of her hand. 'I'm so glad you're here,' she said, flinging her arms round Davina's ample chest. 'Everything's so awful.'

'You poor love, I know what losing a father is like,' Davina murmured.

'It's not just Dad,' Ellie sobbed. 'Although of course that's the worst but her taking the house, and us being homeless, and there's no money because – '

'Darling, wait,' Davina interrupted. 'I'm all confused. Now sit down.'

Davina pushed Ellie back down into the wicker chair and produced a packet of lime green tissues from her enormous handbag.

'Blow!' she ordered. Ellie blew. 'Now,' Davina instructed her. 'Deep breath and tell all.'

Ten minutes later, after Ellie had told her the whole story, Davina stood up, pulled back her shoulders and slipped her handbag over her arm. 'Right,' she said. 'This needs sorting once and for all. Leave it to me.'

'There's nothing you can do, Davina. She's got the law on her side,' Ellie sniffed.

'And you,' snorted Davina, 'have got me. I'll think of something, I promise. Now lead me to the food, angel, will you? And is there alcohol? Your darling father always kept a rather palatable claret, I seem to recall.'

After a drink and a pep talk from Davina, Julia {117} seemed to brighten a bit. She was still at the funeral of the man she loved, of course, but Davina seemed to convince her that she had to take action and that it would make her feel better. So together Davina, Julia and Ellie all slipped into the study, and Julia took out a piece of stationery and a pen and began writing.

'OK, listen to this.' Julia sucked the end of her rollerball pen and began reading the letter she had been scribbling for the past several minutes.

'*Dear Mrs Passmore,*

'*With regard to your letter, which I must confess showed an inherent lack of tact and good taste on your part, I am unable at this point to settle the outstanding bill for fees, owing to . . .*'

'Go on,' urged Ellie.

'That's all I've put,' Julia confessed. 'What should I say – owing to what?' Julia tapped her pen on the table and bit her lip.

'Owing to there being no money, perhaps?' Ellie

suggested. 'You've got to tell her the truth, Mum. I mean, they'll understand. There might be some kind of charity fund for cases like ours.'

'Ellie, you're a genius,' Davina said. 'Of course, that's the answer. I mean, a school like St Ethelreda's is bound to have contingency plans.'

'*Owing to my late ex-husband having died insolvent,*' Julia read out loud as she wrote. 'It does sound very disloyal, written in black and white like that,' Julia murmured, taking a sip of tea.

'Put the bit about bursaries and stuff,' Ellie urged, wishing she could just snatch the notepaper from her mother and do the thing herself.

'*I wonder whether there might be some bursaries, scholarships or distress fund money available since the girls have been with you since the age of five and are, as I am sure you will agree, a great attribute to the school.*'

'That should do it,' Julia exclaimed triumphantly, signing her name with a flourish. 'They can't say no to that, now can they?'

'Surely not!' said Davina.

Ellie smiled, but she well knew they could say whatever they wanted. 'C'mon, back to the guests.'

Julia and Ellie spent the next couple of hours being polite to the remaining guests while Abby and Georgie sat huddled together on a nearby couch. Finally, the last of the guests left.

'I'm so tired I could sleep standing up,' Julia said with a sigh, shutting the door after the last of the mourners. 'Just look at all this mess.'

'We'll all help, Mum,' Georgie said. 'Pandora, you

vacuum, I'll clear the tables and Abby can load the dishwasher.'

'Vacuum?' Pandora stared at them as if someone had suggested she should lead them all in a chorus of 'Rule Britannia'. 'I'm bereaved. I'm going back to bed.'

'*I'm bereaved,*' mimicked Georgie. 'So are we all but it hasn't caused us to lose the use of our arms and legs.'

And with that Pandora sniffed off down the hall. It was the only fitting end to the worst day of their lives.

❧ SECRET NUMBER 12 ❧

*You don't often get to choose the people that come into
your life, but sometimes you get awfully lucky.*

BEFORE THE WEEKEND WAS OVER, Pandora had driven
everyone to screaming pitch. For one thing, she had
decided that Brighton was the pits.

'I'm so used to the London life, you see,' she simpered
on Saturday morning. 'Always something on, something
new to do . . .'

'They call Brighton "London-by-the-Sea",' Julia
pointed out. 'It's very lively – and full of history. There's
the Royal Pavilion and the Lanes and of course, the
Theatre Royal has all the London productions.'

'And it's dead trendy,' Abby added. 'Although of
course at your age I guess that doesn't count for much.'

By lunchtime her moans had switched to the house
itself.

'Are you telling me you don't have a single bidet in
the entire house?' she demanded.

'Be who?' asked Georgie.

'Do you realise that carpets harbour formaldehyde?'
she cried that evening. 'They give off toxic emissions.'

'Rather like you then,' Abby muttered out of earshot.

'This kitchen is like something out of a costume drama,' Pandora said with a shudder on Sunday. 'All this wood is scratched.'

'It's distressed pine,' Ellie explained.

'Not half as distressed as us,' Julia murmured into her left ear.

But it was the plant filled conservatory that was Pandora's real bugbear.

'It's such a health hazard,' she declared, touching the Swiss Cheese plant with the tip of her finger. 'Surely you get insects and things.'

'Oh, dozens,' Georgie said airily. 'But it's only the tarantulas and the cockroaches that cause any real bother.' Georgie waited for her mother to shush her, but all she got from Julia was a broad grin and a wink.

A couple of hours later, with Pandora holed up in her room, and Julia in her garden with Abby and Georgie, all attempting to stay as far away from the house as possible, the phone rang. 'Ellie darling, is that you?'

'Davina!' Ellie beamed as the familiar voice boomed down the telephone. 'Yes, it's me. Shall I call Mum?'

'No dear, just answer me this. What are you doing for A level?'

Ellie frowned. 'French, German, psychology, general studies. Why?'

'And what examining board?'

'Oxford. Davina, what are you on about?'

'Talk soon, dearest one. Got an idea. Must dash. Chin up!'

Ellie set the receiver down, watching it for a moment as though it might reveal Davina's secret. When it didn't, she decided to head outside to track down her mother and sisters in the garden by the old summerhouse.

At first Ellie was annoyed to find Blake there instead. She had planned to take time out to talk with Abby and Georgie, cry a bit and then get herself together for another online search for their new home. But as she walked closer, she saw what he was doing.

'That's amazing!' Ellie's mouth dropped open as she stared at the sketchpad on Blake's lap. 'How do you make it look so real? It's practically like a photo!'

Blake was drawing Holly House – every leaf of the Virginia creeper that clung to its walls, the crack in the leaded-light window halfway up the stairs, the old bird's nest that still perched precariously on top of the rickety drainpipe.

'It's not finished,' Blake said hastily, smudging a corner of the roof tiling with his thumb. 'I can't get the light right – see, the way that shaft of sun hits the window?'

'Well, it looks pretty good to me,' she said.

And so do you, she thought, and then immediately despised herself for even thinking such a thing at a time like this.

'Mum, will you take me driving this evening?' Ellie pleaded later that night. 'My test is only three weeks off and I still can't parallel park properly.'

'Oh Ellie, you'll have to cancel and reschedule,' Julia

said with a sigh. 'I've got far too much to worry about right now without all that.'

Ellie bit her lip and counted to ten. Was sitting in a car for half an hour that demanding? After all the hours Ellie had spent house-hunting online, couldn't she do this one thing for her?

'I could take you,' Blake said, scraping the last of the apricot crumble off his plate. 'I mean, if that's OK with you.'

Ellie felt her insides turn over – so much so she placed a hand on her belly. 'Really? That would be great,' she replied. 'I might not be that good though.'

'Which translates as hang on tight and pray,' Georgie chipped in.

As long as it's me he hangs on to, Ellie thought, and then blushed.

Ellie and Blake shuffled out the car and took off for some of the side streets. Ellie did well, although she was more nervous than usual with Blake there next to her, and she couldn't help but glance at him out of the corner of her eye from time to time. Occasionally, he looked like he was looking at her, rather than the road, as well.

'OK,' Blake said after an hour of driving round the streets of Brighton and Hove. 'Pull into that lay-by for a minute.'

Ellie steered the car into the lay-by and switched off the engine. 'How did I do?' she asked.

'OK,' he said hesitantly. 'But I think we should practise some more. Like every day? Just to be on the safe side.'

'Am I that bad?' Ellie said, sighing.

'Your driving is great,' he said. 'But I need to find out how good you are at other things.'

'Oh, like the Highway Code, you mean,' said Ellie, her mouth for some inexplicable reason going completely dry.

'Not exactly,' he murmured, leaning towards her and touching her hand as it rested on the gear stick.

For one moment, Ellie thought he was going to kiss her. She closed her eyes, but when she didn't feel his lips on hers, she opened them and saw that he was sitting clear on the other side of the car, staring ahead.

'OK,' he said. 'Pull away. Carefully now, watch that cyclist.'

So that's that then, thought Ellie.

'We need to do this every day for a week,' Blake said. 'After school – two hours. OK?'

'Sure,' she said trying to sound dead cool. 'Good idea.'

After that initial lesson, the next couple of weeks were a blur for Ellie – she was still mourning her dad, but her driving lessons were proving a terrific distraction. She Blake began to do other things together, too, and her sisters were very quick to notice.

'You've got paint on the back of your neck,' Georgie told Ellie over supper one evening.

'Art homework,' gabbled Ellie.

'You don't do art,' retorted Georgie.

'And grass stains on your jeans,' chirped Abby.

'Helped mum garden,' muttered Ellie.

'And I'm the pope,' retorted Abby with a smirk.

After all, the Dashwood sisters knew each other all too well.

* * *

Ellie peered in the mirror and frowned at her reflection. OK, so she wasn't stunning, but she wasn't ugly either. She cupped her hands to her mouth, blew and then sniffed. Her breath was OK, so it wasn't that.

So why hadn't he kissed her? It had been two weeks and not even when Ellie had leaned toward him, her eyes closed, pretending to be enjoying the sunshine that was actually making her skin itch, had he kissed her. Nor had she enjoyed a lip-lock when she'd leaned over him to unlock his door, or when she touched his hand, or when he showed her one of his sketches of her laying in the grass.

Never mind that on three occasions now, when they {125} had pulled over in the car up some country lane, he had taken her hand, and leaned towards her and breathed her name – and then pulled back and talked about something totally banal, or suddenly got all businesslike and made her practise her three point turns.

He'd put his arm round her, he'd played with her hair, he'd held her hand as they walked down country lanes. But he hadn't kissed her.

'Ellie, can I borrow your history notes from last – what are you doing?'

'Nothing!' Ellie sprang back from the mirror where she had moved on to practising puckered kisses. 'Don't you ever knock?'

'You've got it bad, haven't you?' Abby demanded, ignoring her question. 'You've taken to wearing lip gloss, mascara and blusher, even for breakfast and now you're kissing yourself in the mirror. Has he kissed you yet?'

Ellie gave up pretending and shook her head. 'No,'

she said. 'He clearly doesn't fancy me – one minute he's coming on strong . . .'

'Is he now?' exclaimed Abby, flopping down on the bed. 'Tell me then – I want all the details.'

For some reason that she couldn't quite work out, Ellie found herself telling Abby everything – how she liked talking to Blake because he was so easy to be with, how she had tried to be really alluring and feminine; about the almost-kisses and about how she worried that she was doing something wrong.

'If you ask me,' said Abby, 'you're on to a loser with that one.'

'So it is me.' Ellie sighed. 'Go on, give it to me straight.'

Abby giggled. 'That's the point – you can't have it straight,' she said, smirking. 'Get it?'

'What are you on about?'

'If you ask me,' Abby pronounced, 'Blake likes you a lot.'

'Really? You're sure?' Ellie's heart lifted.

'Certain,' said Abby. 'Not that it will do you much good.'

'Why? Oh, I get it – oh thanks, Abby. Of course – he's holding back out of respect for my grief. That is so sensitive, so caring, but I really wish he wouldn't.'

'You just don't get it, do you? He's not taking things further because Blake Goodman is, unless I'm very much mistaken, gay.'

Ellie gasped. *Gay?* He couldn't be. I mean, not that it mattered, but Blake? Not Blake, surely? All Ellie could think was, that it would be such a waste.

❧ SECRET NUMBER 13 ❧

Sometimes things really are too good to be true.

'BLAKE! TELEPHONE!'

Georgie yelled across the hall as Ellie and Blake were shuffling out the door, about to go for another drive.

'I'll wait in the den,' Ellie whispered as Blake grabbed the handset. She began to close the door and then stopped as she heard Blake's gravelly tones.

'Blake here – oh, Lucy, it's you.'

Lucy? Who the hell is Lucy?

'What? Oh, I had the mobile switched off. Sorry. No, love, of course I wasn't trying to . . .'

Ellie froze. *Love?* He'd never called her 'love'.

'What? Of course I miss you – yes, yes. How are things?'

Ellie found herself holding her breath as she tried to stop her heart pounding.

'Oh, you poor thing! Well, look, don't worry. I'll pop down soon, OK? What? No, I can't. Not here.'

Ellie strained to catch his words as his voice dropped.

'What? OK then. Yes, yes – of course I love you.' It was the faintest whisper.

He had a girlfriend. Abby was wrong. Blake wasn't gay at all. He was in love with someone else.

Right then, Ellie would have preferred the first option.

As Blake hung up the phone, Ellie slipped outside before she could be caught with her ear to the door. He came outside, and although Ellie couldn't be sure if she was mistaken, he appeared a bit low.

'Actually,' Ellie said, hesitating by the car, 'I think I'll give the driving a miss today. Loads to do!' Like kicking myself for being such a fool or alternatively howling my eyes out.

'No way,' Blake interjected, opening the passenger door. 'You're almost there, and the test's next week.'

He's right, she thought. I need to pass if only to get some freedom. So he's got a girlfriend? So what? Better to find out now. I haven't got time to get mixed up with a guy anyway. Boys have lice. Ellie was willing to tell herself almost anything to thwart off the hurt she could feel inching toward her chest.

'Where shall we go?' Blake asked as Ellie fired the engine. 'Town centre for traffic practice or dual carriage-way for overtaking?'

'Who was that on the phone?' Ellie ignored his question, slammed the car into gear and accelerated down the drive.

She felt Blake stiffen beside her. 'Phone? Oh – no one.'

'C'mon Blake!' she retorted, swinging the car out into the road. 'Of course it was someone – Lucy, didn't I hear you say?'

Blake blushed. Bad sign. 'Yeah – I just meant – well, no one important.'

Ellie's heart lifted a millimetre.

'She's an old friend – of the family, you know? Her mum and my mum are old friends. We practically grew up together.'

As Ellie turned to catch his eye and saw the flush spreading from his neck to his forehead, she had a very nasty feeling that this Lucy was not just a mate.

That night, after they returned from the world's most awkward driving date, Ellie closed the door to her room and sobbed. She'd never liked a boy before – not really, anyway – and now she felt stupid and angry and disappointed all at once. But enough is enough, Ellie told herself, as she opened her door to go to the bathroom to splash water on her face.

'Why are you crying?' Georgie demanded of Ellie as they bumped into one another in the hall.

'I'm not,' Ellie mumbled.

'Oh, cut the crap,' said Georgie.

'Georgie, mind your language!' Ellie snapped.

'Stop being a prude and stop fibbing,' replied Georgie cheerfully. 'You've been crying – is it Dad?'

Ellie shook her head. 'No – I mean, yes,' she muttered.

'Which means no it isn't, but yes you think it ought to be,' said Georgie with a sigh. 'It's Blake, isn't it?'

'What on earth makes you think that?'

'You want a list?' Georgie began ticking off reasons on her fingers. 'One – you, Miss Workaholic, have taken to leaving your homework and going out driving. Two – every time he comes into the room you run your hands through your hair like this.' She put her hands to her head and fluffed up her already unruly locks. 'And three – well, he is rather dishy, isn't he?'

'Yes, I guess he is.' Ellie sighed. 'Not that you normally notice such things.'

Georgie shrugged. 'I like him,' she said. 'He's normal. Which round here is quite a bonus, if you ask me.'

Later that night, when Blake appeared at the front door with Morris, Ellie decided to let the whole thing go. Sure he was the kindest, sweetest, most interesting guy she had ever met, but so what? Clearly he was in love with someone else, and Ellie should never have let her feelings get so out of control – at least that was what Ellie told herself.

'Look, Blake, I'm sorry I was off with you,' Ellie said as Blake unhooked Morris's leash. 'It's none of my business whether you have a girlfriend or not.'

Blake swallowed hard. 'Look, about me and Lucy,' he began. 'I think I should explain . . .'

'Got to dash,' Ellie butted in. 'Loads to do. See you at supper.'

A couple of hours later, Julia tapped a glass with her fork to get everyone's attention. 'I have an e-mail!' she announced.

'How do you know?' Abby asked, shovelling lasagne on to her plate. 'You can't even switch the computer on, never mind print anything.'

'Enough of your cheek!' Julia grinned. 'Ellie loaded down it.'

'Downloaded,' giggled Georgie.

'Whatever,' Julia said. 'Anyway, I think you should all read it.'

Blake jumped up. 'I'll leave you in peace, then,' he said.

'No, stay, Blake,' Julia said. 'We need all the advice we can get. Speaking of advice, I discovered today that according to the law, you're too young to be taking Ellie out for driving practice. Were you aware of that?'

Blake blushed. 'Er . . . no. Sorry, I – '

'But we'll let that pass for now.'

She unfolded a sheet of paper and began reading.

'Dearest Julia,

{131}

'In light of all that's happened, I've come up with solution! And this is it; you remember Ma had that little cottage on our farm? Well, she's in the rest home now, bless her – the stairs were just too much for her and her memory's gone AWOL - but she refuses to sell the place and I thought, why not offer it to you and the girls?

'It's not what you're used to, of course – only three bedrooms and a boiler with a mind of its own, but it would be lovely to have it lived in again. And North Norfolk's got a lot going for it as well – sandy beaches, plenty of space, the odd nice little fish restaurant. I'm on the board of governors of Cromwell Community School; I've checked that all Ellie's subjects are available there and of course, being a state school, there are no fees to pay. What's more they use the same examining board, so it has to be destiny, darling!

'Anyway, angel, let me know what you think. Pop over and see the place at the weekend, why don't you? Oh, and if you agree to slap a bit of paint about the place and mow the lawn, I won't charge rent.

'*Must dash off now – Mother's Union tea at The Grange and I'm on kettle duty!*

'*Love to the girls, and keep your chin up. Love, Davina.*'

'So, what do you think?' Julia eyed her three daughters anxiously.

'Think? I think it's crazy,' Abby shouted. 'Norfolk, for heaven's sake? That's the back of beyond – all sand dunes and farmers with straw hanging out of their mouths.'

'That's so not true!' Blake laughed. 'I go there a lot with – well, with friends, you know. Sailing and stuff.'

'You do?' Ellie said. 'So do you know this school? What's it like?'

'What does the school matter?' Abby butted in. 'Are there clubs? No! Are there huge department stores? No. Is life in Norfolk worth living? No, I don't think so!'

'Abby, if you haven't got anything constructive to say, don't speak,' ordered her mother. 'Georgie, what do you think?'

'Do we really have to leave here?' Georgie's voice was small and filled with emotion, and for a moment she didn't look a day over six years old.

'Yes, darling, I'm afraid we do.'

'What about the letter to Mrs Passmore about the scholarships?' Ellie asked.

'I'm afraid she won't offer them to us,' Julia said. 'I heard last week, but I haven't been able to bring myself to tell you girls.'

'Well,' ventured Georgie, 'I'll go if I can have a horse.'

'The answer is no,' said Julia. 'Could someone please offer something useful to this discussion?'

Blake cleared his throat. 'This friend of yours,

Davina? It wouldn't be Davina Stretton, would it? Lives at Marsh Farm?'

'That's right,' Julia said in surprise. 'Why? Do you know her?'

'Not *know* her, exactly – but I've met her a couple of times because she's Lucy's – she's the friend of a friend of mine,' Blake told her, a frown puckering his forehead. 'Her farm is near Burnham Market.'

'Never heard of it,' Abby cut in, wondering why Ellie suddenly looked as if she could murder someone.

'It's an OK place,' Blake told her. 'Just down the round from Sandringham – the Queen's country house, you know? It's got some cool pubs, sailing club . . .'

'Discos? Nightclubs? Open air raves?' demanded Abby.

'Well, no,' said Blake.

'I rest my case,' Abby said.

'I suppose if none of you is happy about it, we'll have to think again,' their mother said, sighing. 'But this is rent free, and I'll have a ready-made friend, and I'm sure Blake would take you girls out and about a bit.'

'Of course – well, no, actually, I mean I am not up there that often, come to think of it,' Blake stammered. 'But of course, when I am, I'd be delighted.'

I knew it, Abby thought, noting the crestfallen expression on Ellie's face. He's gay, and he doesn't want us to know. It's obvious. Poor Ellie.

'I just don't know what to do,' Julia whimpered, tears welling in her eyes.

'Let's take it!' Ellie said decisively, 'It'll be fun.'

Fun like a terrible rash in summer, thought Abby, though she didn't say a word.

'But what would Dad say?' her mother began. 'I mean, the Dashwoods have lived here for generations and . . .'

'So perhaps it's time we blazed a new trail,' Ellie declared, taking a deep breath. 'Dad would understand. We've got to move on, Mum. We're going to Norfolk.'

❧ SECRET NUMBER 14 ❧

No matter what anyone else says, it really is the thought that counts.

ELLIE RAN HER FINGER LIGHTLY over the picture in her hand and blinked away the tears that it had brought on.

'It's not very good, and I can do better,' Blake told her as he shoved it into her hand, pink with embarrassment. 'But what with you leaving and everything, I thought you might like to have it.'

It was the picture she had seen him struggling with a few weeks before. Holly House in the late afternoon sun. Holding it now, and standing for the last time in front of the home she loved so much, she marvelled at the detail – the robin on the bird bath, the crack in the leaded-light glass by the front door where Abby had hit her rounders ball years before, the straggly ivy and the flowering honeysuckle.

'*For Ellie from Blake with love,*' she read the words scrawled in charcoal in the corner of the picture and bit her lip. Leaving Holly House was so hard. And leaving Blake wasn't exactly easy either. Ellie had passed her driving test, and they'd have only a few weeks of their new school to wrap up before the summer holiday began, but none of that was making Ellie feel much better.

'Right everyone! Ready?' Julia's voice was bright but her shoulders were tense with the pain of leaving as stepped on to the lawn and looked back at the house.

Ellie rolled up the drawing, slid it into a protective tube, and picked up the bag at her feet. 'Thank you Blake,' she said, her voice wavering a bit. 'It means so much.'

Blake didn't say anything, but he did put his arms around her. Still no kiss, but the hug felt wonderful.

'Bye, house,' Abby said softly, tears streaming down her face. 'We're sorry – we never meant to leave you.'

'Come on, Abby. Let's go.' Ellie touched her sister's arm and opened the car door. Concentrate on the good bits, she told herself firmly – like driving your own car without L-plates. Think about being independent, and having a new life. Don't think about what you're leaving or where you're going. Just do it.

And with that, the Dashwood sisters all hugged Blake and with their mother, piled into their two cars filled with their belongings – Ellie driving one, Julia driving the other – and left Holly House behind for the last time.

'This can't be it,' Abby gasped as her mother pulled up outside a small, flint-built cottage. 'It's in the middle of nowhere.'

'Nonsense,' Julia replied briskly, waving to Ellie as she pulled up behind them. 'We've just come through the village, with that lovely church.'

'You call that a village?' Abby retorted. 'More an accident at the side of the road, if you ask me.'

Julia got out of the car and stretched, taking gulps of sea air. From the direction of the sand dunes came the smell of salt and seaweed, mixed with rather less appealing manure from a nearby farm.

'Ellie darling, look at that view,' she said encouragingly, pointing across the marshes to the distant inlet where the white and red sails of dinghies and yachts bobbed in the light breeze. 'Imagine waking up to the sight of the ocean every day.'

'We could see the water before, too,' Georgie interjected sulkily.

Suddenly, the door of the cottage burst open, and Davina, dressed in cord trousers, a baggy sweater and an extraordinary pork pie hat, came down the path and enveloped Julia in a bear hug.

'Welcome to Marsh Cottage,' she cried. 'I just know you are going to love it here!'

'No brain as well as no dress sense,' Abby muttered under her breath. 'It's going to be hell.'

They grabbed some things – a few boxes, the picture of Holly House and one of Max's sculptures – and headed inside. They did all the polite things. Admired the inglenook fireplace and tried to ignore the flowery wallpaper and hideous carpet. Thanked Davina for the pie and cake that was waiting on the chipped Formica-top table in the tiny kitchen, murmured appreciatively as she described the delights of the local sailing club and nearby nature reserve. Agreed that within a few weeks they would have made the place really homely.

They made up the beds, they unpacked their clothes, and drank tea. Georgie sent a text message to Tom, Abby hid her diary under the mattress in the bedroom that she had to share with Ellie, and Ellie vowed silently to work like fury in order to escape to university as soon as she could.

Ellie hung her picture of Holly House in the tiny hallway so that it would be the first thing they saw every time they walked into their new home. And that was when they all gave up trying to be brave and wept in the strange, musty smelling place that they were supposed to call home.

'I can't believe that wretched Pan – ' Abby started, tears streaming down her face.

Georgie interrupted her. 'I think . . .' She paused. 'I rather think we should just forget about her now. Let's never mention her again – she's taken up too much time already.'

Ellie nodded, and after a moment, Abby did too. Julia was the last to agree, but when she did, they all felt a bit stronger for the promise.

Their second evening in the house, they were all but unpacked. Only a few boxes remained untouched, and with the way Julia was turning over the house, Ellie had no doubt they'd be stored soon enough as well.

'Red, definitely red,' declared Abby as she and Ellie pored over a paint chart.

'No way,' retorted Ellie. 'It's bad enough having to share a bedroom with all your mess and junk, without having to take on board your bizarre tastes in décor.'

Ellie stabbed a finger at the chart. '*Blue serenity*,' she read. 'That's much more like it.'

'Oh puh-leese!' Abby retorted. 'It's cold enough in this place without decorating it to look like the inside of an igloo.'

Ellie flung the paint chart to the floor. 'We might as well stick with this awful biscuit-mixed-with-vomit colour, then.' She groaned. 'I think . . .'

Abby held up a finger for Ellie to hold on as her mobile rang. 'Who? Oh, Chloë – hi!' She waved a hand in Ellie's direction and pointed to the door.

'OK, I'm going,' Ellie said, sighing. 'I still say blue is best.'

Ellie trotted down the rickety stairs, and sat down at the kitchen table, her chin resting in her hands and gazed out of the window.

What's wrong with me? There was Abby upstairs, nattering away to her new friend, Chloë, who it had taken her precisely one hour to meet at the local shops. Georgie was out with a guy from her school who she'd apparently met in the first five minutes of her first day, who owned his own dinghy and was teaching her to sail it in the harbour. Even her mother seemed to have got a life overnight – if you could call the local Women's Institute and a flower-arranging class a life.

'Hi, there!' She jumped as the back door opened and Davina burst in. 'Is Mum around?'

'She's gone to the WI.' Ellie shook her head.

'That's where I'm off to,' Davina chortled. 'Running late as usual, the blasted bicycle had a puncture and I hoped Mum would give me a lift.'

'I'll take you,' Ellie said, jumping up. 'I've nothing else to do.'

Davina eyed her closely as she grabbed her car keys and headed for the door. 'What's wrong?'

'Nothing,' Ellie said automatically, slamming the front door behind them and unlocking the car.

'Oh come off it, this is me you're talking to,' said Davina, heaving her ample frame into the passenger seat. 'Homesick, are you?'

The word hit Ellie's brain like a laser beam. 'Yes,' she said, firing the engine. 'That's it – I miss Brighton, I miss my friends, the school here is horrible . . . Oh, I didn't mean to be rude – it's really kind of you to fix us up and . . .'

'Darling, stop apologising,' Davina said, laughing. 'It was bound to be hard going to a new place. So come on, let off steam – what's the worst part?'

'Well, I know it's only been a day, and I'm sure I'll get used to it, but it's just so huge, and so noisy. The building is the pits, all that concrete and muddy brown paint,' complained Ellie, pulling away from the curb. 'And they don't have enough computers and I haven't made a real friend.' Ellie stopped. She knew she sounded like a petulant child.

'It'll get better, sweetheart,' Davina said. 'I promise.'

'I know.' Ellie smiled. She didn't believe a word of it but it seemed the polite thing to say.

They drove along and Ellie took in the sights – the view of the ocean and overgrown grass. It was the type of place that would make a lovely vacation, Ellie realised, so long as you got to leave at some point. She dropped Davina off at the village hall, and was about to pull back out into the road when her mobile bleeped that she had a text message. Ellie punched the 'read' button.

'HI! HOW'S THINGS? HOPE TO BE UP IN NORFOLK VERY SOON – CAN WE MEET? BYE4NOW. B.'

She grinned to herself even though she didn't know what to make of it. It was the third time he'd texted her since she left Brighton, and it hadn't even been forty-eight hours. Her stomach flipped all over again.

✂ SECRET NUMBER 15 ✂

Planning love is like trying to control the weather –
impossible, frustrating and unnatural.

'WHAT ARE YOU DOING TONIGHT?' Chloë asked Abby at
Friday lunchtime, spooning spaghetti down her throat as
if her life depended on it.

'Amusing myself by breathing in and out, probably,'
Abby said with a sigh, as she toyed with her cheese roll.
'There's nothing else to do round here, unless bird
watching turns you on. On a Friday, back in Brighton,
I'd have been going out clubbing or hanging out at the
Pier. There's this guy, Fergus – did I tell you about
Fergus? He . . .'

'You've told the world about Fergus,' Chloë said,
grinning, her freckled cheeks dimpling. 'The one you
dumped, right?'

'Yes,' agreed Abby carelessly. 'He was OK, but I had to
cool it. He came on too strong. But it was fun while it
lasted.'

Chloë looked at her admiringly and Abby told her
conscience that it was only a tiny lie.

'I guess,' she added, raising her voice over the din in

the cafeteria, 'fun is a thing of the past.'

Chloë pulled a face. 'Oh, don't start again,' she said. 'You talk as though nothing happens round here.'

'Well, does it?' Abby stuck a fork into her food.

'There's the Young Farmers' Club – that's neat, we did a raft building competition last week and next month, we're having a dance for charity. You should come along.'

'I don't know,' muttered Abby, ripping the ring pull off her can of cola.

'– and sometimes we go to Fakenham for a movie – or . . .' She was clearly having trouble thinking of any other attractions within a ten-mile radius of the village.

'Anyway,' Chloë said, brightening suddenly, 'there's the disco on Saturday. That'll be ace – it always is.'

Abby stopped fiddling with her lunch and looked up. 'Disco? Where? I didn't know there were any clubs round here.'

'Not at a club. Here, silly,' Chloë said with a laugh.

'Here?' Abby's heart sank. School based discos were always a disaster.

'Sure – it's in aid of Save the Children and Cat-a-clysmic are playing.'

'Who the hell are they?' Abby asked.

'Just the best new sound around,' Chloë said, pushing her plate to one side and fishing an apple out of her bag. 'It's four guys from Year Twelve . . .'

'Oh Chloë – I thought for one glorious moment they were a proper band, not some dumb amateur bunch . . .'

Chloë's chubby face flushed. 'That is such an

up-yourself remark!' she snapped. 'You don't know them, you haven't heard them. You know, I'm beginning to think Samantha was right – you're stuck up.'

Abby touched her arm. 'OK, I'm sorry,' she said. 'I didn't mean it. Are they good?'

'They're amazing,' Chloë enthused, apparently mollified by Abby's apology. 'Ryan's got a sensational voice and Liam plays the keyboard – he's good, too. But of course, it's Nick Mayes that really brings the whole thing together – he's the drummer, and he's dead sexy and – '

'And you fancy him!' Abby grinned.

'How did you know?' Chloë asked, almost choking on her apple. 'Did Amy let on? I'll kill her – or was it Sam – she's a real motor mouth . . .'

'The look on your face told me,' Abby said, laughing. 'I know about these things. So are you two an item?'

'I wish,' she said, sighing. 'Sometimes I wonder if he even knows I exist.'

'So make it so he has no choice,' Abby replied.

'Oh yeah. Like, how?' Chloë demanded.

'Well, go to the disco and flaunt yourself, make him see you, dance funky, be a bit loud . . .'

'I can't – I'm not like that.' Chloë sighed.

'You can act, can't you? Pretend you're playing the vamp in a play,' Abby suggested. 'Works for me every time.'

'I suppose I could try. If we got there early . . .' Chloë bit at her fingernail.

'Hang on,' Abby butted in, 'what's with the "we"? I'm not going.'

'I thought you were bored,' Chloë challenged. 'What, we're not cool enough for you?'

'It's not that,' Abby cried hastily, desperate not to lose the first friend she'd made since moving. 'It's just that – you know, with my dad just having died, going to a disco seems . . .' She paused, remembering how important timing was in moments of deep emotion. 'It seems callous, somehow.'

She saw at once that it had worked. Chloë reached across the table and grabbed her hand. 'Oh, sorry, Abby – I didn't think. But look, maybe coming to the disco would help you move on. I mean, when my mum died – '

'Your mum? I didn't know.'

'She died when I was thirteen,' Chloë said, sighing. 'Cancer. For ages I didn't go anywhere, do anything, except look at old photos and cry.'

'Tell me about it,' whispered Abby, a lump swelling in her throat. Even trying to act cool never managed to totally take away the ache in her heart over her dad.

'But then my dad told me that Mum would hate to see me wasting my life and that I had to live it to the full for her.'

Chloë held Abby's gaze until Abby had to look away from embarrassment at having lied to her new friend about something so awful.

'I guess your dad would feel the same, wouldn't he?'

Slowly Abby nodded. She could almost hear her dad's voice. 'Life's for the living, kiddo,' he used to say.

'So come to the disco,' Chloë urged. 'Everyone else is. It's only four pounds and half of that's for charity. And if you can't hack it, leave early.'

'OK, I'll come, but on one condition,' Abby told her. 'You do everything I say, right? I'm going to make sure that by the end of the evening, this Nick person is panting for you!'

'COMING 2 NORFOLK 4 SAILING WEEKEND. CAN I C U? PICK U UP 8PM SAT? LOVE BLAKE.'

'Yes!' Ellie grinned to herself and punched the 'save' button on her phone.

Tina Gregory leaned across the common room table and peered at her. 'I haven't seen you look so cheerful since you arrived here,' she said with a grin. 'What's up – have you just won the lottery?'

'What? Oh no, it's just a friend – he's coming up at the weekend,' Ellie said, feeling the colour flooding her cheeks as she realised her reactions had been noticed. She'd only just got to know Tina, who was in all the advanced placement classes with her, and while she seemed really genuine, Ellie wasn't about to loosen up too fast.

'He? You never said you had a boyfriend.'

'It's not like that,' Ellie protested, because to be honest she wasn't quite sure what it was like. 'We're not – I mean, it's nothing.'

'Ellie, when someone as buttoned up as you goes all pink around the gills and can't string two words together, it is clearly something,' teased Tina. 'I must say, it comes as a huge relief.'

'What does?'

'The fact that you're human after all,' Tina declared. 'I thought the only guys you were interested in were dead poets. Is he sexy?'

'Sexy? Well, I mean – it's not as if . . . and besides, he's got a . . .' Ellie stumbled uncharacteristically over her words.

'Ellie. Is he sexy? Yes or no?'

'I guess.'

'You guess? Well, I suggest that come the weekend, you find out for sure! Tart yourself up, and give it all you've got, you hear me?'

Ellie took a deep breath and nodded.

'OK,' she said resolutely. 'I think maybe I will.'

This is so cool, thought Georgie, leaning back out of Adam's Topper and feeling the salt spray prick her cheeks. Adam was OK – not like most of the guys at her new school. At least he didn't do soppy chat up lines or try to grope you in mixed football, and truth was, he reminded her a bit of Tom, who she missed a ton already.

The wind was freshening and the little boat cut through the waters of the sand-flanked inlet like a knife through butter. She'd never realised that sailing was so easy – you just had to hook your feet under the strap, lean back, watch the boom and. . .

'Georgie, look out!' Adam's agonised shout broke in on her thoughts. 'To starboard!'

'To what?' Georgie cried, as the wind carried his words away.

Then she saw the red-sailed dinghy bearing down on them, so close she could catch the mischievous grin on the skipper's face.

'Oh help, what do I do?'

'He's taking our wind – heave to!'

She hadn't a clue what he meant but it was too late anyway. She felt herself falling backwards and saw the sail coming towards her like a shroud.

And then she was in the water. Cold, and very, very wet.

'If you tell a living soul, you're dead meat!' Georgie gasped, scrambling back into the Topper. For one thing, she hadn't mentioned Adam or the boat to her mother – she knew the kind of reaction she would get, and for another, falling off a bike or a horse or a boat wasn't in Georgie's nature and she didn't want anyone thinking she couldn't handle herself. 'And stop laughing!' she spluttered.

'I'm sorry,' Adam teased. 'But you looked so funny. It's just as well we were in the harbour. I didn't realise you were clueless about sailing.'

'Watch it!' Georgie protested. 'I've sailed Toppers before. Well, once before.'

'It wasn't your fault, actually,' Adam told her. 'It was that other guy. He should have given way to us. Total moron.'

He manoeuvered the boat up against the jetty. 'But I have to tell – Dad said if I ever had an accident with someone else in the boat, I had to own up. Something about insurance.'

'Come off it – I'm hardly going to sue you, am I?' Georgie reasoned. 'And my mother will have apoplexy if she finds out – she thinks boats are dangerous at the best of times.'

'Everyone round here has one, even if it's only an old rowing boat,' Adam said, and pointed toward the nearby snack bar. 'Are you getting something?'

Georgie shook her head. 'We're poor,' she said. 'I mean, seriously poverty-stricken. No home of our own, no allowances to speak of . . .'

'So get a job,' Adam said, throwing a rope over the mooring post.

'A job? Don't be daft, I'm only thirteen.'

'So? No one takes any notice of that. There are loads of Londoners who come up to sail for the weekend – they stick notices on the club house board, asking people to get boats ready on a Friday night, and then clean them up on Sunday evenings. They pay ten pounds a session if you're lucky.'

Georgie grinned. 'Great. So come on,' she twittered, giving him her hand.

'Come on where?'

'To the boathouse – hanging about here is losing me money.'

✣ SECRET NUMBER 16 ✣

The bottom line is that no person is perfect, but sometimes people are perfect for each other, anyway.

'THAT DOES IT! THIS HAS GOT TO STOP!' Ellie slammed a drawer and glared at Abby.

'What, now?' Abby sighed, wriggling into her black satin trousers. 'OK, so the room's a bit messy . . .'

'Messy? It's an absolute sty,' Ellie protested. 'You've got clothes all over the floor, books on my bed, and you've been using my make-up.'

'Only the tinted moisturiser,' Abby insisted.

'You left the cap off and it's all dried out. How am I going to go out in half an hour looking halfway decent?'

'So that's what all this is about?' Abby asked, laughing. 'Pre-date nerves – it's OK. Quite normal.'

'It's not a date and I'm not nervous,' Ellie said.

'Course not. He's gay. We've established this,' Abby said, blotting her lipstick on a tissue.

'You always think you know everything, don't you?' Ellie snapped. 'He's not gay – he's got a girlfriend!' There. She'd said it.

'A girlfriend? Are you sure?' Abby looked away from the mirror.

Ellie sighed and told her the full story.

'Oh well, that's a relief then, isn't it?' Abby beamed, squeezing Ellie's hand. 'I'm so pleased for you, honestly I am.'

'What? Pleased that he's got someone else? I'm all nervous about some date that's obviously not even a date and you say you're happy for me? Thanks for nothing!'

'Think about it – it'll be easy to wean him off this Lucy person. Changing his whole sexual orientation would have been a tad harder,' Abby explained. 'Mind you, she could just be a token girl – you know, to put people off the scent about his sexuality.'

{151}

'I don't think so, Abby,' Ellie muttered.

'Well, at least you're better off than me. Being single is the pits, but I guess I will have to get used to it,' Abby replied. 'So, what are you wearing on this hot date?'

'Whatever I can find that you haven't borrowed, creased, or sat on,' Ellie said, 'and it *not* a date!'

'Hold your horses,' Abby ordered, yanking open the wardrobe. 'Here – you look good in these.'

She threw a pair of pink satin hipsters at her sister and pulled open another drawer. She yanked open the wardrobe. 'And finish it all off with my Chinese jacket!'

Ellie frowned. 'Isn't that a bit over the top?' She hesitated.

'No, you'll look dead classy,' Abby declared. 'It's all about first impressions – if you've got it, flaunt it.'

'Thanks,' Ellie said. 'Sorry I yelled.'

'Sorry I left the cap off,' Abby countered. 'I wish I was coming with you and Blake instead of going to this dumb – ' She stopped in mid sentence as the door flew open and Georgie burst in.

'You two have got to stand up for me, OK? You've got to make Mum see sense because if you don't, I swear I'll run away and – '

'Georgie, what's going on?' Ellie interupted. 'I'm trying to get ready to go out.'

'I'm not stopping you,' Georgie retorted. 'I'm just letting you know that Mum needs dragging into the twenty-first century – like now.'

The door burst open again and Julia stomped into the room, eyes ablaze.

'Thanks so much for knocking, Mum,' Abby remarked wryly.

'Georgina, you do not run off when I'm trying to have a conversation with you!' Julia stormed, ignoring Abby completely.

'It wasn't a conversation, it was a lecture,' Georgie snapped. 'You should be pleased I've got a job.'

'A job?' Abby gasped, stepping back and standing on a discarded shoe.

'You're too young,' Ellie added, brushing her hair vigorously.

'Don't you start,' Georgie retorted. 'It's just a few hours at the weekend cleaning boats and stuff.'

'Oh, well that's OK,' Ellie said.

'It is most certainly not OK,' Julia snapped. 'What about her school work? And besides, who will you be working with?'

'Ada–' began Georgie. 'Oh, Alice and Emma and a whole gang from school.' She thought it best to keep her mother off the subject of boys.

'And how do I know that the people you'll be working for are suitable?'

'Oh, as if we're really in a position to be choosy!' Georgie shouted. 'I need cash, they need help. I like boats, they've got boats. What's the problem?'

'You're only thirteen . . .'

'Yes Mum, I'm thirteen. So don't treat me like a ten-year-old, OK? You said we all had to knuckle under and make things work here. You said we had to try to make friends, make a new life. That's what I'm doing. Now if you don't mind, I've got to go.' Georgie stormed out of the room and clattered down the stairs.

'Wow!' breathed Abby. 'I think puberty and Georgie Dashwood have finally met up. Could be interesting.'

And even though Ellie didn't often agree with her sister's sense of humour, she winked at her as their mum trotted down the stairs in hot pursuit of their younger sister.

A few minutes later, with Georgie off to goodness knows where, Abby and Ellie shuffled down the stairs, looking fresh and pretty and both a bit nervous.

'Now Abby, have you got your phone? Remember never to put a drink down – it can so easily get spiked. And Ellie dear, are you sure you're going to be warm enough in that skimpy top?'

'Darlings, am I interrupting anything?' A voice crooned in from the doorway. To Ellie's relief, her mother's attention was diverted as Davina, who had taken to calling in unannounced whenever the mood took her, burst through the open back door, carrying a tray of bedding plants.

'These need planting out as soon as poss, Julia dear,' she gabbled. 'My goodness – aren't you two glamorous?' She beamed at Abby and Ellie. 'Off on the razzle, are you? Jolly good for you.'

'Abby's off with her school friends and Blake's taking Ellie out, apparently,' Julia told her. 'He's such a nice boy, that Blake – shame he's related to Pandora.'

'Blake – you mean Lucy's Blake? Blake Goodman?' Davina cried. 'Must be! Heaven knows there can't be that many Blakes around here!'

Ellie swallowed hard, the words 'Lucy's Blake' reverberating round and round in her brain. 'He'll be here to pick me up soon,' she mumbled, avoiding Abby's glance.

'Lucy's Blake, Lucy's Blake.' She repeated the words under her breath as the door bell rang, and Davina and her mum went to greet him.

'That's him!' Chloë grabbed Abby's hand and jerked her towards the corner of the dimly lit hall. 'Isn't he to die for?'

Abby followed her gaze and searched the gaggle of guys setting up the drum kit. She couldn't see anyone remotely worth sacrificing life and limb for.

'Which one?' she shouted, raising her voice over the throb of Chain Gang's latest hit.

'There, the tall one with the fair, curly hair – don't you just yearn to run your fingers through it?'

'Personally, no, but you clearly do,' she said with a laugh, placing her can of Dr Pepper on a table and nudging Chloë's arm. 'So go on – get in there.'

'What do you mean – I can't just go up to him and . . .'

Abby sighed, grabbed Chloë's shoulders and turned her round to face her. 'Watch my lips,' she ordered as the music faded and the DJ left the stage. 'You go over there, you chat for a moment, then just as you walk away, you give him a dead alluring look and say something provocative.'

Chloë chewed her lip and then gasped. 'Oh my God, he's coming this way! I can't look – has he seen me? Is he . . .'

'Oh for heaven's sake!' Abby stepped in front of Nick as he ambled towards the soft drinks bar. 'Hi! You must be Nick Mayes – Chloë's told me what an ace drummer you are.' She gestured to her friend and parted her lips in what she hoped was a winning smile.

'What? Oh. Right. Nice. Thanks.' Nick looked somewhere past her left shoulder. This, thought Abby, is going to be harder than I'd thought.

'So what's your scene?' she asked. 'Garage? Hip-hop?'

Nick stared at her, a small frown puckering his brow. Abby scanned his features.

'Sort of folk-punk-pop, I guess,' he replied with a glimmer of a lopsided smile.

'Cool,' Abby murmured. 'That is just so Chloë's thing – right, Chloë?'

Chloë was standing, cheeks flushed and mouth half open, looking rather like a goldfish who had just found itself outside the bowl. 'Oh me? Yes. Lovely.'

'And have you recorded anything?' Abby went on,

trying frantically to remember the jargon from her *Funk Now* magazine.

'No. Hope to. Soon. Perhaps.' Nick mumbled, grabbing a can of cola.

Hopefully, Abby thought to herself with a sigh, his musical capabilities are superior to his conversational ones.

'Got to go,' he said, glancing at his watch. 'We're on in five.'

Abby kicked Chloë's shin. 'Say something,' she hissed.

'Bye then,' Chloë whispered.

Nick nodded and ambled off, slurping cola as he went.

'I give up.' Abby sighed. 'Was that your best effort?'

Chloë looked offended.

'On the sparkle front, you scored about minus ten,' Abby commented. 'But don't worry, we'll give it another go after they've played.'

She eyed the group who were taking their positions on the stage. The guitarist had acne that could have won awards, and the keyboard player had a shaved head which was so not her style, but Ryan, the vocalist, looked quite cute in a swarthy, Celtic kind of way. And she had to admit that Nick looked passably fit. Hardly a star, but fit enough.

It's going to be a long evening, she thought. But then the band started playing, and Abby surprised herself when she realised was actually dancing to the music – she couldn't help herself.

'They're good,' Abby admitted several minutes later. 'Very good.'

'I said so, didn't I?' Chloë looked as chuffed as if she'd

done the drumming herself. 'Perhaps now you'll stop moaning about Norfolk every five minutes?'

Abby ignored the dig. 'How come,' she mused, 'Nick is such a dweeb to talk to but as soon as he gets drumsticks in his hand, he's passionate and fired up and – '

'You don't fancy him, do you?' Chloë's tone changed instantly as she halted her routine mid hip shake. 'You said he wasn't . . .'

'Of course I don't fancy him,' Abby protested. 'He is so not my type. And anyway, he belongs to you, or at least he will in ten minutes. Come on – and this time, give it your best shot.'

After some more dancing and coaching, Abby {157} dragged Chloë over to the corner of the room where the band was dismantling their kit.

'That was mind-blowing!' Abby began, touching Nick's arm. 'Sensational – you've got a great sound going there.'

'Great sound,' echoed Chloë. 'Dead cool.'

'Thanks.' Nick glanced at her, half smiling, and then looked away.

Abby tried again. 'You know, you should try to get gigs in a few of the clubs round here,' she urged. 'Oh, I forgot, there aren't any clubs round here, are there?'

'Sure there are – well, bars anyhow. You know, Winkles, The Rotten Whelker . . .'

My God, Abby thought, he can do whole sentences.

'I didn't know, I've only just moved here,' Abby said, smiling. 'I'm Abby Dashwood, by the way and of course, you know Chloë, don't you?'

Nick glanced at Chloë and nodded. 'Yes, I guess I've seen you around.'

Abby sighed inwardly. Clearly Chloë hadn't been thrusting enough. She had a lot to learn.

'Not a bad idea, doing a gig,' Ryan, the vocalist, cut in, stuffing sheet music into a bag. 'Get more publicity and stuff.'

'It was Chloë's idea,' Abby said quickly. 'She is just so into the music scene. Right, Chloë?'

'What? Oh, yes, sure,' Chloë gabbled. 'You're ever so good – better than half the bands in the charts.'

'You think so? Really?' Nick sounded enthusiastic. Abby tried to ignore the fact that he was looking at her and not Chloë.

'Sure,' Chloë said. 'Definitely.'

'So let us know when you've got it set up,' she said, running her tongue along her upper lip – she didn't even mean to do it – it was just habit for Abby. 'And we'll be there whipping up the crowds!'

She paused, praying that Chloë would come in with the punchline, or at least mimic her lip-licking routine. But nothing. Prayer, she thought, was very overrated.

'And of course,' Abby murmured, dropping her eyes, 'you'll have to wait to find out what else we can whip up when roused, won't you?'

'Will we, now?' Nick actually began to look animated, winking at Ryan and actually meeting her gaze.

She twirled away, snatching Chloë's hand. Well, at least now he'd remember them.

'OK,' she told Chloë firmly. 'I've done the ground work. Now it's all down to you.'

* * *

At half past eight, Ellie decided that Blake was just being kind, taking pity on her in a new place and doing the right thing by dragging her along to the sailing club to meet his mates. True, he had introduced her to lots of people, showed her the club lounge, took her out on the balcony and pointed out which dinghies belonged to which of his friends, but as the evening wore on, he seemed edgy and distracted. Worse still, every few minutes someone would come up to him and say things like 'Great to see you – where's Lucy?' or 'Lucy still not back then?' while giving Ellie a sidelong glance.

By nine o'clock she had had enough. Well, almost enough.

'I'm sweltering,' Blake said, taking her hand. 'How about we get some fresh air?'

A big part of her wanted to call it quits but a bigger part wanted to be out on the jetty, hand in hand, and hopefully lip to lip with Blake. That was the part that won.

As they shimmied out to the end of the dock, Ellie found herself holding her breath, watching the ripples in the water as they swam away from the boats, willing Blake to tell her something she wanted to hear. And then, he did.

'I really like you, Ellie,' Blake said softly as they stood at the end of the jetty, listening to the jangling of the halyards and the soft cooing of roosting seagulls. He leaned towards her, cupping her chin in his hand.

'No,' she said, pulling away.

'But Ellie . . .'

'What about Lucy? All evening I've heard nothing

but your mates going on and on about Lucy and where she is and why she's not with you.' She took a deep breath. 'So come clean – just what is the score with you two?'

Blake's arms dropped to his side. 'It's complicated.' He sighed.

That, thought Ellie, isn't the right answer. She'd hoped for something along the lines of, 'Lucy? Oh she's history?' or 'Lucy? Am I ever pleased to be rid of her!'

'So explain,' Ellie urged.

'Well, we started going out together ages ago, when we were still at school,' he began uncomfortably. 'You know, just having a laugh but then . . .' He hesitated.

'Then what?'

'Then it got more serious,' he admitted, shifting from one foot to the other as though he had to go to the bathroom. 'But that was ages ago.'

Her heart lifted, and she allowed herself to enjoy the fresh salty air and the perfect night-time temperature for just a moment. 'And now it's over?' She held her breath.

'Yes – well, no, not exactly.'

The fresh salty air suddenly smelled a bit more like stale fish than Ellie had noticed before.

'Oh great! It's not over and you're trying to come on to me? C'mon Blake, I wouldn't have thought it your style.' That's when she realised they were still holding hands and she dropped his.

'It's not like that, Ellie,' Blake protested. 'Lucy's gone away because . . .'

'So she's on holiday and you want someone to fill the gap till she gets back, is that it?'

'You've got it all wrong,' Blake stammered, reaching for Ellie's hand.

'So is it on? Or off?' She was trying hard to keep her cool, but it clearly wasn't working.

'Well, on. Kind of. But . . .'

Ellie took a deep breath and forced a smile on to her lips. 'Fine. Now if you don't mind, I think I'd like to go home.'

She waited for Blake to protest, but instead he turned toward the balcony steps and strode towards the car park.

✄ SECRET NUMBER 17 ✄

*If love is blind, then friendship probably could
use some glasses, too.*

'ANNIE? HAVE YOU GOT A MOMENT?'

'It's Abby, actually, short for Abigail.' Normally Abby would have totally dismissed a guy who couldn't even remember her name, but these were extenuating circumstances. Destiny had clearly instructed Nick to walk across the schoolyard at precisely the moment Abby was heading for the IT suite, and God knows after talking to Chloë that morning and finding out that she still had yet to utter more than a word to Nick, she certainly needed Abby's help.

'Sorry.' He grinned, stuffing his hands in his pockets. 'About that gig idea of yours.'

'Not mine. Chloë's,' Abby said brightly, side stepping to avoid a gaggle of Year Nines in PE outfits.

'Whatever,' Nick went on, 'I wondered – I mean, not if you don't want to – but I'm going to suss a couple of bars on Friday and I thought, well maybe you might like to come.'

'Me?' This was not the plan. He was meant to want

Chloë, not her. She had to get out of this and fast.

'I've got this new car,' he went on eagerly. 'We could go for a meal first if you like and then check out the bars. See which one you think is best.'

'That would be great,' she said, smiling sweetly. 'Only it's not me you want – I'm a new girl round here. Besides, it's Chloë who's got her finger on the pulse of the music scene.'

'Right. So you don't want to come. Fair enough.'

If he hadn't looked so crestfallen, if his hair hadn't at the very second flopped into his left eye and if he hadn't, for one fleeting second, brushed his hand against hers, she would have turned and walked away.

'Of course I want to come,' she said, flicking her hair over her shoulder and briefly touching his arm. 'Tell you what – how about me and Chloë and you and – who's the vocalist guy?'

'Ryan?'

'Yes, him. Team effort – two musicians and two fans – the perfect combination for choosing your launch venue!' She knew she sounded like a paragraph from a badly-written teen magazine, but desperate situations called for drastic solutions. 'Pick us up at seven, yes? I'll tell Chloë. It'll be a blast. What a clever idea of yours!'

On Friday, Nick and Ryan picked up Abby and Chloë and they began their night about town. Abby was fairly certain it was the dullest date she'd even been on, though she was beginning to see what Chloë saw in Nick.

'I just need the loo,' Abby said, stifling a yawn.

'Again?' Chloë gasped. 'Are you ill?'

'No, dimbo,' Abby hissed. 'I'm leaving you two alone. It's called tact.'

Honestly, she thought, pushing her way through the clusters of drinkers in The Rotten Whelker, I give up. Chloë had no technique at all. She sat there drooling at Nick but she never took the initiative.

Abby pushed open the door of the Ladies and joined the queue. Nick was quite sweet really and if Chloë didn't act more assertively, someone else would come along at school and snap him up. She really should get on with it.

She yawned. I'm exhausted, she thought, what with moving seats every time Nick sits beside me and following Ryan to the bar in order to leave the love birds alone. And what does Chloë do? Nothing.

After visiting the toilet for the tenth time that night, and readjusting her ponytail, she left the ladies room and hoped that she'd find Nick and Chloë deep in conversation. No such luck.

'Want a drink?' Nick caught Abby's arm as she headed back from the loo. 'I'm leaving those two alone!'

He grinned, oblivious to Abby's expression of alarm. 'Ryan really fancies your friend,' he said.

'He does?' Abby gasped.

Nick nodded. 'Cool, isn't it?' he murmured. 'Gives us more time to get to know one another.'

'Um, huh, right,' Abby said, glancing at Chloë and Ryan. 'But –' Then, for some reason Abby stopped herself. Maybe it was the way Nick was smiling at her, or the warmth of his hand on the small of her back, but whatever it was, she didn't protest any more.

After checking out the next bar, Abby became more and more certain that perhaps Chloë and Ryan really were the better match, anyway. They certainly weren't having any trouble with conversation, and goodness knows she and Nick had hardly shared a word all night.

'This place has a better feel than the other bar, hasn't it?' Nick shouted over the beat of the band in McGinty's Cavern. 'More upbeat.'

'I don't like it,' Ryan interrupted.

'I do,' Chloë said. 'You're so right, Nick.'

'Well, yes, actually, it is quite good,' Ryan burst out. 'What I meant was I don't like to make a decision on just one evening.' He edged closer to Chloë. 'So how about we do this again?' he asked eagerly.

'We?' queried Chloë, throwing him a withering look.

'I'm dead busy next week,' Nick said.

'Me too,' Abby lied.

'That's fine,' Ryan said enthusiastically. 'Chloë and I could suss out some of the places in Cley or Holt and report back. OK, Clo?'

Bad move, Ryan, thought Abby. Chloë hated having her name shortened.

'Actually, no,' retorted Chloë. 'It's got to be Nick's decision. He's the glue that holds this band together.'

OK, maybe she does still like Nick, then, thought Abby. I can work with that.

'Without him,' Chloë went on, 'the rest of you would be nothing.'

Hang on, Abby thought, cringing. That's a bit hard.

'OK, so how about next Friday?' Nick said hastily.

'I can't do Friday,' said Ryan.

'I can,' Chloë said. 'Abby can't though, can you?' She shot a warning glance across the table.

'No way,' Abby agreed. 'Worst possible night for me.'

'In that case . . .' Nick began.

'Actually, I could do Friday,' Ryan interrupted suddenly.

'Great,' Abby cut in, anxious to get the whole thing over with and go home. 'You don't need me – you two and Chloë give it your best shot and update me afterwards. OK?'

'Cool!' Chloë's grin was as broad as a Cheshire cat.

'I guess,' muttered Nick.

'Fantastic,' said Abby. 'Can we go now?'

Abby was half way up the stairs to bed when her mobile bleeped that it had a message: *WILL U COME OUT WITH ME ON THURSDAY? JUST THE 2 OF US? C U 2MORROW. NICK*

❦ SECRET NUMBER 18 ❧

*The only thing worse than knowing your guy has a
girlfriend is hearing about her. The only thing worse than
that is seeing her.*

'SO COME ALONG, PEOPLE – TELL ALL!'

Davina, faithful to her self-established Sunday
morning after-church ritual, settled herself into one of
the sagging armchairs in the sitting room of Marsh
Cottage and put her feet up on the coffee table.

'The garden's looking so much better, Julia darling –
you are clever. Love those blue things,' she went on.

'Delphiniums,' Julia said with a smile, offering her a plate
of flapjacks. 'They were here already, just buried under a
mass of bindweed. What I plan to do is make a path and
then plant aquilegias, and cranesbill and maybe some
kniphofias and sedums for the autumn, or perhaps . . .'

'And have you made friends, girls?' Davina rushed on,
clearly anxious to avoid a horticultural dissertation. 'I
heard all about you falling out of Adam's boat, Georgie –
sounds hilarious!'

Ellie grinned to herself as Georgie dropped her copy
of *Dinghy Sailing for Beginners* and pulled a frantic-
looking face at Davina.

'Boat? Falling out? Adam?' Julia almost spilled her coffee in alarm. 'Georgie, what's going on?'

'Uh, I didn't mean falling out as in falling out,' Davina replied hastily, mouthing the word 'sorry' to Georgie. 'I meant leaning out, you know, sailing like a real pro! And how about Abby?'

'She's still in bed,' Julia said, sighing.

'Well, not surprising, really,' Davina commented, taking another bite of flapjack. 'I saw her coming out of The Rotten Whelker bar last night and thought she looked a bit . . .'

'Bar?' Julia's coffee was destined to end up all over the carpet. 'I specifically told her . . .'

'Coffee bar,' she said hastily, causing Ellie to wince. 'Type thing, sort of,' she ended lamely. 'And you, Ellie darling – how's school? Have you made any friends?'

'Afraid not,' her mother intervened. 'I can't think why because – '

'Mum?' Ellie squashed the urge to throttle her mother.

'Well, we will have to do something about that,' declared Davina. 'I know – Lucy!'

Every nerve ending in Ellie's body went on red alert. 'Lucy?' she gulped.

'That's right,' Davina went on, biting enthusiastically into one of the biscuits Julia was offering. 'Well of course, you know Blake, so you're bound to meet Lucy soon enough – they come together like ham and eggs, bless them. Anyway, I've got a rather spectacular plan.'

Ellie didn't realise that she had groaned out loud until she got a withering look from her mother and heard Georgie stifle a giggle.

'Lucy will be back soon,' Davina said. 'I'll bring her over and introduce you and then she can take you under her wing – lovely girl – known her since she was a baby. Such a popular little thing. Her mother runs Head Cases, that wonderful hat shop in Burnham Market, father's something rather high up in – '

'Honestly, I'd love to, but – ' Ellie butted in.

'That's settled, then,' Davina carried on. 'She's a pet. You'll just love her.'

Somehow, Ellie thought, I very much doubt it.

'See, I won't be around that much from now on,' Ellie smiled sweetly. 'I've got a job.'

'Job?' Julia's coffee finally connected with the carpet. 'You never said.'

'I only heard yesterday,' Ellie explained, leaping up and grabbing a box of paper tissues from the mantelpiece. 'It's at the sailing club – behind the bar, serving food, that sort of stuff.'

She caught sight of her mother's alarmed expression. 'It's OK – it won't affect my school work,' she assured her. 'Just Wednesday evenings, the odd Friday and Sunday . . .' And every other shift I can get, she added silently.

'Oh Ellie, I don't know that's altogether suitable,' Julia began. 'Bar work – it sounds so – well, rather lower class somehow.'

'Oh Julia, don't be so old-fashioned,' Davina retorted briskly. 'The sailing club is the trendiest place around. What's the word you young people use? Buzzy. That's it, buzzy.' She winked at Ellie. 'And work's work, when all is said and done. Besides, it's the perfect place for Ellie to meet some more young people. And she's sure to hook up with Lucy because she hangs out there all the time in the summer.'

Oh terrific, thought Ellie. Just terrific.

Just then the phone rang and Georgie dashed into the kitchen to get it. A moment later she called for her sister. 'It's Blake!'

Ellie sighed and excused herself from Davina and Mum's chit-chat. 'Hello? Oh, Blake. What? No, we discussed this – you've got . . .' She dropped her voice as she caught sight of Georgie peering over the banisters with a grin on her face. '. . . someone else and . . . Really?'

She gestured to Georgie to go away. Georgie merely grinned.

'Just a chat? As a mate? Yes, OK – well, that's fine. When? Thursday? See you, then.' She replaced the handset.

'Ellie's going out with *Blaaa-ake!* Ellie's going out with . . .' Georgie chanted running downstairs.

'Georgie,' said Ellie.

'Yes?'

'Shut up.'

The next day, back at school, Abby had a different type of run-in to deal with. As she crossed the main lawn, she caught sight of Nick's floppy hair, and strangely, she felt her stomach lurch.

'Nick, wait!' Abby belted across the school forecourt. 'Thanks for the text message, but –'

'Yeah, sure,' he said. 'Oh and by the way, I'm really sorry about your dad. Ellie told me in French today.'

'Thanks. Look, I can't see you on Thursday,' she said.

'Wednesday then?'

Abby shook her head.

'Well, I guess I could do Tuesday if it was . . .'

'No.'

'Is it because of your dad? I mean, we could always go somewhere really quiet – walk along Holkham beach or go over to Brancaster or something.'

'No, I just can't come, OK?' Abby pulled at her ponytail.

'Oh I get it – you're not interested,' he muttered, his mood changing. 'Why can't you just come right out and say so?'

'Because it's not like that.' Abby found herself chewing her lip. 'Look, Chloë really, really fancies you. Surely you know that?'

Nick shrugged.

'And,' Abby went on, 'she's my friend. I can't start going out with the one guy in the entire universe that's she's asked me to help her get her hands on.'

'But I don't want my hands on her,' Nick said. 'I want them – '

'Must dash,' Abby butted in hastily. 'Things to do.'

Abby hurried off, positive she'd done the right thing and that would be that. Of course, three hours, four text messages and two phone calls later, she was feeling a bit differently again. After all, she couldn't very well get Nick to go for Chloë if they didn't spend any time together, and if going out on another double date was the ticket, she was willing to make the effort.

'I'll come, Nick, but it has to be a foursome again. Promise?'

Nick grunted down the phone. 'If that's the only way I get to see you, then I suppose I have to go along with it.' He sighed. 'But don't think I like it because I don't.'

'He's here!'

Ellie jumped and smudged her mascara as Georgie burst into the bedroom and flopped down on Abby's bed on Thursday evening. 'Blake? Here? Now?' Ellie gasped.

'You sound just like Mum,' Georgie giggled. 'Of course Blake – '

'Get off my bed,' Abby butted in, shutting off her hair dryer and running her fingers through her hair. 'You stink.'

'Yacht varnish,' said Georgie happily. 'Me and the gang are helping Mr Dutton do up his boat. Anyway, Ellie, they're in the sitting room and Mum's – '

'They?' Ellie swung round. 'What do you mean, they?'

'Him and this other guy,' Georgie said. 'Piers someone or other – looks really up himself, if you ask me. Wears sunglasses inside the house – I mean, how naff is that?'

Ellie grinned, both relieved that Lucy wasn't there and that her little tomboy sister had noticed what a guy was wearing.

'They're in the sitting room and Mum's just got to the *you will take care of Ellie, won't you?* bit . . .'

'Oh no!' Ellie blotted her lipgloss on a tissue as the ancient bell pull in the porch clanged.

'It's OK, I'll get it,' Georgie said. 'It'll be Emma – she's taking me to Young Farmers. It's a rafting evening but don't tell Mum. She thinks we're bottle-feeding lambs!' She clattered down the still uncarpeted stairs

'Do I look OK?' Ellie pleaded, throwing her make-up

bag on to the bed. 'I mean, not too dressed up and in your face?'

'Quite the opposite,' Abby assured her.

'What? You mean I look a scruff? You could have said – oh, whatever, I don't have time to change right now.'

'No I don't mean that at all,' Abby said, sighing. 'You look classily casual, OK?'

Ellie was half way through the door when Georgie charged back up the stairs. 'It's a guy for you, Abby,' George panted, pushing Ellie out of the way to see Abby. 'Nick Mayes?'

'Nick? From school?' Ellie asked. 'Is this – well, you know . . .'

'No, it is not!' asserted Abby. 'Nick's a mate of Chloë's – he's only picking me up because he's the one with the wheels.'

'Well, he's in the sitting room now, along with Blake and Piers,' Georgie went on, 'and now Mum's moved on to the "*you don't know the hell we've been through in the last six months*" bit. You'd better get down there before she scares them all off for ever.'

'What's wrong?' Abby demanded as Nick drove through the village. 'You haven't said a word since I got into the car.'

He rammed the gears and accelerated. 'I didn't realise all your mates were so flippin' posh.'

'What? Don't be dumb . . .'

'Me? I'm not the dumb one – what about those two with their plummy accents, and their designer label gear? They looked at me like I was a right scruff.'

'Don't be silly,' Abby said. 'Blake's not like that – he's hardly Mr Sophisticated himself.'

Nick sighed. 'And then when your mum asked where I lived, and what my dad did . . .'

'Oh God, she didn't did she?' Abby sighed. 'I'm sorry. She does tend to want a full CV from anyone I even look at.'

'And just so we get everything clear,' he went on, pulling out to pass a woman on a bicycle. 'My mum works in the supermarket in Burnham and my dad's been laid off which is why I don't go around in Burberry and Hugo Boss, OK?'

'Will you shut up and listen?' Abby shouted. 'I reckon you're a really nice guy and I don't give a toss what you wear, OK?'

The moment she had said the words she realised her mistake. She had wanted to make Nick feel good about himself but suddenly he was gazing at her with wide eyed adoration.

'You don't? I mean, you like me?'

'Of course I do,' she murmured. *What else could she say?* 'But Chloë – '

'Chloë nothing. So will you come to King's Lynn with me tomorrow? The Sunday market is great for old vinyl records – I collect them.'

'Why don't you take Chloë?' Abby urged. 'She'd be so into all that stuff.'

'Oh, I get it – You don't want to be seen out with me. Well . . .'

'I'll come,' Abby said. 'Of course, I'll come.'

After all they were mates. Just mates. And it would give her a great opportunity to point out all Chloë's good points.

* * *

'So you're the famous Ellie!' The tall, lean guy with the Armani shades gave a mock bow before vaulting into Blake's MG Midget and perching on the folded soft top. 'I've heard all about you – and I must say, Blake's usually a dark horse.'

'Piers, for God's sake.' Blake flushed scarlet as he climbed into the driving seat and started the engine. 'You're embarrassing Ellie.'

'No he's not.' Ellie smiled.

'This,' Blake went on, glancing over his shoulder, 'is Piers Fordyce who, when he's not playing the fool, is my best mate from school and soon-to-be America's Cup yachtsman.'

'I wish,' Piers said with a laugh, as Blake accelerated down the lane. 'Sorry to play gooseberry, but my car died this morning, and what with Lucy still away, I knew I could cadge a lift.'

Lucy? Why couldn't everyone just stop saying that name all the time? Ellie was quite sure Lucy was the new four-letter word in her life. Her heart plummeted like a stone being dropped off the end of the pier.

'I thought we'd drop Piers off at the sailing club, have a couple of drinks and decide what to do,' Blake said, glancing at Ellie as he turned on to the coast road. 'We could walk along the beach to Allie's Fish Bar or . . .'

'Come off it, Blake,' Piers interrupted. 'Don't tell me that's all you can think of doing with a gorgeous creature like Ellie? Where's your imagination, man?' He leaned forward and punched Blake on the shoulder.' While the cat's away and all that . . .' He chuckled.

Georgie was right – this guy is so up himself, Ellie thought.

'A walk would be lovely,' she told Blake, glancing back at Piers. 'Really good.'

After they dropped Piers off at the club, Blake and Ellie made their way toward the beach, taking their shoes off once they made their way over the dunes.

'I've found this course – art with photography. At Brighton College of Art.' Blake stopped half way along the sands. He turned to Ellie, a broad grin on his face.

'That's ace,' Ellie murmured, her mind still mulling over the Lucy issue. 'And have they got places?'

Blake picked up a seashell and tossed it back and forth in his hands. 'Yes, and what's more, I've got all the right A levels and stuff,' he said, 'I could live with Pandora rent free at Holly House – I mean, oh gosh . . .'

{176}

'It's OK.' Ellie sighed, dragging her big toe in the wet sand. 'I've got used to the idea.'

'Well, it's just that it would be just so perfect.'

'So go for it,' Ellie encouraged, trying to ignore the pang in her chest at the mention of her old home. 'What did your parents say?'

Blake looked at her and raised his eyebrows. 'You want the shortened version, or the whole thing? Mum said, "Oh Blake" which is all she ever says if Dad is within earshot . . . '

'And your father?'

'He told me I was wasting my education, failing the family, opting for an easy life, behaving like an idiot – and those were just the polite bits.'

'Mmm.' Ellie sighed sympathetically. 'I guess you'll just have to go it alone then.'

Blake shook his head, his mood suddenly darkening. 'How can I?' he argued. 'College costs money . . .'

'Get a job in the evenings, take out a student loan,' Ellie began. 'Anything's possible if you really want it enough.'

'I suppose so,' Blake murmured, sounding totally unconvinced. He glanced at Ellie. 'I don't have to decide yet, I guess – not if I take a year off and start next autumn. Dad says I should take the next few weeks while I'm . . . well, I should think about the family reputation, amongst other things. That's when I texted you and said I was coming up. I just wanted to have a sane conversation with a rational human being.' He smiled down at her. 'Trouble is, it's not going to work.'

Ellie frowned. 'What do you mean?'

'I don't want to talk to you about it,' he admitted. 'I just want to kiss you.'

Every cell in her body went on red alert. Remember Lucy, her conscience told her. He's Lucy's Blake – ham and eggs, bless them. She hated liking him so much despite being so angry about what he was doing, and she hated feeling like he liked her too, even though there was someone else.

'Hey, I thought you said something about a fish bar,' she gabbled turning away just as his lips reached her cheek. She backed away and tried to laugh it off, picking up a sea shell and tossing it into the dark water. She didn't want to make the moment any awkward than it already was.

'What?' Blake pulled back. 'I thought . . .'

'Come on,' Ellie said, turning to him with as bright a smile as she could manage. 'I'll race you along the beach.'

She broke into a run and it wasn't until she reached the disused slipway that she realised Blake hadn't joined in.

He was ambling towards her, hands stuffed in his jeans and for a fleeting moment, she couldn't help wishing that she'd had the kiss before acting on her principles.

'Listen, Ellie,' Blake pleaded, as they reached the door of the fish bar. 'Give me five minutes to explain, OK? Just five minutes?'

'What's to explain?' asked Ellie, shaking him off. 'You and Lucy are an item and . . .'

'Just shut up will you?' Blake exploded.

Ellie was too taken aback by the outburst to answer.

'Yes, Lucy and I *were* an item. No, I haven't told her it's over yet. And you know why?'

'It's no concern of mine,' Ellie lied, reaching back into her debate team lingo from St Ethelreda's.

'Because,' Blake went on, ignoring her, 'she's staying in Cornwall with her grandmother who happens to be dying.'

Ellie swallowed. 'Oh,' was all she said because she couldn't think of anything else.

'Lucy's gone down to say her goodbyes – and probably, knowing Lu, to check that's she's in the will!' He attempted a smile.

'I'm sorry,' Ellie apologised. 'I didn't realise.'

'So you see, I can't tell her it's over, can I? I can hardly dump her by phone.'

'I suppose that's true.' Ellie nodded thoughtfully. 'But when she phoned that time at Holly House, you said you loved her.'

Blake's face turned red. 'Well, she kept on asking me if I did and it just seemed easier to go along with it until she got back and I could explain to her face.'

'So when is she coming back?'

'Next weekend, all being well,' Blake said. 'I'll tell her then, I promise.'

'Truly?' Ellie smiled. 'I mean, only if you want to . . . I mean, if you think that you and I could . . .'

'We could,' Blake assured her, leaning towards her and cupping her chin in his hands. ''I'll show you how we could.' His lips were only a millimetre from hers.

'No, Blake!' She pulled away. 'Not now. Not yet.'

'For heaven's sake, I've said I'll tell her, haven't I? What's your problem?' {179}

'The problem,' Ellie retorted, 'isn't mine. It's yours. And she's called Lucy.'

'Fine,' Blake looked at her, with a twinkle in his eye. 'Then lets eat some chips at the very least.'

Ellie agreed and after the waitress brought them over their fish and chips and pints, Blake made her an offer.

'OK, so if I promise not to come on to you, can I see you tomorrow?' He smiled at her playfully. 'I'll keep my hands in my pockets, I'll talk about the weather . . .'

Ellie struggled not to laugh as she took a bite of fried halibut. Blake looked so appealing and pathetic.

'That would be great.' She nodded. 'And Blake?'

'Yes?'

'It's not that I don't like you,' she insisted. It's just, she added to herself, that once I've kissed you I have a feeling there will be no going back.

'Good.' Blake smiled.

❧ SECRET NUMBER 19 ❧

Remember Number 18? Um, yeah.

ELLIE GRINNED AT BLAKE the following afternoon, as they walked barefoot through the sand dunes from Holkham beach.

'I never realised there were so many beautiful beaches round here,' she told him, casting her eyes over the vast expense of seashore with its waving outcops of sea grass and scattered piles of driftwood.

'They used this beach at the end of the movie *Shakespeare in Love*,' Blake told her. 'None of the locals was allowed on it for three days!' He slipped a hand into hers. 'What shall we do now?' he asked. 'Film? There's a good one on in Hunstanton.'

'I've got loads of homework,' Ellie insisted, shaking her head. 'I'm behind as it is.'

'Just an ice cream and a coffee then,' Blake urged.

'OK.' Ellie grinned, turning down the path to the ice cream kiosk. 'What's another ten minutes?'

Blake and Ellie ordered their cones – pistachio and mud pie – and had just shoved one another's cones playfully in each other's faces when a shrill voice from behind made Ellie jump. 'Surprise, surprise!'

'Oh my God!' The colour drained from Blake's face and he lost his grip on his cone. It found the unfortunate landing place of Ellie's foot.

Ellie spun round to find herself staring into the face of a wafer thin, pixie-faced girl with huge brown eyes, blemish free skin and the tightest fitting leather mini skirt Ellie had ever seen. She knew instinctively who it was.

'Blakey darling!' the girl cried, hurling herself at him. Blake looked at Ellie apologetically and hugged her awkwardly.

'Hi, Lucy,' Blake stammered. 'I thought you weren't coming up till next weekend.'

'Couldn't stay away from you,' Lucy piped up, her eyes scanning Ellie from top to toe. 'And who's this?'

Ellie didn't need her psychology text book to understand that Lucy was not exactly thrilled to see her.

'This is Ellie,' Blake began. 'She and I were just – '

'Oh, *Ellie Dashwood*,' Lucy interjected, holding Blake's hand proprietarily. 'Blake's told me all about you.'

'He has?' Ellie was so taken aback that she struggled to get the words out. She wished she was dressed in something smarter than cut off jeans and a sweatshirt.

'Oh gosh, yes,' enthused Lucy. 'He told me all about your tragedy – you poor, poor thing. It must be so hard for you, moving house, not knowing anyone, starting at a crap school . . .'

'How's your grandmother?' Blake cut in, as Ellie was wondering just how often Blake had been speaking to

Lucy in order to impart all that information.

Lucy's eyes sparkled with unshed tears. 'She's gone into a hospice,' she whispered. 'They reckon she's only got a few more weeks at the most.'

Ellie's hard feelings softened. If Lucy was feeling one quarter as bad as she felt about her father . . .

'I'm so sorry, Lucy – Blake told me about it the other day at the sailing club,' she said gently.

'So you two have been out together?' Lucy's grief appeared to evaporate in an instant.

'Oh no – just in a gang,' Blake said quickly. 'With Piers and some others, you know.'

The look of relief on Lucy's face did not escape Ellie's notice. She also found it pretty hard to ignore the anger in the pit of her own stomach – if taking a romantic walk on the beach was hanging in a gang, then Ellie apparently had been confused about the English language for some time now.

'Piers? How is he? Bless him, he phoned me twice last week to see how Granny was getting on.'

'He did?' Blake seemed annoyed. Which he shouldn't, thought Ellie, if he didn't care about Lucy any more.

'I think he fancies me.' Lucy giggled. 'Now don't look so worried, Blakey darling . . .'

She leaned against him and puckered her lips. Blake pecked the top of her head.

'I've got to go,' Ellie burst out. 'Loads of homework to do . . .'

'Homework?' Lucy cried. 'You're not still at school, are you? How dire for you! I'm at college, but I guess Blake told you.'

'No, actually,' replied Ellie, fixing an oh-so-sweet smile on her face, 'In fact, he hardly mentioned you.'

She didn't bother to hang about to see the effect of her rebuff. There was only so long she could keep her cool.

Ellie had just finished her essay on the effects of aroma on supermarket sales, when the doorbell rang. Since everyone else was out, she had no choice but to answer it.

'Hi, it's me!' Lucy stepped over the threshold before Ellie could think up an excuse to shut the door in her face.

'Just thought we could get to know one another better,' she said, fixing Ellie with a steely stare. 'If that's OK with you, of course?'

Not at all, thought Ellie. 'Would you like a drink?'

'No thanks,' Lucy replied. 'Blake's picking me up in half an hour and I have to smarten myself up. You *do* know that Blake and me – we're an item?'

'Yes, he mentioned it,' she stammered.

'That's good,' Lucy grinned. 'He's a sweetie – I mean, I've had loads of boyfriends but he's the sweetest so far.' She eyed Ellie closely. 'So he took you to the Sailing Club, yeah?'

Ellie nodded. 'But only because I applied for a job there,' she said hastily, unsure why she was protecting Blake. I should drop him in it, she thought, he deserves it.

'A job? What for?'

'To earn money,' snapped Ellie.

'Oh sure, I forgot – poverty must be so wretched. Now then, who can we find for you? Someone dishy, with cash of course, who will spoil you rotten!'

'That's really kind but . . .'

'Now there's Piers, he's sweet and terribly brainy. Going to be something clever in the City after uni, part of his father's firm. Loads of money. But he's definitely not your type.'

She eyed Ellie up and down as if finding someone who would deign to go out with her was too much of a challenge.

'There's Miles – you won't have met him yet because he's on his dad's ranch in Montana. His stepmother is a model, she's been on the cover of American *Vogue* and knows absolutely everyone worth knowing. Then there's Jack, lovely but terribly spotty and he hasn't got two pennies to rub together. None of them a patch on Blake, of course.'

At least we agree on something, Ellie thought.

'Blake's dead clever too,' Lucy went on. 'He's going to do law . . .'

'No, art, surely?'

'Oh that – we dealt with that,' she tittered. 'His father had a quiet word with me – said he knew that if anyone could make Blake see sense, it was me – they absolutely confide in me all the time, you know. And as I said to Blake, fiddling about with a paintbrush and a stick of charcoal is great as a hobby but it's hardly a proper job, is it?' She giggled. 'So when we were sailing a couple of weeks back . . .'

'You sail?' Ellie cut in through gritted teeth. She had hoped that Lucy was a landlubber like herself.

'Of course – I was virtually born in a boat.' Ellie thought that if she giggled in that high pitched way once more, she might be forced to throttle her. 'I've got my Coastal Skipper certificate and everything. You?'

Ellie shook her head.

'Really?' Lucy's forehead puckered in a frown. 'How odd. Anyway, just think, in a few weeks' time, I'll be sailing in the Whitsunday Islands.'

'You will?'

'Yes, didn't Blake tell you? It was my great idea for the summer – I've got a mate with two yachts at Byron Bay and . . .'

The striking of the hall clock stopped her in her tracks.

'Oh God, is that the time? I've got to curl my eyelashes and wash my hair and Blake . . . Well, must dash!' She ran down the hall, glancing back over her shoulder. 'So you're OK with all that, yes? It's me and Blake and you can have your pick of the rest.' She laughed but her eyes weren't smiling.

'Fine,' Ellie said with a weak smile.

After all, Blake would deal with it. And by tomorrow Lucy would know she was history. Wouldn't he? He was going to tell her, wasn't he? Ellie tried to squelch the feeling of doubt that was rising in her stomach.

✕ SECRET NUMBER 20 ✕

Love triangles are really anything but lovely.
More hateful, really.

{186}'HI CHLOË, HAVE A GOOD WEEKEND?' Abby slung her school bag under the chair on Monday morning and turned to her friend.

'What's it to you?' Chloë snapped. 'You couldn't give a toss about me, you two-faced cow!'

'What do you mean?' Abby asked, stunned.

'How could you do that to Chloë?' Samantha Carter chipped in, coming up behind her and shoving her out of the way.

'I don't know what you're talking about,' Abby gabbled, praying that it wasn't what she feared it might be.

'Taking her boyfriend off her!' Samantha spat.

'Hang on,' Abby cried, her mind racing. 'He's not her boyfriend . . .'

'Oh, so you do know what I'm talking about, little miss oh-so-innocent!' spat Chloë. 'You said you'd help me get Nick and then you swan off to King's Lynn . . .'

'Yes, I was with him,' Abby admitted instantly. 'But

simply because we're friends and I was trying to him to ask Chloë out.'

'Oh, and you had to go to Kings Lynn to do all that, did you?' retorted Chloë. 'Get real – I wasn't born yesterday.'

Abby tried again. 'We were checking out the Sunday market,' she reasoned. 'Listen, if you don't believe me, wait and see; he's going to ask you out.'

'Really?' Chloë said doubtfully.

'Truly, honestly. It's just that he knows that Ryan fancies you, and Ryan's his best mate and he was in a muddle over how to go about it.' As Abby said the words and saw the glimmer of hope in Chloë's eyes, she knew {187} that she'd got in really deep. She might have saved her own skin – but only if she could get Nick to ask her out, and considering that the time she and Nick had spent together over the weekend had been off the charts, and that she'd felt their chemistry popping like mad all over the place, it wasn't going to be easy. 'You'll see,' she added, spying Nick exiting the corridor at the end of the hall.

Abby shot off after him, and as soon as she caught up she let him know that he'd have to ask Chloë out.

The look on his face as he said 'no' was nothing less than disgusted.

'What do you mean, *no?*' Abby cried, so loudly that a couple of Year Nines warming up on the tennis court missed their shots. 'You have to ask her – I told you . . .'

'I don't have to do anything,' Nick retorted. 'If I'm going to go out with anybody, I want it to be you.'

'But . . .' Abby trailed off, distracted by her thoughts. *He is so cute, the way his bottom lip goes all squashy* when he gets cross. 'Just do this one thing for me. I mean, look – Ryan's dead keen on Chloë, right?'

'He's besotted.'

'Well there you are, then,' declared Abby. 'All you have to do is set up a few dates – you, Chloë and Ryan. Only don't tell Chloë that Ryan's turning up, OK?'

'And then?'

Abby sighed. Some people were so slow on the uptake. 'Then, you start being really off with Chloë, Ryan gets to be extra nice to her and bingo! They're an item and you're off the hook.'

Nick nodded slowly. 'And then you and me . . .'

Abby winked. 'Well,' she murmured, 'if I knew for sure that my best mate was set up with a guy, and you were still free – who's to say what might happen?'

'Well . . .' Nick began taking her hand.

'Don't!' She pulled it away, not daring to risk anyone seeing them looking remotely like a couple.

'Oh great – now you won't even let me touch you,' he said, sighing. 'OK, listen, I really like you, so I'll take Chloë out but only in a gang, but only twice. No arguing – that's the deal. Take it or leave it.'

'And you'll ask her today? Like soon? Very soon?'

'I guess. The sooner I get it over with the better,' Nick said with a sigh. 'And Abby? I'm only doing this because of you.'

He really is sweet, thought Abby. And if Chloë doesn't go for Ryan, then I'm not sure what I'm going to do.

It was all she could think about through most of the next period (not a good thing considering a quiz was scheduled for the following week), but luckily Abby didn't have to wait long for good news.

'Oh my God, Abby!' Chloë cried catching Abby's arm as she headed for the locker room after lunch. 'He's done it, he's done it.'

'Who has done what?' asked Abby, determined to play dumb.

'Nick's asked me out!'

'I told you he would,' she said calmly.

'I know, I'm sorry I ever doubted you,' Chloë gabbled. 'But you have to help me.'

'Hey, I've done my bit,' she protested. 'It's up to you now.'

'Listen, you know we've got a home study day tomorrow? Well stuff studying – come with me to Kings Lynn and help me choose some new gear. Please. I haven't a decent thing in my entire wardrobe. Please.'

'I've got that awful German translation to do, and that maths assignment,' protested Abby.

'Copy mine,' urged Chloë.

'OK, OK, I'll come,' agreed Abby before Chloë could change her mind. The last thing on earth Abby wanted to do on a pleasant Spring day was homework.

'Great!' Chloë grinned. 'The muffins are on me.'

'Mum, you have to sign this now!' Georgie thrust a sheet of bright yellow paper into her mother's hands. 'And I need the cheque for fifty-six pounds,' she added.

Her mother scanned the paper, and Ellie and Abby watched curiously.

'Georgie, this is dated two weeks ago,' she protested.

'Why didn't you bring it home earlier?'

'Just read it, Mum,' Georgie urged.

'CROMWELL COMMUNITY SCHOOL: TRIP TO BRECON BEACONS

'*I hereby give my consent for my daughter, Georgina Dashwood, to participate in the forthcoming camping trip to the Brecon Beacons as part of her school trip to learn survival skills.*

'*In signing this consent form, parents acknowledge that pupils will undergo training in orienteering, map-reading and camp building that will necessitate their being in groups of three or four without full-time supervision of staff* – Good heavens, I'm not signing that!' Julia threw the booking form back at Georgie. 'How can they think of such a thing? Children unsupervised . . .'

'We are *not* children!' Georgie retorted, counting to ten in her head, like all the girls did at times like this. 'We're Year Eight, for heaven's sake. Abby went camping with the Guides when she was eleven and you didn't go ballistic about that.'

'That's true, Mum,' Abby chipped in. 'And Ellie went to France, remember? With Year Eight?'

Georgie threw her a grateful glance.

'That was supervised,' her mother said. 'What if something happened?'

'If you would just read the next bit,' Georgie ordered, 'you'd find out.'

She snatched up the paper and reading: '*However, each group will be equipped with first aid kits and marshals will be positioned at strategically placed checkpoints to ensure that any unlikely emergency is dealt with speedily and efficiently.*'

'So you see, it's fine,' Georgie declared. 'It's totally educational – and character-building and stuff.' She knew her mother was very keen on character building.

'I don't know,' her mother began. 'I'm not sure that your father would have approved.'

'Don't make Dad the excuse! You know he'd have thought it a laugh.' She swallowed hard to get rid of the choking feeling that always came when she thought about Dad. 'Now do you see why I didn't tell you sooner – you always make such a big deal of everything.'

'For goodness sake, sign it, Mum.' Abby grinned. 'That way, the house won't smell of seaweed and yacht varnish for a few days.'

'You can't say no now,' Ellie added, winking at Georgie. 'Think how she'd look in front of her mates – everyone would say you were neurotic.'

'Which I'm not and never have been,' retorted her mother. 'All right, you can go. But you must phone each night and I'll give you a first aid kit and . . .'

'Ace!' Georgie gave her mother a quick hug and headed for the door.

'Wait,' her mother said. 'What about this job down at the boatyard? You can't just ditch that on a whim, you know.'

Georgie beamed. 'It's all sorted. Adam's brother has offered to fill in.' She knew the moment she'd mentioned his name precisely what would happen and it did.

Her mother looked at Ellie and Ellie looked at Abby. 'About this Adam . . .' her mother began.

'Who the hell,' queried Abby at precisely the same moment, 'is Adam?'

The only guy that's half way on my wavelength since Tom, that's who, thought Georgie defiantly. 'Just this boy in my class.' She shrugged. 'No one special.' She dashed out of the room before the family inquisition could really take off.

'That,' she heard Abby say as she took the stairs two at a time, 'means he's special.'

'Get stuffed!' Georgie shouted back. 'That is so not true!' She heard the sound of muffled laughter and then Abby's voice once more.

'I rest my case,' Abby said.

❧ SECRET NUMBER 21 ❧

*Sometimes love really does find you when you least
expect it (and thus are not properly dressed).*

NO ONE TOLD ABBY THE BUS took three quarters of an
hour to get to Kings Lynn. Not only did it stop in every
village and hamlet, but every few minutes someone
would stick out an arm, the driver would pull up and
collect parcels and then yabber for ages about the
weather or some woman's bunions or the success of the
village flower show. It was like finding yourself in the
middle of a Jane Austen novel.

Accordingly, she was fifteen minutes late when the
bus finally pulled up at the Market Square. It was
pouring with rain as Abby grappled with her umbrella
and began heading toward the shops. She ran across the
Square, past the Guildhall, dodging between the crowds
of tourists and shoppers and cursing herself for wearing a
skirt as passing cars splashed mud up her legs.

'I'm looking for Top Shop,' she gasped to a girl in a
leather mini skirt who looked as if she might be clued up
about fashion. 'Do you know it?'

'Sure. The quickest way is . . .' But then she broke off

and waved to someone the other side of the road. 'Just coming, sweetie!' she trilled.

'Top Shop?' Abby urged.

'Oh sure! You just cut through that alleyway opposite, go across Queen Street and it's facing you. You can't miss it.'

'Thanks, you've saved my life.' Abby pushed her already sodden hair out of her face and started running again, her head bent against the driving rain as she struggled to stop her umbrella from blowing inside out. So much for enjoying a spring day.

One minute she was running down Queen Street, relieved at finally having glimpsed the gaudy 'Sale Now On' banners draped across the windows of Top Shop, the next she was face down in a puddle of water, the contents of her bag sprawled across the cobbles and two booted feet three inches from her left nostril. She was suddenly soaking wet.

'Hell, are you OK?' Abby was vaguely conscious of a guy's voice in her right ear. A firm hand gripped her arm and began hauling her to her feet. 'I know that girls make a habit of throwing themselves at my feet, but this . . .'

'Get stuffed!' Abby yanked her arm away, brushing away tears of frustration and embarrassment with her other hand. 'That is so . . . ouch! My foot!'

'You're hurt!' The guy grabbed her other arm and turned her towards him.

'Not half as much bloody pain as you'll be in if you don't – ' But she stopped as she laid eyes on her rescuer. Tall, broad-shouldered, huge grey eyes, wavy chocolate brown hair, the faintest trace of Hugo Boss – it all hit her consciousness in a millisecond.

'Wow! Fiery as well as sexy – it must be my lucky day.' The guy grinned at her and tightened his hold on her arm. 'Hunt Meade-Holman, short for Hunter – and you are?'

'Abby Dashwood, short for Abigail,' she said sweetly. 'Pleased to meet you.'

Ten minutes later, after he had bought her a coffee (she had declined an éclair because cream on the chin is not exactly a turn-on), some thrilling conversation and a near kiss, she remembered Chloë.

'I've got to go,' she cried, leaping to her feet and then sinking back into her seat as her ankle gave way beneath her. 'Ow! Cripes!'

'You can't go yet, we're only just getting to know one another.'

'I'm supposed to meeting a friend,' she began.

'Male or female?'

'Female,' she replied with a smile.

'Thank God for that,' Hunter said, looking deep into her eyes. 'Otherwise, I'd be forced to do away with the competition.'

'I have to go.' Abby insisted on trying not to let her delight at his remark show on her face. 'I had a falling out with my best mate and if I let her down again – which I suppose I already have by not turning up on time – well, I don't know what she'll do.'

'So? The damage is done. Anyway, you've got a watertight excuse.'

'Yes, but . . .'

'No buts,' Hunter said firmly. 'My car is parked just a couple of streets away. I'm driving you home.'

Abby said nothing while a battle raged in her head. Chloë had probably given up and gone home herself, but then again she could be wandering round Top Shop waiting for Abby. Abby owed it to her to keep her part of the bargain.

'I'd love a lift home please,' she told him with what she hoped was an alluring smile, 'but first, there's something we have to do.'

* * *

Abby convinced Hunter to drop her by the shop, though she received a less than warm welcome a few minutes later.

'About flaming time too!' Chloë, her arms full of clothes, glared at Abby. 'You're half an hour late – hey, Abby? What's wrong?'

Abby pressed her lips together and tried a brave but weary smile. 'I had a fall,' she murmured, limping a few steps to push her point home. 'I've knackered my ankle.'

'Oh gosh, sorry, poor you. Is it very painful?'

'Pretty much. Hunter wanted to call an ambulance but I told him I had to get here to help you and . . .'

'Hunter?' Chloë asked. 'Who is Hunter?'

Abby leaned towards her. 'You promise you won't tell? I mean, seriously promise?'

Chloë's eyes widened in anticipation. 'Of course.'

Abby jerked her head in the direction of the doorway, where Hunter was hovering, his head buried in a copy of *Car City* magazine.

'He's my boyfriend,' she whispered, wincing again for

good measure as she hobbled on one foot. 'New boyfriend, but whatevs. Isn't he a dish?'

'Boyfriend!' Abby was gratified to see that the word had precisely the effect on Chloë that she had planned. 'So you and he – you're not – I mean, Nick and you . . .'

'*Nick?* How many times do I have to tell you, Chloë? It really hurts that you don't believe me.' Thankfully the very real pain in her ankle enabled her to look on the point of tears without too much effort.

'I do, I do.' Chloë was positively radiant as she gave Abby a quick hug. 'It's just that you never mentioned this Hunter person.'

'Well, you know, it all happened quite fast,' Abby said, ignoring precisely how fast it had actually happened. She rubbed her ankle pathetically.

'Look, I'll be fine,' Chloë assured her, dead on cue. 'You go and get that ankle sorted. But first, look, this is what I've chosen. What do you think?'

Don't tell her what you think, Abby thought, gazing at the mish-mash of clothes of all styles and fabrics in Chloë's arms.

'The black's the sexiest but the red is the most unusual,' she said, smiling. 'Depends exactly what image you're going for.'

'Sexy.' Chloë grinned. 'Definitely sexy.'

'Black then,' Abby said quickly, catching sight of Hunter out of the corner of her eye as he glanced at his watch for the third time. 'And if you really don't mind, I do feel a bit faint.'

'Of course I don't – and thanks, Abby. I'm sorry about – well, you know.'

'Don't give it another thought!' Abby said breezily. 'I'm just so happy to have been of help.'

'Abby, what were you thinking of?' Julia demanded, rifling through her first aid box for some arnica cream. 'Getting in the car with a total stranger – anything could have happened! You don't know the first thing about him.'

'I do now,' replied Abby dreamily, resting her foot on the kitchen stool. 'He's eighteen . . .'

'He looks older,' her mother retorted suspiciously.

'. . . his father's the local MP,' Abby continued, ignoring her, 'they live at a place called Fairfield Court . . .'

'Fairfield Court? That gorgeous Georgian house on the Fakenham Road?' Julia gasped, dabbing cream on to Abby's bruised ankle. 'Davina took me there – the gardens are open to the public. It's an amazing place.'

'Hunt left school last summer – Winchester, actually . . .' Abby knew full well that dropping in the name of a top independent school would add to his status in her mother's eyes.

'Well, admittedly he did seem to have lovely manners,' her mother conceded, pulling the wrapper off a crêpe bandage with her teeth.

'Well, you'll see him again soon,' Abby said quickly. 'He's picking me up at seven. We're going out.' She held her breath, willing her mother to think it was a wonderful piece of news.

'Going out? Don't be so ridiculous – you can't go out. I've hardly exchanged a dozen words with the boy.'

'When he comes, you can do the full interrogation, can't you?' Abby said patiently, wincing slightly as her mother began binding her ankle with unnecessary vigour. 'And he's taking me for a drive so I won't have to walk. Oh Mum, he's so lovely and I think he really likes me . . .'

Julia shook her head slowly and touched Abby's cheek. 'How could anyone not like you, darling? But don't get your hopes up.' She switched into her doom-laden voice. 'If everything you say is true, he'll probably turn his nose up at the way we're forced to live these days.'

That was not what Abby wanted to hear. The look of fleeting surprise and the momentary frown on Hunter's face as they had pulled up outside Marsh Cottage hadn't escaped her.

'He's not like that,' she retorted defensively. 'Anyway, I told him all about what happened . . .' She paused, suddenly realising that she was digging herself into a rather deep hole. 'But I made him promise not to mention it to you, because you'd get upset.'

'That was thoughtful, darling,' her mother remarked. 'And I agree, it's best left in the past.'

Absolutely, thought Abby, especially since I doctored the truth a little. So what if Hunter thought they'd leased Holly House out to a film company for a year or so while they fought Pandora in the courts? What if Julia was supposedly recovering from a nervous breakdown following Max's death and thus, she mustn't be upset? Abby figured that by the time she had to tell him the truth, Hunter would be madly in love with her, and it would no longer matter at all. Abby had a way of justifying things.

Abby was on cloud nine. At last, after all those false starts, she was experiencing love in glorious Technicolor. She realised now that the way she had felt about Fergus – about every boyfriend she had ever dated – had just been childish infatuation, silly crushes that had nothing to do with true, adult, womanly love. Hunter was perfect; he had it all – looks to die for, sex appeal oozing from every pore, money that kept flowing no matter where she wanted to go or what she wanted to do, and a car that was the envy of all her mates.

And thanks to Chloë, she had mates. Chloë had been out with Nick and Ryan not twice but four times and had told everyone that it was all down to Abby that she had found the love of her life. Even Amy and Samantha looked at Abby with new respect and asked her for advice on tactics for pulling guys, on top of everything else. Plus, Abby didn't even have to cope with her mother's usual neurosis.

'I think Hunter is a delightful young man,' she had pronounced after Abby's third date. 'Such lovely manners and such clean fingernails.'

Abby knew that even the state of his digits wouldn't have counted for anything, had it not been for the way Hunter played her mother like a violin.

'Your garden, Julia,' he enthused, 'is quite stunning. We could do with you at Fairfield Court.'

'This carrot cake is the best I've ever tasted – my mother's a hopeless cook.'

'I love coming here – everything is so much more cosy than at home.'

Within a week, he had Julia eating out of his hand. She didn't even complain that Abby was out three nights a week. The fact that most evenings involved a session at the sailing club seemed to set her mind at rest.

'Ellie will keep an eye out for you,' she murmured by way of justification. Abby didn't bother mentioning that once they'd left for smoochy drives round the country-side or dimly-lit night clubs in Norwich, there was precious little Ellie could do. In fact, Ellie seemed to be the one person that Hunter couldn't charm.

'So what does Hunter do exactly?' Ellie asked her one morning after Abby and Hunter had made a brief appearance at the club house while Ellie was working.

'Nothing,' Abby shrugged, looking up from her last minute attempts to tackle the causes and effects of the Vietnam War. 'He left school last summer and he's taking time out to decide what to do next.'

'Lucky him,' muttered Georgie.

'Very sensible,' Julia murmured, pouring a cup of coffee. 'Make sure he follows the right course.'

Ellie frowned. 'Well, he's had a whole year – surely he must know by now.'

'Some people don't spend their whole lives worrying about tomorrow,' she retorted, quoting verbatim Hunter's phrase to her from the night before. 'The world is too preoccupied with work and achievement. He's trying to find the essence of him.'

'Sounds like a cop out to me,' Ellie said with a shrug. 'So, if he hasn't got a job, where does he get all his money from?'

'His father gives him an allowance, if you must know,' snapped Abby. 'He's dead wealthy and . . .'

'Just like we were once,' Julia said, sighing. 'Life is so much easier with money.'

'Isn't his father the guy who is up before that select committee for supposedly accepting bribes about something or other?' Ellie ventured.

'Surely not?' Julia looked alarmed.

'That,' spat Abby, quoting Hunter again, 'is just a load of hyped-up media hysteria. Nothing's proven. Anyway, what's that got to do with me and Hunter?'

'It just sounds a bit dodgy,' Ellie ventured. 'I don't want you to get hurt.'

'Oh, stuff it, Ellie!' snapped Abby. 'I don't tell you how to behave with Blake, do I?'

'Blake?' Ellie shrugged, pushing her plate away and getting up. 'What's Blake got to do with anything?'

'Clearly,' Abby said with a sigh as she glanced at Georgie, 'Blake has a whole lot to do with everything.'

'Ellie? Blake here.'

Ellie's heart soared as she pushed her homework to one side. Keep calm, she ordered herself firmly.

'Hi, how are you?' She hoped she sounded really laid back.

'Cool,' he replied. 'You?'

Time to cut to the chase, she thought.

'So did you tell Lucy?' Sugar – now she sounded too keen.

'Not exactly,' Blake confessed.

'Well, either you did or you didn't,' Ellie retorted,

pressing the phone closer to her ear. So much for calm and laidback.

'No, I didn't,' he said. 'See, she had a call when we got to the restaurant – her gran died that afternoon.'

'Oh no!' Ellie immediately felt racked with guilt for her impatience. 'Of course you couldn't say anything.'

'The funeral's on Wednesday,' Blake explained. 'She's in a right state, poor kid.'

Ellie tried very hard not to feel jealous of the compassion in his voice. But he had called her 'kid', which was promising.

'So when we get back from funeral . . .'

'We?' Ellie's voice came out as a squeak.

'I'm driving her down,' Blake said. 'Her parents are already there and she's too much of a mess to drive. What else can I do?'

Buy her a train ticket, thought Ellie savagely. And then spent the rest of the evening despising herself for being so callous.

On their second date, Hunter had kissed her.

On their fourth date, he had taken her to meet his parents. Sadly they were out, so they had kissed for a very long time on the chaise longe in the sitting room which he said was antique and worth a small fortune. And last night, on their sixth date, he had bought her a ring, a twisted silver band with a tiny green stone in the middle.

'Just to show the world you're mine,' he had whispered as he slipped it tenderly on to the middle finger of her left hand and kissed her. The next day at school Abby slipped it on to her fourth finger.

'Are you engaged?' Chloë gasped.

'Not as far the world is concerned,' Abby admitted. 'But between the two of us . . .'

She let the words hang in the air and her street cred with Year Eleven soared overnight. If there was anything she could teach her sisters it was that spin is everything – Abby would likely end up as head of a marketing company one day.

❧ SECRET NUMBER 22 ❧

Sometimes the perfect guy for you isn't the perfect guy for everyone else. And sometimes — and here's where it gets sticky — he thinks he is.

'WHAT THE HELL IS GOING ON?' Nick stood blocking the door to the science block, his face flushed and his sandy eyebrows knitted together in an angry frown.

'I've got to get to biology,' Abby began but Nick wasn't listening.

'We had an agreement, right? I would take Chloë out twice — twice, remember? And then you and me would get back together. Well — yes, or no?'

'Yes, but – '

'Yes but you set me up!' he snapped. 'You had already found someone better, hadn't you? Someone with a flash car, someone too stuck up to wipe his own arse.'

'Nick! It wasn't like that.' Abby felt her stomach churning at the sight of Nick's ever reddening face.

'Oh, give me a little credit!' He dropped his voice as one of the lab technicians pushed past them, glancing pointedly at his watch. 'Chloë told me she saw you with Hunter Meade-Holman the day you went shopping with her — you told her he was your boyfriend.'

'Yes, but I didn't really mean – '

Nick interrupted, 'So even then, you were conning me and – '

'I'd only just met him that day,' Abby protested. 'And anyway, you took Chloë out four times, not two like you said, so I assumed you had fallen for her big time and – '

'Is that really likely? When it's you I . . . Oh forget it,' he snapped, turning away. 'If Hunter Meade-Holman is the sort of guy you want, have him. See if I care – the stuck up, self-opinionated – '

'You don't even know him,' Abby began.

'Everyone round here knows Hunter!' Nick spat the words out. 'He makes sure of that. No matter, though. I'm telling Chloë tomorrow.'

'Telling her what?' Abby gasped.

'That I'm dumping her,' he said. 'That I fancy someone else.'

'You won't tell her who?' The moment she had said the words she regretted them. Nick looked at her for one very long moment and then shook his head. He let the door swing closed in her face.

For the rest of the day, Abby tried to tell herself that she was blameless, that she'd never meant for Nick to fall for her, that she'd acted out of the best of intentions.

Somehow, it didn't seem to work.

The following afternoon Hunter sprang his surprise.

'I've got a new cat,' he announced, the moment the front door had shut behind her. 'She's amazing – you just have to come and see her.'

Abby looked at him in amazement. He looked as excited as if he had just won the lottery. This completely proved Nick wrong – Hunter was an animal lover! How sweet was that!

'I've got a cat,' she cried. 'I love them.'

Hunter grabbed her hand and kissed it spontaneously. 'You do?' He fired the engine and accelerated so fast down the lane that Abby had to dodge the overhanging branches of the hawthorn hedge from hitting her through the open window.

'I knew you were the girl for me! What kind is yours? Mine's a Tiger.'

'Oh, Manderley's not at all fierce. She's Persian crossed with next door's tabby.' She laughed.

{207}

The expression on Hunt's face told her at once that she'd made a blunder. 'Oh for God's sake!' he snapped. 'I'm not talking about some dumb animal. Cat – catamaran? For sailing?'

Abby's brain went into instant Situation Survival mode. 'I know that, silly!' She tossed her hair and grinned at him, praying that she would look convincing. 'I was just teasing.'

Hunter looked slightly mollified. 'So – do you or don't you sail?'

'Sail? Of course I do,' she replied breezily. 'Doesn't everyone?'

'Great,' Hunter said with a grin. 'We'll take her out right now. She handles like a dream – eighteen feet long and her speed in the open water is amazing.'

'Well, I'm not really dressed for – '

'Don't worry,' Hunter interrupted, 'you can hire a

wetsuit at the sailing club.' He eyed her closely. 'Are you up for it or not?'

'Do you really need to ask?' Abby said, but she thought, Please God don't let me be seasick – vomit is so unsexy.

Ellie eyed herself in the mirror of the staff changing room at the sailing club. There was no doubt about it – the uniform suited her. Tight denim shorts, striped T-shirt, white deck shoes and a lanyard with her name in mock sail stitch.

She walked through to the bar, pausing to gaze out of the huge picture windows overlooking the marina and the sand spits. From the barbecue deck below, above the sound of the halyards jangling in the light breeze, she could hear voices raised in friendly banter, bets being taken on who would win that afternoon's 470 Class races. She was about to head for the bar for the lunch time shift when her mobile phone rang.

'Ellie? It's me – Lucy.'

'Lucy? How did you get my number?'

'Davina, silly. Anyway, listen – is Blake with you? His mobile's switched off.'

Ellie shook her head and then realised that Lucy couldn't see through the phone. 'No – why would he be?' she asked.

'He's not where he's supposed to be,' Lucy replied curtly. 'He's supposed to be taking me sailing and he hasn't picked me up.'

Sailing? You're supposed to be devastated about your gran's death, Ellie thought.

'Perhaps he's caught up in traffic,' Ellie suggested and hated herself for covering for him all over again. 'Oh, and I'm sorry about your grandmother.'

'Thanks,' Lucy said without much feeling. 'And Blake is most definitely not with you?'

'I haven't seen him in ages,' Ellie replied.

'Oh good.' Lucy sighed. 'That's OK then. Ciao!'

Abby was wriggling into her wetsuit and trying to stop the butterflies that were suffocating in her stomach when her mobile phone bleeped.

R U COMING 2 GIG 2NITE? SO XCITED. CHLOË

No way, thought Abby, wondering whether rubber clad bums were a turn on. Not if tonight's the night that Nick dumps her – I want to be as far away as possible.

Then again, Abby reasoned, Chloë was a friend. As Abby dragged her feet out to the dock she weighed her options. As she approached Hunter at his new cat, however, her thoughts turned to the task in front of her.

The quay side at the sailing club was a hive of activity with boats being rigged, crew yelling instructions to one another and dinghies manoeuvering out into the open sea. Abby was conscious of the strengthening breeze and the foam crested waves and wondered yet again whether this was, after all, such a good idea.

'Isn't she a beauty?' Hunter said proudly. 'She's going to slay the opposition at the regatta next week.' He glanced at his watch. 'Come on, let's get going. Here's your harness . . .'

'Harness?' Abby tried to hide her fear by tying up a ponytail.

'For the trapeze, silly.' He eyed her closely. 'You have been out on the trapeze before, haven't you?'

Abby swallowed hard. She'd seen people at the Brighton Marina hanging over the edge of their boats, their heads practically skimming the surface of the water, and she had always labelled them totally and irretrievably insane.

'Look, Hunt, I was just thinking . . .' She jumped as a hand landed on her shoulder.

'Abby? I thought it was you – this is amazing!'

The voice in Abby's left ear sounded vaguely familiar. 'Blake!' she cried, turning around. 'You never said you were coming up this weekend.'

Hunter straightened up from rigging the boat and frowned. 'Hi Blake, haven't seen you in ages – you two know each other?'

'Sure,' Blake nodded. 'My aunt's . . . '

'Blake's aunt is keeping an eye on Holly House for us,' Abby blurted out, throwing Blake a pleading look.

'Living there, actually,' Blake remarked, holding Abby's gaze.

'Well, yes, obviously – you can hardly keep an eye on something if you're not there can you?' Abby gabbled.

A look of recognition flashed across Hunter's face. 'Oh I get it – during the filming?'

'Filming?' Blake frowned and stared at Abby. 'I don't – '

Abby planted her left foot firmly on his toes. 'Can we get going?' she begged, clambering on to the boat. She didn't want to sail but she reckoned the terrors of the ocean were as nothing compared to Blake blowing her story about Holly House clean out of the water.

'Hunt, you're not taking that out on your own, surely?' Blake looked at them questioningly.

'No, Blake, if you look carefully, you will observe that I have Abby with me,' Hunt retorted sarcastically.

'But Abby doesn't sail,' Blake replied, turning to face her. 'And I don't think it's quite safe . . .'

'Doesn't sail?' Hunt's head jerked up. 'Abby?'

For a moment, Abby had to fight the desire to pitch Blake head first into the harbour. But then as a gust of wind blew, she saw two dinghies almost capsize as they caught the cross wind, and reckoned that she had in fact been saved in the nick of time.

'Ellie said you hated the water and gave up after three lessons,' Blake reminded her.

OK, she thought, glaring back at him. No need to go into all the sordid details.

'For God's sake!' Hunter hurled the rope into the boat and yanked on the zip of his wetsuit. 'Why didn't you say? This whole day is turning out to be a disaster.' He bit his thumbnail and then brightened. 'You come, Blake – I'll show you how she handles.'

'You know I can't.' Blake shook his head. 'For one thing, I'm waiting for Lucy and for another, I'm not part of the syndicate.'

'Syndicate?' Abby frowned.

'The boats belongs to six of the members,' Blake said. 'Hunt's dad is one of them so he's OK, I guess, but . . .'

'I thought you said the boat – cat – was yours,' Abby said accusingly.

Hunt shrugged. 'Dad's, mine, what's the difference?' he said assuredly. 'Anyway, I need a drink. Want one?' He didn't wait for an answer and strode down the jetty.

'Don't worry,' Blake said, as Abby turned to follow. 'You're better off on dry land than on water with that maniac. He is a complete prat in a boat.'

'How dare you speak about my boyfriend like that,' Abby snapped, quickening her pace.

'Boyfriend?' Blake looked gobsmacked. 'You're going out with him?'

Abby nodded, crossing her arms dramatically across her chest.

'I didn't know,' Blake murmured. 'So is this why you've spun some dumb story about Holly House – to impress Mr Up Himself?'

Abby was about to tell Blake where to go, but realised he was grinning at her. She shrugged. 'OK, so I was stupid,' she admitted. 'But he's got this big house, and knows all these double-barrelled people and I thought . . .'

'You thought you'd hang on to him if you impressed him,' Blake finished for her. 'You won't, you know – Hunter doesn't, well, hang on, for very long.'

'Well, that's where you're wrong!' Abby retorted, more to convince herself than anything. 'What would you know about it, anyway? You don't have a clue about love or romance or else you'd have got it together with Ellie by now!'

'Don't talk about stuff you don't understand!' Blake snapped, a flash of anger across his face.

'Look, I don't know what the problem is but she's in the bar right now and you're here, so for God's sake, go and see her and get your act together!'

'Leave it, Abby,' retorted Blake, looking quite a bit more serious than she'd ever seen him before. 'Just leave it.'

'A large apple juice and soda water, please.'

Ellie knew who it was before she turned round. Play it dead cool, she told herself, picking up a half pint glass and turning to face Blake. 'Well, hi there,' she said.

'How's it going?' Blake asked, nervously glancing over his shoulder.

'Cool,' she replied. 'Ice? Lemon?'

He nodded. 'Look,' he said, 'about us.'

'Blake, no – you've said all that needs to be said.' Ellie picked up another glass.

He leaned across the bar and took her hand. 'No, that's the whole bloody point,' he stressed, raising his voice above the CD playing in the background. 'What I haven't said is that I think I'm falling . . .'

'Blake! Shit – where have you been!' Lucy, purple in the face and with teeth clenched, belted up to the bar and grabbed his hand, wretching his whole body away from Ellie.

'Lucy, cool it,' Blake began. 'You're the one who's late.'

'No – you were supposed to pick me up, remember? And as for you,' she said, wheeling round to face Ellie, 'You liar! You said you hadn't seen Blake. And here you are with your nasty little beer wench paws all over him!'

'I hadn't seen him,' Ellie protested, cocking her fist on her hip. 'He only just turned up. Looking for you. Worried because he couldn't find you.'

She glared at Blake, daring him to contradict her. You deserve each other, thought Ellie.

'Well, I'm here now,' Lucy said. 'Take me sailing and I might forgive you.'

Blake gave Ellie an apologetic shrug.

I hope she falls in, thought Ellie, slamming glasses on to the bar. Close to a very hungry shark. And I might just hope he falls in after her.

✂ SECRET NUMBER 23 ✂

Never turn down a date.

'A GIG? AT THE PUB? Oh Abby, it'll be dire.' Hunter pulled her towards him and ran her hands down her back, resting them lightly on her bottom. Abby found this particularly rewarding since it had taken all afternoon, a lot of snogging in the sand dunes and all her feminine wiles to pacify Hunt and make him forget her lie about knowing how to sail. 'And besides, you promised we could have some real us time – somewhere romantic,' he breathed, gently nibbling her left ear lobe.

'I know but . . .'

He pulled away. 'Clearly you don't feel for me what you said you did.' His tone was icy.

'I do, you know I do,' Abby pleaded.

'So show me,' Hunt whispered, cupping her face in his hands. 'I'll be off to Scotland next week.'

'Scotland?' Abby's heart dropped like a stone.

'My grandfather's estate,' Hunt said rather grandly. 'I'm going straight after the ball. I've got us tickets, by the way – so you owe me.'

'How much?' Abby began scrabbling in her purse.

'Not in money, silly – in favours!' He ran his lips over the back of her neck and shivers of electricity shot through her body.

'Well, we'll have to see, won't we? So what's this about Scotland?' Anything to change the subject, thought Abby.

'It's a great place – grouse shooting, deer stalking – and there's a dry ski slope at Glenshee . . .'

'That's something I can do!' Abby interjected. 'I'm good at it – truly. And I've done clay pigeon shooting with my dad.' Ask me to come with you, she pleaded in her head. 'I'm free all summer,' she added with a sigh. 'And without you . . .' She let the words hang in the air.

'So, make the most of me while I'm here,' Hunt challenged with a grin. 'Forget this stupid gig and come back to the house with me. My parents will be out. No prying eyes . . .'

Abby's stomach lurched at the innuendo in his voice. 'Well, what if we go and get something to eat at the sailing club, then go to the gig, just for an hour, and then I promise we'll leave?'

'And if I say yes, you promise that you'll – you know? And this time, you won't back off?' Hunt sighed.

Abby took a deep breath. 'Mmm,' she mumbled, trying to tell herself that he didn't mean what she knew full well he meant. 'Come on – I fancy pizza with a whole load of chips!'

'Ellie Dashwood, you have been polishing that glass for the last five minutes to my certain knowledge!' Casey, the supervisor, grinned at her and gave her a friendly nudge. 'Which one are you drooling over then? If it's Piers, here he comes – so I'll leave you to it . . .'

Ellie turned to protest but not quickly enough. Piers leaned over the bar and touched her arm. 'Are you working tonight?'

Ellie shook her head. 'No – why?' She slammed a couple of schooners down on the counter top with unnecessary vigor.

'Just that we're all meeting up at The Jolly Sailor – some new band's playing and they've got a barbecue running. Coming?'

'No thanks.' Ellie shook her head.

Piers eyed her closely. 'Why not? It'll be a blast.'

Oh sure, Ellie thought. Yet another hour of watching Lucy wrap herself round Blake like a boa constrictor on speed and standing by while my sister gets chatted up by the second hottest guy in the room (well, possibly even the sexiest if you go for that sort of up-yourself arrogance). No thank you. 'Not in the mood.'

'Are you in a strop about something?' Piers asked with a grin. 'Is it Blake?'

'Why would it be Blake?' she retorted. 'I've just got heaps to do.' A weak excuse but it would have to do.

'I just thought that Blake was rather keen – oh, well never mind,' Piers murmured. 'But do come to the pub – for my sake? Please?'

'What do you mean, for your sake?'

Piers sighed. He said, 'Because otherwise I'll be there, all alone, no one to talk to and all this charm unused and going to waste and . . .'

Ellie giggled despite herself. 'You're an idiot,' she said, grinning.

'This is very true,' said Piers. 'I make idiocy into an artform. So you'll come?'

'Yes,' she smiled. 'I'll come. See you there at nine o'clock.'

Later that night, Ellie stopped dead as she came out of the loo at the back of The Jolly Sailor – she'd heard a familiar voice but she didn't think she liked the sound of what it was saying.

'What on earth did you have to go and ask her for?' Blake was leaning against the bar wall glaring at Piers.

'I thought you'd be pleased.' Piers shrugged.

'You just have to interfere, don't you?' Blake grunted. 'I've spent the last two months trying to get rid of – Oh, Ellie! Hi!'

Blake leaned forward and planted a quick kiss on Ellie's cheek. Act natural, Ellie told herself clenching her hands together to stop them from shaking. Don't let him see that you heard.

'Can I get you a drink?' Blake asked edging a little closer to her and peering anxiously into her eyes.

'Drinks? Oh, darling, thank you! Vodka and tonic, please.' Lucy appeared from the corner of the room as if zapped to his side by remote control.

'Mine's a shandy,' Piers interjected.

'And you, Ellie?' Blake repeated, the colour in his face rising by the second.

'No thanks,' she murmured. 'Actually I was just leaving because – '

'Nonsense!' Piers interupted. 'You promised me you'd stay.'

'And now she wants to leave,' Lucy interrupted. 'So let her.'

There was something in Lucy's tone that set Ellie on edge, but she also got the distinct feeling that she did the same thing to Lucy. It was too good not to give up.

'OK,' she replied, giving Piers the brightest smile she could manage. She turned to Blake. 'J$_2$O please, with loads of ice. I'm driving.'

Blake pushed his way through the crowds of drinkers to the bar, Lucy close on his heels with her arm hooked through his, gazing up at him adoringly. Much as she wanted to, Ellie found she couldn't tear her eyes away from them.

'Nick, listen, please!' Abby stepped over the tangle of leads and loudspeakers and tried again. 'There's something I need to say,' she pleaded. 'It's important.'

'Like what? Go and get lost, Nick? Go out with four of my mates, Nick?' He grappled with his drum kit, turning his back on her just as Chloë jumped up on to the makeshift stage and shoved a plate of barbecued chicken and corn in his hand.

'Hi, darling, I got you some food!' She planted a kiss on the back of his neck and Abby saw him visibly pull back. 'I'm *sooooo* proud of you!'

Even Abby had to admit she was a bit cringe-making.

'My very own pop hero!' Chloë practically screamed.

'Actually,' Nick cut in hastily, 'there is something you could do. Get me a cola – I'm parched.'

'Sure!' She blew another kiss and headed for the bar.

'The moment this gig's over, I'm telling her,' he muttered to Abby. 'I can't pretend any longer.'

Abby took a deep breath. 'Don't say anything to her tonight, please,' she pleaded. 'If you promise not to say anything to Chloë tonight, I'll go out with you again.'

Nick gave short sarcastic laugh, and Abby hated herself for suggesting something so rude.

'If you remember, you are already going out with someone,' he replied. ' Or has he chucked you?'

Abby caught the note of hope in his voice. 'No, but . . .'

'Well I'm not sharing you, OK? You may think two-timing is a big deal – I do! And I don't go for cheap bribes, either. Now if you don't mind, we've got a gig to finish.'

'Come on, Ellie, let's dance!' Piers grabbed her hand and dragged her on to the tiny space that passed for a dance floor.

She was about to make some excuse but then saw that Blake had turned from the bar and was watching her.

'Sure,' she said, laughing and swaying in time to the beat and waving her arms above her head. She put a hand on Pier's shoulder and shimmied closer.

Blake was still watching.

'Answer me one thing straight, OK?' Piers asked her, brushing his lips close to her ear. 'Do you fancy Blake? Because he says – '

'He says he wishes I was a million miles away because he's with Lucy,' Ellie snapped. 'I realise that now, and frankly I couldn't give a damn. As far as I'm concerned, he can go to the other side of the world on a one way ticket.'

'So you do fancy him!' Piers laughed. He pulled her closer to him and glanced over her left shoulder to the bar. 'That's good.'

'What do you mean, that's good?'

'You're a great mover, you know,' he murmured, putting his finger to her lips and then running his hands down her back to her bottom.

'At it again, are you?' Lucy appeared at her elbow glaring at Ellie. 'Can't keep your hands off men, can you?'

'What's it to you? You've got Blake, remember?' Ellie startled herself with the note of acerbity in her voice.

'My turn I think,' Lucy hissed, turning to Piers.

'Hi, gorgeous!' Piers dropped Ellie's hand and winked at Lucy. And with that, she pulled him on to the dance floor, her hips already swaying to the beat of the song the DJ had put on in between the band's sets.

Ellie was still staring after them and catching her breath, when Blake shoved a glass in her hand.

'Your drink,' he said abruptly, handing it to her.

'Have a nice day sailing?' she asked sarcastically.

'Nope,' Blake said. And disappeared into the Gents, leaving Ellie alone for only a moment.

A firm hand clasped her shoulder and she turned to find Hunter, a beer glass in one hand and a plate of sausages in the other. 'Ellie, what is it with your sister? I get Abby a plate of food and what does she do? Swans off to chat up that adolescent drummer guy.' He gestured towards the stage where the band was taking a short break.

'That's Nick – he's a friend of hers,' Ellie said, still watching Lucy who was pushing through the crowd towards the bar, hand firmly holding on to Piers. No wonder Blake looked miffed. If he was mine, I'd never treat him like that, she thought.

'The band's good, isn't it?' she muttered, in an attempt to put Blake out of her mind and appear normal.

Hunter shrugged. 'Compared to what?' He took a swig of beer, wiped his mouth with the back of his hand and sighed. 'Frankly, this is all pretty dull, isn't it?'

'Compared to what?' Ellie snapped back at him, her bottled up emotions finally spilling out. 'Do you have to practice being so obnoxious or does it come naturally?'

Hunter took a step backwards and held up her hands in mock fear.

'Chill out!' he parried. 'I was just making conversation. What's with everyone tonight? Blake's as jumpy as hell, Abby's uptight, Lucy's even more . . .'

'You know Lucy?' Ellie could have kicked herself for showing interest.

'Of course, everyone round here knows Lucy,' he said with a laugh. 'I used to go out with her – well, so did Piers and most of the rest of the crowd, to be honest.' He took another gulp of beer. 'Now she's with Blake, although God knows what she sees in him – no style, that guy, no style at all. Whereas Lucy . . .' He took a bite out of a sausage and glanced appreciatively at Lucy's bottom perched on the bar stool. 'She's a real little raver when she gets going. Mind you, I have high hopes of your sister given time.'

There was something about the way his lips

transformed into something between a smile and a sneer that turned Ellie's stomach.

'Great potential,' he murmured, draining his glass and dumping it on a nearby table. 'Pity she doesn't sail – but she can go like the wind in other departments!'

'You . . .' Ellie bit her tongue and thanked her lucky stars that she was here to keep an eye on her sister.

Falling in love is the greatest adventure there is – which, incidentally, can make it quite dangerous. After all, a broken heart can hurt more than a broken leg.

{224}   ABBY SAT ON THE END OF HER BED, scribbling in her diary, the words smudging as tears fell on the page.

Dear Diary,

My life is over. I've been totally humiliated – and by my own sister at that. Hunt stormed off last night and it's nearly midday and he hasn't phoned. We always go out on Sundays. He thinks I'm a kid; I knew I should have given in when he wanted to – well, you know. I can't write it down because to be honest it doesn't feel right – but I know that's what guys want you to do and I kept making excuses. I love him so much but I was scared and now I've lost him for ever. I should never have gone to the gig, never have bothered about Chloë and Nick.

She paused as her mobile phone bleeped from the pocket of her jeans. '*Let it be him, let it be him,*' she whispered, flipping open the cover and seeing the text message alert flashing.

NICK'S CHUCKED ME. SAYS THERE'S SOMEONE ELSE.

WHAT DID I DO WRONG? I NEED YOU LIKE NOW – RING ME PLEASE. CHLOË.

Abby stared at the screen. She couldn't phone Chloë; she couldn't talk to anyone. She had her own problems to sort out, and anyway, Chloë's feelings about Nick were only puppy love, whereas her own . . .

'Abby? Hunter's here!' Julia's voice wafted up the stairs. 'And he's in a hurry!'

The diary and the phone crashed to the floor as Abby leaped up from the bed and dashed towards the door, her heart beating wildly. It was when she caught sight of her reflection in the dressing table mirror that she stopped dead. Puffy eyes, snot on the end of her nose and mascara streaks down her cheeks – she couldn't let Hunter see her like this.

But she couldn't let Hunter not see her, either.

'Hang on! In the loo!' she shouted, stuffing the diary back in its hiding place and grabbing her phone. 'Give me five minutes.'

This, she thought, dashing to the bathroom, never happens in the movies – no one's face ever swells up like a bloated pig when they sob. She splashed cold water on her face, blew her nose and went to work with the concealer.

'Abby! Hunter can't hang about – what are you doing?' Julia hollered.

Abby plastered on the lip gloss, looked in the mirror, pouted her lips as sexily as she could and flew down the stairs, ignoring the distant shrilling of her phone from the bedroom.

As Abby scrambled through the sitting room she could hear Hunter chatting to her mother in the kitchen.

'. . . so I'm off to Ballater tomorrow,' she heard him say.

Tomorrow? He wasn't supposed to go to Scotland till after the ball.

'Look, if Abby's not ready, I'll have to make tracks – so much to get done . . .'

No way, thought Abby. You can't leave.

'Hi, darling!' she cried brightly, pushing open the kitchen door and remembering the instructions for dealing with relationship crisis in her latest copy of *Heaven Sent* magazine. 'What are you two nattering about?'

'Hunter's off to Scotland,' Julia said. 'He . . .'

'What about the ball?' Abby gasped.

'I'll probably fly down for that,' he said airily. 'See how the mood takes me.'

'I've always wanted to go to Scotland,' Abby declared wistfully. 'All that walking and shooting. Just my scene.'

'Oh Abby, really!' Her mother burst out laughing. 'You take a bus to the end of the road, given half a chance. And if you remember, when Dad took you clay pigeon shooting you spent half the time with your hands clamped over your ears!'

Hunter laughed, nodding in agreement. 'I guess Abby is just not your outdoors, sporty type, is she?' he replied, as if she had suddenly become invisible. 'Better at indoor sports, eh, Abby?'

Abby flushed scarlet and held her breath, waiting for her mother to shout him down.

'That's right,' Julia said, beaming placidly. 'She's very good at table tennis, and a real dab hand at cards, aren't you, darling?'

Hunter stifled a laugh and turned to Abby. 'Fancy a trip to Hunstanton?' he asked her.

'I'm all yours.' She smiled sweetly. Apparently there were advantages to having a mother who had never mastered the double entendre, after all.

'I've got to stop,' Georgie panted. 'I'm totally out of breath.'

She flopped down on the scrubby grass halfway up Pen-y-Fan, and wriggled her arms free of her rucksack.

'Me too.' Her teammate, Harriet, sighed and unlaced her walking boot. 'Thank goodness this is the last day of hiking – I've got blisters, my shoulders hurt and . . .'

'It's ace up here, isn't it?' Georgie butted in, unscrewing her water bottle and gazing at the barren peaks of the Brecon Beacons all around her. She turned to Adam who was poring over their OS map.

'Well,' Adam said, 'we're not in the lead but I've got an idea. If we take the higher path and then cut down by the waterfall here.' He prodded the map with his thumb. 'I reckon we could cut off a corner and get in front.'

'Let's do it, then,' urged Georgie, taking a swig from the bottle. 'I bet Jeanie Cross my Mars bar that we'd beat her lot. Come on.'

'We can't do that,' Harriet protested. 'What if we get lost? No one will ever find us.'

'Oh, get a grip,' Georgie scoffed, wishing for the tenth time that day that she hadn't been lumbered with the class wimp for the day. 'There are over fifty of us on this mountainside – we're hardly likely to disappear without trace. Anyway, where's your spirit of adventure?'

'I haven't got one,' Harriet retorted. 'I wish I'd never come – Mum said I'd hate it.'

'Well, you'll just have to grin and bear it,' Georgie told her, 'because if we don't get going we're going to lose time points, OK?' She hitched her rucksack on her back and began striding along the path.

'No – wait,' Adam called, stuffing the map in his back pocket. 'We can't expect Harriet to do something she doesn't feel comfortable with.'

'Are you going soft or what?' Georgie glared at him.

Adam was going to be a sports instructor, and obviously liked being with her because she was one of the guys. And now here he was going all slushy over Harriet who made a drama out of a small blister.

'Are we in this to win or aren't we?' Georgie snapped crossly.

Adam pulled a face and winked at her before turning to Harriet. 'Look, there's your mate Claire, with Sally over by that rock,' he said, shading his eyes from the sun and pointing along the path. 'Why don't you join them? I'm sure they could do with someone else now that Paul's had to drop out with his sprained ankle.'

The look of relief on Harriet's face was almost comical. 'OK, then,' she said. 'And that way, if you never turn up at the checkpoint, I can alert the emergency services.'

Georgie struggled not to laugh out loud. 'Great idea, Harriet!' she said with mock enthusiasm, as Harriet slithered down the slope to join her friends, and Adam walked over to join Georgie.

'I know this is supposed to be an endurance test, but we deserve a medal for putting up with her.' Georgie declared. 'That was dead clever, the way you got rid of her.'

Adam grinned and pointed to the marks he'd penciled in on the map. Georgie perched on a nearby boulder and frowned.

'That's not a short cut,' she objected, peering at the map. 'It's just a parallel route to this one. In fact, it could even be longer.'

'I know,' Adam confessed. 'But it has one major advantage over all the other paths.'

'What's that?'

'I get to be on my own with you,' he murmured, kicking a stone out of his path.

{229}

He stretched out a hand to pull Georgie to her feet. And when he didn't let go, she decided that if he was going to be slushy, then it was only right that he did it with her and no one else.

'You don't love me, do you?' Hunter pulled into a lay-by on the outskirts of the village and turned to face Abby. 'You never really did.'

Abby quashed the rising panic she felt and pulled him towards her. 'Of course I love you, Hunt – how many times do I have to tell you?'

Hunter stiffened and pulled away. 'Words are easy,' he said, flicking a stray leaf off the dashboard. 'It's actions that matter.'

'What do you want me to do to prove it?' Before she had finished the sentence, she knew it was precisely the question he'd hoped she'd ask.

'Show me,' he said, his shadowed eyes gazing into

hers. 'Come back to the house now – my parents are at a constituency rally – we'll have the place to ourselves.'

'But you said you had shopping to do,' Abby reminded him.

'Forget shopping,' Hunter retorted. 'I made that up to get you to myself.'

For a moment, Abby said nothing.

'You see?' Hunter burst out. 'All you want is to play little girl games. We're not kids any more, you know, Abby . . .'

'No,' she said, her heart pounding. 'It's not like that. I've never loved anyone the way I love you.'

'So prove it,' Hunter said, pulling her to him and kissing her rather harder than she would have liked. 'I love you and you love me,' he murmured nibbling her ear lobe and cupping her breast in his hand. 'Please, Abby. I've been so patient – you can't treat me like this.'

Abby could feel her throat closing with unshed tears. She did love him, but she just didn't feel ready yet. 'I can't,' she whispered. 'Not yet.'

The force with which Hunter shoved her away from him almost knocked the breath out of her. 'Your decision,' he snapped. 'There's a name for girls like you, you know that?' He leaned across her and threw open the passenger door. 'I think you should get out.'

'Hunt, no,' Abby implored. 'Don't be like that – it's not fair.'

'Fair? You're a fine one to talk about being fair,' he thundered. 'Now either you stop messing around with me and come back to the house, or you get out of my car right now.'

She wasn't sure where it came from, but she was glad

when it did – suddenly her whole being was filled with red hot anger.

'Then I'll get out,' she screamed, stepping out of the car and slamming the door shut. 'When I do make love to someone, it'll be because I know they really care about me and you clearly . . .'

Her voice cracked and to her intense irritation, she could feel tears rolling down her cheeks.

'I'm out of here,' he yelled through the window, ramming the key into the ignition. He started the engine.

'No, Hunt, stop!' Abby went to open the car door again, but at the same moment she saw Hunter buzz it locked.

Her cries of 'Hunter, come back,' were drowned out by the noise of his car accelerating away into the distance.

❧ SECRET NUMBER 25 ❧

*Sometimes the more you ignore love, the move
seriously it hunts you down.*

ELLIE WAS LYING ON HER BED, trying to make sense of her German homework, when her mobile phone bleeped. Even now, knowing what she did, she always hoped every text message was from Blake. She flipped the cover and squinted at the screen.

TICKETS CAME 2DAY! 6 DAYS AND COUNTING – OZ HERE WE COME! CAN'T WAIT DRLG. LUV U LUCY XXX

She felt as if her body had been frozen. She sat motionless, reading and re-reading the words. It was clearly not meant for her – Lucy had obviously pressed the wrong button and sent her the message.

'I'll be sailing in the Whitsunday Islands,' Lucy's voice echoed in her head as clearly as if she had been sitting next to her. 'Yes, didn't Blake tell you? It was my great idea for the summer . . .'

'You idiot, you stupid idiot!' Ellie shouted the words at her reflection in the dressing table mirror. 'He's going to Australia with Lucy. And he didn't even have the guts to tell me.'

She clamped her hands to her mouth and took a few long, deep breaths.

'That's that, then,' she told herself firmly. 'That's that.'

Abby trudged along the lane, her eyes blinded by tears. She'd left her mobile phone on the bedroom floor, she had no money on her and it was a five-mile walk home.

'Abby? Abby?'

She was conscious of a car pulling up beside her, but she wouldn't look around. She knew it was Hunter, but after what he's just done, she wasn't sure she wanted to see him any more. Of course she wanted to see him eventually again and eventually, she even wanted to do all of the things he obviously couldn't wait to do, but not yet. She just couldn't. Was she abnormal? She knew loads of girls at school had done it, and most of them said it was amazing and life-changing.

But she was scared. Did that mean she was frigid? Maybe she should she just do it and get it over with . . . Yes, then she could stop thinking about it and surely it wouldn't be nearly so big a deal once they just did it, right? Yes, that was what she would tell Hunter – that they could have sex, and that she was ready, even though she was fairly certain she wasn't.

'Abby, what's wrong? Are you hurt?'

She turned. It wasn't Hunter. It was Nick.

'Come on, in the car,' Nick said taking her arm. 'I'm taking you home.'

'I'm fine,' she told him shrugging him off.

'Really?' Nick looked at her sceptically. 'I'd hate to see you on a bad day then. Was it Hunter?'

She wanted to tell him where to go, she wanted to say that everything was fine with Hunter, but for some reason she couldn't. There Nick was, looking at her with big understanding eyes, so Abby simply dropped her head and sobbed. And when she felt Nick's arms go round her she didn't pull away. She just let the tears fall.

'Can someone get that phone?' Ellie shouted as the telephone in the hallway shrilled persistently. 'Oh for heaven's sake!'

She clattered down the stairs, French textbook in hand and grabbed the handset.

{234}

'Hello? Oh Chloë – no, sorry, she's out, I'm afraid. With Hunter, yes.'

She paused, trying to catch what Chloë was saying. She sounded as if she had an awful cold.

'Her mobile? No you won't catch her on that, she's left it behind – typical Abby, yes. Are you OK? Oh. Right. Yes, I'll tell her. Yes, I promise. Bye.' She replaced the handset just as the front door bell clanged. 'Now what? Forgotten her key as well, I suppose!'

She yanked the front door open, venting her bad mood on the creaking hinges.

'Blake!' Look casual, she told herself.

'Hey, Ellie.'

She tried not to notice his floppy combats and his cute new trainers. She willed herself to keep acting normal, not look into his eyes, not to let him know how crushed she really felt. 'What brings you here?'

'You, actually,' Blake looked nervous. 'Can I come in?'

'Well, I'm really busy and . . .'

'It won't take a minute,' he said stepping into the hallway. 'I just need to explain stuff.'

'What stuff?' Ellie asked, reluctantly closing the front door and waving him into the sitting room.

'Well, Lucy and me . . .'

'Oh that! I thought you were going to tell me something interesting.' She knew she sounded vicious and sulky but she couldn't help it.

'Ellie, listen – what happened was – '

Ellie interrupted, 'I'm not interested in what happened. And I'm really busy so – '

'But about you and me . . .'

Ellie took a deep breath and tried desperately to swallow the lump that was blocking her throat. 'You and me?' she queried. 'There is no you and me, Blake – You've made that quite clear.'

{235}

Blake stepped towards her, a pleading expression on his face. 'Ellie, listen, for just one minute, please. You see the thing is, I won't be around for a bit because . . .'

'Because of your trip with Lucy?' Ellie interrupted brightly. 'Great, isn't it? I'm sure you'll have a blast. They say Australia is wonderful at this time of year.'

'You knew?' Blake's face paled in horror.

'Yes,' she replied. 'Pity you couldn't have told me yourself. All that pretence about dumping her – seems a waste of breath.' Ellie whipped her mobile phone from the back pocket of her jeans, thrusting it under Blake's nose. 'I got this text from Lucy – clearly meant for you.'

Blake's eyes scanned the screen and she saw, with a degree of satisfaction, the look of embarrassment flooding his face. 'Oh God, no – I mean, I got the same message, but how come it got through to you?'

As the reality of the situation hit her, Ellie wondered why it had taken her so long to grasp the truth.

'Because Lucy wanted me to be damn sure that you were out of bounds,' she said with as much hardness as she could manage. 'Well, you can tell her from me that she needn't have bothered – I don't go snatching other girls' boyfriends.'

'Ellie, I never meant . . .' Blake started and then petered out.

'Never meant what, Blake? Never meant to tell me? Never meant it to mean anything when you tried to kiss me? Never meant it when you said you were dumping her? Is that what you never meant, Blake?' Ellie suddenly realised she was yelling.

'Ellie, if you will just listen for five seconds,' he pleaded, shoving the phone back into her hand. 'It's because her grandmother . . .'

'Oh yes, I forgot the grandmother!' Ellie feigned forgetfulness, slapping her forehead. 'Well, she's dead now, isn't she? Or are you taking her ashes to Sydney?'

'Oh for God's sake . . .' Blake began.

The door burst open and Julia beamed at them while she wiped her muddy hands on her gardening apron.

'I thought I heard voices,' she said. 'Blake! Lovely to see you. Coffee? Cake?'

'He's just leaving,' Ellie said edging towards the door. 'He's off to Australia. With Lucy.'

Go on, squirm. You deserve it.

'Australia? With Lucy?' Ellie wished her mother would either construct an entire sentence or leave the room.

'Just for a few weeks,' Blake said weakly. 'I've got relatives out there and my father . . .'

'Don't let us hold you up,' Ellie butted in, because hearing even the vaguest outline of their plans made her feel sick to her stomach.

'I'll see you when I get back,' Blake murmured as Ellie opened the front door.

'Whatever,' she said, wishing he would go so that she could cry.

'Take care, Ellie,' he whispered. 'I'll get everything sorted, I promise.'

It wasn't until she was upstairs, lying face down on her bed howling her eyes out, that she began to wonder what on earth he had meant.

❧ SECRET NUMBER 26 ❧

Friendship can lead to love, but it doesn't usually work the other way around.

'THAT WAS SUCH A COOL TRIP,' Georgie enthused as the coach trundled along the M6 on the journey home. 'I wish it wasn't over.'

'Me too,' Adam agreed. 'Actually, I was thinking. . .'

'Careful,' Georgie teased. 'You don't want to hurt yourself.'

'Right, ha,' Adam looked lore than a little uncomfortable. 'Georgie?' He dropped his voice to a whisper and leaned towards her.

'Yeah?'

'Will you go out with me?'

'Out with you?' Georgie's stomach appeared to be lodged somewhere in the middle of her throat. 'As in out-out?'

'I mean, nothing heavy, just to have a laugh and hang out and stuff.'

Georgie couldn't help thinking how cute he looked when he blushed. 'I don't know,' she began, not because she didn't like him – she did, almost as much as she had liked Tom – but because no way did she fancy the gooey, kissy-kissy bits that boys always seemed to go for.

'I thought,' Adam ventured, 'that we could go to the new skateboard park over at Hunstanton.'

'Oh yes, ace!' Georgie cried at once, not entirely realising if she was yelping for joy at the prospect of the skatepark, or of Adam becoming her boyfriend. 'I've got this wicked board my dad gave me and I've hardly used it since he died.'

'So let's do it.' Adam grinned. 'It would be a bit off to let him think he'd wasted his money, wouldn't it?'

She looked at him long and hard. He was talking about Dad like he was just around the corner, like he could hear them chatting. That was so cool.

'Will you come, then?' He suddenly looked hesitant and small.

'I will,' she said with a grin. By the time she realised she was giving him a hug, it was too late to pull back. Not that it mattered. Hugs didn't count. Hugs were quite nice really.

Georgie and Adam let go of each other, but Georgie could still see that Adam had something on his mind.

'What is it, then?' Georgie asked, suddenly. 'I think there's more – I can tell.'

'Well, now that we're seeing each other . . .' Adam began.

'Yes?' Georgie asked skeptically.

'There's this ball, and I was thinking – '

'A ball? Oh come on, Adam, that's not my scene at all!' I knew this going out thing was all wrong! she thought.

'Um, right, but it's not really a ball,' Adam assured

her. 'More a glorified disco. I just thought the money would be useful, especially if we're going to the skate park.'

'Money? You pay them, dimbo, not the other way round,' she said with a laugh.

'That's where you're wrong,' he countered. 'I told you my dad's got a catering company? Well, they're doing the food and running the bar for the ball, and if we're prepared to help out for the first two hours, we get ten pounds.'

'Each?'

'Each.'

'Well, why didn't you say so?' She laughed and then frowned.

'What now?' He sighed.

'I guess we have to dress up, right?'

'Afraid so.' Adam nodded. 'I've got to put on my brother's hand-me-down tuxedo. But it's worth it for a tenner.'

'True,' Georgie said. 'I wouldn't do it for less though.'

'You won't say anything to anyone? You promise?' Abby demanded as Nick pulled up outside Marsh Cottage.

'Of course not,' he said. 'Although why you don't want the whole world to know what a slimeball Hunter is beats me.'

'Just leave it, OK?' Abby said, terrified that she would start crying again. 'It was sort of more my fault, really, than it seems – I'll call him and . . .'

'Abby, don't – he's not worth it,' Nick began.

'You're just saying that because you want me to

yourself,' Abby said impatiently opening the car door.

'True,' Nick murmured quietly. 'Anyway, I'm here if you need me.'

Abby felt guilty for snapping. After all, Nick had taken her out to lunch, walked along the beach for hours listening to her ranting and raving and he hadn't once blown his top or got fed up. He'd told her he broke things off with Chloë, and even though Abby felt heartbroken for herself, she felt it for Chloë, too – Nick really was a catch, even Abby could see that.

'Thanks,' she said. 'I mean it – thanks for today and bringing me home. I'll see you around.'

She slammed the door and turned to go, but Nick {241} leaned across and touched her hand through the open window.

'About the sailing club ball,' he said. 'I've got tickets and if Hunter doesn't show . . .'

'Of course he'll show,' Abby said, sounding a lot more confident than she felt. 'I told you – it's just a blip.'

But when she glanced back at Nick – all red-faced, and twisted-looking – she could help but feel a bit of a knot in her heart.

'What's the matter with Abby?' Georgie demanded of her mother a couple of hours after arriving home. 'She's hardly said a word to me since I got back and she's playing loads of morbid songs in her bedroom and sniffing a lot.'

'It's Hunter,' her mother said, sighing. 'He's leaving for Scotland tomorrow and Abby's – Oh there you are, darling!' She broke off as Abby, crumpled tissues in hand, came into the kitchen.

'Feeling better?' Julia asked her. 'How about some tea and toast?

Abby shook her head.

'Darling, this is silly,' her mother went on. 'Hunter has only gone for a few days – he'll be back for the ball.'

'What's he doing in Scotland anyway?' Georgie asked.

'Grouse shooting with his grandfather,' Abby replied.

'He's what?' Georgie spat toast crumbs across the table in her disgust. 'How could you go out with someone who kills innocent little birds for fun? That is just the worst thing.'

'What do you know?' Abby retorted. 'You eat chicken – you don't think they die a natural death, do you?'

'No, but I don't go out with the guys that wring their necks, do I?' Georgie parried, proud of herself for her quickness of thought. 'Anyway, I'm thinking of turning vegetarian.'

'Don't be so ridiculous,' her mother snorted. 'What on earth gave you that idea?'

'Adam says that you should never eat something you are not prepared to kill,' she replied. 'But then Adam is an animal lover and a conservationist.'

'I knew it,' Abby burst out, a smile interrupting her sour face. 'Georgie and Adam are an item.'

Her mother's eyebrows shot heavenwards. 'Nonsense,' she retorted. 'She's only thirteen – he's just a friend, right, Georgie?'

'Right,' she agreed. Telling the truth would only get her mother's blood pressure up, and besides, Abby was right after all: secret love is the most exciting.

✂ SECRET NUMBER 27 ✂

*Absence can do two things to love: make it stronger,
or allow you to pretend it never existed at all.*

'ELLIE, DARLING, SHOULDN'T YOU BE GETTING READY?'
Julia demanded at seven o'clock on the night of the ball.
'The bathroom's free at last.'

'I don't think I'll bother going,' Ellie said with a yawn.
'I'm tired and besides, it's not much fun on your own.'

'Now just you stop that right now,' Julia admonished
her. 'If you don't go, you won't meet new people and
besides, do you think I want Georgie on her own at a
place like that?'

Georgie had finally spilled the beans about Adam and
the ball the day before, and since then Julia had been a
wreck about the whole thing.

'Mum, she'll be fine – Adam's parents will be there,'
Ellie said with a laugh.

'Yes, well, they will be busy, and besides, you need to
get out.' Julia eyed Ellie closely. 'You've been looking
very peaky lately – all this studying is all very well but
you need some fun. And you are supposed to be on
holiday.'

'OK, OK, I'll go,' Ellie said with a sigh, knowing that her mother wouldn't stop nagging until she gave in.

'You look stunning.' Chloë stood behind Abby as they gazed at their reflections in the full-length mirror in Julia's bedroom. 'If Hunter *does* come . . .'

'He will come, I know he will,' Abby assured her, twirling round to admire the sexy swing of her new black net skirt. Chloë had shown up heartbroken over Nick the same afternoon that Hunter had left Abby at the side of the road. And even though Abby hadn't exactly told Chloë that she'd already heard the other side of the story from Nick, she did offer Chloë a shoulder to cry on, and helped her hatch a plan to get Nick back. Somehow, after the afternoon Abby spent with him, and everything that had happened with Chloë, Abby felt like she owed it to her.

'Well, if he does, he'll be bowled over,' Chloë finished. 'Did he reply to your messages?'

'No.' Abby shook her head. 'But then of course, as Mum said, there probably isn't a signal in the mountains and I guess his grandfather won't be hooked up to the internet so he won't be checking e-mail.'

'True.' Chloë didn't sound as convinced as Abby would have liked. 'Oh God, I'm so nervous.'

'What have you got to be nervous about? You look great, you're a cool dancer, and you're going to have an entire evening in the same room as the guy you fancy.' Abby smiled a bit mischievously. 'Plus, we've got a plan.'

'Yes, but what if it doesn't work?'

'Well, that's down to you, isn't it? I've done all I can.

I've arranged for him to fetch us – and believe me, that was hard enough because he wanted to go with Liam and Ryan and all the kit in the van – '

'And he knows I'm coming along?' Chloë urged.

Abby paused. She mustn't lie. Not this time. 'Not exactly,' she said. 'It's the surprise element, you see. He won't ever have seen you dressed up to the nines before, and it's your opportunity to sweep him off his feet.' Abby cringed inwardly at her own clichés, but Chloë seemed impressed.

'That's neat,' Chloë cried. 'Thanks, Abby.'

'That's OK,' Abby replied. 'Now will you please put your face on and let's get downstairs? He'll be here any minute.'

{245}

After a few more minutes of lip gloss application and another layer of perfectly tinted bronzer, Abby and Chloë swooshed down the stairs in their gowns. Before they'd even reached the bottom step, the doorbell clanged.

'Just in time!' said Abby as she dove for the door.

Upstairs Ellie was playing music a bit louder than she usually did, so Abby had the unusual good fortune of slipping out without her mum quizzing the boys on their every intention for the evening.

'Hey, Nick!' said Chloë enthusiastically as they shuffled out of the house.

'Hey, Chloë,' Nick said, and then turned to Abby and gave her a withering look.

They drove to the ball in near silence, and as soon as Chloë disappeared to the Ladies' room at the sailing club, Nick grabbed Abby's shoulder. 'If you think you're going to get me to start up again with Chloë, let me tell you right now it's a non-starter.'

'I don't,' Abby assured him. 'I was wrong about you two – you're not suited, anyway. She just needed a lift that's all. Honestly.'

'That's OK then,' Nick muttered. 'Ryan will be all over her anyway. Got to go – we're on in ten minutes.' He gave the thumbs up sign to Liam and Ryan who were beckoning him urgently from the stage. 'Hang on to my car keys and wallet, will you? I hate clutter when I'm drumming.'

She shoved them into her new oh-so-chic quilted clutch bag. 'Good luck,' she whispered and gave him a quick kiss on the cheek.

'Thanks.' Nick's fingers went up to his face and when he smiled, Abby noticed how his whole face relaxed. 'See you during the break, yeah?'

'Yeah.' Abby smiled.

'Lovely to meet you, Georgie dear,' Adam's mother cried, shoving a plate of canapés in her hand. 'Now hand these round, will you? Start with the VIPs, in the Captain's corner, and then do the rest of the crowd. Refills in the back kitchen, OK?' She darted off to stir a vat of soup.

'Come on,' Adam said. 'The sooner we get rid of all the appetisers, the sooner we get our ten quid!' He kicked open the swing door with a foot to let Georgie through.

'Wow,' Georgie breathed.

She gazed at the room which had been transformed into an underwater world with sea-green voiles hanging at the window, huge silver fish covering the dim lights and piles of seaweed and shells stacked around upturned lobster pots at every table.

'Doesn't it look amazing?' she said with a gasp, turning to Adam.

'So do you,' he mumbled, his face flushing. 'Really – you do.'

'I feel stupid,' she admitted, tugging at the spaghetti straps of her lavender shift dress and gazing down at her legs, the bruises from skateboarding not totally hidden by her tights. 'I don't really do dresses.'

'Well, you should,' Adam said. 'You look like – well, pop starry or something.'

Georgie squirmed and fiddled with the sequinned necklace that Abby had lent her. 'Get real,' she muttered, shoving the dish of canapés under the nose of the first person she passed. 'Oh, it's you.'

Georgie grinned up at Ellie who was chatting to a guy in a maroon tux. 'This is my sister, Ellie,' Georgie said, turning to Adam. 'The one I was telling you about with the complicated love life.'

'Georgie,' Ellie hissed.

'This is your little sister?' Georgie realised then that the guy with Ellie was the one who had turned up at the house with Blake weeks before. 'Remember me? Piers?'

'Oh sure,' nodded Georgie. 'Say – you two – you're not . . .?'

'Georgie?' said Ellie.

'Yes?'

'Go and serve your canapés, OK?'

* * *

After collecting some food on a plate from the buffet, Piers and Ellie settled at a table alongside another few guests. But before long, the other partygoers began drifting toward the dance floor again, and Ellie found her mind drifting off as well.

'Ellie? Come back – you were miles away.' Piers touched her arm across the table, and Ellie jerked her thoughts away from mental images of aeroplanes taking off and back to the dance floor of the sailing club.

'Sorry,' she said. 'What were you saying?'

'Just that it's a pity Blake's not here,' Piers commented, picking chicken off a drumstick with his teeth. 'His name's on the prizewinner's list.'

'It is? What for?'

'Winning the Open Laser Challenge,' Piers answered. 'Of course, it was all down to the superb quality of the guy at the helm.'

'Who was that?' Ellie said, pushing coleslaw salad round her plate.

'Me,' Piers said laughing. 'I'm surprised Blake didn't tell you.'

'Why would he tell me anything?' Ellie asked. 'It's not as if – '

'Not as if you're crazy about him?' Piers teased, eyeing her closely as she fiddled with her earring. 'No, of course it's not.'

Ellie wanted to shout him down and tell him where to go, but she was so close to tears that she didn't dare open her mouth.

'I'll tell you one thing,' Piers went on, 'you'd be much better for him than Lucy. Those two aren't remotely suited, you know.'

'Don't you think so?' Ellie tried to sound dis-interested.

'No way,' Piers asserted, topping up Abby's wine glass. 'Lucy needs a guy who knows how to chill, someone with a bit of spunk.'

'Blake's got spunk,' she cut in.

'Oh sure, like a warthog's top of the glamour stakes,' he said with a laugh.

'I thought he was your friend,' Ellie replied.

'He is – he's a great guy, just not Lucy's type. He'll kill her spirit and . . .'

'Well, it doesn't seem to bother her, does it?' Ellie {249} retorted, giving up all attempts at eating as she pushed her plate away. 'She is flying halfway round the world with him as we speak isn't she?' Ellie visibly cringed at the idea of Blake and Lucy sitting in first class together, sharing an Ipod and drinking ginger ale.

'Jealous, are you?' Piers smiled at her.

'Of course I'm not jealous!' Ellie spat right back at him.

'That's good,' Piers commented calmly as she scanned the room for a sign to the loos. 'Since it's your fault he's gone.'

'My . . . ? How do make that out?'

'Come off it, Ellie,' he protested. 'There's only so many times you can give a guy the brush off before he gets the message.'

'What are you on about? Like I'm expected to two time another girl?'

'It wasn't like that,' Piers began. 'It's complicated.'

'No it's not,' Ellie said. 'It's dead simple. Blake wanted to be with Lucy and I don't give a damn.' I'm getting like Abby, she thought, quoting old movies in times of stress. 'Get the message?'

Piers grinned. 'The message as in you're crazy about him and he's besotted with you? Oh, sure – I get it. The question is, what are we going to do about it?'

Ellie wheeled round and began pushing her way to the loo. She had to get there before the tears came. No one, least of all Piers Fordyce, was going to see her cry.

'Ryan's singing better than ever,' Abby said to Chloë as the band broke for the interval and Chloë came storming toward her. 'He's quite cute isn't he? He's dead keen on you.'

'How could you do that to me?' Chloë demanded. 'I saw you – you kissed Nick!'

'I gave him a good luck peck,' Abby protested. 'A peck doesn't mean a thing.'

'I suppose,' Chloë said, sighing. 'Ryan just gave me one before going on as well, but I just don't feel it for him, you know? He's much nicer than I thought at first, but he's not Nick, is he? I mean, if you didn't have Hunter . . .'

Which right now I don't, thought Abby.

'. . . which one would you choose? Nick or Ryan?'

'Nick,' Abby said before she could think straight. What? It was the truth.

'See what I mean?' replied Chloë. 'No contest is there?'

But before Abby could find a way to temper her reply

in Ryan's favour, she was distracted by the double doors which had just swung open with a party of latecomers. And at the back, towering above the rest and with his arm round a tall, chestnut-haired girl with a plunge neckline and a cleavage to die for, was Hunter.

❧ SECRET NUMBER 28 ❧

You'll never forget your first kiss.

'IT'S NICE OUT HERE, ISN'T IT?' Georgie said, listening to the jangling of the halyards on the boats lined up by the jetty. When they had finished serving the guests Adam had suggested they come outside, and now Georgie was glad he did. 'Do you go sailing?'

'No,' Adam said. 'But I thought I might give wind-surfing a go – or water-skiing. Cheaper and less complicated, I guess.'

'I fancy that,' Georgie said. 'We could do it together.'

Adam put his hand on her shoulder. 'There's lots we could do together,' he said, and his voice was so husky that Georgie wondered if he had caught a cold.

But when he pulled her gently towards him and kissed her, ever so lightly, on the lips, all thoughts of his state of health evaporated on the spot.

Hunter had his hands round the girl's waist as Abby sashayed up to them, puckering her lips and blowing a kiss in his direction. She took a giant gulp of wine to give her courage, and she realised she'd just emptied her third glass.

'Hi, darling – how was Scotland? Missed you big time,' Abby trilled as she approached.

'Oh it's you.' Hunter seemed amused but hardly overwhelmed by passion.

'And who is this?' The girl clinging to his arm spoke with a soft Scottish burr and looked at Abby as if she had crawled out from under a rotting log.

'I'm Abby,' Abby said as charmingly as she could. 'I'm Hunter's girlfriend.'

'How extraordinary,' the girl said. 'I'm Fiona, and I'm Hunter's girlfriend. Now one of us must be wrong, and it certainly isn't me.' She turned to Hunter who was watching them in amusement. 'Is this the girl you were telling me about? The one with the crush on you?' she asked.

'Yes, this is Abby,' he said, in the tone of voice one might use when talking about a rather senile old lady. 'Abby, meet Fiona. And yes, she's my girlfriend.'

She put out a hand to grab a chair because for some reason the floor was moving like waves on a rough sea.

'You . . . you can't . . . I'll do what you wanted . . . you . . .' Abby's voice cracked.

'Sorry, sunshine,' Hunter said, sidling up to Fiona. 'I need someone a bit more sophisticated than a school girl, if you catch my drift.'

'Ladies and gentlemen, please make your way to the podium – the prize-giving is about to take place.' Everyone turned as the announcement boomed from the speaker system.

'Come on Abby, let's go,' Piers urged, suddenly appearing at Abby's side. They didn't know each other well, but Piers was quickly developing a soft spot for the Dashwood girls. 'He's an idiot – don't let him get to you.'

'Leave me alone,' Abby shouted. 'Hunt, listen to me . . .'

'Hysterical as well as immature,' Fiona said, grinning. With that, she wound her arms around Hunter's neck and began kissing him in the kind of way that gets movies an 18 Certificate.

Whether it was the effects of the wine or simply the fact that she realised she had nothing else to lose, she didn't know, but before she could think Abby grabbed Piers's glass and threw its burgundy contents all over Fiona. Abby watched, pleased, as the red liquid ran down Fiona's neck and into her milky white cleavage. It looked, she thought with satisfaction, very much like blood.

'For God's sake!' Hunter leaped back as droplets of wine splattered his dinner shirt. 'What the hell's going on?'

'She's crazy!' Fiona wailed. 'This dress – it's ruined. It cost me three hundred pounds.'

'Well, it was a waste of money,' Abby yelled. 'It just makes you look like the tart you are!'

'Abby, what on earth's going on?' She heard Georgie coming in from the patio, and felt someone pulling her back. She wrenched herself free.

'Get lost!' she shouted, pushing past Hunter and Fiona. Fiona grabbed her arm.

'Not so fast,' she began. 'You'll pay for this.'

Abby swung her arm, hitting Fiona on the cheek with her handbag. With that, she ran across the room, burst through the doors and sped as fast as she could, blinded with tears, into the car park.

'Go and find Ellie,' Piers ordered Georgie urgently. 'I think she's in the loo. I'll go after Abby.'

Georgie rushed to the Ladies and found Ellie, both hands resting on a washbasin, staring at her reflection in the mirror.

'Come quickly,' Georgie gabbled. 'It's Abby – she hit this girl and now she's run off.'

'Hit what girl? What are you on about?' Ellie gasped, as Georgie grabbed her hand and pulled her through the swinging doors.

'I just came in from outside, and Abby was yelling at this girl and then she threw wine over her and now she's run off. And Piers thinks she's been drinking.'

Ellie pushed through the crowd gathering for the prize-giving, ran to the door and out into the night. A blast of cool, salty air hit her burning cheeks and she struggled to focus in the unaccustomed darkness.

'I can't see her,' Piers said, panting up to them. 'I went down to the jetty but she's not there. The state she's in, if she fell into the water . . .'

He didn't bother to complete the sentence.

They were all laughing at her. Abby could hear them in her head, imagine them staring after her as she ran through the car park. She could hear someone calling her name, saw a dark shape striding along the jetty, but she couldn't face anyone. She had to get away. She ran across the car park and that's when she saw it: Nick's battered old car.

And she had the keys.

Her hands shook as she fumbled in her bag. If she sat in the car and kept her head down, she'd be safe. No one would find her.

She opened the door, shut it as quietly as she could and sat, catching her breath and choking on her sobs.

'Abby, Abby!' The shouts were coming nearer.

She stared at the keys in her hand. She wouldn't go far. Just down the road, away from here.

She could only just reach the pedals and she struggled to remember what to do. She'd driven her dad's old car up and down the drive before. She'd even had a go behind the wheel of Hunter's car down by Holkham beach. Surely if you could drive one car you could drive any car.

She pressed the accelerator and the engine revved. As she let the handbrake off, she caught sight of a familiar figure run wildly from the door of the club.

Ellie.

She had to go. Now.

She pressed the pedal harder and the car lurched wildly forward.

❧ SECRET NUMBER 29 ❧

There is no worse combination than a broken heart and too much champagne. The headache is more than you can take when your heart hurts so much already.

'WE'VE GOT TO FIND HER,' Ellie cried, looking frantically around. {257}

'I'll get Adam and go round the back,' Georgie said. 'You check the boat house and look behind . . .' Her words were drowned out by the spluttering of a car engine.

'That's Nick's car,' Ellie said. 'Stop him – tell him to look out for Abby. She might be trying to walk home.'

Piers sprinted towards the car, Ellie hard on his heels, shielding her eyes from the headlights as the vehicle swung sharply around.

'No!' Piers gasped.

The car reversed wildly, hitting the bumper of a blue Mercedes and then bouncing off the bonnet of a Ford Fiesta.

'For God's, sake what's he doing?' Ellie shouted above the engine noise. 'Nick, stop!'

Piers grabbed her arm and spun her round to face him. 'Ellie, it's not Nick,' he stressed urgently. 'It's Abby.'

'But Abby can't drive,' she stammered. 'She wouldn't?' But Ellie knew: *she would*.

Nick's car was lurching towards the exit, swerving haphazardly from side to side.

'Get your car, follow her,' Ellie pleaded. 'Quickly.'

Piers shook his head. 'I can't – I've had too many drinks. Don't worry, I'll find someone else to drive my car.'

'Hurry,' Ellie sobbed as Nick's car disappeared out of sight. 'Please hurry.'

Abby hadn't realised it would be so dark. Even with the headlights on, she could hardly see where she was going, and the tears streaming down her face weren't helping. A motorcyclist came towards her, blaring his horn, and she swerved, narrowly missing a ditch.

The road from the sailing club was really no more than a track, rutted in places and sprinkled with shingle. She hit a pothole and rammed her foot down. The car sped forward. She drove on. The shingle gave way to tarmac and the lane widened slightly. Ahead of her was the main road, traffic thundering past, headlights piercing the darkness.

She began to pull out into the road but the speed of the traffic scared her. Headlights streaked by her in every direction.

And then a sudden, piercing light blinded her. A horn blared. A huge, black shape with silver bars bore down on her. For a split second she saw a face frozen in terror.

Then she felt herself spinning, tipping, falling.

{258}

A searing pain shot through her body. Someone screamed.

And then she fell into a huge, black silent pit.

'What took you so long?' Ellie said as Piers ran up to her with Nick behind him. 'She's been gone fifteen minutes.'

'The speeches were on,' Piers panted. 'And everyone I asked had had a drink. Then I found Nick.'

'Which way?' Nick grabbed Piers's car keys and jumped into the driving seat.

'She turned left,' Ellie said, sobbing, and climbed into the back with Piers. 'Are you sure you're OK to drive?'

{259}

'Fine,' Nick said. 'I've been on lemonade all night – always am when I'm playing.' Nick jammed the keys into the ignition.

Please God, Ellie prayed, let us find her. Let her be OK.

'What about Georgie?' Piers asked suddenly.

'Adam's parents are keeping an eye on her,' Ellie said. 'I've told her not to phone Mum, at least not yet. Not till we've found Abby.'

Nick accelerated gently up the shingled lane.

'Keep looking,' he said. 'She might have parked up in a lay-by.'

They didn't speak for several minutes.

'The main road,' Nick said finally. 'Which way?'

Afterwards, Ellie would never remember who saw it first. Was it her, when she screamed at the sight of blue flashing lights? Was it Nick's 'Dear Jesus' that had tipped her off? Or was it Piers, who shouted 'Stop!' and then put his hand over Ellie's eyes?

What she *would* remember for weeks to come was the sight of twisted metal, the image of the other driver on his knees on the side of the road and the voice of the burly police officer. 'She's trapped. We're going to have to cut her out.'

A siren wailing. Then jolting. And pain. Someone crying.

'Mum, Mum,' over and over.

Then faces, coming and going. All in a blur.

'You're in hospital now.'

Familiar voice. Mum.

'I'm here, darling. Right beside you.'

Hospital. Going to see Dad. Dad's getting better? No. Dad is dead. Hospitals are where people die. Pain everywhere.

And then a prick in the arm. And nothing.

It was happening all over again. Just like before. Sitting, waiting, in the relatives' room, wanting them to come, but dreading what they'd say.

'Oh, why are they taking so long? Ellie said for the tenth time. 'The police can tell us about your car, but no one says anything about my sister . . .'

Nick swallowed.

'The police – they asked me if I wanted to press charges,' he said. 'Like I care about the damn car. All I care about is Abby.'

Ellie smiled faintly and nodded. 'You do, don't you?'

she murmured, shivering with delayed shock. 'You really care.'

Nick turned and Ellie saw he was struggling not to cry.

'I love her, Ellie.' He got up and paced the room. 'If anything – ' He paused as the door flew open and Julia stood, tears streaming down her face.

'Do you ever pray?' Georgie sat in Adam's kitchen, cradling a mug of hot chocolate and staring at the clock.

'Sure,' Adam replied. 'I mean, there has to be someone in charge, doesn't there? Otherwise we'd all have messed up eons ago.'

'Yes, but when Dad died,' she began, stuttering over the word, 'we all prayed like crazy and it didn't make any difference.'

{261}

'You don't always get what you want, I guess,' Adam said, stifling a yawn. 'But it can't hurt to ask, can it?'

'So will you – I mean, could we . . . ?' Georgie ventured.

'Pray? Sure.' Adam wiped his nose with his sleeve and put his mug on the table. 'Look God, Georgie's sister had a car crash and we're all dead worried about her. You can cure anything so if possible, could you get to work on Abby right now? She's in Kings Lynn hospital, but I guess you know that. Thanks for listening. Amen.'

Georgie stared at him. 'That didn't sound like a prayer,' she protested. 'That was just like normal talking.'

Adam shrugged. 'That's just the way I do it,' he said. Julia's tear-stained cheeks looked brighter under the fluorescent hospital lighting.

'Oh God, Mum, what?' Ellie froze.

Julia flung open her arms and hugged her. 'She's going to be fine,' she wept. 'Oh Ellie, she's going to be all right.'

❧ SECRET NUMBER 30 ❧

*Surviving a broken heart requires that same thing as
recovering from any injury – time and love.
(And a little ice cream doesn't hurt.)*

'I DON'T WANT TO SEE ANYBODY, MUM.' Abby blinked
back the tears and squeezed her mother's hand. Two days
had passed but still everything hurt. 'Promise me, you
won't let anyone come.'

'But darling,' her mother protested, shifting her
position on the chair beside the bed.' You said that
yesterday and Ellie and Georgie so want to be here . . .'

'No, mum!' Abby shouted. 'Yesterday I kept praying
I'd remember what had happened. Now I can – and I
realise that amnesia is no bad thing. I just want to die.'

Julia stood up and leaned over the bed. 'Now Abby,
you listen to me and you listen well,' she stressed. 'I don't
want to hear that kind of talk again, you understand me?
I know you feel dreadful about what happened, and I
know you wish you could wind the clock back. But you
can't.'

Abby's tears flowed faster. 'Everyone's going to hate
me,' she sobbed, shifting her plastered leg gingerly. 'Even
you are getting cross.'

'Only when you say silly things about dying,' Julia murmured, her voice breaking. 'And no one will hate you – if you think that you underestimate your sisters and your friends.'

'What friends?' Abby retorted. 'They're not going to want to know me now, are they?'

'Oh really?' Julia replied, plunging her hand into a large carrier bag at her feet. 'So that's why there's a card and some chocolates from Chloë, a couple of magazines from Piers and a note from Nick. He's come by here waiting for you to wake up quite a few times, you know.'

Abby stared at the pile her mum had made at the foot of her bed. 'And Hunter? Is there anything from Hunter?'

Julia shook her head. 'Hunter's not a friend, darling,' she said softly. 'The one person Hunter adores is Hunter.'

Abby closed her eyes.

'I was taken in by him too, you know,' Julia said. 'But Piers and Nick have been putting me straight.'

'You've seen Nick?' Abby asked, opening her eyes. 'He must hate me. That letter must be legal papers suing me for stealing his car!'

'Darling,' Julia said patiently, 'he didn't leave the hospital on the night of the accident till four in the morning – he hardly seemed concerned about his car. In fact, he blames himself for not telling you from the start what Hunter was like.'

'He tried,' Abby sniffled. 'I just thought he was jealous.'

Her mother smiled. 'He does seem very fond of you,' she admitted. 'So let him come – he'll cheer you up.'

'I couldn't even if I wanted to,' she said, just to put an end to her mother's nagging.' Chloë would kill me – she's got a thing about him and . . .'

'Chloë wants to come too – she said Ryan would bring her tonight.'

'Chloë? Ryan?' Abby asked, running her hand along her cast. 'Mum, you've got it all muddled up – Chloë can't stand Ryan.'

'Oh, really?' Her mother smiled. 'So is that why Chloë came round holding hands with a rather nice looking boy whom she introduced as Ryan? Lovely lad. He said my carrot cake was the best he'd ever tasted. But then, I've heard that before – haven't I? Now then, will you have visitors?'

'Do I have a choice?' Abby sighed.

'No,' her mum said with a smile. And as if on cue, there was a light *tap tap tap* on the door.

'Hello?' Nick came in the door just behind his voice. 'The nurse said you were awake, so . . . Oh hi, Mrs Dashwood.'

'Hi, Nick,' Julia said mischeivously as she slipped out the door behind Nick. 'I'll just leave you two alone.'

'Nick, I'm so sorry,' Abby began, 'but I'm afraid I can't – '

'Let me guess – see me?' Nick asked, sounding much less perturbed than Abby would have expected. 'Well, you have to.'

'Why's that?' Abby asked, surprised by Nick's assertiveness.

'Because you've got a broken leg.' Nick smiled at her. 'So I'm afraid you can't get away.' Nick sat down at the chair next to the bed and took her hand. 'Abby, I love you. And I know you love Hunter, much as it makes me want to puke to say it.'

'Nick – ' Abby tried to interrupt.

'No, Abby, listen,' Nick said. 'I know you think Hunter is great, but he's not, and besides, the rumour is that he's going back to Scotland with that girl.' Nick paused, but Abby didn't interrupt. 'And I'm here. So how about you give me a shot, eh? For a few weeks, until your leg heals and you can run away from me if you want to?'

Abby was very quiet, and Nick's hopeful expression dropped. 'What about your car?' she finally asked.

'To hell with the car. What about what I just said?'

'Well, it's just that . . .' Abby stammered, 'What with Chloë and all . . .'

'Forget Chloë. This is about you and me, Abby!' Nick practically stomped his feet on the linoleum floor.

Abby looked at Nick, who was looking at her with more love than Hunter ever had, and suddenly knew what she had to do. 'Just let me sort a few things, OK?'

Nick twisted his mouth up, unsure whether or not this was a good sign. 'OK,' he said. 'I guess that's OK.' Nick turned to go but before he left he bent over Abby, and very gently, he kissed her.

Abby's eyes were open the whole time – she couldn't believe he'd just done that! But then again, it was quite nice really. Abby realised she could imagine doing quite a bit more of that with Nick. He left without saying another word.

Abby lay back on the pillow and closed her eyes. How

could he be so nice after everything she'd done? And he was quite cute, really. Plus, he had seen her all goobery, with runny mascara, over another guy and he still liked her.

'Abby, you've got a visitor.' The nurse stuck her head round the door a few minutes later. 'I'll tell her to come up.'

'No,' Abby began but the nurse had left. Who else could it be?

I'll pretend to be asleep, she thought, but as she screwed up her eyes, the door flew open and Chloë burst into the room, flowers in one hand, and started talking before Abby could even say hello.

'Oh God, Abby, if I hadn't forced you to get Nick to drive us to the ball, you wouldn't have had his keys and . . .'

'Hey, come on,' Abby said, the saliva drying in her mouth. 'I was the dumb idiot who took the car and ruined the party and caused so much worry. Everyone must hate me.'

'Certainly not! Because of you, I've got a boyfriend.' Chloë flopped down on the bed.

'Ouch! Not on the bed.' Abby winced as a pain shot through her leg.

'Sorry.' Chloë jumped up and started pacing the room. 'It's Ryan.'

Abby was gobsmacked. *Ryan!?* 'But, Chloë, you've been rotten to Ryan. You loathe the guy.'

'I know but that was before the ball. You see, after you drove off, I was crying and he comforted me. He said you'd been drinking . . .'

'Don't.' Abby winced at the memory.

'Well, anyway, we got talking and I said you were my best mate in the whole world and that if anything happened to you, I couldn't bear it . . .' Chloë said animatedly.

'You said that?' Abby sat up a bit in bed.

'Of course, it's true, so why wouldn't I say it?' Chloë asked. 'Anyway, we started looking for you with a lot of the others.'

Abby groaned from the embarrassment.

'Anyway, the next day Ryan phoned me and we went by your house to find out how you were doing, and then we went for a drink, and he said that Nick had been up all night and was sick with worry. That's when I knew.'

'What?' Abby asked.

'That no matter what I did, Nick wouldn't fall for me because he'd already fallen for you,' she said, surprisingly brightly. 'OK, it hurt a bit at first but then Ryan and I talked some more and then he asked if maybe I'd like to meet up again, which we did, and then tonight – '

'So you like him?' Abby interrupted, trying to get a hold on Chloë's long-winded report.

Chloë nodded, her eyes bright and her normally pallid cheeks flushed.

Abby paused and took a deep breath. 'More than Nick?'

Chloë bit her lip. 'Not entirely,' she whispered. 'But I think I could. I mean, it's early days and everything but it's a lot nicer being with someone who really wants to be with you. I mean, when I saw how totally devastated Nick was about your accident, it hit me that he would never feel that way about me. And Ryan – well, he's quite hot, isn't he?'

'Chloë, you promise you're not still angling for Nick? Promise on your honour?'

'I swear it – why?' Chloë looked concerned.

'Because if you don't mind, I think I might rather like to have him,' Abby confessed.

✄ SECRET NUMBER 31 ✄

Sometimes a kiss says more than words can
(no matter how good a talker you may be).

'I'M SO BORED,' ABBY SAID with a sigh, lying on the sofa ten days later as Nick drew cartoons on her leg plaster. 'I feel like one of those Victorian invalids who die in darkened rooms for want of sunlight and stimulation.'

Nick burst out laughing. 'Abby, you're so dramatic,' he teased. 'You want to go out? Let's go then.'

'I can't,' she protested. 'I can hardly walk on those awful crutches and thanks to me you don't have a car. Mum's out serving tea to the old ladies, Ellie's down in Brighton seeing old schoolmates . . .'

'Wheelchair! My great gran's old one is still in our shed. Wait here. Oh well, I suppose you don't have a choice do you?' He grinned at Abby. 'I'll be back in an hour.'

'Is that Georgie?' Nick asked as he pushed Abby in the wheelchair down to the jetty. 'With that guy by the rowing boats?'

Abby shaded her eyes against the glare of the late

afternoon sun. 'Yes,' she said. 'I can't see who the guy is, though.'

'Must be Adam, I guess,' Nick remarked.

She shook her head. 'He's gone to Liverpool to see his grandparents,' she told him, cupping her hands to her mouth. 'Hey, Georgie – over here!'

Georgie waved and ran along the jetty towards them. 'Hi,' she panted. 'Hey, wheelchair – neat idea. Can I have a go?'

'No, you can't,' retorted Abby. 'I'm the invalid, remember?'

'As if you'd let us forget,' Georgie teased. 'Anyway, you'll never guess who I'm going rowing with – Tom!'

'Tom?' Abby shielded her eyes again. 'What's Tom doing here?'

'Surprise visit,' Georgie said. 'He missed me.'

Abby couldn't help seeing the smug look on Georgie's face. 'But what about Adam?'

'I like Adam, I do,' replied Georgie calmly, 'but Tom and I have been rather close for quite a long time.'

Abby could see the twinkle in Georgie's eye. She smiled at her little sister who suddenly seemed rather grown up.

'And,' Georgie went on. 'I reckon Tom and I have always had a bit of something special, don't you think?'

'You know, Georgie, I do.'

Ellie fumbled in her jeans pocket for her door key, slipped her sunglasses over her eyes to cut the glare of the sinking sun, and kicked the gate open with her foot.

'Hi.'

'What the . . . ?' She jumped back, dropping her bag, her heart pounding as a figure stepped out from behind the laurel bush.

'Sorry – I didn't mean to scare you.'

Blake. She stood motionless, her mind in turmoil. He was in Australia – or, at least, he was *supposed* to be in Australia.

'I had to come to see you,' he said taking a step towards her. 'Then when I got here, I didn't have the nerve to ring the bell.'

Ellie exhaled deeply. 'I'd have thought,' she said, ramming her key into the lock, 'that compared to flying round the world at the drop of a hat, bell ringing would be a doddle. Aren't you meant to be somewhere else?'

'Not any more,' he murmured. 'Look, can I come in?'

No you can't, Ellie muttered silently in her head. No way. 'Yes, of course. Come on.' The truth was, no matter what she tried to make herself think, Ellie's feelings for Blake were not so simple.

As Ellie led him into the kitchen and flipped on the hot water, Blake took a seat at the kitchen table.

'I told her.' Blake handed her the empty mug she'd just absentmindedly set in front of him, his eyes holding Ellie's gaze.

'You told who, what?' She knew full well he meant Lucy, but she wasn't about to let him off that easy.

'I told Lucy. About how I really felt. About you.' Blake spoke in sentences that quite resembled Julia's in times of stress.

'You did?' A surge of joy flooded Ellie's heart, and she turned toward the coffee machine to hide a smile. She was suddenly doubly thankful that the rest of the family was out of the house and not bursting into the room.

Blake nodded. 'In Hong Kong. I wanted to go to see this amazing exhibition that was on – about Asian art, you know? Anyway, Lucy kept on and on about how it was pointless since any idea of me being an artist was stupid. And that was when . . .' He hesitated, chewing his bottom lip. 'Well, I flipped out. Told her that no way was I doing law, that I'd probably be penniless for years till I got established, but that I'd be happy and that was all that mattered.' He laughed dryly. 'I told her straight out that I didn't want to be on the trip with her in the first place,' he confessed.

'So why were you?' The image of Blake and Lucy together on the other side of the world – even if it was of them fighting – was cooling the feeling she'd had a moment before.

'It was arranged ages ago, when we were still an item,' Blake said. 'Lucy's parents and my lot got together and decided it would be an ace idea, in the way that parents do, and they paid for the air tickets and everything . . .'

'And then when Lucy's gran died, you felt you couldn't back out, is that it?' Ellie asked, with a touch more acerbity in her voice than she intended.

'Well, yes . . .' Blake nodded. 'I know it was pathetic, I know I took the easy option – but if you'd been just a bit more encouraging . . .'

'Hang on a minute, don't you go blaming me!' Ellie protested. 'I'd been perfectly cl – '

'Oh no, you certainly hadn't!' Blake said to her, more loudly than she'd expected him to. 'But, let me finish for once, will you Ellie?'

Ellie nodded, taking a seat across from him.

'I told her that if she wanted money, status and all that hip lifestyle, she should be with Piers and not me. Which I always knew was the truth and I think they both did as well.'

Ellie shook her head in bewilderment. 'I don't get it,' she stammered. 'Where does Piers come into it?'

As she asked the question, snippets of the conversation she'd had with Piers at the ball filtered back into her confused brain. '*He's a great guy, just not Lucy's type . . . he'll kill her spirit . . . it's your fault he's gone . . . only so many times you can give a guy the brush off . . .*'

Blake leaned forward and reached out for her hand. Ellie edged back into her chair. Not so fast, buddy.

Blake retreated, but kept talking. 'Before I went, I told Piers how I've wanted to be with you ever since I met you that evening at your old house,' Blake began.

'Come off it,' Ellie protested. 'You had heaps of opportunities . . . '

'Sure I did, and what happened?' Blake raised his voice and Ellie saw him clench his fists. 'You ran off – remember that night on the beach? You wouldn't let me get near you. Whenever I tried to talk to you about the real reason I was going to Oz with Lucy, all you could say was, "There is no you and me! Australia's wonderful at this time of year!" Hardly the sort of thing a girl who's keen on you comes out with, is it?'

Ellie swallowed. 'I thought – I mean, you two were an item and I . . .' Ellie paused before remembering something. 'At the bar that time, I heard you say to Piers that you'd been trying to get rid of me for months.'

'Not you!' Blake practically laughed. 'Lucy! I'd been trying to get rid of Lucy for months! Ever since I first met you, in fact,' he added, his voice softening. 'So can we start over? Will you go out with me?'

'What about Lucy?' Ellie asked – she knew she wasn't cut out for any more confrontations with her, and after all of this back and forth, she wanted to be damn sure things were over between she and Blake.

'If you'd *ever* let me finish,' Blake said, grinning, 'I'd have explained. Lucy's in Australia. Waiting for Piers.'

Ellie's protests were cut short by the touch of Blake's lips against hers.

'I love you, Ellie Dashwood,' he whispered. 'And even if you say no, I'll pester you until you change your mind.'

'But – ' It was when he kissed her for the second time that she decided that saying no would simply be a waste of breath.

EPILOGUE

*'Y*OU LIKE IT?' BLAKE ASKED, a worry-crease set between his eyes.

Ellie nodded her head and brushed the tears from her eyes. 'Mum, Abby, Georgie, come and look!' she called.

'What is it?' Julia gasped as she and Georgie dashed into the sitting room, followed by a slightly limping Abby. She clamped her hands to her mouth and stared at the painting lying on the coffee table.

'It's all of us – you, me, Abby, Georgie,' Ellie breathed. 'And Dad.'

Even Georgie let out a little throttling sound in her throat.

'Oh, Blake – it's beautiful.' Julia beamed at him.

Blake smiled. 'I sketched Max while I was living with him and Pandora in London,' he explained. 'He was laughing at *Only Fools and Horses* on the TV. I added the rest of you later.'

'We'll hang it next to your painting of Holly House,' Julia declared. 'We'll start a Blake Goodman gallery and when you're world famous, we can say that we knew you in your early phase!'

'Look,' he said, fumbling with a button on his shirtsleeve. 'You guys know that I'll be starting at art school next week in Brighton, and living at Holly House. And, well, I know it's awkward, but Pandora's going away for a couple of months – some crystal therapy course – and I wondered if you'd like to come? You know, visit your home?'

For a moment, no one spoke.

'Not me,' Julia finally replied brightly. 'I've got so much to do here what with being on the garden society committee, and playing in the bridge tournament . . .'

'Um, I think I'll stick around here at weekends,' Abby agreed. 'You know, with Nick playing at gigs and stuff . . .'

'Yeah,' said Georgie, 'Tom's coming up again for a visit, and I've already got my hands full with Adam, so . . . 'fraid not. Thanks, though.'

'Ellie?' Blake's voice was hardly more than a whisper.

'I don't think so.' She smiled into Blake's anxious eyes. 'This is our home now,' Ellie said softly. 'I reckon we're finally fine where we are.'

And with that, everyone slowly nodded. Ellie was right – this was home now, and with the picture of Holly House smiling down on them from the wall, the new portrait of all five of them together again, and a year's worth of secrets of love finally uncovered, it finally felt that way.

If you would like more information about
books available from Piccadilly Press and how
to order them, please contact us at:

Piccadilly Press Ltd
5 Castle Road
London
NW1 8PR

Tel: 020 7267 4492
Fax: 020 7267 4493

Feel free to visit our website at
www.piccadillypress.co.uk